Counseling and Coaching in Times of Crisis and Transition

Counseling and Coaching in Times of Crisis and Transition explores how threats and challenges caused by rapid social and technological changes require counselors and coaches to rethink their usual ways of working, and, in some cases, even abandon their traditional theoretical anchors. The authors of this forward-thinking book argue that practitioners who aim to help others strengthen their resources can no longer afford to wait for clients in their offices or offer them protected, objective and neutral professional relationships.

Contributors from around the world argue that there is a real need for new counseling and coaching actions to be delivered in different contexts: counselors and coaches should be able to use heterogeneous languages and interventions, as well as numerous relationship modalities and activities to streamline the support that they offer to people in sectors as diverse as health and wellbeing, life and career design, prevention and community inclusion, work inclusion, and schools. The book provides an evidence-based framework, with numerous counseling and coaching examples that are capable of promoting people's strengths, whether face-to-face, in groups or online.

This book will appeal to academics, researchers and postgraduate students in the fields of counseling and coaching, as well as those with an interest in psychological, social and educational science. It should also be essential reading for practitioners and policymakers in a diverse range of contexts, including those working on intervention and support for vulnerable people, nontraditional and disadvantaged students, and people with disabilities.

Laura Nota is Professor in the Department of Philosophy, Sociology, Education and Applied Psychology at the University of Padova, Italy. She is Delegate of the Rector for Inclusion and Disability. Her research interests concern the ields of career counseling and coaching, and psychology of inclusion.

alvatore Soresi is Professor in the Department of Philosophy, Sociology, ducation and Applied Psychology at the University of Padova, Italy. His esearch activities concern counseling, career counseling and career coaching, nd psychology of disability and inclusion.

Counseling and Coaching in Times of Crisis and Transition

From Research to Practice

Edited by Laura Nota and Salvatore Soresi

Routledge
Taylor & Francis Group
LONDON AND NEW YORK

First published 2018 by Routledge

2 Park Square, Milton Park, Abingdon, Oxfordshire OX14 4RN
52 Vanderbilt Avenue, New York, NY 10017

Routledge is an imprint of the Taylor & Francis Group, an informa business

First issued in paperback 2018

British Library Cataloguing-in-Publication Data
A catalogue record for this book is available from the British Library

Library of Congress Cataloging-in-Publication Data
Names: Nota, Laura, 1966–, author. | Soresi, Salvatore, author.
Title: Counseling and coaching in times of crisis and transition : from research to practice / Laura Nota and Salvatore Soresi.
Description: Abingdon, Oxon ; New York, NY : Routledge, 2018.
Identifiers: LCCN 2017014359 | ISBN 9781138290082 (hardcover) | ISBN 9781315266596 (ebook)
Subjects: LCSH: Counseling psychology. | Personal coaching.
Classification: LCC BF636.6 .N67 2018 | DDC 158.3—dc23
LC record available at https://lccn.loc.gov/2017014359

ISBN: 978-1-138-29008-2 (hbk)
ISBN: 978-0-367-20391-7 (pbk)

Typeset in Bembo
by Apex CoVantage, LLC

Contents

Figures

Tables

Contributors

Laura Aleni Sestito is Full Professor of Developmental Psychology at the Department of Humanities of the University of Naples Federico II. Research activity currently covers mainly psychology of adolescence and in particular developmental tasks related to the formation and consolidating processes of identity (namely, Identity Functions, Identity Capital, Identity Distress, and Vocational Identity); narrative approach to identity formation processes; transition processes from late adolescence to adulthood and assumption of adult roles in contemporary society. The main aspects related to the identity formation processes, according to recent debate in Europe and internationally, are being examined in collaboration with researchers from other universities and research institutions in Italian and foreign companies.

Chiara Annovazzi. After her postgraduate Master's Degree in Psychology of Social Processes, Decision-making and Economic Behavior, she started her PhD and is currently a PhD student in Social, Cognitive and Clinical Psychology, at the Department of Psychology, University of Milano-Bicocca. She is member of the International Association of Applied Psychology (IAAP), of the University Network for Counseling (Uni.Co) and of the Italian Society for Vocational Guidance (SIO). Research interest deals with academic self-efficacy, gender issues and psychosocial counseling for students, parents and offspring at the university.

Marco Bani. School of Medicine and Surgery, University of Milano-Bicocca (Italy). He teaches Clinical Psychology and Health Psychology. His research interests are on Cognitive counseling intervention, in particular on treatment effectiveness.

Bianca Beersma is Full Professor in Institutions and Identity at the VU University in Amsterdam. Her research focuses on how the dilemma between individual and collective interests can be managed to foster cooperation, collaboration, and effective group performance. For group members, collaborating means they have to find a balance between their own interests and those of the group. This can both create challenges and opportunities, and she examines the ways in which individuals and groups deal with this. As such, her studies focus on the motivational and contextual factors that drive behavior in settings such as teamwork, negotiation and interpersonal conflict.

Martina Bernardi obtained a Cellular and Molecular Medicine degree at the University of Bristol. She then undertook a second degree in Psychology at the University of Royal Holloway, London. After concluding her Master's degree in Clinical and Health Psychology at the Vita-Salute San Raffaele University, she conducted an internship at the San Raffaele Hospital in Milan within the psycho-oncology field. She has published various articles within the Clinical and Health Psychology Department. She now works at the University of Parma in the Linguistics department.

Steven D. Brown is Professor Emeritus in the School of Education at Loyola University Chicago. He is a fellow of the American Psychological Association and the Association for Psychological Science. Dr. Brown is also the recipient of the John L. Holland Award for Outstanding Achievement in Career and Personality Research, the Best Science Award, and the Leona Tyler Award for Life-Time Contributions to Counseling Psychology (all from the Society of Counseling Psychology of the American Psychological Association) as well as the Distinguished Achievement Award from the Society for Vocational Psychology. He developed, along with Drs. Robert W. Lent and Gail Hackett, Social Cognitive Career Theory and co-edited (with Dr. Robert Lent) four editions of the *Handbook of Counseling Psychology* and two editions of *Career Development and Counseling: Putting Theory and Research to Work*.

Elisabetta Camussi is a Senior Associate Professor in Social Psychology at the Department of Psychology, University of Milano-Bicocca (Italy). Here she teaches Social Psychology and Psychology of Gender Differences. Research interests deal with Gender Stereotypes, Vocational Guidance and Career Counseling, Public Engagement, Common Sense and Everyday Knowledge, Qualitative Research Methods, Action-Research. She is Scientific Coordinator of the University Network for Vocational Guidance and a member of the Italian National Expert for University Public Engagement Evaluation (ANVUR).

Letizia Carnelli graduated from the Vita-Salute San Raffaele University in Clinical Psychology. She is a Psychotherapist and Researcher at this university. Since 2012, she works for the Clinical and Health Psychology Service of the San Raffaele hospital as a psychologist for both the Gynaecology and Obstetrics departments, where she is involved in both clinical aspects and research. She is the author and co-author of numerous scientific articles for both Italian and international journals in the field of medical and health psychology. Moreover, in her role as a psychologist who helps and supports oncological patients, she also participated in the founding of the project Salute allo Specchio (Health in the Mirror), dedicated to the humanization of treatment in oncology.

Ilaria Di Maggio is a PhD student at the Doctoral School of Psychological Sciences at the University of Padova. Here she received her Master's degree in psychology and her postgraduate Master's course in "Life design and career counseling". She is member of the SIO (Italian Society ofVocational Guidance). Her research activities regard the analysis of factors involved in professional and social inclusion of young and adults with vulnerability (namely, individuals with substance use disorder, unemployed, and immigrants). Special attention is devoted to the development and adaptation to the Italian context of assessment instruments and to the development of career counseling and career education programs.

Valentina Di Mattei obtained a Psychology degree at the Vita-Salute San Raffaele University, Milan. She also obtained her Specialist Certification in Clinical Psychology, cum laude, at theVita-Salute San Raffaele University in Italy. She was awarded a Research Fellowship at the San Raffaele University Department of Cognitive Neurosciences. As Assistant Professor of Psychodynamic Psychology and Health Psychology in the Faculty of Psychology at the San Raffaele University, she is the author of many publications in the Health Psychology research field.This is also her clinical practice area.

Tiziana Di Palma got a first title of Doctor of Research in Psychological and Pedagogical Sciences at the University of Naples Federico II in 2012. Currently, she is a PhD student in Mind, Gender, and Languages. She is part of the research group in Developmental Psychology studying identity processes in adolescence and in the transition to adulthood, with specific regard to Mediterranean and Italian populations. Her research interests focus on identity processes during adolescence and transition to adulthood and, in particular, on vocational identity processes during transition from high school to work and/or university.

Maria Eduarda Duarte is Full Professor at the University of Lisbon, CICPSI, Faculty of Psychology, where she directs the Master Course in Psychology of Human Resources, Work, and Organizations. Her professional interests include career psychology theory and research, with special emphasis on issues relevant to adults and the world of work. She is research director of Career Guidance and Development of Human Resources Services. Her publications and presentations have encompassed topics on adult career problems, testing and assessment, and counseling process. Since 2005, she is Chair of the Portuguese Psychological Society; she also served on editorial boards for some Portuguese, European, and Iberia-American journals. She was the Director of the National Institute of Guidance (2009–2014). She is President of Counseling Division, IAAP. She received the Fellow

Award – IAAP (2014) and ESVDC award 2015. She is also National Defence Adviser, since 2006.

Giovanna Esposito is a post-doctoral researcher at the Center for Active and Integrated Inclusion of Students – SInAPSi – University of Naples Federico II, Italy. Her research interests concern the study of reflexive competences, the promotion and evaluation of mentalization in counseling and psychotherapy, and the use of multimodal narrative devices in clinical psychology interventions.

Lea Ferrari is Associate Professor at the Department of Philosophy, Sociology, Education and Applied Psychology, University of Padova, where she teaches Diversity Management in the Workplace, and Psychology of Work Inclusion for people with disability. Research activities are related to the study of career construction across the lifespan according to the latest approaches of life design and the sociocognitive model. Her interests focus on disability management and the processes of job placement and job search in adults at risk for their vulnerabilities.

Maria Francesca Freda is an Associate Professor of Clinical Psychology at the Department of Humanities, University of Naples Federico II, Italy. Her research interests regard clinical psychological intervention within the institutional framework, mentalization, narrative methods, the combined medical and psychological interventions in the health sector, trauma elaboration during illness.

Rachel Gali Cinamon is Professor for Career Development at the School of Education, Tel Aviv University, Israel. She is the head of the Career Development Lab, and head of the post master career-counseling program. Her research areas within career development are career development of at-risk populations (women, minorities and people with special needs), the work-family interface, exploration process in the period of emerging adulthood and career interventions. She published more than 50 papers and chapters in books and presented more than 100 papers at international conferences. She is involved in several international research studies and projects, and serves at the editorial board of several international journals. One of her recent papers, Whiston, S., & Cinamon, R. G. (2015), "The Work-family interface: Integrating research and practice," *Career Development Quarterly*, *63*(1), 44–56, got the best paper award for 2015. She is married and the mother of three children, and a runs long distance. www.education.tau.ac.il/profile/cinamon; https://education.tau.ac.il/yeuts_career_lab

Maria Cristina Ginevra is a Research Fellow at the Department of Psychology, University of Milano-Bicocca. She is also an Adjunct Professor at the Department of Philosophy, Sociology, Pedagogy and Applied Psychology, University of Padova, where she teaches Educational Psychology. She collaborates with LaRIOS Laboratory (Laboratory of Research and Intervention in Career Guidance and Counseling), University of Padova. In 2015, she received the Young Research Award 2015 from the European Society for Vocational Designing and Career Counseling (ESVDC). She is a full member of ESVDC-European Society for Vocational Designing and Career Counseling, SIO-Italian Society for Vocational Guidance, and AIP-Italian Association of Psychology.

Moshe Israelashvili is an Associate Professor in the School Counseling Program, School of Education, Tel Aviv University (Israel), where he received his PhD in Social Psychology. His research focuses on prevention and inoculation programs, resilience promotion, fostering life skills in educational context, adolescents' coping and counseling people in transition. Prof. Israelashvili is intensively involved in the development, implementation and evaluation of prevention programs, especially in the context of children and youth resilience and substance abuse prevention. He is a consultant to major institutions in Israel, such as Israel Ministry of Education/Psych-Counseling Services, Israel Anti-Drug Authority and Israel Internet Association. He published numerous papers and chapters on his fields of expertise; recently (with Prof. John L. Romano, from the University of Minnesota, USA) he edited *The Cambridge Handbook of International Prevention Science* (Cambridge University Press; February 2017).

Vladimer Kobayashi is a PhD student at the University of Amsterdam. His work in Learning Analytics (LA) lies at the junction of Education and Labour Economics. He is investigating how LA can be used to uncover education-labour market linkages. The perceived outcome of his study is that of the labour industry and the education system mutually benefiting each other. He uses big data across multiple disciplines.

Robert W. Lent is a Professor at the Department of Counseling, Higher Education, and Special Education, University of Maryland. He received his MA and PhD at the Department of Psychology, Ohio State University. He is author with Drs. Steven Brown and Gail Hackett of the Social Cognitive Career Theory. His research interests concern the applications of social cognitive theory, career development, work satisfaction and adjustment, choice of and persistence in scientific and technical fields, school-to-work transition, work-family balance, subjective and psychological wellbeing, psychological coping, counselor development and training, and research training.

Lorenzo Montali is Assistant Professor of Social Psychology at the Department of Psychology, University of Milan-Bicocca. His research interests are in the area of attitude formation and social representations, focusing in particular on how the public opinion/nonexperts understand/manage/have experience of scientific and technological issues, and on the relationship between experts and public opinion on these issues. He has developed a specific competence in methodology, particularly in the use of qualitative methodologies for discourse analysis. Since 2004, he teaches Qualitative Methodologies in a Master's course at the Department of Psychology and Social Psychology. In 2013, he has been Visiting Scholar at the International Institute of Qualitative Methodologies, University of Alberta (Canada).

Giorgio Rezzonico is full professor of Clinical Psychology, at the School of Medicine and Surgery, University of Milano-Bicocca (Italy). He is director of the ANSCo, the Swiss National Association of Counseling. His research area includes personality disorders, eating disorders, client/counselor relationship. He is co-editor of the Italian reference textbook on cognitive-relational counseling at School of Medicine and Surgery.

John L. Romano is Professor Emeritus of Educational Psychology at the University of Minnesota (USA). His current scholarship focuses on Prevention Science and International Psychology. He is the author of *Prevention Psychology: Enhancing Personal and Social Well-Being* (APA, 2015), and co-editor of *The Cambridge Handbook of International Prevention Science* (Cambridge University Press, 2017). Dr. Romano is a Fellow of the American Psychological Association (APA; Divisions of Counseling Psychology and International Psychology). Among his awards and recognitions are Inaugural Lifetime Achievement Award, from Prevention Section of APA's Society of Counseling Psychology, Distinguished Contributions to Counseling Psychology recognition from the Society of Counseling Psychology, APA's International Psychology Division International Mentoring Award, and the American Counseling Association Research Award. Dr. Romano is a licensed psychologist, and has been a visiting professor, consultant, and external evaluator/assessor for several universities across the globe.

Sara Santilli is a Research Fellow at the University of Padova and psychologist, has a postgraduate degree in Career Counseling at the University of Padova, collaborates with La.R.I.O.S. (Laboratory of Research and Intervention in Vocational Guidance) and University Centre for Disability and Inclusion, University of Padova, Italy, in the organization of vocational guidance projects and research concerning disability, career guidance, counseling and job placement. Vice-President of the Italian Society for Vocational Guidance (SIO), she is a member of the Italian Society of Behavior Analysis and Modification and Cognitive Behavioral Therapy – AIAMC.

Kate Scorgie is Professor (retired), School of Education at Azusa Pacific University where she taught courses in educational psychology, research for educators, and motivation and learning. Her research interests include families of children with disabilities, self-determination of persons with disabilities, participative case study pedagogy and transformative learning.

Sarah Scorgie is a grant writer in San Diego specializing in issues of health and human services. Her study interests include disability disclosure, self-identification, employer practices, and inclusion.

Teresa Maria Sgaramella is a Research Associate at the Department of Philosophy, Sociology, Education and Applied Psychology, University of Padova. Here she teaches master-level students on Rehabilitation Counseling and Psychology of Disability and Inclusion, and Coaching for Inclusion in the Workplace in the postgraduate course on counseling and coaching for inclusion. Research activities deal with life design construction in complex living conditions due to disability or psychological distress. Her interests focus on strength assessment and on counseling and coaching preventive actions for inclusion and participation.

Karrie A. Shogren is a Professor in the Department of Special Education, Director of the Kansas University Center on Developmental Disabilities, and Associate Director of the Beach Center on Disability. Dr. Shogren's research focuses on self-determination and systems of support for students with disabilities and she has a specific interest in the multiple, nested contextual factors that impact student outcomes. Dr. Shogren has published over 85 articles in peer-reviewed journals, is the author or co-author of 10 books, and is one of the co-authors of *Intellectual Disability: Definition, Classification, and Systems of Support*, the 11th Edition of the American Association on Intellectual and Developmental Disabilities' seminal definition of intellectual disability (formerly mental retardation) as well as the Supports Intensity Scale-Children's and Adult Version. Dr. Shogren has received grant funding from several sources, including the Institute of Education Sciences (IES) and National Institute on Disability, Independent Living, and Rehabilitation Research (NIDILRR). Dr. Shogren is Co-Editor of Inclusion and Remedial and Special Education, and Associate Editor of Intellectual and Developmental Disabilities and Research and Practice for Persons with Severe Disabilities.

Luigia Simona Sica is senior assistant professor of Developmental Psychology at the Department of Humanities, University of Naples Federico II in Italy. Research interests include developmental psychology, vocational and personal identity formation processes in adolescence and emerging adulthood, and advanced learning technologies. Specifically, she has research experience on identity formation processes in adolescence, in particular on vocational identity domain for youth in European countries affected by economic crises and in normative/not-normative development contexts, using both quantitative and qualitative research methodologies. A number of researches on these fields were published in ISI international psychology journals.

Maria Grazia Strepparava is Associate Professor of Clinical Psychology at the School of Medicine and Surgery University of Milano-Bicocca (Italy). She coordinates the University Counseling Service for Students. Her teaching and research activities deal with clinical psychology, with particular reference to patient-doctor communication, health psychology, counseling and cognitive psychotherapy.

Tim Theeboom is assistant professor at the University of Amsterdam. In his research, he mainly focuses on the effects of coaching. As a consultant and researcher, he constantly aims to bridge the gap between research and practice, scholars and practitioners. Translating (positive) psychological knowledge into organizational practice (on both the organizational and individual level) as a consultant, trainer and coach is his main strength and source of energy. His main topics being: Coaching (Topic of his PhD); Personal and Professional Development; Careers and Employability; Wellbeing. As a consultant, he has mainly (but not exclusively) worked in the public sector.

Terence J. G. Tracey received his BA at Cornell University in 1974, his masters at the University of Kansas in 1977 and his Ph.D. from the Counseling and Personnel Services Department at the University of Maryland, College Park, in 1981. He then was employed as a Counseling Psychologist at the University Counseling Service at the State University of New York at Buffalo from 1981–1983. Following this, he joined the faculty of the Counseling Psychology Program in the Department of Educational Psychology at the University of Illinois at Urbana-Champaign where he also served as Division Chair and Department Associate Chair. He moved to become a Program Leader of the Counseling and Counseling Psychology Programs at Arizona State University in 1999. His scholarship has focused on the topics of client-therapist interaction in psychotherapy and its relation to outcome, interpersonal models of personality and psychotherapy, the structure and development of vocational interests, and minority student academic success. He has published over 150 refereed empirical studies and book chapters in these areas.

Annelies E. M. van Vianen is Full Professor Organizational Psychology and she is the Chair of the program group Work and Organizational Psychology at the University of Amsterdam. She was the Editor of the Dutch scientific journal *Gedrag en Organisatie* (Behavior and Organisation) and she is serving or has served in the editorial boards of Personnel Psychology, International Journal of Selection and Assessment, Academy of Management Journal, and Academy of Management Review. She is the (co)author of about 160 national and international scientific articles, book chapters, and professional articles on topics including person-organization fit, gender and work, intelligence, justice, self-regulation, and career development. Her research interests cover a broad area of issues in organizational and personnel psychology. Central to her research is the interaction between persons and their environment. She studied this subject at different levels, i.e. the interaction and fit between: (1) individuals in teams (person-person fit), (2) individuals and their organization, and (3) individuals and the national culture they are employed in. Her current research projects concern: determinants of people's fit perceptions, self-regulation during unemployment, career development, organizational justice and health, and leadership.

Michael L. Wehmeyer is The Ross and Mariana Beach Professor in Special Education and Chair, Department of Special Education; and Director and Senior Scientist of the Beach Center on Disability all at the University of Kansas. His areas of research include self-determination, positive psychology and disability, transition to adulthood, the education and inclusion of students with severe disabilities, and applied cognitive technologies. He is a Past-President of the Board of Directors for and a Fellow of the American Association on Intellectual and Developmental Disabilities (AAIDD); a past president of the Council for Exceptional Children's Division on Career Development and Transition (DCDT); a Fellow of the American Psychological Association (APA), Intellectual and Developmental Disabilities Division (Div. 33); and Vice-President for the Americas and a Fellow of the International Association for the Scientific Study of Intellectual and Developmental Disabilities (IASSIDD). From 2005 to 2010, he was Editor-in-Chief for the journal Remedial and Special Education and currently co-edits, with Dr. Karrie Shogren, the AAIDD e-journal Inclusion. He obtained his undergraduate degree and a Master's in special education with a focus on intellectual disability from the University of Tulsa and also holds a Master's degree in Experimental Psychology from the University of Sussex in Brighton, England. His doctorate is in Human Development and Communication Sciences from the University of Texas at Dallas.

Robert Zwitser is Assistant Professor at the Psychological Methods group of the University of Amsterdam. His research is focused on modern test theory, adaptive testing, differential item functioning, and large-scale educational assessment. He is teaching applied statistics within the Bachelor programme Psychology and he is the coordinator of the Master's track Behavioural Data Science. Furthermore, he is statistical advisor in the Department of Psychology, and he is member of the Psychology's Study Program Committee.

Counseling and coaching in times of crisis and transition

An introduction

Today's challenges

In times of deep uncertainty and socio-economic crises like the one we are experiencing, scholars and professionals of counseling and career counseling have to do their best to show that with renewed sensitivity and up-to-date instruments, they can help people, organizations and contexts identify, with hope and confidence despite everything, new goals to pursue and opportunities to seize, whilst updating the strategies and techniques to be used.

The uncertainty typical of our present and future requires also the so-called help professions (among them coaching and counseling, highlighted in this volume) to pay special attention to the issues of "change" and of complexity by considering the impact that they have on the wellbeing of people, groups and communities. Change can no longer be seen as an exceptional event, as a one-off, like in the past. Nowadays it permeates our contexts, from work to education to communication, triggering unexpected opportunities but also causing much discomfort and exclusions to a number of individuals – such as those belonging to the middle class – that we had been able to defend in many countries.

The complexity that we are here referring to concerns many of the issues that we have to deal with, from inequalities to poverty, from increased rates of immigration and emigration to the strong competitiveness and precariousness increasingly ruling the labor market, and it often goes so far as to inhibit the aspirations of many people, especially the young, for decent and satisfactory occupations, with worrying consequences also about their individual and relational wellbeing.

As Taleb (2008) has well argued, the real threat is not so much what can be predicted, which we can be ready to tackle, but rather what cannot. Indeed, not all the variables in play are adequately known and not all the consequences produced by actions can be mastered or all their effects restricted (Cheung-Judge & Holbeche, 2011).

In all of this, a central role seems to be played by what is called *disruptive innovations* (see Bertelè, 2013; Bower & Christensen, 1995; Downes & Nunes,

2014), which would move following market rules decidedly different from the usual ones. The latter, in fact, generally aim to satisfy the requests coming from the needs of their current clients and would obtain short- or very short-term usefulness, neglecting what would be necessary to future needs. A particularly apt example of "disruptive innovation" is the huge diffusion of *smartphones* and *tablets* and *their ability* to offer myriads low-cost applications, as also underlined by Bertelé when introducing to the Italian reader the successful book written by Downes and Nunes, the main creators of *Big-bang disruption*. By introducing alternative *business models, disruptive innovation* has "disruptively" sanctioned the end of entire productive sectors and shaken up traditional economic and competitive logics. Suffice to mention, for example, the impact that the latest wave of digital technologies has been producing on labor and on people's lifestyles, actually thanks to the often low cost of these innovations and the easiness and quickness of their spreading all over the world. Witness, often with painful occupational outcomes, the slump in sales of compact digital cameras and of portable GPS systems – now easily and freely downloadable – although both products had been put on the market only at the beginning of this century. Under everybody's eyes is also the crisis of daily newspapers, of the printing industry and of everything connected with printing and the occupations associated with it. E-books have become increasingly popular over the last few years, and in 2011 U.S. sales of e-books had already overcome those of printed books. In addition, we must also mention the online sales of almost every product, from foods to clothing, to products associated with work, studying and leisure time. We should also mention the financial and banking sector, in which most payments are soon expected to be made via a smartphone, the health system, with the planning of remote health check-ups, the education system, with the expectation of online courses made available to a large number of users.

These examples are only a few that can be provided to witness the *disruptive* effects of the latest technological innovations. Clearly justified are the reasons behind the worries that many have about employment and the idea that the greatest risk is run especially by the occupations typically carried out by the middle class. This warning was also sounded by, among others, the Davos World Economic Forum in 2016, when in Switzerland they were debating on the consequences of the so-called fourth industrial revolution, "thanks" to which an ever-increasing number of human beings are being substituted in the workplace by machines, without in the meantime being possible to envisage some sort of feasible outplacement for them (today's estimate is that 45% of jobs could be replaced by automation). Such a situation can also mean a further increase of the Gini index (see note), which shows the gap between the richest and the poorest components of the population, thereby putting at risk democracy itself, which, according to political analysts, has its foundations in the middle class.

Frey and Osborne (2013) have stated that the consequences of computerization on the world of work are clearly mentioned in the literature and document the slump in occupations where tasks need specific procedures that are easily carried out by algorithms. By taking into account advances in Machine Learning (ML) – including Data Mining, Machine Vision, Computational Statistics and other sub-fields of Artificial Intelligence (AI), and Mobile Robotics (MR) – Frey and Osborne (2013) have devised a way of placing occupations into categories according to how vulnerable they are to computerization and concluded that "sophisticated algorithms could substitute for approximately 140 million full-time knowledge workers worldwide" (p. 19). For instance, in the health care sector diagnoses and diagnostic tasks are already being computerized; computerization has started to move into the legal and financial field, with sophisticated algorithms able to carry out tasks usually performed by paralegals, contract and patent lawyers (Markoff, 2011).

The intertwining of experienced situations has brought about very significant challenges: (1) economic ones with financial crises in many countries, high unemployment rates, considerable disparities between Northern and Southern hemisphere countries (Thompson & Reuveny, 2009); (2) ecological ones with climate warming, an oncoming water crisis, extinction of living species, etc. (Fotopoulos, 2007); (3) human ones with what the International Labor Office has called a "deficit of decent work" (International Labor Office, 2001, 2006); (4) a world demographic explosion and massive migrations of populations who cannot survive within their native environment (Ehrlich & Ehrlich, 2009); (5) increased mental health issues, with feelings of discomfort and insecurity suffered by an ever increasing number of individuals, and with the World Health Organization (WHO, 2011) estimating that depression and mental health problems will be the 2nd highest medical cause of disability by the year 2030 (Nota & Soresi, 2015).

The conditions just mentioned require the triggering of what economists call "tipping point" or turning point, a situation in which innovation is given impulse and concentrated on, with the creation of a new balance -aiming at development and growth- which will tend to feed itself. This contrasts with what is defined as "path dependency" – in other words, the dependency on the path already trodden, on one's own past – which, as we have already seen, unfortunately stops us from improving.

We believe that counseling and coaching can become significant instruments in the 21st century to give impulse to new forces and new energies and to facilitate a sort of social regeneration, able to take advantage from the ongoing changes to improve social and human conditions. However, for counseling and coaching to be able to fulfill such a task, brave actions are needed on the part of those that study and practice them.

Despite the presence of threats, hardships and difficulties, which are often intense and unexpected, practitioners who aim to help people persist in strengthening their resources can no longer afford to "wait" for clients in their offices and offer them particularly "protected", "objective" and "neutral" professional relationships. They should more and more frequently try to intercept also those individuals who do not spontaneously approach counseling services, who are not advancing explicit requests for help and who often are not even able to bear the costs for receiving it.

It is increasingly necessary to create new counseling and coaching actions to be delivered in different contexts (wellbeing and health, learning, training and school, guidance, life and career design, work inclusion, prevention and community inclusion), for different categories of people using heterogeneous languages, tools and interventions (helping relationship, training/education, information, prevention, support and supervision), as well as numerous relationship modalities and activities (face-to-face, small and large groups, online, counselor-free, and so on).

Counseling and coaching: from the past to the present

Speaking about counseling, we must remember that it is part of a broader landscape. In the psychosocial context we have two major strands, one related to counseling and one related to psychological counseling.

In the Western context, in the last decades of the last century counseling was considered as a way to help people cope with difficult situations; several international associations were created, such as the American Counseling Association, the Australian Counseling Association, the European Association for Counseling, the British Association for Counselling and Psychotherapy; and several Journals were established (Journal of Counseling & Development (JCD), Adultspan Journal, The Career Development Quarterly (CDQ), Counseling and Values (CVJ), Counselor Education and Supervision (CES), etc.). In 2016 the American Counseling Association writes:

> According to 20/20: A Vision for the Future of Counseling, the delegates comprised of 31 counseling organizations agreed upon a unified definition of counseling: Professional counseling is a professional relationship that empowers diverse individuals, families, and groups to accomplish mental health, wellness, education, and career goals.

In parallel, also psychology has begun to deal with counseling, identifying this as an area of development for the profession. Several actions followed: the realization of research activities, the creation of counseling psychology departments, the creation of dedicated journals, like for example the Journal of Counseling Psychology and The Counseling Psychology, as well as specific divisions in the most famous and recognized international associations, Division 17 of the American Psychological Association and Division 16 of the International Association of Applied Psychology, gave birth to the field of psychological counseling. For division 17 of APA (Society of Counseling Psychology, 2017) "Counseling Psychology is a specialty within professional psychology that maintains a focus on facilitating personal and interpersonal functioning across the lifespan. The specialty pays particular attention to emotional, social, vocational, educational, health-related, developmental, and organizational concerns. The practice of Counseling Psychology encompasses a broad range of culturally-sensitive practices that help people improve their wellbeing, alleviate distress and maladjustment, resolve crises, and increase their ability to function better in their lives. Over time, scholars have also tried to differentiate counseling from other sectors, such as clinical psychology".

Always with counseling in mind, it must be considered that by looking up the word "counseling" in scientific literature, we can see that other scholars and professionals are interested in it. A discipline that shows interest in counseling is pedagogy. Drawing on a database recognized by the pedagogical sector, the Educational Resources Information Center (ERIC), and considering the past 10 to 15 years, we found almost 20,000 articles whose key words included counseling, with an average of more than 1,500 articles per year.

Another discipline that has made room for counseling is philosophy. Philosophical counseling is defined as that set of actions aiming to create a dialogue with the client centered on encouraging different ways of thinking about one's own reality and condition. The Philosopher's Index gathers scientific publications in this sector: over the last ten years on average 15 to 20 writings a year are devoted to counseling.

Then there is the counseling studied in the medical field: genetic counseling, health education counseling, nutritional counseling, patient counseling, contraception counseling, counseling for diseases like cancer and HIV, counseling to control smoking and the diet, telephone counseling (with more than 40,000 publications found in PubMed over the last 10 to 15 years). Specialized publications can be found also in the economic field. The financial sector is indeed one of the ambits where counseling is studied most, and researchers actually reference specific definitions of it in their publications. We would like to recall one of them: Financial counseling is "the process of advising, instructing, and motivating clients concerning creative and effective use of all resources" (Credit Counseling Centers, Inc., 1981, p. 21).

Similar heterogeneity can be found also when analyzing coaching in depth. Grant (2008) maintains that contemporary professional coaching is an interdisciplinary methodology and therefore not "owned" by any single group or professional association. Diversity and the multidisciplinary quality of coaching make it particularly difficult to devise shared definitions, theoretical models, instruments, and efficacious evaluations.

For example, coaching can be defined as the process that enables *learning and development* to occur and thus performance to improve (emphasis added) (Parsole & Wray, 2000). Also it can be understood as a collaborative, action-oriented conversation that facilitates the enhancement of life experiences, goal attainment, self-directed learning and performance in the coachees' professional and personal life (Spence & Grant, 2007).

In their 2014 meta-analysis, Lai and McDowall addressed this issue and concluded that it is possible to distinguish between "general" and "psychological" coaching. They stated that *coaching refers to* "a reflective process between coaches and coachees which helps or facilitates coachees to experience positive behavioral changes through continuous dialogue and negotiations with coaches to meet coachees' personal or work goals" (p. 124).

> "Coaching psychology refers to a process that aims to help or facilitate the nonclinical populations for sustained behavioural changes through psychological evidence-based interventions and process. These interventions will help the coach to get deeper and richer pictures of coachees' behaviours, motivations, values and beliefs during the coaching process and facilitate coachees to achieve their goals".

Similar to what happened in the case of counseling, a number of studies and in-depth analyses on coaching have been carried out by scholars from different disciplines, such as psychology (papers published in PsycINFO in 2014–2016: 0.4%), pedagogy (papers published in ERIC in 2014–2016: 0.9%), medicine and biomedics (papers published in PubMed in 2014–2016: 0.05%), and economics (papers published in EconLit in 2014–2016: 0.03%).

Notwithstanding what was said previously, we wished to expand on the contributions that counseling and coaching can give as we believe they can help us find novel, original, low-cost answers to assist larger and larger groups of individuals with brief, friendly supports centered on goals and wellbeing.

Actions for the near future

The different study sectors of counseling and coaching raise several important issues for scholars and researchers. For example, a question is certainly to what extent we can consider counseling and coaching as a prerogative of only one discipline; how advantageous or reductive, if not even downright improper, this perspective can be; and what interdisciplinary interactions may be requested of future studies. It can be legitimately asked to what extent proposed actions in counseling actually differ, and how, from other forms of psychological/pedagogical interventions. Another question could also be about what differentiates the aims, objectives and techniques of counseling and coaching. In this connection, we can say that much overlapping can already be noticed. For instance, in attempting to differentiate between career counseling and career coaching, Duarte (in this volume) states that "it seems obvious then that more similarities than differences exist, across all definitions" and that it would make more sense to say that "what really matters here is to sift and separate what is good counseling/good coaching from what is not good counseling/not good coaching".

Reid (2016) maintains that career counselors and career coaches actually share similar vocabulary; that they deal with similar issues, including career planning, career adjustment, implementation of career choice; that they tend to follow common procedures, such as the establishment of a work alliance, confidentiality, with a number of similar session aims.

As may well be imagined, the road to find exhaustive answers to these questions is long and complicated.

With this book, we have therefore decided to focus the attention of readers, colleagues, and professionals on some important aspects that may help them from the very beginning realize interventions that are significant for individuals.

First of all, the counseling and the coaching of the near future must be able to help individuals cope with their current challenges and keep in tune with the aims and the objectives set out by the international organizations that deal with overall development. We will recall the 2020 objectives of the European Union, the United Nations 2030 Agenda for sustainable development, the recommendations of the International Labor Organization (ILO), to mention but a few official documents that encourage focusing on quality of life and on the rights of everyone to full participation and to a decent occupation. They also advocate the use of innovative social models attentive to everybody's good and centered on civic virtues that take into account sustainability, biodiversity, heterogeneity and the uniqueness of fundamental inalienable values.

Thus, also counseling and coaching should facilitate the transition from *homo economicus* to *homo empaticus* who can promote solidarity, inclusion, civil responsibility and take care of the natural world that surrounds him in favor of a common good that overcomes selfishness as well as visions anchored only in here-and-now satisfaction, starting from greater attention to the most vulnerable individuals and creating pathways and initiating actions in the most disparate contexts.

The actions of counseling and coaching in the present and in the near future will have to:

- take an interest not only in those that explicitly ask for help but also in the reality of many people in difficulty who do not ask for that kind of help or "spontaneously" approach the services maybe because of cultural reasons or prejudice or because they have little faith in interventions and professions associated with counseling;
- focus on group or online interventions, which may be more easily accessible, with definitely lower costs, to a great number of people who could associate with counseling aims and objectives massively ascribable to education and to the strengthening of personal resources and competences;
- privilege environmental and situational views also in cases where, at least theoretically, there is a declared inseparability between individuals and their past and present life contexts;

- take on a preventive role, since individuals who are not experiencing high levels of discomfort are extremely unlikely to explicitly look for help from people considered potential "allies" of counseling and coaching, such as persons from their relational setting (friends' and relations' network) and some contexts (schools, communities, workplaces, health and social services);
- understand and use different languages and collaborate in multicultural complex environments often requiring multidisciplinary approaches, by working in the street, on trains, at home and more and more from a distance in favor of small and large groups and less and less in closed offices and in face-to-face interactions.

Also, in light of what was said earlier about complexity, it is becoming increasingly important to reflect on the fact that the idea of counseling and coaching characterized by autonomous professional profiles able to provide answers to a range of diverse problems appears now obsolete. We need professionals (doctors, educators, financial experts, etc.) able to empower people to deal with specific problem situations (educational, financial, legal, etc.) by using counseling actions whenever necessary. Such actions in different professional activities are characterized by the peculiarity of the issues dealt with, require specific knowledge of the discipline, and must necessarily be associated with other professional competences in the area in which and for which professionals have been trained. For instance, a financial expert may decide to implement actions of financial counseling for a client who, among other things, needs suggestions on how to invest their money. In order to be credible some characteristics are indispensable: specialized knowledge and abilities to correctly carry out the counseling action, but also additional special competences, such as the ability of financial analysis to be used when necessary without any hesitation. To be efficient and efficacious, the function of financial counseling must be done by individuals who have, above all, great knowledge and specific competences in that field. The same goes for any type of counseling (pedagogical, genetic, psychological, etc.).

At the same time, the function of counseling in the diverse professional areas requires the ability to be just as proficient at adequately handling the professional-client relationship and be able to listen to clients' needs and verify their understanding of them, activate their personal resources and their coping and self-determination abilities, and implement active behaviors such as giving suggestions and information, stimulate available resources, search for and identify possible allies, initiate educational activities. In other words, there is the need to master some psycho-educational abilities. We can say that what was mentioned previously gives a "multidisciplinary" coloring to the function of counseling.

Last, especially attractive today seem to be those theoretical models that look at people and groups from "positive" perspectives, and that emphasize their strengths, their abilities and their functioning. Models whose worldview is positive and life affirming focus on spotting success and abundance, rather than focus on spotting deficits and failures.

According to Polly (2015), conversations on strengths between managers and workers increase performance by 68% and people tend to be more motivated by the opportunity to use their strengths. Individuals should be prepared to find the best in themselves and in others and to express and present these aspects. They must be helped to learn, or learn again, to reflect on themselves and on their contexts, concentrate on the very best they have had, lived or experienced, on their potential allies and on what allows them to exploit to the full their own strengths, their own determination, persistence and moral courage. Attention to positive aspects also facilitates the underscoring of resources and consequently investing in the future. By doing that, we hope people may be able to determine a "dense future zone", that is to say, devote time to finding zones – also diversified – of future, alternative spaces to be filled with plans, hopes and aspirations. This ability can encourage acting now in ways that are in line with the desired future. Interesting is also the notion of savoring, "the capacity to attend to, appreciate, and enhance the positive experiences in one's life" (Bryant, Ericksen, & DeHoeck, 2008, p. 857).

In all this, counseling and coaching will necessarily find themselves using constructs that are very dear to the so-called positive psychology because they will often need to strengthen personal resources, instill confidence and hope, encourage, sustain and strengthen resilience, problem-solving abilities and abilities to cope with difficulties that might unexpectedly come up.

Contents of this volume

This volume is the result of the collaboration of international scholars who wish to spread the belief that some models and some good counseling practices can help people deal more confidently with the challenges and threats that the future seems to increasingly have in store for many of them. In the Introduction, the conditions and effects of the current economic crisis on the wellbeing and the quality of life of large segments of the population will be recalled. The editors of this work will then suggest that some important contributions and supports can come from models and innovative practices of counseling and coaching which – while containing costs – can help people cope with the hardships of these times in school, in community contexts, and throughout their working life.

The reflections and the proposals of the various authors who, notwithstanding their differences and specificities, have shared this project have been organized into three sections:

1 The first, entitled **Approaches, methodologies and techniques for counseling and coaching,** focuses on the need that counseling and coaching models have to be heterogeneous and flexible to adapt to changes.

Attention will be devoted to some original and current trends that can be used to enrich the range of actions useful to face current challenges. Different ways to promote wellbeing in a time of crisis will be considered. Modalities to promote reflexivity, theory-driven innovative strategies and methods in counseling, as well as what can make coaching effective, will be deepened. This section will include the contributions of researchers from the University of Naples Federico II and the University of Milano-Bicocca, Italy, and of researchers from Tel Aviv University, Israel, and the University of Amsterdam, The Netherlands.

2 The second section, **Career counseling and counseling for professional life,** deals with working life in current and future contexts and with effective strategies to manage it satisfactorily. Starting from threats and challenges to our working life, recent approaches will be considered, underlining the wealth of visions but also of solutions and ideas for practice in career counseling and coaching, together with the need for actions and assessing their effectiveness. The colleagues included in this section come from the University of Lisbon, Portugal; the University of Maryland, the University of Chicago, the University of Kansas, Arizona State University, USA; and the University of University of Naples Federico II and the University of Milano-Bicocca, Italy.
3 The third section, **Counseling and coaching actions for wellbeing and inclusion,** examines the awareness that health, wellbeing and inclusion are also at risk in current times. There is an increasing need for counseling and coaching models that emphasize attention to prevention, set up inclusive contexts and give emphasis to self-determination, for the development of rich and courageous identities. In this section, too, colleagues from universities in different countries have given their contributions: the University of Minnesota and Azusa Pacific University & San Diego, USA; Tel Aviv University, Israel; the University of Padova, and the Vita-Salute San Raffaele University, Milan, Italy.

At the end of the volume, some conclusive reflections are added on some ideas for the future of counseling and coaching. Recalling what was presented in the different chapters, such reflections intend to highlight some trend lines that the counseling and coaching of the future should continue to cultivate to become – notwithstanding possible difficulties, problems and threats – real anchorages, and instruments able to strengthen the abilities of many individuals and of different contexts.

Note

Gini's index of concentration is an indicator that offers a measure of the concentration of transferable quantitative variables, as is the case with income. The closer it is to 0 the more we would be in a situation of fairly homogeneous distribution of the considered variable (fair distribution of wealth in our case). On the contrary, when the index is close to 1 the distribution would be particularly inhomogeneous/unequal as the value 1 corresponds to the maximum possible concentration, that is to say, when only one person would hold the whole income of the country. The calculation procedures of Gini's index are on the whole fairly simple (see Gini, 1921; Lanza, 2015).

References

American Counseling Association. (2016). *20/20: Consensus definition of counseling*. Retrieved from www.counseling.org/

Bertelè, U. (2013). *Strategia* [Strategy]. Milano: EGEA.

Bower, J. L., & Christensen, C. M. (1995). Disruptive technologies: Catching the wave. *Harvard Business Review, 73*(1), 43–53.

Bryant, F. B., Ericksen, C. L., & DeHoek, A. H. (2008). Savoring. In S. J. Lopez (Ed.), *Encyclopedia of positive psychology* (pp. 857–859). New York, NY: Wiley/Blackwell.

Cheung-Judge, M-Y., & Holbeche, L. (2011). *Organization development: A practitioner's guide for OD and HR*. London: Kogan Page.

Credit Counseling Centers, Inc. (1981). *Credit counselor training handbook*. Southfield, MI: Credit Counseling Centers.

Downes, L., & Nunes, P. (2014). Big bang disruption: Strategy in the age of devastating innovation. New York, NY: Penguin.

Ehrlich, P. R., & Ehrlich, A. H. (2009). The population bomb revisited. *The Electronic Journal of Sustainable Development, 1*(3), 5–13.

Fotopoulos, T. (2007). The ecological crisis as a part of the present multidimensional crisis and inclusive democracy. *The International Journal of Inclusive Democracy, 3*(3). Retrieved from www.inclusivedemocracy.org/journal

Frey, C. B., & Osborne, M. A. (2013). *The future of employment: How susceptible are jobs to computerisation*. Oxford Martin School, Working Paper No. 7.

Gini, C. (1921). Measurement of inequality of incomes. *The Economic Journal, 31*(121), 124–126.

Grant, A. M. (2008). Past, present and future: The evolution of professional coaching and coaching psychology. In S. Palmer & A. Whybrow (Eds.), *Handbook of coaching psychology: A guide for practitioners* (pp. 23–29). London: Routledge.

International Labour Office. (2001). *Reducing the decent work deficit: A global challenge*. Retrieved from www.ilo.org/public/portugue/region/eurpro/lisbon/pdf/rep-i-a.pdf

International Labour Office. (2006). Showcasing tool and experiences in labour administration and the informal economy. Geneva: ILO.

Lai, Y., & McDowall, A. (2014). A systematic review (SR) of coaching psychology: Focusing on the attributes of effective coaching psychologists. *International Coaching Psychology Review, 9*(2), 118–134.

Lanza, G. (2015). *La misurazione della disuguaglianza economica: Approcci, metodi e strumenti* [Measuring economic inequality: Approaches, methods and instruments]. Milano: Franco Angeli.

Markoff, J. (2011, March 4). Armies of expensive lawyers replaced by cheaper software. *The New York Times*.

Nota, L., & Soresi, S. (2015). *Il counseling del futuro* [Counseling of the future]. Padova: Cleup.

Parsole, E., & Wray, M. (2000). Coaching and mentoring: Practical methods to improve learning. London: Kogan Page.

Polly, S. (2015). *Building strength: Tools for the positive psychology practitioner.* Paper presented at workshop at Fourth World Congress on Positive Psychology, Orlando, FL.

Reid, H. (2016). Usefulness and truthfulness reviewing the limitations and promoting the benefits of constructivist approaches for career counselling. In M. McMahon & Patton (Eds.), *Career counselling: Constructivist approaches*. London: Routledge.

Society of Counseling Psychology. American Psychological Association Section 17 (2017). *What is counseling psychology*. Retrieved from www.div17.org/

Spence, G. B., & Grant, A. M. (2007). Professional and peer life coaching and the enhancement of goal striving and wellbeing: An exploratory study. *The Journal of Positive Psychology*, *2*(3), 185–194.

Taleb, N. N. (2008). The black swan: The Impact of the highly improbable. London: Penguin.

Thompson, W. R., & Reuveny, R. (2009). *Limits to globalization: North-South divergence*. London: Routledge.

World Health Organization. (2011). Global burden of mental disorders and the need for a comprehensive, coordinated response from health and social sectors at the country level. Retrieved from http://apps.who.int/gb/ebwha/pdf_files/EB130/B130_9-en.pdf

Part I

Approaches, methodologies and techniques for counseling and coaching

Looking back, we can certainly say that the times we are living in are very different from the past and are also especially challenging. The Western world is now looking with concern at the high levels of discomfort and malaise being experienced because of social, economic, and environmental crises that are more frequent and intense than those of the past century.

In addition, our life contexts contain such highly complex elements that they are not so easily understandable with our current instruments of analysis, which continue to hypothesize the existence of prevalently linear causal relationships among events. Thanks to the contributions of the theories of complexity, we are realizing that reality is mostly made up of systems characterized by a great number of elements affecting one another via micro influences, which can trigger causal relationships that are not easily predictable. In all of this, a significant role is attributed to the new technologies that are characterizing educational settings, professional contexts, and leisure actions.

Many people are, therefore, looking for advantageous ways to cope with our current times and with the most widespread forms of difficulties and discomfort. Counseling and coaching can be helpful modalities to assist people in this task if they can free themselves from their "old consolidated operational ways" to promote opportunities for growth and improvement in increasingly heterogeneous contexts. This will have to done by using new conceptual and operational instruments derived from our ability to theorize the best from different knowledge domains, from research areas and different applicative sectors traditionally competing with one another.

In the following pages, we present approaches, methodologies and techniques which, albeit their diversity, have responded in a heterogeneous and flexible way to current needs and priorities.

In Chapter 1 of the first section, much space is devoted to an ability considered particularly important in our times: reflexivity. Giovanna Esposito and Maria Francesca Freda present the Narrative Mediation Path, which, by promoting reflection and reflexivity, originates a process that helps to build new meanings and orient actions in a different way. The examples that they propose underscore how a multimodal narrative approach that integrates different narrative modes, as well as the individual and the group process of meaning reconstruction, becomes an innovative approach able to help students who may need to develop reflexive competences to impact their academic performance.

In Chapter 2, Maria Grazia Strepparava, Marco Bani, and Giorgio Rezzonico focus on cognitive and behavioral approaches to counseling, paying attention to some skills about thought reformulation, emotion regulation, and mindfulness that can be useful for healthcare professionals and for those who work in a healthcare environment. Particular emphasis is given to train health practitioners and students in counseling skills to help them to communicate adequately with patients and relatives and to provide a set of basic tools of self-regulation and self-care to treat properly different emotionally challenging situations and to adapt to the professional requirements of the caring professions.

The next author, Moshe Israelashvili, offers a further example of originality in Chapter 3. Starting from the observation that children and adolescents are intensively engaged in dealing with these new technologies and that a prominent feature of engagement in these new technologies is visual, he underlines that this has major implications for the future of (school) counseling. So he briefly reviews the well-documented features of visualized communication and describes two studies that explore the implementation of visualization in a school-related setting, the first on the feasibility of using YouTube in mental health counseling, and the second on the integration of pictures in counseling parents of high-school graduates.

The section closes with a contribution in Chapter 4 by *Tim Theeboom, Annelies E.M. van Vianen, Bianca Beersma, Robert Zwitser,* and *Vladimer Kobayashi* who focus on the practitioner's perspective to better understand the process of coaching. Starting from the acknowledgement of the increased popularity of coaching, together with the relatively costly individualized nature of coaching, they underline the importance of considering the coaching success indicators that coaches refer to. The awareness and the consideration of such indicators can provide information that may be used to increase the alignment between coaching practice and research and therefore help researchers and professionals choose objectives and practices that value effectiveness to be better able to respond to the real needs of individuals.

Chapter 1

Counseling and reflexive processes

Role of multimodal narrative devices in promoting reflection and reflexivity in a university context

Giovanna Esposito and Maria Francesca Freda

Introduction

According to the recent European guidelines (Council of the European Union, 2013), underachievement among university students is a phenomenon currently hampering the processes of inclusion and participation of many European students in universities. As this is a growing issue, with 35% of European students at a risk of dropping out due to their academic performance, there is an increased need for developing novel intervention models that can help deal with underachievement in higher education (HE).

Underachievement is commonly seen as a discrepancy between the level of students' performance and their academic potential. Accordingly, underachieving students are those who often present with low academic performance by not passing any examinations over a long period of time, achieving low scores in examinations, or presenting with a low Grade Point Average (GPA) or a low European Credit Transfer System (ECTS) score (a standard for comparing study attainment and performance of students in HE throughout the European Union). Such discrepancies may not be the direct result of a diagnosed learning disability and may persist over an extended period of time (Reis & McCoach, 2000). There is not a single cause of underachievement; rather, it is influenced by numerous factors such as teaching methods, personality traits, and impairments in relational or reflexive competences (e.g., Rimm, 2003). Underachieving students are often nontraditional students or disadvantaged students; for example, they may be first-generation students, working students, or immigrants.

The European Commission has called for the need to develop and implement innovative approaches, such as guidance and counseling, to help underachieving university students fully reap the benefits of tertiary education. To respond to these needs, we implemented the Innovative Solution to Acquire Learning to Learn (INSTALL; please see Note) European Project, which involved 198 underachieving students enrolled in four European university degree programs (Italy, Romania, Spain, and Ireland). For this project, a model of narrative group counseling, the Narrative Mediation Path (NMP), was created. It aims at the overall improvement in students' reflexive processes to influence their academic performance, which is considered to be the main indicator of academic inclusion (e.g., Muskens, 2011).

The relevance of reflexivity in the field of HE is not new in the literature, and reflexivity is deemed useful for encouraging critical thinking and supporting student academic productivity (Taylor, 2011). In particular, underachieving students often face reflexive difficulties with regard to specific developmental tasks (e.g., failing an exam) and strategic utilization of their time at university (Padykula & Horwitz, 2011). Moreover, narration is nowadays considered an important device for developing reflexive competencies among underachieving students. This is because narrative devices play a key role in facilitating the reassignment of meaning to the events of one's own life (Lieblich, 2012).

In this chapter, we present the theoretical background of NMP counseling by discussing a semiotic and psychodynamic conceptualization of reflexive processes that distinguish between two levels of different complexity (reflection and reflexivity) and that ascribe to multimodal narrative devices a key role in promoting reflexive processes. We then discuss the NMP approach and present various narrative excerpts taken from the transcripts of one group of underachieving students who participated in the counseling sessions.

A semiotic and psychodynamic conceptualization of reflexive process: reflection and reflexivity

Throughout the years, many models of reflexive process have been developed (e.g., Bleakley, 2006) and reflexive processes have been equated with metacognition, introspection, and critical thinking (Moore, 2011).

Many of these models concur in describing reflection as the result of various levels of complexity. For example, in pedagogy, Mezirow (1990) distinguished four levels of increasing complexity (habitual action/non-reflection, understanding, reflection, and critical reflection). Burkitt (2012) identified two levels in sociology: self-reflection and reflexivity.

Moreover, there has been a shift in conceiving of reflexive process from an individual function (often defined as self-reflection and linked to the concept of introspection) to the idea of the reflexive process as an intersubjective product that emerges through dialogical exchange among people who share the same context (Valsiner, 2007).

We have recently presented a conceptualization of reflexive process that fits within the debate on reflexivity and that has many dimensions and is an intersubjective process. According to this conceptualization, reflexive processes are to be discussed within a semiotic and psychodynamic perspective and may be conceived as constituted by two distinct levels of complexity (Esposito & Freda, 2016; Esposito, Freda, & De Luca Picione, 2016; Freda, De Luca Picione, & Esposito, 2015). The conceptualization is based on two issues that have been poorly addressed in the literature on reflexive processes: a conception of emotions as regulators of sense-making processes and an intersubjective declination of emotions that considers the relationship between individual and context.

Rather than being identified as variables that interfere or threaten the linearity and rationality of relational processes, emotions may be understood as the matrix of thought (Matte Blanco, 1975), an unconscious mode of operation of the mind that generalizes and homogenizes the field of experience. This process of categorization that does not focus on the characteristics of the specific event but instead treats it in terms of class or category of similar experiences is referred to as "emotional semiosis" (Freda, 2011; Salvatore, 2011). Moreover, the affective process cannot be understood in intra-psychological terms, as being confined to the head, since it has a semiotic and dialogical nature. Affective meaning is a collective product, performed through individual minds, and it emerges through and in terms of how people combine signs according to the cultural context they are part of and that they contribute to building (Salvatore & Freda, 2011).

We assume reflexive processes to be ever more analytical and complex mechanisms of experience differentiation. Furthermore, we propose a distinction between two levels of reflexive process: reflection and reflexivity.

Reflection is the psychological process through which individuals are able to gain new understandings of themselves and recognize themselves as subjective entities of semiotic production (i.e., they reflect themselves). Take the case of an underachieving university student who states the following:

> "I have always thought myself to be a victim of the ugliness of some professors and of some mates. Now I realize I am just an insecure and weak person."

The narrative informs us of a new way to give meaning to the self within a specific context (weak, insecure) that contrasts with the role of victim the student has previously conformed to.

Reflection has been conceived as an important step toward reaching reflexivity. Reflexivity is a semiotic process of transformation by considering one's own perspective and the way it directs the self, giving meaning to relational processes. Through reflexivity, subjects are able to think about the relational processes in which they are involved. The subject is consequently able to give a new meaning to a process (not to the self) and to recognize the active role assumed in guiding events. This equates to understanding that one co-constructs relationships not only because of external causes but also because of internal reasons and desires that drive human action. For example, recall the case of the female student who describes her feeling of being insecure and weak. She continues the same narrative by saying:

> "the more I thought I was a victim, the more I could not change my situation of isolation from everyone. Now I realize that conceiving of myself as a victim of professors was just an excuse to be noticed, to say that I exist

at the university. It seems paradoxical, but I tried to hide in order to be noticed, I hoped someone, sooner or later, would notice me and invite me to participate in group class work."

In this narrative, the student is not so much involved in a process of signification as a way of being but is instead immersed in a way of acting within a relational context. She acknowledges the emotional dynamic enacted; she had directed her complaints against the university and defined herself as a victim to be noticed by others.

Multimodal narrative methodology and reflexive process

The relevance of narrative approaches in counseling is not new. Many narrative models (e.g., Savickas, 2005) focus on various problems and integrate different counseling intervention settings (Richardson, 2012). According to Murdock, Dual, and Nilsonn (2012), the narrative approach to counseling presents a well-defined theoretical structure supported by a considerable body of empirical research. Several authors have acknowledged the centrality of telling stories and have described how narratives play an important role in giving meaning to one's own experience (Bruner, 1990). Subjects are conceived as active storytellers who organize their multiple life experiences into coherent stories that they share with others in an intersubjective process of meaning construction.

Thus, narration plays a key role in the promotion of reflexive processes, as this requires that the information presents itself in the form of representation. It requires that the information represents itself (from the Latin *re-ad-praesentare* = representation, make present again). Representation allows the activation of a reflexive process. According to a semiotic model of the mind (Valsiner, 2007), the construction of a text is a semiotic process generated by emotions while, at the same time, symbolizing them by representing them as words (Freda, 2011).

Several examples have been provided in the literature regarding the use of multiple narrative devices in the same intervention for the promotion of reflexive processes. When this happens, it is preferable to define the narrative approach as a multimodal narrative approach (Pink, 2011). Multimodality uses multiple modes and media associated with specific sensory channels. It has been considered effective in promoting reflexive processes (Pink, 2011). Multimodality is "a new multi-semiotic form in which meaning is produced through the inter-relationships between and among different media and modes" (Dicks, Soyinka, & Coffey, 2006, p. 78). Using multiple media makes it possible to create new realities of meaning and knowledge to promote an understanding of the complexity of experiences, thereby enabling an in-depth analysis that would not be otherwise available.

A novel counseling approach: the narrative mediation path

Given the reflexive potential of multimodality approaches, we devised and trialed the NMP, a novel narrative counseling that was implemented among underachieving students who were at a risk of being excluded. The NMP comprises seven weekly group counseling sessions integrating the group and individual narrative levels through the use of four narrative modes: metaphoric, iconographic, writing, and bodily.

Each narrative mode had its own medium: the metaphoric mode involved proverbs and mottos. Students were asked to choose the one that represented their university experiences (e.g., "He who makes his bed must lie in it," "Yes, we can!"). Metaphoric media allowed students to identify the "problem," namely their difficulties in the academic experience, by focusing on what had not yet been placed in the spotlight or focused on. The metaphoric mode provided an anchor to cultural connotations of the formative self that was necessary early along the counseling path when the students had yet to test their relational fields and verify its *holding* capacity (Winnicott, 1971).

In the iconographic mode, six vignettes were given, each featuring a character engaged in a typical situation at university (e.g., enrolment, attending a class, self-study, an informal moment at university, a written examination, or an oral examination), and students were asked to select one character, put themselves in his/her shoes, and write a speech balloon containing the character's thoughts or feelings for each vignette. At the end of the task, each student was requested to reflect on the representation of the student that emerged from what they had written in each balloon, and the group was invited to comment on it. The iconographic mode encouraged the analysis of the university experience at a diachronic level; unlike the previous mode that focused on the "problem," through vignettes, students were encouraged to ask themselves about what they usually "did" to overcome the problem in various university experiences. Specifically, the vignettes were projective stimuli that became a sort of *transitional object* (Winnicott, 1971) that belonged to but was also separate from the students.

In the writing mode, in accordance with McAdams's (McAdams et al., 2006) narrative model, three narrative assignments were given (writing about a *low point, high point,* and *decisional turning point* in the students' university experiences). The writing mode aimed to analyze the connection between students' past actions within the university and the competencies used to realize them. Unlike the previous modes, writing media explicitly invited students to narrate their past actions and assume a more subjective position, namely to be both the subject and object of their narration.

Finally, in the bodily mode, the students were asked to create a sculpture from the bodies of all group members to reflect their future at the university. The bodily mode conveyed a symbolic and nonverbal representation of students' university future and focused on learned competences and changes that occurred due to their participation in group counseling. Sculpture mobilized the body and symbolically allowed students to "take action" by working on how to perform to achieve academic goals.

Moreover, over each session, a common methodological sequence was adopted: first, the *narrative medium* (proverbs, vignettes, etc.) was presented; then, each group member engaged in the *narrative construction of the experience* and was asked to give meaning to it; thereafter, a *group-level narrative meta-discourse* was elaborated from each member's narration; and finally, each participant *reconstructed the narrative experience* and was asked to elaborate a new meaning based on the previous individual and group narrative meta-discourse.

Similar to the personal narratives, the members of the group were conceived as "reflexive mirrors" who allowed students to think about their relationship in the university context and to identify new ways to cope, construct sense, and favor a reprioritization of university goals. Members were asked to be participants in each other's stories and be performers and audience members at the same time to re-author their personal stories and account for the other alternatives (Freda, Gonzàlez-Monteagudo, & Esposito, 2016).

In NMP counseling, the counselor aims at promoting these processes of individual and collective meaning reconstruction. The counselor is considered to be a "reflexive social mirror" (Bateman & Fonagy, 2012) who holds students' narratives, encourages member participation, and contributes to co-constructing meaning in the inter-subjective group setting. The counselor supports participants in opening into new possible and functional actions in the university context (Esposito et al., 2016). In other words, the counselor recursively moves from subjectivity to intersubjectivity by supporting individuals in reflecting on their personal narratives and by involving members of the group in co-constructing a new meaning to give to individual narratives (Freda & Esposito, 2017).

To assess the efficacy of NMP counseling groups, some *ad hoc* questionnaires were developed and administered in three evaluation phases (pre-test, post-test, and follow-up). Specifically, the academic performance scale was administered in the pre-test phase (at the beginning of the NMP's first session) and approximately one year from the end of the counseling period. The questionnaire included several questions regarding the year of enrollment, the degree program, the highest and the lowest scores obtained in the examination, the number of failed examinations, their number in the ECTS, the number of examinations passed, and the GPAs of each student.

During the post-test phase (at the end of the NMP's seventh session), the satisfaction questionnaire was administered, which included questions regarding the students' degree of satisfaction. The students were asked to answer on a seven-point Likert scale (ranging from extremely satisfied to extremely unsatisfied) questions related to several dimensions of group counseling (i.e., overall satisfaction, accessibility and cleanness of the counseling location, availability and courtesy of the counselor, time of the intervention, utility of counseling in achieving personal university objectives, and satisfaction with the efficacy of counseling).

Examples of NMP practices

To exemplify how NMP counseling promotes reflection and reflexivity, we now present various narrative excepts taken from the transcripts of one group of Italian underachieving students who participated in the NMP counseling sessions.

The group comprised seven students (women = four; men = three) enrolled in different degree courses (including law, engineering, and biology) at the University of Naples, Italy. The mean age of the students was 22.35 years (SD = 1.75). Three students were taking longer than usual to complete their master's degree, while two students were enrolled in the third year and two students were enrolled in the second year of the bachelor's degree program. All the students were considered underachievers as, at the time of their enrollment in the NMP group counseling, they had a GPA of less than 23 and had gained less than 50% in the ECTS. Moreover, two students did not pass any exam for one year, while the others passed only one or two exams in the year before their participation in the counseling sessions.

The group counseling sessions were held from October to December 2014. The group counseling was free and did not offer any issuance of university's ECTS. Instead, each student was given a certificate of participation in the INSTALL project. Moreover, all the students signed an informed consent form that allowed researchers to use both the narrative materials and audio recordings from the sessions for training and research purposes. Regarding the assessment of the efficacy of this NMP group counseling, from the pre-test to the follow-up phase, there was a significant increase in the ECTS ($Z = -2.201$; $p = 0.028$) and the number of examinations passed ($Z = -2.214$; $p = 0.027$). Moreover, regarding the satisfaction of the group counseling, all the group members acknowledged overall satisfaction (N = 6 extremely satisfied; N = 1 very satisfied).

Furthermore, we discuss the narrative passages of reflection and reflexivity that emerged in the student narratives. Names have been changed to protect the privacy of the participants.

Metaphoric mode

During the first session, Maria chose "Yes, we can!" as her motto in the metaphoric mode. She motivated her choice by narrating:

> "I do not exactly know why I have chosen this motto! I am now realizing that for me the aspect of 'we' is fundamental! I don't like to stay alone, but,

> mostly important, I have to care of many people, such as my brothers, my husband and also my colleagues. I gave them my class notes even if they do not ask me to do it. I am an altruistic person but I don't know if it's a good thing!"
>
> (Reflection)

Through choosing the proverb and explaining her motivation, Maria understood the meaning the medium acquired in relation to her own university experience and redefined herself as an altruistic person.

As a result of the request of the counselor to explain why she behaved in such an altruistic way, Maria said:

> "Sincerely I don't know why I behave in such a way. Maybe my altruistic behavior is just a way to relate with others because I do not know other ways to keep in touch with people. Maybe I hope that my altruism can allow people to recognize me but, in such a way, I cannot understand which are my own desires, wishes and plans for the future."
>
> (Reflexivity)

Maria gained access to a reflexivity process through recognizing the active role assumed in guiding her "altruistic" behavior at the university. She understood that she enacted an emotional dynamic characterized by her need to be seen and recognized and also realized that this behavior could be unproductive for her personal and academic growth.

Iconographic mode

During the fourth session of the iconographic mode, Diego read what he wrote in the vignettes. In his first vignette on enrollment, he stated:

> "I chose the boy near the desk and I inserted several question marks because when I enrolled at university I had many doubts on my decision. I chose this degree course because some friends of mine suggested [it to] me. I do not know what I have to do, what I like. . . . I am an insecure and confused student, sometimes I think I will never be able to take a clear decision."

The vignettes provided an opportunity for Diego to have access to a reflective process by giving a new meaning to his role as a confused and insecure student.

Invited by the NMP counselor to read the other vignettes, Diego said that the last one, the oral examination, was the vignette that better explained his academic difficulties, stating the following:

> "I chose the boy who goes away from the class. I am afraid to be evaluated and I usually escape! I think that this happens because I have several doubts, even on my competences! Very often I said that I escape because

> that professors were insensitive to me, but now I realized that my behavior is just a way not to face with my difficulty in removing doubts about myself."
>
> (Reflexivity)

In this narrative, Diego recognized that his behaviors were not caused by the insensitivity of some professors but were instead due to his difficulty in removing doubts and assuming a clear position with regard to his university experience.

Writing mode

A student, Sara, described in the high point narrative an episode in which she was happy about a successful performance in an examination. The counselor asked why she thought the experience was so positively significant, and Sara stated:

> "I realized that I am not a stupid student, I have some competencies! I always thought [I was] inferior to my colleagues as they frequently passed examinations with a higher rate".
>
> (Reflection)

The writing media promoted a representation of Sara as a capable student that differed from the "stupid" student she had believed herself to be. Sara's reflection triggered a series of processes within the group, and the other members asked her about the origin of her belief of being incapable. She stated:

> "When I was at high school I had the same idea. But I also think that this rigid belief was an excuse to not improve and not to study: it was easier for me to think that I cannot achieve good academic results because I was limited; in such a way I could avoid [the commitment to] study."

Bodily mode

During the bodily mode, the group sculpted a route to reach the degree. Each student decided to sculpt an obstacle along the route, such as insecurity, stubbornness, or weakness. A member of the group, Paolo, sculpted the stubbornness, and the counselor asked him to justify his choice and comment on what he felt and thought during the sculptural representation. Paolo stated:

> "I sculpted the stubbornness because it's my problem. While I was sculpting, I felt that my body had to be rigid. I am rigid, stiff, stubborn, it's very difficult for me to change an idea, even when the others try to convince me that I am wrong".
>
> (Reflection)

Through the sculpture, Paolo redefined himself as a stiff and stubborn student who had to work in the future to attenuate this problem. A group member, Gloria, commented that Paolo, particularly in the latter sessions, had gradually reduced his tendency to be stubborn as he had often listened to other members' suggestions. In the following excerpt, the positive redefinition by Gloria allowed Paolo to gain access to a reflexive process and to recognize how his stiffness had contributed to his poor academic performance, stating:

> "It's a pleasure you noted this change! Maybe it really means that something [has] changed! My stubbornness has created too many university problems and many difficulties in my social relationships."
>
> (Reflexivity)

Conclusion

Despite the existence of several examples of a narrative approach to counseling, we believe that the NMP is characterized by specific aspects that constitute its advantages: (a) it adopts a multimodal narrative approach that integrates different narrative modes as well as the individual and the group process of meaning reconstruction; (b) it aims at developing reflexive processes of different complexity; and (c) it targets underachieving college students who may need to develop reflexive competences to influence their academic performance.

Nevertheless, the NMP has some limitations. From a technical and procedural perspective, the NMP processes/formats have been developed primarily for HE. To extend the model to other educational contexts, further adaptation of the NMP would be required. This is mainly because the narrative stimuli developed for each of the four modes (metaphoric, iconographic, writing, and bodily) are directly connected to academic experience. For example, the vignettes used for the iconographic mode require the recollection of typical events from academic experiences. Therefore, if this process were to be used in other contexts, such as a school, all narrative mode stimuli would need to be refocused toward the shared common experiences of the users involved.

Moreover, many students may not benefit from this type of approach because they may suffer from clinical psychopathologies that require treatment in a specific psychotherapeutic setting, or because they may be extremely uncomfortable with some modes and media (e.g., bodily mode) or with the group setting. As explained earlier, all four modes and the related media have to be used to achieve effectiveness, and there is a specific order of model stages that must be followed.

In conclusion, despite its limits in terms of adaptability, the use of the NMP has interesting implications for HE policies and practices. There has been a recent surge in demand for the implementation of innovative methods at universities to promote reflexive competence. This competence has been considered to be fundamental for the critical thinking needed to support complex learning processes (Taylor, 2011) and has also been important for employability (Esposito, Freda, & Bosco, 2015). Narrative methods are a useful tool in intervention settings designed to reach these aims because narrative is a functional tool for reflecting on the limitations that hinder academic productivity. Narrative also hints at the resources required for investing to implement actions that lead to academic inclusion.

Finally, the NMP could be a useful approach for professionals devoted to supporting students struggling with aspects of their university lives and who have to deal with the difficulties intrinsic in their professional tasks. Counselors need to focus on more than just low levels of academic performance. In addition, they should assist students in understanding and dealing with the critical phases that threaten their academic path. For example, it is important to aim at promoting both the reflexive processes (reflection and reflexivity) to allow students to give new meanings to their representations of themselves as students and to the role they assume in orienting their university underachievement. This means constantly stimulating group discussions about each student's university story by posing simple questions that involve all members in a process of meaning co-construction.

As mentioned earlier, each member of the group may assume a key role in allowing students to reflect on their own university experience by assuming a different perspective. Moreover, the counselors in each narrative mode must balance the descriptive and elaborative levels in the students' narratives to allow them to describe their university experience and reflect on it by giving new meanings to that experience. Many students, for example, experience a high level of difficulty in narrating their present or past stories: they seem blocked with regard to returning to their stories and tend to avoid opportunities to gain access to thoughts and feelings connected with such experiences. The work of the counselor is to allow students to recover this descriptive ability by posing specific questions aimed at expanding upon these narratives (e.g., "What happened? Tell me more about this event") or by initiating interventions that foster counterfactual thinking. By inserting an unexpected element (e.g., "What would have happened if . . ."), the counselor can redirect students toward thinking about their experiences from a different perspective. Moreover, the counselor must focus on the relationship between reflexivity and agency, as this could be conceived as the outcome of the reflexive awareness. This will allow students to gain access to the reversibility of their choices to perform effectively at the university and plan new actions that will help them strategically achieve their learning goals. For example, it could be helpful to adopt particular counseling techniques that will enable students to describe whether they have assumed a more agentive stance by performing new actions from one session to another or by dealing with their university problems. The counselor could support the assumption of an agentive stance by supporting students in scheduling future plans due to their reflexive awareness and by focusing on what they are willing to do to overcome their university problems.

Acknowledgments

The European Commission supported this work [Grant Agreement 2011–4040 Project 517750-LLP-1–2011–1-IT-ERASMUS-ESIN].

Note

The project was funded in 2011 within the ERASMUS Multilateral Project initiative and ended in March 2014. The SInAPSi center of the Federico II University took the lead in the partnership with three other European universities: US (Spain), NUIM (Ireland), and NSPSA (Romania). This project was funded with support from the European Commission. This publication reflects the views only of the author, and the Commission cannot be held responsible for any use which may be made of the information contained therein.

References

Bateman, A. W., & Fonagy, P. (Eds.). (2012). *Handbook of mentalizing in mental health practice*. Arlington, VA: American Psychiatric Association.

Bleakley, A. (2006). From reflexive practice to holistic reflexivity. *Studies in Higher Education, 24*, 315–330. doi:10.1080/03075079912331379925.

Bruner, J. (1990). *Acts of meaning*. Cambridge, MA: Harvard University Press.

Burkitt, I. (2012). Emotional reflexivity: Feeling, emotion and imagination in reflexive dialogues. *Sociology, 46*, 458–472. doi:10.1177/0038038511422587.

Council of the European Union. (2013). *Council conclusions on the social dimension of higher education*. Retrieved from www.consilium.europa.eu/uedocs/cms_data/docs/pressdata/en/educ/137144.pdf

Dicks, B., Soyinka, B., & Coffey, A. (2006). Multimodality ethnography. *Qualitative Research, 6*, 77–96. doi:10.1177/1468794106058876.

Esposito, G., & Freda, M. F. (2016). Reflexive and agentive functions of narrative writing: A qualitative study on the narratives of university students. *Integrative Psychological and Behavioral Science, 50*, 333–357. doi:10.1007/s12124-015-9323-5.

Esposito, G., Freda, M. F., & Bosco, V. (2015). Examining perception of competency through practicum competencies outline. *European Journal of Training and Development, 39*, 700–720. doi:10.1108/EJTD-05-2015-0037.

Esposito, G., Freda, M. F., & De Luca Picione, R. (2016). Reflexivity or "Reflexivities" in higher education: Conceptualizing unique reflexive process. In M. F. Freda, J. Gonzàlez-Monteagudo, & G. Esposito (Eds.), *Working with underachieving students in higher education: Fostering inclusion through narration and reflexivity* (pp. 32–42). Abingdon: Oxon; New York, NY: Routledge.

Freda, M. F. (2011). Understanding continuity to recognize discontinuity. *Integrative Psychological & Behavioral Science, 45*, 335–346. doi:10.1007/s12124-011-9169-4.

Freda, M. F., De Luca Picione, R., & Esposito, G. (2015). Reflexivity: Applying a reflexive process to an educational context. In G. Marsico, R. Ruggeri, & S. Salvatore (Eds.), *YIS: The yearbook of ideographic science – reflexivity and psychology* (pp. 195–225). Charlotte, NC: IAP- Information Age Publishing.

Freda, M. F., & Esposito, G. (2017). Promoting reflection and reflexivity through narrative devices: Narrative mediation path qualitative multimodal method. *Qualitative Research Journal, 17*(1), 2–19. doi:10.1108/QRJ-06-2016-0039.

Freda, M. F., Gonzàlez-Monteagudo, J., & Esposito, G. (Eds.). (2016). Working with underachieving students in higher education: Fostering inclusion through narration and reflexivity. Abingdon: Oxon; New York, NY: Routledge.
Lieblich, A. (2012). Healing plots: Writing and reading in life-stories groups. *Qualitative Inquiry, 19*, 46–52. doi:10.1177/1077800412462982.
Matte Blanco, I. (1975). *The unconscious as infinite sets: An essay in bi-logic*. London, UK: Gerald Duckworth and Company Ltd.
McAdams, D. P., Bauer, J. J., Sakaeda, A. R., Anyidoho, N. A., Machado, M. A., Magrino-Failla, K., . . . Pals, J. L. (2006). Continuity and change in the life story: A longitudinal study of autobiographical memories in emerging adulthood. *Journal of Personality, 74*, 1371–1400. doi:10.1111/j.1467-6494.2006.00412.x.
Mezirow, J. (1990). *Transformative dimensions of adult learning*. San Francisco, CA: Jossey-Bass.
Moore, T. (2011). Critical thinking: Seven definitions in search of a concept. *Studies in Higher Education, 36*, 1–17. doi:10.1080/03075079.2011.586995.
Murdock, N. L., Dual, C., & Nilsonn, J. E. (2012). Emerging approaches to counseling intervention. theory, research, practice, and training. *The Counseling Psychologist, 40*, 966–975. doi:10.1177/0011000012460663.
Muskens, G. (2011). Inclusion and education in European countries: Methodological considerations. *Quality and Quantity, 47*, 237–255. doi:10.1007/s11135-011-9514-1.
Padykula, L. N., & Horwitz, M. (2011). Using psychodynamic concepts to measure interpersonal competencies during social work training. *International Journal of Applied Psychoanalytic Studies, 9*, 48–61. doi:10.1002/aps.312.
Pink, S. (2011). Multimodality, multisensoriality and ethnographic knowing: Social semiotics and the phenomenology of perception. *Qualitative Research, 11*, 261–276. doi:10.1177/1468794111399835.
Reis, S. M., & McCoach, D. B. (2000). The underachievement of gifted students: What do we know and where do we go? *Gifted Child Quarterly, 44*, 152–170. doi:10.1177/001698620004400302.
Richardson, M. S. (2012). Counseling for work and relationship. *The Counseling Psychologist, 40*, 190–242. doi:10.1177/0011000011406452.
Rimm, S. B. (2003). Underachievement: A national epidemic. In N. Colangelo & G. A. Davis (Eds.), *Handbook of gifted education* (pp. 424–443). Boston, MA: Allyn and Bacon.
Salvatore, S. (2011). Psychotherapy research needs theory. Outline for an epistemology of the clinical exchange. *Integrative Psychological and Behavioral Science, 45*, 366–388. doi:10.1007/s12124-011-9180-9.
Salvatore, S., & Freda, M. F. (2011). Affect, unconscious and sensemaking: A psychodynamic, semiotic and dialogic model. *New Ideas in Psychology, 29*, 119–135. doi:10.1016/j.newideapsych.2010.06.001.
Savickas, M. L. (2005). The theory and practice of career construction. In S. D. Brown & R. W. Lent (Eds.), *Career development and counseling* (pp. 42–70). Hoboken, NJ: John Wiley.
Taylor, C. A. (2011). More than meets the eye: The use of videonarratives to facilitate doctoral students' reflexivity on their doctoral journeys. *Studies in Higher Education, 36*, 441–458. doi:10.1080/03075071003714115.
Valsiner, J. (2007). Culture in minds and societies: Foundations of cultural psychology. New Delhi: Sage Publications.
Winnicott, D. W. (1971). *Playing and reality*. London, UK: Tavistock.

Chapter 2

New issues in cognitive counseling

Counseling skills in health care

Maria Grazia Strepparava, Marco Bani, and Giorgio Rezzonico

Introduction: counseling and health

In their everyday activities, healthcare professionals use a wide range of counseling skills, mainly communication and relational skills. These skills are crucial for medical doctors, nurses, midwives, and physical and rehabilitation therapists for implementing preventive and supportive interventions concerning their patients' health: to assist patients in stopping wrong habits and in changing those attitudes that prevent treatment adherence, to foster cooperation in treatment choice, to guide the patient's decision in informed consent, to communicate adequately in difficult or critical situations, such as in breaking bad news (Buckman, 2011). Good relational attitudes and high levels of interpersonal sensitivity are also crucial for performing all those clinical activities to the highest level. Burnard (2005), in describing the counseling skills needed by health professionals, focuses his attention on three major areas: (a) *listening and attending skills*, that is, the ability of being truly focused on the other, consciously making ourselves aware of what the other person is saying; (b) *client-centered skills*, the set of skills and attitudes based on the assumption that the client is the best authority on her/his own experience, and that he/she is fully capable of changing and growing, but the changes need favorable conditions in which to bloom and blossom, conditions often lacking in crisis situations; and (c) *helping with feelings skills*, the set of techniques we may use to identify, explore, express, and regulate feelings and emotions. The first area is basically relational and involves a set of attitudes, the second and third are more "technical" as they imply the knowledge and the ability to use some practical skills to adequately explore the client's subjective experience of facts and emotions. These skills can be taught and learned, just like any skills that can be disassembled into small discernible parts that can be easily assessed. On the contrary, attitudes can be only assessed in a global way and they are learned mainly from direct experience.

Communication and counseling skills are indicated as mandatory requirements for health professionals in several clinical guidelines for many different health problems such as smoking prevention (Raw, McNeill, & West, 1998, 2000), management and prevention of obesity (AA.VV., 2007), breastfeeding, oncology, e.g., primary breast cancer (Senkus et al., 2013), specific aspects of medical treatment that have an influence on adherence (Ollie, Foster, & Maher, 2015), genetic counseling (Caldas et al., 1999), and palliative care (Rudilla Galiana, Oliver, & Barreto, 2016). According to several healthcare authorities and medical associations (see note), palliative care interventions, must be integrated early in the illness trajectory, but this requirement is often neglected (Siouta et al., 2016). The 2007 survey on the genetic counseling guidelines of 18 international, regional, and national organizations (Forrest, Martin, Delatycki, & Aitken, 2007) strongly emphasized that communication from health professionals is the best way to *support* individuals exposed to highly stressful decision-making situations. These findings imply that clinicians absolutely need to be adequately trained in communication and relational skills, during their academic education or later.

In this chapter, we present and describe some "ready to use" skills coming from the well-established cognitive and behavioral psychological tradition that can be of use for healthcare professionals and for those who work in healthcare environments. We focus on skills about thought reformulation, emotion regulation, and mindfulness. The skills for working on thought reformulation are useful because patients' behavior, in many situations of physical illness, is driven by unrealistic thoughts or unfounded assumptions concerning health, illness, therapy, the present, or the future. Skills for working on emotion regulation are helpful because often the patient's subjective reaction to illness – mild or severe – is accompanied by high emotional arousal. For many patients, the experience of high emotional activation is scarcely sustainable and, in many situations, their suffering is intolerable. Practitioners need to know how to explore their patients' emotional discomfort and what strategies to suggest for managing this negative arousal. Mindfulness is the last topic. We choose it because mindfulness has demonstrated its effectiveness in reducing suffering, stress levels, and also, in some cases, physical pain, dramatically improving patients' quality of life in many different clinical situations, from cancer to chronic back pain (Kabat-Zinn, 1990).

Cognitive and behavioral approach: past, present, and future

A relevant contribution to the acquisition of counseling skills in healthcare settings comes from cognitive and behavioral psychological science. Cognitive and Cognitive-Behavior Therapy (CBT) have a long tradition of research and conceptual modelling (Beck, 1976; Ellis, 1970). Core issues of these approaches are the emphasis on the empowerment of the client, the focus on positive thinking, and the use of different strategies for improving self-knowledge. When the client's awareness of the dysfunctional thinking processes and mental schemata increases, previous attitudes and behaviors are modified, suffering is reduced, and personal improvement is supported. One core aspect of classical CBT is the assumption that our thoughts and mental schemata shape our behaviors, emotions, and mental states and that suffering is generated by wrong or dysfunctional thoughts. The most important point in clinical intervention is how to modify dysfunctional thoughts to change the subject's mental experience. The role of the therapist is to identify, by using the Socratic dialogue, what is wrong in the client's thinking processes and to show more useful alternatives. The same general background and assumptions underlie the traditional cognitive approach to counseling (Palmer, Dainow, & Milner, 1996): a counselor is an expert on human suffering who helps the client to identify the wrong thoughts and assumptions that shape his/her behavior. In classical CBT counseling, awareness and understanding of wrong attitudes is the first step toward finding a new perspective, new thoughts, and, therefore, new behaviors. Usually a cognitive counselor works on the client's ability to (a) clarify problems or difficulties, (b) recognize thoughts, and (c) foster a better understanding of the reasoning schemata behind what is perceived as a critical or unsolvable situation. It is obvious that such a process can also be applied in health contexts, for example in a smoking cessation intervention, or in a post-surgical rehabilitation.

As O'Donohue and Fisher (2008) wrote in their book "Cognitive behavior therapy (CBT) is an approach to human problems that can be viewed from several interrelated perspectives: philosophical, theoretical, methodological, assessment oriented, and technological" (p. 1) and, from the technological point of view "the presence of such a large number of major distinctive techniques leaves no doubt as to the *multifactorial* nature of contemporary CBT" (p. 3). The book is an interesting collection of almost all the main techniques used in delivering CBT, ranging from the oldest and the classical ones – as, for example, behavioral activation, contingency management, or cognitive restructuring – to the newest ones – such as cognitive defusion or mindfulness practice. Obviously, only a subset of them is eligible for counseling interventions, even if the blurred boundary between low-intensity-CBT intervention and CBT-counseling is not so easy to draw.

The main, and the most useful, set of CBT techniques concerns the strategies for exploring the cognitive distortions that guide our thinking processes, commonly considered as some sort of *fallacies* we tell ourselves several times a day. In the CBT approach (Trower, Jones, & Dryden, 2015), the most powerful conceptualization is the ABC model for analyzing critical events: *A* for Activating Event (the actual event), *B* (Beliefs about the event), and *C* (Consequences). In the classical CBT approach, the beliefs about the event were described as rational or irrational, with a negative nuance, as some sort of "distortion". In the more recent approaches, this perspective has been considered excessively judgmental and it is now preferred to describe the subjective perception as "dysfunctional", that is, a more neutral and not-judgmental description that enhances the functional consequences of the mental representation that the person has of his lived reality (Guidano, 1991; Rezzonico and Meier,

2010). Illness perception and subjective reaction to illness are colored by dysfunctional thoughts concerning the causes and the potential consequences of the disease, and these thoughts shape the patient's emotional reaction to the illness and the patient's behavior in following or not following healthcare advice. Imagining any possible physical change affects the person's mental representation of his/her future life: its quality, its quantity, wellbeing, also the need to be supported by a caregiver for normal activities, or the loss of independence. These are only some of the many worries affecting patients. Being able to detect, recognize, analyze, and defuse useless preconceptions, or being able to address those behavioral changes that, if not accomplished, will threaten the patient's life, is a set of skills healthcare providers must possess to do their best work. The cognitive approach to counseling gives many practical suggestions that are ready-to-use for healthcare providers. However, what we want to underline is the need for appropriate training, covering both the theory and the applications. For this purpose, self-practice and self-reflection are valuable training strategies that involve professionals applying the skills to themselves, reflecting on the process, and sharing this reflection with colleagues. In the next pages, we will give a short summary of some old and new ideas we hope will be of help for health professionals and counselors working in healthcare settings.

In the last decades, there have been several changes in traditional cognitive therapy: the introduction of mindfulness (Kabat-Zinn, 1994), Acceptance and Commitment Therapy (ACT) (Hayes, 2004), Dialectic Behavior Therapy (DBT) (Lineean, 1993, 2014), the *cognitive-relational* approach, that give a central role to attachment (Guidano & Liotti, 1983), and the cognitive-constructive approach (Guidano, 1987, 1991; Mahoney, 2003). All of these approaches have been labelled as "third wave cognitive therapy". Third wave approaches have a strong emphasis on (a) emotion regulation, changing partially the way in which emotions are conceptualized; (b) behavioral changes, as changing the behaviors imply parallel changes in the underlying thoughts; (c) learning strategies to calm the mind when overwhelmed by negative thoughts; (d) an emphasis on the positive role of acceptance of reality, for reducing the negative impact of worthless thoughts arising from the useless struggle with things that cannot be modified; and (e) decreasing the self-blaming attitude that accompanies this fight. In the last decade, many relevant changes have occurred in cognitive training and the original set of therapeutic tools is now enriched by new techniques. In the meantime, the *role of the therapist* changed, shifting from that of an expert that knows the right and the wrong, whose goal is to correct inappropriate thoughts, to the role of a compassionate human being helping clients to find strategies for being more regulated, more self-aware, more compassionate towards themselves, totally aware of each lived experience, and of the present moment (Gilbert, 2010). Cognitive counseling is, therefore, evolving in the same direction, adding new tools, techniques, and attitudes – new skills – for many different applications.

We now move to the first of the three sets of skills we believe could be useful for those who work in a healthcare environment: how to work on dysfunctional thoughts.

Working with thoughts

Dysfunctional thoughts are the more accessible dimension of subjective experience and they are the best candidates for the type of interventions that the health professionals can do in their daily activities when confronted with patients' reactions to symptoms, treatment options, side effects of therapy, changes in the health situation, or in their autonomy level. The skills are also needed when they have to help people in palliative care or end-of-life choices. Here we have a list of the most common examples of dysfunctional thoughts that a proper counseling intervention can reduce, ameliorating individual reactivity to illness:

Dichotomous Thinking or "the black-and-white" attitude: this is the propensity to think of things in terms of binary opposition, not being able to see the shades of grey, being intolerant of ambiguity or of uncertainty (e.g., "if my blood test is not good, I have cancer"). Real life is full of grey areas, and ambiguity or uncertainty is normal, certainty is rare in human affairs. Challenging the client on this point, suggesting, with examples, a totally different point of view is the first step to gain a wider perspective (e.g., "your blood test is out of the range, but this can be due to different reasons; I think that probably . . .").

Overgeneralizing: Often we make statements beginning with "always" or "never": "I always have some health problems", "I never succeed in reaching my goals", but these statements are often wrong: in some cases, we can have health problems that generate anxiety but they are generally temporary and are not severe. Identify all the overgeneralizations as soon as they appear in the discourse, stop the conversation and encourage the person to find at least one counterfactual example. Help to scale down the description, to reach a more realistic perspective, and to support the patient ("I'm aware that is a difficult situation, but I want to remember that last year we have faced and solved the same problem, and I'm confident that we have a good chance to stay well"). The feeling of being overwhelmed by things too heavy or too big and the feeling of helplessness is reduced.

Filtering: Another dysfunctional way of thinking is looking only to the dark side of something ("my tests are normal, but the doctor was doubtful about my headache, this means that I have a serious problem"). It is a typical habit in depression, but several people have a general tendency to focus on the negative elements of events and to forget the bright (positive) side, that is always possible to find in every situation, even in the worst one. This attitude emerges easily when people are confronted with health problems or when they are asked to change some well-established habits. The role of the health professional is, in this case, to remind the client what he/she is forgetting, enhancing the positive side left unexpressed.

Catastrophizing: It not easy to be confronted with critical or challenging situations, but some people react impulsively, immediately imagining the worst-case scenario, all the possible obstacles and the negative consequences ("I've lost two kilos this month, I'm sure it's stomach cancer"). When involved in this negative perspective, people tend to avoid the situation. If and when they try to confront the experience, they feel overwhelmed by intense negative emotions (fear, anxiety, and worry), they react and perform at a lower level than usual. Showing that the dramatic scenario is *just one among many possible* future scenarios, recognizing that it is a mental representation and not an actual reality, helps people to maintain a more realistic attitude, reducing the negative emotional activation and fostering a more realistic perspective ("losing weight can be a sign of a change in eating habits, or in physical activity or perhaps you're having a distressing period at work").

Making unfair comparisons: When we are dissatisfied with something, it is common to make a comparison with someone we think has a better situation than we have. In this way, our thoughts amplify a set of negative emotions: feeling inferior, feeling a loser, feeling envy, feeling sad. The strategy is to help the patient to find a more balanced attitude, making a positive comparison, looking for winning situations, not staying stuck on the negative and looking at the complexity of life ("try to image you have a friend with your same problem; what do you say to him?").

Confusing fact with feeling: Cognitions and emotions are deeply interrelated, as result of evolutionary pressure. This bond is helpful in everyday life, as in many situations this will facilitate decision making, relationship management, affective interaction, prosocial behavior, and empathy. But, in some situations, when the emotional mind leads our reactions, it is difficult to separate facts and feelings. Our subjective reaction, the feelings we have, is easily transformed into something real outside our mind ("if I feel fear for my health, this mean that there's a threat"). The intervention is to help people to separate the two realms – facts and feelings – to gain a more balanced perspective.

Personalizing or the self-blame game: It is probably one of the most common sources of suffering, when we get involved in obsessive and intrusive thoughts of regret, guilt, responsibility, without the light of forgiveness. When we remain in this negative attitude, it becomes impossible to escape from suffering and we lose the chance to find any possible solution to the problem. In the medical setting, it is easy to see people in the blame-loop, defeated by the feeling of being responsible of their own illness, stuck on self-judgement, guilt, and self-criticizing ("Why isn't my wife answering? She's angry with me; due to my health problem, I'm also going to ruin her life"). Therefore, they need help to see and appreciate the role of objective or external variables in what has happened and to shift from an internalized attribution style to a more balanced one that takes into account many causes, not just one.

Labelling: Language is a powerful way of building realities of very different quality. The problem is that we easily confuse the action a person does with the person. On many occasions, it is easier to think, "I'm a loser" or "he/she is dumb" instead of thinking "I lost the race" or "he/she made a mistake". Sensitivity to language is crucial for healthcare providers in detecting, isolating, and disclosing to the patient every self or other judging statement, deconstructing the reification process, bringing the person back to the facts. For example, there are different ways of saying "I'm ill": "I have a disease, but I'm not my disease"; the first label is more self-judging than the next one.

Working with emotions

One of the most relevant changes in the cognitive therapy model derives from the research done on severe illnesses, such as posttraumatic stress disorders (PTSD) or personality disorders (PD), given that the classic CBT approach is ineffective in the majority of cases. PTSD symptomatology mainly concerns traumatic memories. Emotional memory traces are the result of a process of elaboration that reduces the affective charge, integrating the factual aspect in autobiographical, cortical memory networks. In the case of traumatic memories, the process of memory consolidation seems to fail. The memory trace remains located in subcortical and primary perceptual areas, lacking the appropriate integration in autobiographical, cortical memory networks. Exposure to a trigger results in an involuntarily retrieved memory trace, hard to verbalize and consisting for the most part of primary sensory information, such as images, smells, or sounds (Brewin, 2011; van Marle, 2015). These findings show that there are some emotional states not directly generated by thoughts, but as a result of the reactivations of ancient memories, deeply rooted in sensory and perceptual information, re-enacted by factual experiences. The main point here is that some dysfunctional mental states or states of intense emotional activation are generated by other central – neither linguistic nor thought-related – emotional states. These mental states emerge like a pop-up in the mind, without any link to thoughts or beliefs. These findings challenge the CBT primacy of thoughts on emotion. Some schema-therapy interventions (Jacob, Van Genderen, & Seebauer, 2014; Young, Klosko, & Weishaar, 2003; van Vreeswijk, Broersen, & Nadort, 2015) are based on non-linguistic strategies, using corrective bodily experience for inducing emotional and cognitive changes. Schema therapy is one of the newest approaches of the third wave cognitive therapies, developed to treat cases resistant to the classical CBT: a schema is an organized pattern of thoughts, behaviors, and emotions we use to organize and perceive new information. Suffering derives from early maladaptive schemas, defined as "self-defeating life patterns of perception, emotion, and physical sensation" (Young et al., 2003) established from childhood and repeated throughout life. These negative schemata concern experiences and memories of past hurt, fear, abuse, neglect, unmet safety needs, abandonment, or lack of normal human affection in general. Bodily sensations are deeply associated with such emotional memories and are easily activated when some internal or external trigger stimulates them. Early maladaptive schemas can have different levels of severity and pervasiveness. The more severe the schema, the more intense the negative emotion when the schema is triggered and the longer it lasts. The more pervasive the schema, the greater the number of situations that trigger it. Rarely are they suitable for counseling since they need psychotherapy. Healthcare professionals must be very careful in managing these patients, given their clinical complexity, properly identifying the critical situations that must be re-addressed to expert clinical psychologists. However, there are several simpler situations in which it is not only possible, but very useful, to work with the client on their emotional reactions. Some of these strategies are derived from the process model proposed by Gross (1998, 2013) and include:

- *Attention deployment* refers to influencing emotional responding by redirecting the client's attention to a different subject within a given situation; looking at medical information (often available online) can increase the level of anxiety, thus it can be useful to suggest some reliable website rather than saying, "stop looking at online information!".
- *Distraction* involves a shift in attention either away from the emotional aspects of the situation or away from the situation altogether; for example, during a medical procedure (injection or magnetic resonance) the doctor can talk with the patient to help him/her to displace the attention.
- *Reappraisal* involves changing the subjective meaning of a situation in such a way as to induce a change in the person's emotional response to that situation.
- *Response modulation* refers to influencing physiological, experiential, or behavioral responses directly: physical exercise or relaxation (e.g., simple deep breathing exercises) may be used to decrease the physiological aspects of negative emotions.

Since 2010, an emotion-based protocol, derived from the Gross processual model, is routinely applied in the counseling service for students at our university. It is implemented by skilled psychotherapists and it is of proved efficacy in reducing stress levels and suffering intensity (Strepparava et al., 2016). Here is a brief summary of our intervention: we start from the identification of the most critical personal themes in the first encounter; next, counselors teach self-observation techniques to increase students' awareness of dysfunctional cognitive, behavioral, and emotional schemata; then, the counselor and client explore alternative emotion regulation strategies and focus on reappraisal – that is, the cognitive re-evaluation of the situation. Together, they develop goal-oriented problem solving strategies, and at the end of the process, they reprocess the shared achievements or any other aspects that need further investigation. Obviously, if required by the student, or if the clinical problem cannot be addressed within the limits of counseling treatment, the students are readdressed to more appropriate services.

Mindfulness: How to quiet the mind

Mindfulness is probably one of the most diffused and known third wave approaches. Mindfulness can be considered an *enhanced attention to* and *awareness* of current experience or present reality. Usually, we are conscious of thoughts, motives, and emotions as well as sensory and perceptual stimuli. Consciousness encompasses both awareness and attention. Awareness is the background "radar" of consciousness, monitoring the inner and outer environment while attention is a process of focusing conscious awareness, providing heightened sensitivity to a limited range of experience (Brown & Ryan, 2003). Mindfulness is related to emotional intelligence (Salovey, Mayer, Goldman, Turvey, & Palfai, 1995) and to aspects of the Openness to Experience dimension of personality (Costa & McCrae, 1992) and to empathy (Strepparava, Ardenghi, & Corrias, 2015). Mindfulness is an attribute of consciousness long believed to promote wellbeing (Kabat-Zinn, 1990). Everyone has the capacity to attend and to be aware, but individuals differ in their propensity or willingness to be aware or to sustain attention to what is occurring in the present and dispositional mindfulness is variable within persons.

We may depict our mind as a beautiful place, full of memories and future plans, full of love, warmth, and joy. However, when a negative style of thinking emerges, the thoughts of the internal dialogue become negative and the dark side becomes more persuasive and dominant than the bright side, and supportive thoughts lose their energy. Obsessive, intrusive, and repetitive thoughts are very powerful and tend to fill the mind with negative ideas. As a consequence, we become unable to concentrate and we experience a feeling like picking up marbles on a rolling ship (Johnstone, 2012). In this situation, we need to quiet the mind, change our attention focus, and calm down our thoughts. Mindfulness is a way in which we can easily quiet our mind by focusing our attention on the present moment (Kabat-Zinn, 1994), allowing thoughts to pass by, like clouds in the sky that are blown away by the wind. This shift of attention can also be obtained by key images, like a scuba diver sitting on the sea bottom during a storm: on the surface of the ocean the wind blows, the waves break, but at the sea bottom everything is calm and quiet. There are some self-help books that are useful for introducing people to mindfulness that can be very useful in counseling, because they are full of drawings and images: the perceptual component helps a lot to explain and transmit the deep meaning of the basic principle of mindfulness like intrusiveness of thoughts, focalized attention, the present experience, and their relation with anxiety and depression (Johnstone, 2012, 2013). Mindfulness principles are sometimes difficult to understand or to apply, when transmitted only by words, while if supported by images, people easily understand the main message and the background attitude can be improved.

Having a mindful attitude is paying attention to present experience without adding thoughts or images to the pure sensations, just noticing what is happening internally and externally. In mindfulness, we regulate the attention shift, not the mental contents. To be mindfully in the present and acting mindfully means to do one thing at a time; to concentrate the mind; to focus only on what works, not on preconceptions or presuppositions; to let go of distractions, to act as skillfully as is possible, always keeping an eye on the objective; to assume a nonjudgmental attitude in every situation; to see but not to evaluate what is seen, ungluing opinions from facts, acknowledging if something is wholesome or harmful, without judging and without judging one's own judging.

In many psychological interventions, like in dialectical behavior therapy (DBT; Linehan, 1993, 2014), mindfulness processes have an important role and demonstrate empirical benefits in the management of crises, emotion dysregulation, hyper reactivity, and impulsive behavior. In order to avoid being overwhelmed by negative emotional activation, a person has to take a step back from his/her emotions, looking without judging the feelings, with an open mind, accepting what is coming just as it is. Learning and being trained in mindfulness is a long process; it is not easy and it needs hours of practice to be effective. Mindfulness is an activity requiring a high level of engagement and commitment and participants are often asked to complete personal mindfulness practices at home. We believe, anyway, that the previously listed points can be, at least partially, used as behavior guidelines by everyone. Often, we are not able to apply them to ourselves and we need the help of an expert to remind us of these behaviors and attitudes – e.g., being not judgmental – so that we are more capable of confronting challenging situations or events. Some hints, suggestions, or images usually adopted in practicing mindfulness, like the scuba diver or the spaceman in his spaceship in the wide, silent space, can be used to help people to form the idea of the optimal attitude and may help in reducing some negative behaviors and in implementing positive attitudes. For example, we suggested two self-help books at the end of a two-hour seminar for a medical student, illustrating mindfulness principles, and followed this with a brief practical experience. This short experience was enough to induce the student's curiosity, their reflection on some of their dysfunctional mental mechanisms, the desire to learn more positive strategies and to foster participation in mindfulness groups organized by the clinical psychology unit of the nearby teaching hospital.

There are several empirical proofs that mindfulness programs and practices can improve physical and psychological health, promoting overall wellbeing in many different health settings and on many types of patients with physical illness (Matchim & Armer, 2007; Matchim, Armer, & Stewart, 2011; Proulx, 2003). Workplace stress is high among healthcare professionals and it is associated with reduced psychological health, lower quality of patient care (Prins et al., 2009; Shanafelt, Bradley, Wipf, & Back, 2002; West, Tan, Habermann, Sloan, & Shanafelt, 2009), and patient satisfaction (Anagnostopoulos et al., 2012, Argentero, Dell'Olivo, Santa Ferretti, & Burnout, 2008; Halbesleben & Rathert, 2008). Many systematic reviews on healthcare providers revealed that practitioners who incorporate mindfulness into their personal and professional lives demonstrated an improved sense of wellbeing and ability to employ self-care strategies Escuriex & Labbé, 2011; Irving et al., 2014; White, 2013). Mindfulness-based interventions seem to have the potential to reduce stress among healthcare professionals. Also, to confirm the previous findings, some researchers report the need for long-term follow-up measures to determine any continuing effects of mindfulness training on stress outcomes (Burton, Kramer, Ritchie, & Jenkins, 2016).

The high workload and personal demands can change the bright years of medical school into a stressful experience. Medical students already report symptoms of psychological distress and burnout before graduating. They experience more psychological distress than age matched peers (Strepparava et al., 2016). Problems expand after graduation: the stress level during medical school seems to be predictive of lower work satisfaction and more work-related problems after graduation (Finset et al., 2005). Teaching medical students how to learn resilience attitudes such as self-awareness of stress signals and of unhelpful automatic responses is potentially of great benefit. Several studies show the benefit of teaching mindful practices and implementing mindfulness-based interventions at university for medical or nursing students (Dobkin & Hutchinson, 2013). The main problem is determining which format is more useful. Recent research shows that clinical clerkship students have higher interest and participation rates than preclinical students. A training in mindfulness given during clerkships probably results in better opportunities for integrating the exercises in daily hospital practice and it is therefore more effective for future clinical activity (van Dijk, Lucassen, & Speckens, 2015).

In our opinion, a short training in mindfulness is of great help for all those practitioners who work daily with patients or difficult clients as they can find supportive strategies for helping people, but also for taking adequate care of themselves.

Conclusion: Take care of ourselves so that we can care for others

We hope that this brief overview can be of help to all those practitioners who are engaged on a daily basis with suffering people. It is our intention to give them suggestions for deconstructing the many mental assumptions that underlie people's thoughts and that so often fill their minds – our minds – with worthless suffering and to provide a general idea of the old and the new in the cognitive field.

Health practitioners and healthcare professionals do a lot of counseling with their patients or their patients' relatives and they absolutely need to be properly trained to do that. If this does not happen, they are at risk of being ineffective or dangerous. A good training in counseling skills is important not only for patients' safety but for health practitioners' safety, too. In our activity as medical educators, we spent several years in training many actual and future health practitioners: students (of medicine, nursing, and midwifery) and professionals (medical doctors, nurses, and several other healthcare providers). In doing this job, we have three main educational goals: The first goal is to help the health practitioners to learn how to communicate with patients and relatives in many different situations, improving their ability to manage motivational interviews, supporting decision making, regulating emotional discomfort, and helping people to be aware of and to disclose their own feelings about health, illness, impairment, therapies, life, and death. Several basic counseling skills are essential for all health professionals in the majority of clinical situations they encounter. Health professionals should build a therapeutic alliance and reach concordance on therapeutic strategies and behavioral modifications that are needed for the successful delivery of care, not just for adherence to treatment. Physicians, nurses, midwives, and physical and rehabilitation therapists must possess the ability to use active listening, reformulation, and supportive talk when interacting with patients and they must develop attitudes and sensitivity to interpersonal relationship, being able to identify the relational pattern arising in the most common clinical situations.

The second goal is to help healthcare providers to be more aware and sensible to their inner mental states, their thinking processes, their behavioral habits, and their emotional realm. Strengthening their competence in emotion regulation, teaching them how to calm the mind, make them learn to self-regulate and not to react impulsively to negative stimuli is, in our opinion, a mandatory intervention to ameliorate their capability to manage stressful and difficult interactions and clinical relationships.

As a third goal, while teaching the students and the health practitioners the previously mentioned set of basic tools for self-regulation and self-care, we implemented a sort of preventive intervention aimed at reducing their vulnerability to stress, and fostering a better adaptation to the professional requirements of the caring professions. Medical education in Italy is a six-year journey of hard learning and deeply challenging experiences. Medical practice is performed in a stressful working environment. Any activity linked to health and illness and to hospitals places people in front of the basic challenges of every human life: physical and emotional suffering, death, impairment, loss, and loneliness. The teaching of some ready-to-use resources to face these hard and most common stressors to healthcare practitioners or students, during, or after, their medical education, could make the difference between a difficult and unbearable working life or a difficult but manageable professional experience.

Note

World Health Organization, WHO; the European Society of Medical Oncology, ESMO; the American Society of Clinical Oncology, ASCO; the National Comprehensive Cancer Network, NCCN.

References

AA.VV. (2007). 2006 Canadian clinical practice guidelines on the management and prevention of obesity in adults and children. *Canadian Medical Association Journal, 176*, 1–13.

Anagnostopoulos, F., Liolios, E., Persefonis, G., Slater, J., Kafetsios, K., & Niakas, D. (2012). Physician burnout and patient satisfaction with consultation in primary health care settings: Evidence of relationships from a one-with-many design. *Journal of Clinical Psychology in Medical Settings, 19*(4), 401–410.

Argentero, P., Dell'Olivo, B., Santa Ferretti, M., & Burnout, W. G. (2008). Staff burnout and patient satisfaction with the quality of dialysis care. *American Journal of Kidney Diseases, 51*(1), 80–92.

Beck, A. T. (1976). *Cognitive therapy and emotional disorders*. New York: International Universities Press.

Bennett-Levy, J., Richards, D. A., Ferrand, P. (2010). Low intensity CBT interventions: a revolution in mental health care. In J. Bennett-Levy, D. A. Richards, & P. Ferrand, H. Christensen, K. Griffiths, D. Kavanagh . . . & J.Proudfoot (Eds.), *Oxford Guide to Low Intensity CBT Interventions* (pp. 3–18). Oxford: Oxford University Press.

Brewin, C. R. (2011). The nature and significance of memory disturbance in posttraumatic stress disorder. *Annual Review of Clinical Psychology*, 7, 203–227.

Brown, K. W., & Ryan, R. M. (2003). The benefits of being present: Mindfulness and its role in psychological wellbeing. *Journal of Personality and Social Psychology, 84*(4), 822–848.

Buckmann, R. (2011). Practical plans for difficult conversations in medicine: Strategies that work in breaking bad News. Baltimore, MD: Johns Hopkins University Press.

Burnard, P. (2005). *Counselling skills for health professionals*. Cheltenham, UK: Nelson Thornes.

Burton, A. M., Kramer, R. S. S., Ritchie, K. L., & Jenkins, R. (2016). Identity from variation: Representations of faces derived from multiple instances. *Cognitive Science, 40*, 202–223.

Caldas, C., Carneiro, F., Lynch, H. T., Yokota, J., Wiesner, G. L., Powell, S. M., & MacLeod, P. (1999). Familial gastric cancer: Overview and guidelines for management. *Journal of Medical Genetics, 36*(12), 873–880.

Costa, P. T., Jr., & McCrae, R. R. (1992). Revised NEO Personality Inventory (NEO PI-R) and NEO Five-Factor Inventory (NEO-FFI): Professional manual. Odessa, FL: Psychological Assessment Resources.

Dobkin, P. L., & Hutchinson, T. A. (2013). Teaching mindfulness in medical school: Where are we now and where are we going? *Medical Education, 47*(8), 768–779.

Ellis, A. (1970). The essence of rational psychotherapy: A comprehensive approach to treatment. New York, NY: Institute for Rational Living.

Escuriex, B. F., & Labbé, E. E. (2011). Health care providers' mindfulness and treatment outcomes: A critical review of the research literature. *Mindfulness*, *2*(4), 242–253.

Finset, K. B., Gude, T., Hem, E., Tyssen, R., Ekeberg, O., & Vaglum, P. (2005). Which young physicians are satisfied with their work? A prospective nationwide study in Norway. *BMC Medical Education*, *5*(1), 19.

Forrest, L. E., Martin, B., Delatycki, L. S., & Aitken, M. (2007). Communicating genetic information in families – a review of guidelines and position papers. *European Journal of Human Genetics*, *15*, 612–618.

Gilbert, P. (2010). Compassion focused therapy: Distinctive features (CBT distinctive features). New York, NY: Routledge.

Gross, J. J. (1998). The emerging field of emotion regulation: An integrative review. *Review of General Psychology*, *2*, 271–299.

Gross, J. J. (2013). *Handbook of emotion regulation*. New York, NY: Guilford Press.

Guidano, V. F. (1987). *Complexity of the self*. New York, NY: Guilford Press.

Guidano, V. F. (1991). *The self in progress*. New York, NY: Guilford Press.

Guidano, V. F., & Liotti, G. (1983). Cognitive processes and emotion disorders: A structural approach to psychotherapy. New York, NY: Guilford Press.

Halbesleben, J. R., & Rathert, C. (2008). Linking physician burnout and patient outcomes: Exploring the dyadic relationship between physicians and patients. *Health Care Management Review*, *33*(1), 29–39.

Hayes, S. C. (2004). Acceptance and commitment therapy, relational frame theory, and the third wave of behavioral and cognitive therapies. *Behaviour Therapy*, *35*, 639–665.

Irving, J. A., Park-Saltzman, J., Fitzpatrick, M., Dobkin, P. L., Chen, A., & Hutchinson, T. (2014). Experiences of professionals health care enrolled in mindfulness based medical practice: A grounded theory model. *Mindfulness*, *5*(1), 60–71.

Jacob, G., Van Genderen, H., & Seebauer, L. (2014). *Breaking negative thinking patterns: A schema therapy self-help and support book*. Malden, MA: John Wiley & Sons.

Johnstone, M. (2012). Quiet the mind, an illustrated guide on how to meditate. Sydney: Pan Macmillan.

Johnstone, M. (2013). *Capturing mindfulness*. Sydney: Pan Macmillan.

Kabat-Zinn, J. (1990). Full catastrophe living: Using the wisdom of your body and mind to face stress, pain, and illness. New York, NY: Delacourt.

Kabat-Zinn, J. (Ed.). (1994). Wherever you go there you are: Mindfulness meditation in everyday life. New York, NY: Hyperion.

Kabat-Zinn, J. (2003). Mindfulness-based interventions in context: past, present, and future. *Clinical Psychology: Science & Practice* *10*(2), 144–156.

Linehan, M. M. (1993). Cognitive-behavioral treatment of borderline personality disorder. New York, NY: Guilford press.

Linehan, M. M. (2014). *DBT® skills training manual*. New York, NY: Guilford Press.

Mahoney, M. J. (2003). *Constructive psychotherapy: A practical guide*. New York, NY: Guilford Press.

Matchim, Y., & Armer, J. M. (2007). Measuring the psychological impact of mindfulness meditation on health among patients with cancer: A literature review. *Oncology Nursing Forum*, *34*(5), 1059–1066.

Matchim, Y., Armer, J. M., & Stewart, B. R. (2011). Effects of mindfulness-based stress reduction (MBSR) on health among breast cancer survivors. *Western Journal of Nursing Research*, *33*(8), 996–1016.

O'Donohue, W., & Fisher, J. E. (2008). Cognitive behavior therapy: Applying empirically supported techniques in your practice (2nd ed.). Hoboken, NJ: John Wiley & Sons.

Ollie, M., Foster, J., & Maher, J. (2015). The role of behavioural modification and exercise in the management of cancer-related fatigue to reduce its impact during and after cancer treatment. *Acta Oncologica, 54*(5), 581–586.

Palmer, S., Dainow, S., & Milner, P. (Eds.). (1996). *Counselling: The BACP counselling reader* (Vol. 1). Thousand Oaks, CA: Sage.

Prins, J. T., Van Der Heijden, F. M. M. A., Hoekstra-Weebers, J. E. H. M., Bakker, A. B., Van de Wiel, H. B. M., Jacobs, B., & Gazendam-Donofrio, S. M. (2009). Burnout, engagement and resident physicians' self-reported errors. *Psychology, Health & Medicine, 14*(6), 654–666.

Proulx, K. (2003). Integrating mindfulness-based stress reduction. *Holistic Nursing Practice, 17*(4), 201–208.

Raw, M., McNeill, A., & West, R. (1998). Smoking cessation guidelines for health professionals: A guide to effective smoking cessation interventions for the health care system. *Thorax, 53*, 1–19.

Raw, M., McNeill, A., & West, R. (2000). Smoking cessation guidelines for health professionals: An update. *Thorax, 55*, 987–999.

Rezzonico, G., & Meier, C. (Eds.). (2010). *Il counselling cognitivo relazionale* [The relational cognitive counseling]. Milano, IT: Franco Angeli Editore.

Rudilla, D., Galiana, L., Oliver, A., & Barreto, P. (2016). Comparing counseling and dignity therapies in home care patients: A pilot study. *Palliative and Supportive Care, 14*(4), 321–329.

Salovey, P., Mayer, J. D., Goldman, S. L., Turvey, C., & Palfai, T. F. (1995). Emotional attention, clarity, and repair: Exploring emotional intelligence using the Trait Meta-Mood Scale. In J. W. Pennebaker (Ed.), *Emotion, disclosure, and health* (pp. 125–154). Washington, DC: American Psychological Association.

Senkus, E., Kyriakides, S., Penault-Llorca, F., Poortmans, P., Thompson, A., Zackrisson, S., & Cardoso, F. (2013). Primary breast cancer: ESMO Clinical Practice Guidelines for diagnosis, treatment and follow-up. *Annals of Oncology, 26*(suppl. 5), 8–30.

Shanafelt, T. D., Bradley, K. A., Wipf, J. E., & Back, A. L. (2002). Burnout and self-reported patient care in an internal medicine residency program. *Annals of Internal Medicine, 136*(5), 358–367.

Siouta, N., Van Beek, K., Siouta, N., Preston, N., Hasselaar, J., Hughes, S., . . . Menten, J. (2016). Integrated palliative care in Europe: A qualitative systematic literature review of empirically tested models in cancer and chronic disease. *BMC Palliative Care, 15*, 1–16.

Strepparava, M. G., Ardenghi, S., & Corrias, D. (2015). A study on the association between mindfulness, empathy and patient-centeredness in Italian medical students. In *Association for Medical Education in Europe (AMEE), Scottish Exhibition and Conference Centre (SECC)*, Glasgow.

Strepparava, M., Bani, M., Zorzi, F., Corrias, D., Dolce, R., & Rezzonico, G. (2016). Cognitive counselling intervention: Treatment effectiveness in an Italian university centre. *British Journal of Guidance & Counselling, 44*(4), 423–433.

Trower, P., Jones, J., & Dryden, W. (2015). *Cognitive behavioural counselling in action*. Thousand Oaks, CA: Sage.

Van Dijk, I., Lucassen, P. L., & Speckens, A. E. (2015). Mindfulness training for medical students in their clinical clerkships: Two cross-sectional studies exploring interest and participation. *BMC Medical Education, 15*, 1–8.

Van Marle, H. (2015). PTSD as a memory disorder. *European Journal of Psychotraumatology, 6*, 1–3.

Van Vreeswijk, M., Broersen, J., & Nadort, M. (2015). *The Wiley-Blackwell handbook of schema therapy: Theory, research and practice*. Hoboken, NJ: John Wiley & Sons.

West, C. P., Tan, A. D., Habermann, T. M., Sloan, J. A., & Shanafelt, T. D. (2009). Association of resident fatigue and distress with perceived medical errors. *Jama, 302*(12), 1294–1300.

White, L. (2013). Mindfulness in nursing: An evolutionary concept analysis. *Journal of Advanced Nursing, 70*(2), 282–294.

Young, J. E., Klosko, J. S., & Weishaar, M. E. (2003). *Schema therapy: A practitioner's guide*. New York, NY: Guilford Press.

Chapter 3

The increasingly prominent role of visualization in counseling

Examples and implications for school counseling

Moshe Israelashvili

Establishing good communication with the client has always been a critical step in moving the counseling process forward. In order to facilitate the development of a positive communicative relationship with the client, counselors are willing to use all possible channels of communication. Among the various possible channels, oral communication always has been and still is the major form of communication used (e.g., Nouri, & Rudd, 2014), and this is also the case in the school counseling setting (e.g. Nelson, Bein, Huemer, Ryst, & Steiner, 2009). Thus, traditionally, novice counselors are trained to pay attention to words – i.e., in terms of how and when the client expresses himself/herself, the content expressed, as well as how the counselor should express himself/herself to the client, to achieve the counseling goals. However, recent technological and social developments challenge the taken-for-granted importance of words in human communication. Rather, it seems that images are playing an increasingly prominent role in the way people communicate with each other. This shift, from the written and spoken word to the visualized word and image, has major implications for counselors' training as well as for the content and sequence of counseling sessions and interventions. The current chapter will briefly review the well-documented features of visualized communication, outline several of the potential implications of these features for counseling, and describe two studies that explored the implementation of visualization in a school-related setting. The chapter concludes with a general recommendation to further discuss the theoretical and applied implications of the "visualizing age" for counseling in general and especially for school counseling.

The current role of visualization in people's lives

One does not need to be a historian to notice the major and dramatic change that the world has undergone in the last 25 years. Here are three examples of inventions that have played a part in this process of change: First, it would be a cliché to say that the internet has changed the world. Yet, it is worth noting that a recent survey on internet use indicates that in more than 60% of the world's countries, the rate of people who use the internet exceeds 50% of the population (Internet Live Statistics, 2016). Second, it would also be trivial to mention that the wide expansion of cell phones, even in undeveloped areas and among disadvantaged populations, has further changed the world. The widespread use of cell phones, and the internet that is accessible from them, is so intensive that recently several cities in the world (e.g., Sydney, Australia; Augsburg, Germany) made the decision to install traffic lights on the ground at pedestrian crossings, to help "mobile phone zombies" pay attention to the walk/stop signs. Third, another invention that should be mentioned is the digital camera. The invention of the camera and the ability to take still pictures triggered many social and technological global processes, such as reaching a better understanding of nature, documentation of historical events, etc. However, the invention of the digital camera – i.e., a camera that records and stores still photographic images, sounds and videos digitally *(WhatIs.com)* – changed the invention of the camera into a dramatic personal revolution in individual lives – i.e., leading to the extensive documentation of oneself and of others (see next). Hence, a recent book by King (2016) describes how imagery has taken over the role of words in today's politics and media. In his book, King describes the major role that images play in the U.S. administration, as represented by pictures featured in both the written and visualized media. King gives detailed examples of how certain pictures that appeared in the media, either well-planned in advance or spontaneously, have later led to significant political and social implications. For King (2016), current media is about optics, rather than language, and governing is more about the prevention of image collapse.

Yet, while many people would declare that these three technological developments changed the world, few people really comprehend what kind of a new world was created by these three technical developments, alongside many other technical developments and applications that emerged from them.

While many other examples of recent innovations could be listed, these three examples are mentioned here, as the combination of them has led to further new developments and applications that have intensified our shift from being "thinking-figures" or "verbal creatures" into "visual creatures"; i.e., creatures whose eyes are the dominant acting organ in the body, throughout daily activities. Some of these developments and applications are listed below (the definitions are based on WhatIs.com):

- *YouTube* – a video-hosting website that allows members to store and serve video content.
- *Instagram* – a mobile photo application that uses a cell phone camera to take pictures, after which users can upload, edit and share photos with other members through the Instagram website, email, Twitter, Facebook, Tumblr, Foursquare and Flickr.
- *WhatsApp* – a cross-platform instant messaging application that allows iPhone, BlackBerry, Android, Windows Phone and Nokia smartphone users to exchange text, image, video and audio messages for free.

- *Snapchat* – a mobile app that allows users to send and receive "self-destructing" photos and videos. According to the Snapchat Blog, it is used by over 100 million people every day.

The above-mentioned tools are only a few examples of ways in which "ordinary" people spend *additional* time – i.e., in addition to watching TV, looking at their computer screen, watching movies, following the WAZE road guide, etc. – using their visual sense to a greater extent than their other senses. With the increasing role that visual media plays in current society, there are two recently developed popular trends that are of particular interest and emphasize the visual perspective as the essence of interpersonal communication: (1) selfies and (2) emojis.

A *selfie* is a self-portrait, typically a photograph, that is posted online. Originally, many painters painted their self-portraits. Several explanations were given, such as the self-portrait as a way of saving the cost of a model, the painter's willingness to archive his/her own portrait, narcissistic observation, etc. However, unlike painters, in recent years the trend of taking one's own picture has dramatically expanded. The most common places for selfies to be documented are blogs, social networking sites, such as Facebook, and photo-sharing websites, such as Instagram. People are so eager to take selfies that some would even risk their lives to do so – i.e., 27 people died in 2015 while trying to take a "special" selfie (International Business Times, 2016). The flourishing of selfies is grounded in the vast technological development that led to the transformation of the cell phone into the smartphone, and the smartphone into a walking-computer, easily handled and inexpensively used anytime, all the time. Thus, selfies are not only a derivation of new technological tools; rather, they have become the new way in which people communicate with each other, present themselves to world, advertise their positive characteristics and leave their mark on the history of humankind. Moreover, somehow taking selfies seems to also be a way in which people communicate with themselves (Frosh, 2015). All of these (partially exaggerated) qualifications of selfies actually represent the new expression of an old acronym: "a picture is worth a thousand words". Yet, the other side of the coin (i.e., phenomenon) is the sudden decline in the use of words to describe oneself and/or to present personal qualifications and characteristics.

The term *emoji* refers to a selection of (currently 1,851) miniature paintings that people use in digital communication, either as an addition to, or even in replacement of, the written language. This set of paintings originated in Japan, as a way to communicate and express icons from Japanese culture (e.g., a white rose, as a symbol of innocence or devotion). Accordingly, the original meaning of the word emoji was *pictograph*, and resulted from the merging of two Japanese words *e* (絵, "picture") + *moji* (文字, "character"). Table 3.1 presents some types of Emoji.

The use of emojis has intensively expanded in the last two years, up to the point that the introduction of a new emoji is regulated by an organization

Table 3.1 Types of emoji

Examples of the general categories of Emoji:
Smileys & People, Animals & Nature, Food & Drink, Activity, Travel & Places, Objects, Symbols and Flags
Examples of events to which Emoji refers:
Birthday, Fall/Autumn, Graduation, New Year's Eve, Olympics, Wedding/Marriage
http://isoftjar.blogspot.com/2013/03/emoji-free-iphone-free-download.html

(Unicode), that formally presents all the legal shapes of emojis that can be used along with their variations (see: http://unicode.org/emoji/charts/full-emoji-list.html); has developed a special search engine for emojis (Emojipedia) as well as Emoji Applications (Apps), which are constantly being developed; has declared July 17 to be the formal World Emoji Day (see http://worldemojiday.com/); etc. Thus, one of the major points that should be mentioned is, again, that the use of emojis replaces the use of the spoken or written words. Hence, children and youth feel more comfortable in seemingly drawing their feelings, rather than verbally expressing them. In light of the prominent role that visual aspects of communication now have, it is important to examine whether counseling, as a profession, has adapted itself to this change.

Past discussions of the role of visualization in counseling

The significant role that images, symbols and visualization may play in the counseling process is not at all a new realization. Rather, both theories of counseling, as well as practical guidelines for counselors, have already highlighted its importance, such as Jung's (1997) approach to analytical psychology and Ivey's (Ivey & Authier, 1978) microskills approach to counselor training.

Jung's analytical psychology was established following his personal debate regarding Freud's psychodynamic approach. One of the major arguments that Jung raised against Freud's psychoanalytical approach was the cumbersomeness of words, both in revealing the client's problem, as well as in helping the client to change. Jung conceptualized the unconscious as much more vibrant, rich and free of the limitations that (spoken) words might impose on a person's (conscious and unconscious) mental activity, especially when in relation to children. According to Jung, images, symbols and signs are better representations of the unconscious than words. Accordingly, Jung encouraged the counselor to explore the client's inner world by referring to the client's world of imagery, as would be represented by significant symbols, personal drawings, etc. (Jung, 1997). Unsurprisingly, Jung is frequently mentioned as one of the major theorists that paved the way for art therapy (Malchiodi, 2006). Finally, it should be noted that, to some degree, other psychoanalysts share Jung's critique of the need to overcome the limitations that words impose on the inner world, such as Winnicot's suggestion (1971) to use scribbled drawings (i.e., an unfinished drawing) as a way to explore children's inner worlds.

Ivey's (Ivey & Authier, 1978) microcounseling approach incorporates visualization in counseling from a different point of view. According to Ivey, a comprehensive understanding of the client's problem and ways to counsel him/her are achieved when the counselor gradually uses a variety of microskills (e.g., asking, reflecting, focusing, confrontation, influencing, etc.). Among these skills, which the counselors are expected to acquire during training, is a skill referred to as "client observation" – i.e., how to observe and understand the client's appearance. Another related skill is "attending behavior" that refers, among other things, to the ability to properly behave and comprehend topics that are related to body language. These two categories of skills highlight the need to properly understand and represent images, alongside words.

Thus, these two examples represent the general notion, clear to all counselors, scientists, as well as practitioners, that counseling does give homage to images, visions and pictures. However, it should be emphasized that in the counseling literature, words are still dominant – i.e., the consideration of visions and images are only secondary, or at most equal, to the use and analysis of words. Is it possible that while the counselor tries to "lead the client along the road to healing" the client's attention is held by his/her smartphone screen? Or, most importantly – is the "new generation of clients" (i.e., youth) able to comprehend ideas without watching them on a screen? While it seems that, naturally, at the individual level, many counselors also use these and other technological developments, the theory and especially practice of these phenomena in counseling are still far behind the times.

The major theorem of the current chapter is that the relative importance of words versus images is changing, with words taking on a secondary role to images. Namely, recent technological developments are gradually transforming the way in which people not only communicate with each other but also "communicate with themselves". Thus, the speedy invasion of these new technologies and especially their implications for the context and practice of counseling is somehow unacknowledged or even ignored. Specifically, the growing need for a greater understanding of the major role that visions and images play in many clients' lives is evident.

Current knowledge on visualization in counseling

Awareness regarding the domination of digital media and imagery has been recognized in several scientific domains for a relatively long time. One prominent example is the development of M-health (e.g., Istepanian, Laxminarayan, & Pattichis, 2006; Kay, Santos, & Takane, 2011). M-health, the achievement of health through mobile technologies, is currently a major determinant of medical companies' strategic plans and future development goals (e.g., Aitken, 2016).

This is due to the many advantages of M-health, such as: increased efficacy; a reduction in waiting lists; 24/7 availability; equity; anonymity; lower cost; etc. (see Olff, 2015). An example that demonstrates many of these advantages is Sullivan, Jones, Kishore, and Stephenson's (2015) study on the role that smartphones can play in HIV prevention. However, M-health is not related to physical health alone; for example, with the increasing range of available apps, there is a gradually growing number of new apps dedicated to the treatment of mental health problems, such as depression (e.g., *Black rainbow*) and bipolar disorder (*MoodRhythm*; see Leigh & Flatt, 2015), schizophrenia (MindFrame; Terp, Laursen, Jørgensen, Mainz, & Bjørnes, 2016) and others.

Interestingly, however, the number of studies which address the intensive preoccupation with visualization in our society is far from being satisfactory. Practically speaking, an exploration of the number of studies conducted on relevant topics – as represented by checking the combination of the term "counseling" along with several related terms in PsycNet (retrieved on June 5, 2016) – yielded the following results:

- 123,985 studies address internet use, among which 3,305 are related to counseling (37:1)
- 1,181 studies which report on cell phone use, among which only 33 are related to counseling (36:1)
- 36,293 studies have reported on digital camera use, among which only 5 are related to counseling (58:1)
- Finally, only two studies have ever been reported in PsycNet on emojis.

An interesting exceptional case, with a relatively large number of references relating to the new "world of imagery", is the case of virtual reality (VR). VR is defined as "an artificial world that consists of images and sounds created by a computer and that is affected by the actions of a person who is experiencing it" (Merriam-Webster Dictionary). A sub-case of VR is augmented reality (AR), in which the computer simulates artificial objects in the real environment (while VR creates an artificial environment). A common way to create VR is by using a head-mounted display (HMD), through which the person can see visions that are, at least partially, different from reality and he/she can begin to relate to the VR as if it were true. As mentioned earlier, unlike the other visual digital media developments, it seems that counselors and related professionals have already begun to try to utilize the power of VR and explore its incorporation within various types of interventions. In a recent literature review, Valmaggia, Latif, Kempton, and Rus-Calafell (2016) report on 1,160 studies, conducted on VR, among which 24 were control studies, in which the utility of using virtual reality in psychological treatment (VRT) was experimentally examined. Valmaggia et al.'s review confirmed the effectiveness of VRT, in comparison to conventional treatments. For example, in a study conducted among PTSD patients, a re-experiencing-focused intervention was manipulated by using virtual reality exposure (VRE) treatment. Findings of this study (Maples-Keller, Price, Rauch, Gerardi, & Rothbaum, 2016) demonstrated that VRE is a powerful tool for addressing recurring symptoms, which in turn is a key component of overcoming PTSD. Other studies have demonstrated the power of using VR for reducing pain (Kenney & Milling, 2016); for improving children's cognitive modifiability and flexibility (Passig, Tzuriel, & Eshel-Kedmi, 2016); etc.

However, while not de-evaluating the potential importance of VR for the improvement of various psychological difficulties and/or functions, it seems that VR is only one instance of a rather large spectrum of topics that are gradually being influenced by contemporary visualized reality. This notion stems from the fact, as mentioned earlier, that new technologies have led to the intensified use of images rather than words, manifested in our preoccupation with producing and consuming images (i.e., pictures and videos, such as selfies), with growing attention to one's own and others' appearance (e.g., in Facebook), adopting a new language, as represented by emoji symbols, and being connected to the world through the smartphone screen. This, in turn, has led the development and mastery of visual skills to a greater degree than oral and verbal skills.

Meanwhile, the field of counseling is still deeply embedded in listening and speaking skills, as the major determinant of counseling outcomes, and hence also as a major goal in counselors' training (Moyers & Miller, 2013). In light of the new visualized world, a comprehensive reconsideration of counseling theory and practice is needed. Sporadic visualized alternatives to the spoken language have been suggested (e.g., Boender & Thraen, 2016). However, counseling is still far behind the reality of people's lives today. Next are a few examples of the new challenges that counseling researchers and practitioners, especially those who work in school settings, face:

Establishing relationships

A major challenge in every counseling session is to establish an open and trustworthy relationship with the client (Bachelor & Horvath, 1999). In order to achieve this goal, numerous suggestions have been made, such as the cognitive-behavioral approach's recommendation that the counselor prepare in advance for the first meeting(s) with the client (Ormhaug & Jensen, 2016). Needless to mention that Facebook and other channels of social networking would enable the counselor to collect a large amount of information about the client, as well as vice versa. Such a process of collecting information out of a person's Facebook page is extremely common in daily use (such as before starting to date someone), and using it. Yet, counselors rarely receive comprehensive guidance about how to explore other people's (i.e., the potential or actual client) Facebook pages: how to analyze and consider the pictures that are posted on an individual's Facebook wall and/or Instagram account; to what extent the visualized materials that are presented in the social media (e.g., pictures, selfies and videos) can be trusted; what information can be drawn from them; how and when to share one's knowledge about the client's information, as retrieved from the social media, in the course of the sessions' progress; whether it is recommended for the counselor to share his/her own visualized materials in one or more of the social media channels; what would be considered is an ethical use of client's Facebook; etc. Doing the "visualized" homework properly can ease and foster the establishment of open communication between the counselor and the client, and vice versa – i.e., being outdated about social media and the visualized world, misunderstanding the role of visualization in the client's life or ignoring the importance of that specific emoji, presented by the client or by the counselor to the client, for the client's happiness are only a few examples of the mistakes that a counselor can make in pursuing communication with the client. However, needless to mention that more sophisticated use of the client's world of images shouldn't lead to ignoring the more traditional channels of getting and exchanging communication, between the client and the counselor, but rather should be added to them.

Conveying a sense of empathy and caring

Sometimes it is difficult to help the potential client (e.g., adolescent who's been "forced' to join his/her parents and attend a counselor) be willing to move from the waiting room into the counselor's treatment room (Rosenthal, 2016). Yet, moreover, it might be even harder to make the client, who is already in treatment room, feel that the counselor really understands him/her. However, the increasing power of images in many (especially young) people's lives make it even more complicated than it used to be to convey empathic acceptance to the client. While it is still generally recommended to be warm and supportive, it seems that the old method of conveying these attitudes through words (and silence) should be secondary, to a certain extent, to conveying it through images and gestures. One possible, though relatively rudimentary, derivation of this notion is the even greater importance that should be attributed to the decorum of the counselor's room. Additional and more important ways of conveying warmth and acceptance through imagery are through symbols, signs, sights, pictures, videos, etc. that should be more intensively incorporated into the sessions of the counseling process themselves, to help the client better understand the message that the counselor is trying to convey. In this context, it is of special importance that the counselor be familiar with popular and/or common contexts, related to the counselor's clients and/or specialty, that are presented on YouTube and similar video channels.

However, to be able to sophisticatedly incorporate the visualized world into the counseling process, counselors – especially novice counselors – should have the proper guidance on how and when to incorporate or avoid the use of visualization. For example, recent findings suggest that even though using e-counseling – i.e., the use of internet-based components – is an efficient tool in counseling people with medical problems, using it at an early stage of the counseling process might be problematic (Zandbelt, de Kanter, & Ubbink, 2015).

Counseling people who are in need

In relation to videos, in some cases, the counselor might encourage the clients to prepare a video of their own, in which the client would either present their problem in the way they want it to be presented, present solutions they wish to promote (realistically or idealistically) or simply tell/document their story for future use. Another option would be to help the client prepare a video to be posted in WhatsApp, to deliver a message and/or get future consideration from family, peers, class, school, etc. However, awareness of people's intensive engagement in visualization is not just a justification to explore new ways of incorporating and/or considering related tools within the counseling session, rather it is also a call for a renewed evaluation of old, well-established theories and procedures in counseling. Practically speaking, next are two examples of counseling approaches that gain further importance in the presence of the current visualization era: (a) *Play Therapy*: Play therapy has long been a useful technique in counseling children who are in need. Accordingly, a recent review of studies on the utility of child-centered play therapy indicates its positive impact on a large scope of problems (Lin & Bratton, 2015). However, it should be noted that the healing component of play therapy is not only the joint play between the counselor and the troubled child but rather that the counselor and the child together consider actual and visible events, in relation to which they react and reflect. Hence, play therapy seems to be an even more appropriate tool for helping people today, especially children who have more experience with visual rather than oral communication. In light of this notion, it seems reasonable to suggest that future counselors should also be trained in various forms of play therapy. While counseling children would be based on the more traditional ways of conducting play therapy, counseling adults could be based on the more modern forms of play such as playback theater (Murphy & Neimeyer, 2014), both as players and as observers. (b) *Analytic Psychology*: Recent trends in theories counseling demonstrate the growing attention that analytic psychology receives from counselors, researchers and practitioners (Huskinson & Stein, 2015). However, the importance that Gustav Jung attributed to images – e.g., symbols, signs, dreams and the visual arts – calls for further reevaluation of analytic psychology's utility in helping people who are in need. For example, at the very practical level, (1) it seems that several emojis have already been "incorporated" into many children's collective unconsciousness or subconscious, and already serve as buffers to either positive or negative mood and associations. (2) Counselors, scientists and practitioners as well should reassess long-standing assumptions regarding the similarities and differences, as well as the sources of such differences, among the various cultures. This is not just a recommendation to reach a better understanding of the emic and epic in cultures (Newland, Patel, & Senapati, 2015); rather, it is a suggestion to explore the possibility that visualized (i.e., external) signs play a greater role in culturally based self-definition. Should such an exploration reveal that people attribute greater importance to external signs, it would help counselors to better understand and better counsel the help-seeker. (3) The arts, a field that Jung and his followers intensively explored, has become an even more powerful way of understanding the client's problems and ways to overcome them. The arts not only represent visions that the beholder – i.e., the artist – has; rather, it is also an efficient way to express oneself when the arsenal of words is limited, such as the case of a meeting between strangers/foreigners. Hence, especially during the current era of intensive exposure to visual screens, the use of arts in counseling and therapy would not just be a matter of using "the power of creativity" (Dean, 2016), but rather of using "the power of habit" (i.e., the habit of watching pictures, figures, shapes and symbols) as well.

Career development

Recent technical and internet-based development has changed the career world in numerous ways. The emergence of new occupations and the decline of traditional ones have already been extensively discussed. Here, one example of visualization in relation to *career decision-making* will be mentioned. Recent research findings highlight the negative impact of personal difficulties on decision-making, career planning, and career development (Gati & Levin, 2014). However, the possible contribution of visualization to difficulties in career decision-making still awaits intensive research. One possibility, that should be further explored, is that current access to endless videos and pictures enables better decision-making when used properly. Namely, that if the career counselor was to encourage the client to explore the concrete visualization of a potential occupation and related aspects, through all channels of social media, the process of decision-making would be easier and based to a greater extent on reality. However, another possibility, that should also be explored, is that current access to endless videos and images makes decision-making much more problematic, since the client is exposed to too many images and visualized situations, that are related to the given occupation, to the point that these images might become confusing and difficult to process, both cognitively and emotionally. Moreover, it is possible that some people may become too preoccupied with searching for visualized demonstrations of the potential occupation (or relevant situation, such as a potential date, etc.), leaving them with no time, energy or awareness for the parallel need to explore themselves, in terms of personal values, personal needs, etc.

Progressing toward visualization – two explorations

As mentioned previously, counseling should take the new "visual age" more seriously. This means not only being aware of it and/or mentioning it but rather implementing its meaning and implications within revised models of counseling and change, to find new innovative ways of intervening among clients who are in need of help, and accordingly, updating the training given to novice counselors.

Next are two examples in which the possible uses of visualization in counseling are explored; one relates to the use of YouTube and the other to the use of selfies.

Incorporating YouTube in counseling depressed clients

A preliminary survey that was administered to adolescents and emerging adults (Israelashvili, 2014b) showed that 58% of the study sample (N = 716) watch movies on YouTube and a considerable number reported that they also use YouTube as a source for gaining information on various issues that bother them. It should be noted that YouTube is an open video-hosting website, in which anyone can post his/her video (under minimal content restrictions). Hence, it is plausible that people might post misleading videos and/or their own personal experiences that might be far from the common (i.e., normal) experience. Another, closely related question refers to the utility of using such free videos in the course of counseling, e.g., to expose a client to the ways in which other people cope with a problem she/he has encountered. Indeed, a study was conducted (Israelashvili, 2014a) in which the content and features of free YouTube videos on coping were analyzed. As mentioned, the study had two goals: (1) To evaluate the type of messages that YouTube videos on stress and coping convey; (2) To evaluate whether they could be used as a component in intervention to promote people's coping mechanisms in stressful situations. The criteria for inclusion of videos in the study were: videos that deal with social anxiety; non-advertisement; videos including a monologue; a video (i.e., not a PowerPoint presentation); videos that present a real event; English-speaking; focusing of stress and depression (and not presenting comorbidity); and a message that is delivered by people who are between the ages of 10 and 30. The selection of videos that met these criteria was conducted by three observers: two graduate counseling students and a senior counseling psychologist. These three people viewed the videos independently, and the top 20 videos that were selected by the three of them were included in the study. An example of such a video can be found in www.youtube.com/watch?v=x0MFaNmnJg0. Table 3.2 presents the criteria according to which each of the videos was independently rated by these three observers.

Analysis of the video content, features and counseling messages indicated that: 75% of the monologues describe coping mechanisms, in which about 35% discussed problem-focused coping mechanisms only and most of the others (55%) described mix-forms of coping. The monologues could be divided into three general groups: (a) 35% that reflect hopelessness; (b) 30% that exhibit hopefulness; and (c) 35% that display neither hope nor despair. The general conclusion that could be drawn from the study's findings was that occasional exposure to YouTube monologues on social anxiety plus coping could be informative to

Table 3.2 Criteria for ranking the videos

The setting
- Location
- Photography technique
- Context
- Sex
- Age
- Marital status
- Seemed to be in stress
- Way of speaking
- Eye contact
- Length
- Numbers of viewers
- Music

The content
- Purpose
- Ways of coping
- Future expectation:
- Receiving therapy
- References to family . . . to occupation . . . to friends
- Aggressive verbalization

Intensity
- Has other videos
- How many of them deal with anxiety
- Focus more on anxiety . . . on coping
- Professional relatedness to anxiety

General impression
- Video quality; Message quality; Support coping;
- Foresting hopelessness . . . Helplessness

the audience, but would not necessarily promote personal resilience. However, it was evident that careful guided exposure to selected monologues could serve as an enriching component in programs designed to promote coping behavior and resilience among adolescents and emerging adults who suffer from social anxiety. This was especially relevant for counseling sessions in which CBT, or another therapy from the related family of therapeutic techniques (e.g., ACT), is implemented. Thus, despite the potential risk that people who post videos on YouTube might, intentionally or unintentionally, mislead naïve people or, especially, people who are in need of help, the study's findings indicate that there is greater probability that the YouTube viewer would benefit from watching such monologues. Assuming that this conclusion can be generalized beyond the scope of social anxiety, an assumption that should be validated in the future, this conclusion opens a large variety of options for utilizing visualization to counsel people with various problems. One such an option is to teach coping skills by giving the client visualized homework, rather than discussing it in the treatment room.

Incorporating selfies when counseling parents

Instructing parents on how to raise their children, especially in times of difficulty, is one of the counselor's major roles. Indeed, providing parents with guidance can make a difference in preventing a child's maladjustment (e.g., Gewirtz & Youssef, 2016). One such event that can be a stressful time for many families (Young et al., 2011) is an adolescent's transition from high school. Parents often have mixed feelings about the adolescent's coming departure; on the one hand, they may understand the need to continue on, while on the other hand, parents are frequently worried about the child's ability to manage in the future. Moreover, in many houses a debate begins to take place concerning the preferred path of development for the child; i.e., the best subject and/or occupation that the adolescent should pursue (Bahrassa, Syed, Su, & Lee, 2011). Such tension is especially present in Israeli families, since the majority of the Israeli-Jewish adolescents are obliged to join compulsory military service upon graduation from high school. In order to advise parents on how to manage this period of time, group counseling was offered to parents of 12th graders in Israel, as a complimentary support "to those parents who wish to share their thoughts and feelings about it". Generally speaking, the goal of the group counseling was to help the parents differentiate between their own and their adolescent child's feelings of stress, perceptions and desires, as a preliminary goal to finding the meeting point between parent and child. Details regarding the other goals and components of this counseling process are described elsewhere (for more details see Israelashvili, 2006). However, over the years one of the group counseling sessions gradually shifted from its original structure to a visualized one, taking advantage of the popularity of selfies. In this group, an effort was made to help parents become more aware, and if possible understand more accurately, their adolescent child's strengths and weaknesses. Practically speaking, after three group meetings, in which the general issue of transitions and the specific topic of transition from high school were discussed, each parent was asked to bring one picture of their own child. Parents brought all kinds of pictures – i.e., some parents brought an old picture of the child, such as a picture taken when the (adolescent) child was in kindergarten; other parents brought a picture of themselves with the child (sometimes the child was hidden behind them); etc. The parents were divided into pairs, in which one parent described his/her child to the other parent, and afterward vice versa, the other parent presented his/her child to the first parent. Each pair was instructed to make a list of the child's strengths and a list of the child's weaknesses, as seemed to be represented by the picture the parent had brought. A discussion of the strengths and weaknesses that were listed in each of the pairs concluded the meeting. The parents were then asked to bring another picture to the following meeting – a selfie that the child selected and gave them. The parents were instructed to tell the child that she/he can either give the parent an existing picture or make a special selfie for the group meeting. The next meeting began with a similar process of discussion of the pictures in pairs. However, this time the parents were asked to also list the "surprises" they discovered, by comparing the picture they brought to the previous meeting and the selfie they received from their child. Many times, other parents made significant comments on the similarities and differences between the picture the parent brought and the selfie the child gave the parent. The major point to be remember is that the use of pictures, and especially the comparison between the parents' preferred picture versus the adolescent's preferred selfie, was a very dramatic way of prompting a general discussion on the extent to which parents know their adolescent children, his/her preferences, self-esteem, future plans, etc. Needless to say, that following this discussion the parents received homework – to have "a serious, in-depth discussion" with their adolescent child about the child's true preferences, strengths and weaknesses, as a basis for mutual decision-making.

Concluding comments

The old saying that "one picture is worth a thousand words" has been frequently used as a way of encouraging the use of pictures, illustrations or symbols that illustrate the message one wishes to convey. However, contemporary society emphasizes the visual, with the average individual living in Western society exposed to thousands of images a day. In light of this reality, the counselor – especially school counselors – is requested to look up from his/her smartphone and consider the implications of the new visual age upon counseling models and practice.

It is suggested that the prominent feature of engagement in these new technologies is that for many children and youth the visual, rather than the written or spoken word, is the dominant form of communication. This notion has major implications for the future of counseling, in terms of counselors' training, counseling methods, measurement and evaluation in counseling, priorities in counseling youth, priorities in using e-counseling versus traditional face-to-face counseling, the need to develop visually-oriented M-counseling (i.e., similar to M-health) and especially the future of school counseling. These tasks are not challenges for the future but rather of critical current necessity in keeping (school) counseling relevant to people's lives.

References

Aitken, M. (2016). Why life sciences companies need to tap technology to gain a competitive edge – and what that means for the chief information officers (CIO) role. *mHealth*, *2*(10), 1–3.

Bachelor, A., & Horvath, A. (1999). The therapeutic relationship. In M. A. Hubble, B. L. Duncan, & S. D. Miller (Eds.), *The heart and soul of change: What works in therapy* (pp. 133–178). Washington, DC, US: American Psychological Association, doi:http://dx.doi.org/10.1037/11132-004

Bahrassa, N. F., Syed, M., Su, J., & Lee, R. M. (2011). Family conflict and academic performance of first-year Asian American undergraduates. *Cultural Diversity and Ethnic Minority Psychology, 17*, 415–426. doi:http://dx.doi.org/10.1037/a0024731

Boender, J. A., & Thraen, E. S. (2016). Representative images of values/views on sex: Talking about sex through images. In C. F. Sori, L. L. Hecker, & M. E. Bachenberg (Eds.), *The therapist's notebook for children and adolescents: Homework, handouts, and activities for use in psychotherapy* (2nd ed., pp. 201–207). New York, NY: Routledge/Taylor & Francis Group.

Dean, M. L. (2016). Using art media in psychotherapy: Bringing the power of creativity to practice. New York, NY: Routledge/Taylor & Francis Group.

Frosh, P. (2015). Selfies | the gestural image: The selfie, photography theory, and kinesthetic sociability. *International Journal of Communication, 9*, 22.

Gati, I., & Levin, N. (2014). Counseling for career decision-making difficulties: Measures and methods. *The Career Development Quarterly, 62*, 98–113.

Gewirtz, A., & Youssef, A. M. (2016). Family-based prevention: Efficacy, effectiveness, and widespread implementation of parenting programs to reduce child behavior problems. In M. Israelashvili & J. L. Romano (Eds.), *Cambridge handbook of international prevention science* (Ch. 12). Cambridge, UK: Cambridge University Press.

Huskinson, L., & Stein, M. (Eds.). (2015). *Analytical psychology in a changing world: The search for self, identity and community*. New York, NY: Routledge/Taylor & Francis Group.

International Business Times. (2016). Selfie deaths: 27 die in global picture craze in 2015. Retrieved June 5, 2016, from www.ibtimes.co.uk/selfie-deaths-27-die-global-picture-craze-2015-1538172

Internet Live Statistics. (2016). *Internet users by country*. Retrieved June 4, 2016, from www.internetlivestats.com/internet-users-by-country

Israelashvili, M. (2006). The school-to-army transition: Interventions for high-school students and their families. In P. Buchwald (Ed.), *Stress and anxiety: Application to health, community, work place, and education* (pp. 325–346). Cambridge: Cambridge Scholar Press Ltd.

Israelashvili, M. (2014a). *Internet-focused coping*. Research Report. Submitted to Israel Internet Association.

Israelashvili, M. (2014b). YouTube monologs on anxiety, stress and coping: What can be learnt from it? In *35th International Conference of the Stress and Anxiety Research Society*, Cluj, Romania.

Istepanian, R., Laxminarayan, S., & Pattichis, C. S. (2006). *M-health*. New York, NY: Springer Science + Business Media, Incorporated.

Ivey, A. E., & Authier, J. (1978). Microcounseling: Innovations in interviewing, counseling, psychotherapy, and psychoeducation (2nd ed.). Oxford, UK: Charles C Thomas.

Jung, C. (1997). *Jung on active imagination*. Princeton, NJ: Princeton University Press.

Kay, M., Santos, J., & Takane, M. (2011). mHealth: New horizons for health through mobile technologies. *World Health Organization, 64*, 66–71.

Kenney, M. P., & Milling, L. S. (2016). The effectiveness of virtual reality distraction for reducing pain: A meta-analysis. *Psychology of Consciousness: Theory, Research, and Practice, 3*(3), 199–210. doi:http://dx.doi.org/10.1037/cns0000084

King, J. (2016). Off script: An advance man's guide to white house stagecraft, campaign spectacle, and political suicide. New York, NY: St. Martin's Press.

Leigh, S., & Flatt, S. (2015). App-based psychological interventions: Friend or foe? *Evidence-Based Mental Health, 18*, 97–99. doi:10.1136/eb-2015-102203

Lin, Y-W., & Bratton, S. C. (2015). A meta-analytic review of child-centered play therapy approaches. *Journal of Counseling & Development, 93*, 45–58. doi:http://dx.doi.org/10.1002/j.1556-6676.2015.00180.x

Malchiodi, C. A. (2006). *The art therapy sourcebook*. New York, NY: McGraw-Hill Professional. ISBN 978-0-07-146827-5.

Maples-Keller, J. L., Price, M., Rauch, S., Gerardi, M., & Rothbaum, B. O. (2016). Behavior therapy investigating relationships between PTSD symptom clusters within virtual reality exposure therapy for OEF/OIF veterans. *Behavior Therapy, 48*, 147–155. doi:10.1016/j.beth.2016.02.011

Moyers, T. B., & Miller, W. R. (2013). Is low therapist empathy toxic? *Psychology of Addictive Behaviors, 27*, 878–884. doi:http://dx.doi.org/10.1037/a0030274

Murphy, V. R., & Neimeyer, R. A. (2014). Playback theatre: Grief and the expressive arts: Practices for creating meaning. In B. E. Thompson & R. A. Neimeyer (Eds.), *Grief and the expressive arts: Practices for creating meaning. Series in death, dying, and bereavement* (pp. 89–94). New York, NY: Routledge/Taylor & Francis.

Nelson, K. L., Bein, E., Huemer, J., Ryst, E., & Steiner, H. (2009). Listening for avoidance: Narrative form and defensiveness in adolescent memories. *Child Psychiatry and Human Development, 40*, 561–573. doi:http://dx.doi.org/10.1007/s10578-009-0144-y

Newland, J., Patel, N., & Senapati, M. (2015). Professional and ethical practice in a multiethnic society. In J. Morrissey & R. Tribe (Eds.), *Handbook of professional and ethical practice for psychologists, counsellors and psychotherapists* (2nd ed., pp. 183–192). New York, NY: Routlege.

Nouri, S. S., & Rudd, R. E. (2014). Health literacy in the "oral exchange": An important element of patient – provider communication. *Patient Education and Counseling, 98*, 565–571. doi:http://dx.doi.org/10.1016/j.pec.2014.12.002

Olff, M. (2015). Mobile mental health: A challenging research agenda. *European Journal of Psychotraumatology, 6*, 1–7.

Ormhaug, S. M., & Jensen, T. K. (2016). Investigating treatment characteristics and first-session relationship variables as predictors of dropout in the treatment of traumatized youth. *Psychotherapy Research*. Advance Online Publication. 1–15. doi:10.1080/10503307.2016.1189617

Passig, D., Tzuriel, D., & Eshel-Kedmi, G. (2016). Improving children's cognitive modifiability by dynamic assessment in 3D immersive virtual reality environments. *Computers & Education, 95*, 296–308. doi:http://dx.doi.org/10.1016/j.compedu.2016.01.009

Rosenthal, H. (2016). The goat story: The royal road from the waiting room to the counseling couch. In C. Sori, L. L. Hecker, & M. E. Bachenberg (Eds.), *The therapist's notebook for children and adolescents: Homework, handouts, and activities for use in psychotherapy* (2nd ed., pp. 216–219). New York, NY: Routledge/Taylor & Francis Group.

Sullivan, P. S., Jones, J., Kishore, N., & Stephenson, R. (2015). The roles of technology in primary HIV prevention for men who have sex with men. *Current HIV/AIDS Reports, 12*, 481–488.

Terp, M., Laursen, B. S., Jørgensen, R., Mainz, J., & Bjørnes, C. D. (2016). A room for design: Through participatory design young adults with schizophrenia become strong collaborators. *International Journal of Mental Health Nursing, 25*, 496–550. doi:10.1111/inm.12231

Valmaggia, L. R., Latif, L., Kempton, M. J., & Rus-Calafell, M. (2016). Virtual reality in the psychological treatment for mental health problems: A systematic review of recent evidence. *Psychiatry Research, 236,* 189–195. doi:http://dx.doi.org/10.1016/j.psychres.2016.01.015

Whatis.com. Retrieved June 5, 2016, from http://whatis.techtarget.com/definitions/A.

Winnicott, D. (1971). *Therapeutic consultation in child psychiatry*. London: Hogarth Press.

Young, R. A., Marshall, S. K., Valach, L., Domene, J. F., Graham, M. D., & Zaidman-Zait, A. (2011). *Transition to adulthood: Action, projects, and counseling*. New York, NY: Springer Science + Business Media.

Zandbelt, L. C., de Kanter, F. E. C., & Ubbink, D. T. (2015). E-consulting in a medical specialist setting: Medicine of the future? *Patient Education and Counseling*, *99*, 689–705. doi:http://dx.doi.org/10.1016/j.pec.2015.11.005

Chapter 4

A practitioner's perspective on coaching effectiveness

Tim Theeboom, Annelies E.M. Van Vianen, Bianca Beersma, Robert Zwitser and Vladimer Kobayashi

In past decades, coaching – which involves a "result-oriented, systematic process in which the coach facilitates the enhancement of life experience and goal-attainment in the personal and/or professional life of normal, non-clinical clients" (Grant, 2003, p. 254) – has grown into a $2 billion industry worldwide (International Coach Federation, 2012). In order to facilitate the personal and professional development of their employees, organizations increasingly rely on coaching as a human-resource development (HRD) tool (Theeboom et al., 2014). Not surprisingly, this increase in the popularity of coaching together with the relatively costly individualized nature of coaching (e.g., as compared to training) has raised the question whether coaching can indeed be effectively used as a human resource development methodology and whether the investments in coaching can be justified (Bono, Purvanova, Towler, & Peterson, 2009). Consequently, the question of how coaching effectiveness can be measured is a central topic of discussion in both coaching practice and research (Grant, 2013).

Currently, there is no unified answer to this question because researchers have used diverse indicators of coaching success. In a meta-analytic review of the empirical coaching literature, Theeboom et al. (2014) described five overarching *coaching success indicators* (CSIs) that emerged from existing effectiveness research: individual performance, wellbeing, coping, work-related attitudes, and self-regulated goal attainment. In essence, this classification represents a "bottom-up" approach and serves as a summary of the outcomes that had previously been investigated in coaching effectiveness studies.

Other meta-analytic investigations have taken a "top-down" approach and have classified CSIs based on either existing or newly developed theoretical frameworks. Jones, Woods, and Guillaume (2016) sought to integrate the effectiveness research on coaching with the broader literature on training and development by classifying coaching outcomes based on (an adaptation of) Kirkpatrick's (1979) well-known four level training evaluation model (Kraiger, Ford, & Salas, 1993). Specifically, they opted for four overarching CSIs: affective outcomes (e.g., satisfaction), cognitive outcomes (e.g., problem-solving strategies), skill-based outcomes (e.g., leadership skills), and results (e.g., goal achievement). Taking a slightly different approach, Sonesh and colleagues

(Sonesh et al., 2015) subdivided CSIs into only two categories; "relationship outcomes" (e.g., satisfaction with the relationship) and "goal-attainment coachee outcomes" (e.g., behavioral change), and meta-analytically investigated whether relationship outcomes are predictive for the more distal goal-attainment outcomes.

All three meta-analytic investigations showed that coaching can have positive effects (Jones et al., 2016; Sonesh et al., 2015; Theeboom et al., 2014) and that the different classifications are useful for their specific purpose (e.g., summarizing the literature vs. testing a predictive model). However, the CSIs represented in all three classifications represent a purely academic point of view. To date, there is no research that investigated whether these CSIs are actually utilized by coaching practitioners to evaluate the effectiveness of their interventions. Hence, the viewpoint of practitioners is missing in determining relevant CSIs.

For two reasons, we believe that this is an unfortunate state of affairs. First, investigating a practitioner's perspective on important CSIs may provide information that can be used to increase the alignment between coaching practice and research. Coaches will utilize CSIs that they view as relevant for generating sustainable individual change in the personal and/or professional lives of their coachees. However, these practiced CSIs may not fully converge with the CSIs that academics use in studies that aim to inform and support coaching practices. This could mean that researchers' findings do not resonate with the particular interests of coaches and thus do not contribute to improving coaching practices. Moreover, it could lead to practitioners utilizing CSIs that have a high face validity but are – according to existing research – hardly predictive for clients' sustained adaptation and/or improved functioning at work. For example, coaches might strive to foster a coachee's conscientiousness (being persistent, organized, and goal-directed; Costa & McCrae, 1992) because they adhere to the popular belief that being highly conscientiousness is positively related to job performance (Le et al., 2011). However, research indicates that the relationship between conscientiousness and job performance may be curvilinear (and a moderate level of conscientiousness is desirable), because highly conscientious individuals tend to become rigid and get lost in details while overlooking more important goals (Lepine, Colquitt, & Erez, 2000; Mount, Oh, & Burns, 2008).

Second, coaches who work in organizational settings often need to work with the desires and needs of both their individual clients (the coachee) and the client's organization (Ely et al., 2010). Although coaching should aim to align these different needs, discrepancies and tensions between these needs might still exist or develop during the coaching process. For example, while the ultimate goal of coaching may be to foster both functioning (e.g., job performance) and wellbeing (e.g., work-life balance), the organization may particularly value the former while the coach (and/or the coachee) may be mostly concerned with the latter. An investigation of the relative importance that practitioners ascribe to different CSIs could shed light on how coaches deal with the multifaceted nature of coaching and the complexity that is inherent to coaching in organizational settings (Ely et al., 2010).

In summary, we believe that investigating which CSIs practitioners use could enrich the debate about the measurement of coaching effectiveness. As such, this study uses a concept-mapping approach to shed light on the CSIs that coaching practitioners use to assess the effectiveness of their own interventions and the relative importance that these practitioners ascribe to these CSIs. It is important to note that we do not aim to offer any causal claims about coaching effectiveness. Rather, we intend to explore and describe practitioners' mental representation of coaching effectiveness.

Concept-mapping

Concept-mapping is a structured mixed-method research methodology that enables researchers to visualize and categorize participant-generated statements relevant to a particular topic (e.g., descriptions of CSIs) into clusters based on conceptual similarity as perceived by the participants themselves rather than the researchers (Trochim, 1989). This ability to capture the conceptual thinking and meaning-making schemes of participants and to minimize the influence of investigator bias have made concept-mapping a popular tool for marketing research (e.g., Bigné, Aldás-Manzano, Küster, & Vila, 2002). However, its potential has also been recognized by investigators in the fields that share commonalities with coaching such as counseling (Bedi, 2006) and psychotherapy (Tracey, Lichtenberg, Goodyear, Claiborn, & Wampold, 2003). For example, Tracey et al. (2003) used concept-mapping techniques to categorize the "common factors" (factors that are present regardless of the specific psychotherapy approach such as the therapist-client relationship) that contribute to psychotherapy effectiveness as conceived by 21 experts in the field.

Generally, concept-mapping procedures consist of five steps: (1) determining the focus and selecting the participants, (2) creating units of analysis, (3) sorting and rating the units, (4) multidimensional scaling, and (5) finding a cluster solution and labeling the clusters (Jackson & Trochim, 2002; Trochim, 1989). Steps 1 to 3 will be described in more detail in the methods section. Steps 4 and 5 will be discussed in the results section.

Method

Focus and participants (Step 1)

The focus of our study was to explore indicators that professional coaches use to determine whether their coaching interventions are successful. An online questionnaire was sent to 118 coaches who were certified as senior practitioners by the NOBCO, a Dutch professional body for coaches recognized by the European Mentoring and Coaching Council (EMCC). Sixty-six of these senior practitioners filled out the initial questionnaire (response rate 56%). The mean age of the participants was 53.86 years (SD = 7.15) and 44 of them were female (66.67%). On average, the participants had 14 years of experience (SD = 6.93) and on average spent 17.53 hours per week (SD = 7.35) on coaching. Finally, 31 of the participants (47%) indicated that they had engaged in psychological training. The questionnaire included questions about the participants' background (demographics, engagement in psychological training, years of experience as a coach) and, in line with previous concept-mapping studies (e.g., Behfar, Peterson, Mannix, & Trochim, 2008) asked the participants to respond to a single open question: "Coaching can be more or less successful. For you as a practitioner, what indicates whether your coaching has been successful?" We indicated that it was allowed to give multiple answers and that there was no limit to the number of words the participants could use to respond.

Creating units of analysis (Step 2)

Initially, our open question resulted in a total of 218 answers. A review of the answers showed that the majority of the respondents interpreted the question as intended. However, the answers also showed that some respondents had interpreted the question differently. Some seemed to have interpreted the question as "what methods do you use to evaluate the success of coaching" and responded accordingly (e.g., "an evaluation form"). An alternative (but related) interpretation was "which aspects of the coaching *process* indicate whether coaching is successful", which provided answers such as "the coachee completes all the sessions". Finally, some respondents interpreted the question as "what determines whether coaching is successful", eliciting answers such as "a good relationship with the coachee" and "the coachee feels safe". All statements reflecting an alternative interpretation of our open question were excluded from the concept-mapping process. For the remaining statements, one additional inclusion criterion was used. That is, statements were only included when the content/subject of the change within the coachee was explicitly specified rather than being purely evaluative. For example, a statement such as "the coachee changes" was excluded. One exception was made for statements referring to the "attainment of personal goals" because of the central role that goal-attainment scaling plays in the measurement of coaching effectiveness (Grant, 2013). Thus, statements such as "when there is considerable progression to the goals that were set up front" were included regardless of whether the personal goals were further specified.

When the answers represented a single concept (e.g., "the coachee has attained his/her predefined goal"), we directly used them as units of analysis. When the participants gave multiple and/or double-barreled answers (e.g., "the coachee feels better and performs better"), we unitized these answers by breaking sentences into single-concept phrases (e.g., (1) the coachee feels better, (2) the coachee performs better) as suggested by Jackson and Trochim (2002).

In those cases where there was doubt about the inclusion and/or unitization of answers, the first and third author discussed the cases until they could come to a mutual agreement. These procedures resulted in a total of 98 unique statements which is considered a suitable amount of units for concept-mapping procedures (Trochim, 1989).

Sorting and rating (Step 3)

From the original 66 participants who participated in the first part of the study, 14 participated in the sorting and rating stage. These participants were asked to sort the 98 statements (see earlier) into different piles (categories) using Usability card-sorting software. For this sorting task, five conditions were set based on the concept-mapping literature (Trochim, 1989): (1) all statements should be sorted into a pile, (2) it is not allowed to create a junk and/or miscellaneous pile, (3) there has to be a minimum of two piles, (4) the piles should be formed based on content/meaning rather than other properties (e.g., the length of the statements), and (5) each pile should be given a name that most accurately represents the statements in it.

Six weeks after they completed the sorting procedure, the same 14 participants were sent a list of all the 98 statements (in random order), and were asked to rate "how relevant the statement is as an indicator of coaching success" on a 1–7 Likert scale. This was done because this rating can inform decision-making when a final cluster solution needs to be chosen (Trochim, 1989) and it can provide information regarding the centrality of the clusters for the topic of interest. The six-week interval between the sorting and the rating of the statements was incorporated to prevent participants from using their own relevance ratings as a reference for categorization rather than the content/meaning of the statements.

Results

Multidimensional scaling (Step 4)

Based on the sorting procedure outlined previously, a similarity matrix was produced for each of the 14 participants. The matrices were 98 x 98 binary square matrices in which both rows and columns represent statements (similar to a correlation table). Cell values represented whether statements were sorted together (1) or not (0). The similarity matrices were then aggregated by adding together the 14 individual matrices created by the participants. From that aggregated matrix, MDS procedures created a two-dimensional map (see Figure 4.1) of the distances between each statement.

By choosing a two-dimensional solution, we followed recommendations by Kruskal and Whish (1978) and chose the solution that has been found to be most useful for subsequent cluster-analyses and concept-mapping procedures

Figure 4.1 Multidimensional scaling point map of statements

in general (Trochim, 1989). Statements (represented by numbers) that are closer together on the map were judged (by the participants) to be more similar than statements that lie further apart. It is important to note that the position (left, right, bottom, top) of the individual statements is not relevant for the interpretation, only the distance between the statements (Jackson & Trochim, 2002).

Cluster-analysis: labeling and ratings (Step 5)

In order to determine the appropriate number of clusters for the statements sorted by the participants, a hierarchical agglomerative cluster analysis (Ward's method) was conducted on the MDS map coordinates of each statement. Because there is "no sensible mathematical criterion that can be used to select the number of clusters" (Jackson & Trochim, 2002, p. 316), we used two types of output to aid our decision-making: the MDS map and a dendogram that visually displays different cluster solutions and gives an indication of the sum of the (squared) within cluster-distances. The first and the second author inspected a range of (7–13) solutions and judged the conceptual coherency and feasibility of each solution. The authors finally decided on a 10-cluster solution as it displayed the best fit with both the dendogram and the MDS map. Both merging into less (e.g., nine clusters) and splitting into more clusters (e.g., 11 clusters) did not result in more conceptual clarity and/or coherence. Figure 4.1 provides a graphical display of the 10 clusters on the MDS map.

During the sorting of the statements into the different piles, we also asked the participants to come up with names for these piles. We used these participant-generated pile names as input for labeling the different clusters. The first and second author first independently searched for the most appropriate label for each cluster and then discussed discrepancies until they fully agreed on the appropriate cluster labels. Finally, the following labels were agreed upon: responsibility/autonomy, self-awareness, self-concordance, goal-attainment, wellbeing, learning, behavioral change, coping/development, metacommunication, and performance improvement.

Cluster-ratings. In order to determine the (relative) perceived centrality of the clusters, we first calculated the mean centrality rating of each cluster by taking the mean of all individual statements within that cluster (as rated by the participants). We then used a Monte Carlo simulation (100.000 trials) to compute the 95% confidence intervals of the means and the ranking position for each statement. For that simulation, we assumed that the cluster scores are multivariate normally distributed. An exemplary statement for each cluster, the mean ratings, the ranking and the 95% confidence intervals for both the mean rating, and the ranking of each cluster are displayed in Table 4.1.

In general, the results show that all CSIs are considered to be important and that there is not much differentiation between the clusters: the 95% confidence intervals for both the mean ratings and the ranking positions are largely overlapping. The notable exception is that the performance improvement cluster was consistently rated as the least central to coaching success. We will elaborate on these results in the discussion section.

Additional analyses: Coaches' educational background and experience

In addition to the concept-mapping procedures, we used R software (R Core Team, 2013) to explore whether the CSIs that coaches use relate to their educational background and experience. First, since there is an ongoing debate about the differences between psychologists and non-psychologists coaches (e.g., Grant, 2006), we investigated whether there are differences between the CSIs of psychologists and non-psychologists. Second, it has been argued that a coach's level of proficiency is linked to the degree to which they use their own conceptual models, see the bigger picture, and focus on fundamental (rather than surface-level) problems (Peterson, 2011). Therefore, we also investigated possible differences between the CSIs of more versus less experienced coaches.

Table 4.1 Exemplary statements, mean ratings, ranking, and 95% confidence intervals for each cluster

Cluster	*Example*	*Mean rating (1–7)*	*95% CI*	*Ranking*	*Ranking 95% CI*
Responsibility/autonomy	"Coachee takes responsibility for change"	5.60	5.23–5.98	1	1–5
Self-awareness	"Coachee has become aware of his/her own change process"	5.53	5.06–5.99	2	1–7
Self-concordance	"Coachee acts in accordance with his/her own needs"	5.43	4.98–5.88	3	1–8
Goal-attainment	"Coachee attains preset goals"	5.35	4.78–5.94	4	1–9
Wellbeing	"Coachee feels better"	5.31	4.96–5.66	5	3–7
Learning	"Coachee has really learned something"	5.30	4.77–5.82	6	1–8
Behavioral change	"Visible changes in the coachee's behavior"	5.21	4.75–5.68	7	2–9
Coping/development	"Coachee recovers from burn-out"	5.04	4.50–5.58	8	4–9
Metacommunication	"Coachee is able to explain his/her own process to others"	4.93	4.42–5.45	9	5–9
Performance improvement	"Coachee adds value to the goals of the organization"	4.30	3.74–4.86	10	10–10

First, we checked whether educational background and experience were related to the number of criteria that coaches mentioned. For these analyses, we used the 218 statements originally generated by the practitioners. We only found a difference based on coaches' level of experience. Specifically, a Welch Two Sample t-test showed that coaches who had equal to or more than 13 years of experience ($n = 32$) mentioned significantly more CSIs ($M = 2.96$, $SD = 2.37$) than coaches who had less than 13 years of experience ($n = 34$, $M = 1.86$, $SD = 1.06$; $T(1, 32) = 2.14$, $p = .04$). We did not find significant differences based on whether the coaches had a background in psychology and neither did we find an interaction between experience and psychological background.

Discussion

With this study, we provide insight into practitioners' mental representation of coaching effectiveness. The concept-mapping analyses indicated that practitioners distinguish 10 conceptually different clusters of CSIs: responsibility/autonomy, self-awareness, self-concordance, goal-attainment, wellbeing, learning, behavioral change, coping/development, metacommunication, and performance improvement. In general, all clusters were considered to be equally important as CSIs. One exception is that the performance improvement cluster was consistently rated the least central to coaching success. Finally, additional analyses indicated that on average, experienced coaches mentioned more CSIs than less experienced coaches. Next, we will discuss how these findings contribute to two aims of our study: (1) investigating to which degree coaching research aligns with coaching practice in terms of measuring coaching effectiveness and (2) uncovering how coaching practitioners balance the needs of different stakeholders in measuring the effects of their interventions.

Regarding the first aim, our findings demonstrate both similarities and differences between the dominant CSIs in the coaching literature and the CSIs as identified by the coaching practitioners in our study. Practitioners use similar CSIs that have previously been studied in coaching effectiveness research such as self-awareness (e.g., Bozer & Sarros, 2012), self-concordance (e.g., Burke & Linley, 2007), goal-attainment (e.g., Grant, 2003), wellbeing (e.g., Grant, Curtayne, & Burton, 2009), learning (e.g., Grant, 2008), behavioral change (e.g., Kochanowski, Seifert, & Yukl, 2010), coping (e.g., Grant, Green, & Rynsaardt, 2010), and performance improvement (e.g., Smither, London, Flautt, Vargas, & Kucine, 2003). Generally speaking, validated measures are available for these constructs. As our study shows that practitioners value and utilize these outcomes, we hope that coaching practitioners and researchers continue to collaborate. Specifically, we hope that practitioners will start (or continue) to use validated measures (which can be provided by researchers) to assess the effectiveness of their own interventions and that researchers can then use the collected data for further research on (long-term) coaching effectiveness.

Notably, practitioners identified two additional CSIs that (to our knowledge) haven't been addressed in previous research: metacommunication and responsibility/autonomy.

The metacommunication cluster mainly included statements that referred to the coachee's ability to verbalize and explain his/her own development during the coaching process and its outcomes. Interestingly, research in the area of learning and education has shown that the ability to generate and verbalize explanations about certain events or information is positively related to learning outcomes (e.g., deep-level learning) in young children as well as adults (Van Blankenstein, Dolmans, Van der Vleuten, & Schmidt, 2011). Thus, metacommunication could (together with the learning and self-awareness CSIs) serve as a proximal indicator of the "transfer of coaching": the degree to which the coaching will have long-lasting effects. We suspect that research opportunities in the area of metacommunication are plentiful. In coaching practice, it is not uncommon for coaches to ask their coachees to write down and explain their experiences of the coaching and change process in diaries and other forms of written reflections. For instance, it would be interesting to see longitudinal studies in which diaries and written reflections are used to assess the validity of metacommunication as a predictor of sustainable change (e.g., sustained increases in wellbeing and/or functioning).

The second CSI that emerged, and has not yet been used in previous coaching effectiveness research, is the responsibility/autonomy cluster. This CSI mainly includes statements that refer to the degree to which coachees feel ownership of their problem(s) and the degree to which they are willing and able to take responsibility for solving those problems. Multiple scholars have argued that such feelings of ownership and responsibility are important antecedents of sustained motivation in a coaching context (Moen & Federici, 2012; Moen & Skaalvik, 2009; Oades & Spence, 2011). The broader psychological literature seems to provide indirect evidence for this argument. For example, research has shown that having an internal locus of control (the degree to which individuals believe in their ability to control events and behavioral results that happen in their lives; Rotter, 1966) is positively related to persistence (Joo, Joung, & Sim, 2011) and the utilization of proactive problem-solving strategies (Dijkstra, Beersma, & Evers, 2011). Likewise, research in the area of the Self-Determination Theory (Deci & Ryan, 1985) has shown that being autonomously motivated for change (striving for a goal because it is intrinsically rewarding) is related to commitment, wellbeing, and performance in organizational and educational settings (Sheldon & Houser-Marko, 2001; Vansteenkiste et al., 2007).

In summary, we believe that the responsibility/autonomy CSI could be an important addition to the coaching effectiveness literature and that it is worthwhile to explore how this CSI can be measured in research and practice. Coaches can support their coachees' autonomy in different ways. For example, coaches can invite coachees to set the agenda for both the overall coaching engagement and for each session. Furthermore, coaches can try to minimize imperative language (Oades & Spence, 2011). Finally, as asking questions is one of the main tools that coaches use in the coaching process, coaches can aim to ask inquiring rather than suggestive questions. Future research could measure these different autonomy supportive behaviors (e.g., by using observational methods) and investigate how those behaviors could foster feelings of problem ownership in the coachee, and more distal long-term outcomes.

The perceived relevance ratings of the different CSIs provide insight into the way in which coaches balance the needs of different stakeholders of workplace coaching (i.e., the coachee and the coachee's organization). On the one hand, the results indicate that all CSIs are considered to be important to coaching effectiveness. The lowest mean rating (performance improvement) is still 4.30 on a 7-point Likert scale. On the other hand, it is interesting to note that this same performance improvement CSI is the only CSI that is consistently rated to be the least important to coaching success. Based on the included statements (e.g., increased performance, contributing to the effectiveness of the organization), the performance improvement CSI seems to refer to outcomes that are beneficial for the coachee's organization. As such, our data suggests that coaches focus mostly on the individual stakeholder rather than the organization.

Future research needs to investigate whether this finding is generalizable beyond the Dutch/European context of our study. Coaching in Europe has been strongly influenced by humanistic psychotherapy approaches and has a strong psychological and individual focus (Kets de Vries, 2011). Coaching in the European regions has been found to be less goal-focused and result-focused than, for instance, coaching in the U.S. (David, Clutterbuck, & Megginson, 2014). Although we recognize the potential drawbacks of being too goal-focused (see Boyatzis & Howard, 2015), we believe that in order for coaching to be taken seriously as a human resource development strategy, it is necessary for coaches (in all regions) to search for ways to balance and align the needs of coachees and their organizations.

Finally, additional analysis showed that experienced coaches mentioned more CSIs than less experienced coaches. This finding is in line with Peterson's (2011) ideas about coaching expertise. Based on the five-stage model of expertise (novice, advanced beginners, competent, proficient, and experts), Peterson proposes that more experienced coaches are more inclined to focus on underlying principles (rather than on surface characteristics of problems) and are better equipped to deal with complex and multifaceted issues (and thus, are able to focus on multiple CSIs). Although our results should be interpreted with caution because of the exploratory nature of our study, our results indicate that experienced coaches indeed think differently about the multifaceted nature of coaching and have a broader view of relevant outcomes. Although it has been argued that psychologists and non-psychologists differ in their conceptualization of coaching practice and coaching effectiveness (Bono et al., 2009; Bozer, Sarros, & Santora, 2014; Grant, 2006), our results do not support that notion.

In summary, our results raise several questions and issues that need to be addressed in future research. Besides these specific questions and issues, we hope that this study more generally inspires future researchers to investigate the practitioner's perspective on coaching effectiveness. We believe that insight into the CSIs that practitioners utilize might not only advance the alignment between coaching research and practice as discussed earlier but that it could also reveal more about what happens behind closed doors in coaching. That is, the goals that practitioners strive for may tell us something about the implicit mental models that guide coaching practice and explain why coaches choose to use certain interventions (Barner & Higgins, 2007). For example, a coach that sees increased self-insight as the most important CSI will most likely engage in other interventions (e.g., reflective dialogue) than a coach that believes that changes in the coachee's overt behaviors are the most important CSI to strive for (e.g., role-play). In other words, identifying the CSIs that coaches use and consider as important may enhance our understanding of coaches' "theories in use" and the interventions that they tend to use in their coaching practice.

This study provides some initial insight into the CSIs that coaching practitioners use to monitor the effectiveness of their own coaching engagements. In general, it is encouraging to see that there is considerable agreement between coaching researchers and practitioners on the criteria that can help to determine whether coaching interventions are successful. Nonetheless, this study revealed additional CSIs and information about coaches' dominant focus of attention. Specifically, the emergence of new CSIs (metacommunication and responsibility/autonomy) and the focus on the individual (rather than the organizational stakeholder) provide interesting directions for future research. At the least, this study shows that incorporating the practitioner's perspective can foster our understanding of coaching and the development of coaching effectiveness research.

Implications for coaching practice

This study also has some implications for coaching practice. As the effectiveness of coaching hinges on clear and attainable coaching goals, practitioners could pay particular attention to specifying the outcomes of coaching for each individual coaching trajectory. First, this could be done at the start of the coaching process by means of discussing the overall coaching outcomes as well as more intermediate outcomes with the coachee and important stakeholders such as, for example, a coachee's supervisor. All parties in the coaching process – and not only the coach and coachee – could clarify what they expect from a coaching intervention in terms of (tangible) outcomes and how these outcomes could be assessed in the end. Most likely, the organization (i.e., the supervisor) will express her concern with observable improvements in a coachee's skills and performance. By discussing these expectations, the parties could exchange whether and when expectations can be met, who will be involved in assessing a coachee's accomplishments, and how this can be measured. A transparent contract between all stakeholders will help coaches and their coachees to remain alert on an organization's return on investment. At the same time, we would advise coaches, coachees, and organizational stakeholders to be flexible with regard to the goals as goals may change due to developments in the coaching process. Coaching is a dynamic process that should allow for adjustments in goals when involved parties agree this ultimately benefits the coachee and his/her organizational context.

Besides discussing the "ultimate", or long-term outcomes that the coaching intervention should achieve, during the coaching process, the coach and coachee could further discuss the "short-term" outcomes they want to attain in a specific stage of this process. Both research and practice tend to focus on the ultimate outcomes of coaching rather than the sub-outcomes that are necessary for attaining these ultimate outcomes. However, Hackman and Wageman (2005) argued that coaching should be viewed through a temporal lens because different coaching interventions may be relevant and effective during different stages of the coaching process. Based on our current findings, we agree that this would be a good approach. Some theoretical models that can be applied to coaching already take such a temporal perspective into account. For example, the Trans Theoretical Model of Change (TTM, Prochaska & Velicer, 1997) describes five stages individuals may go through during change interventions. In the first (precontemplation) stage, individuals become aware of a need for change; in the second (contemplation) stage, they explore their motivation; in the third (preparation) stage, they set specific goals and make plans for action; in the fourth (action) stage, they set the first steps toward the attainment of goals; and in the fifth (maintenance) stage, they consolidate their progress (Grant, 2012; Prochaska & Velicer, 1997). Each coaching stage requests specific competencies coachees must develop to move through subsequent stages of the coaching process. Hence, each stage should be focused on specific stage-relevant outcomes that are identified at the onset of a specific stage. Subsequently, the coach could employ interventions that facilitate the development of focal competencies in each stage.

Finally, our finding that experienced coaches mentioned more coaching success indicators than less experienced coaches underlines that much could be gained from intervision, supervision, and mentorship among coaches. Through mentorship, experienced coaches could guide less experienced coaches, not only with regard to the development of coaching skills and techniques, but also with setting, specifying, and measuring coaching outcomes. Furthermore, mentor and mentee coaches could critically discuss the extent to which a mentee's coaching goals were accomplished and how coaching success was measured. Feedback about the coaching process and its outcomes from an experienced mentor coach is important because it could facilitate deep-level learning and transfer (Van Blankenstein et al., 2011).

Inexperienced coaches may primarily use their coachees' feedback to evaluate the effectiveness of their coaching interventions. However, this feedback is not sufficient for measuring the effectiveness of coaching. For example, a coachee may report having developed greater responsibility for and confidence in solving his problems while in fact he remains to lean on the guidance of others in his work environment. Hence, in addition to letting coachees verbalize their progress, coaches should use techniques that bring coachees' actual behaviors to the surface. After all, effective coaching should be a dialogue-based as well as an evidence-based change methodology in the workplace.

Note

Portions of this chapter were presented at the World Educational Research Association Focal Meeting, Edinburgh, Scotland, 2014, and at the American Educational Research Association Meeting, Philadelphia, PA, 2014. In addition, the negotiation template has been presented in graduate courses in education and leadership studies.

References

Barner, R., & Higgins, J. (2007). Understanding implicit models that guide the coaching process. *Journal of Management Development, 26*(2), 148–158. doi:http://doi.org/10.1108/02621710710726053

Bedi, R. P. (2006). Concept mapping the client's perspective on counseling alliance formation. *Journal of Counseling Psychology, 53*(1), 26–35. doi:http://doi.org/10.1037/0022-0167.53.1.26

Behfar, K. J., Peterson, R. S., Mannix, E. A., & Trochim, W. M. K. (2008). The critical role of conflict resolution in teams: A close look at the links between conflict type, conflict management strategies, and team outcomes. *Journal of Applied Psychology, 93*(1), 170–188. doi:http://doi.org/10.1037/0021-9010.93.1.170

Bigné, J. E., Aldás-Manzano, J., Küster, I., & Vila, N. (2002). The concept mapping approach in marketing: An application in the travel agencies sector. *Qualitative Market Research: An International Journal, 5*(2), 87–95. doi:http://doi.org/10.1108/13522750210423724

Bono, J. E., Purvanova, R. K., Towler, A. J., & Peterson, D. B. (2009). A survey of executive coaching practices. *Personnel Psychology, 62*(2), 361–404. doi:http://doi.org/10.1111/j.1744-6570.2009.01142.x

Boyatzis, R. A., & Howard, A. (2015). When goal setting helps and hinders sustained, desired change. In S. A. David, D. A. Clutterbuck, & D. Megginson (Eds.), *Beyond goals: Effective strategies for coaching and mentoring* (pp. 211–228). Dorchester: Gower Publishing Limited.

Bozer, G., & Sarros, J. C. (2012). Examining the effectiveness of executive coaching on coachees' performance in the Israeli context. *International Journal of Evidence Based Coaching and Mentoring, 10*(1), 14–32.

Bozer, G., Sarros, J. C., & Santora, J. C. (2014). Academic background and credibility in executive coaching effectiveness. *Personnel Review, 43*(6), 881–897. doi:http://dx.doi.org/10.1108/PR-10-2013-0171

Burke, D., & Linley, P. A. (2007). Enhancing goal self-concordance through coaching. *International Coaching Psychology Review, 2*(1), 62–69.

Costa, P., & McCrae, R. (1992). Normal personality assessment in clinical practice: The NEO personality inventory. *Psychological Assessment, 4*(1), 5–13. doi:http://doi.org/10.1037//1040-3590.4.1.5

David, S., Clutterbuck, D., & Megginson, D. (2014). Goal orientation in coaching differs according to region, experience, and education. *International Journal of Evidence Based Coaching & Mentoring, 12*(2), 134–145.

Deci, E. L., & Ryan, R. M. (1985). *Intrinsic motivation and self-determination in human behavior.* New York: Springer Science & Business Media.

Dijkstra, M. T. M., Beersma, B., & Evers, A. (2011). Reducing conflict-related employee strain: The benefits of an internal locus of control and a problem-solving conflict management strategy. *Work & Stress, 25*(2), 167–184. doi:http://doi.org/10.1080/02678373.2011.593344

Ely, K., Boyce, L. A., Nelson, J. K., Zaccaro, S. J., Hernez-Broome, G., & Whyman, W. (2010). Evaluating leadership coaching: A review and integrated framework. *The Leadership Quarterly, 21*(4), 585–599. doi:http://doi.org/10.1016/j.leaqua.2010.06.003

Grant, A. M. (2003). The impact of life coaching on goal attainment, metacognition, and mental health. *Social Behavior and Personality: An International Journal, 31*(3), 253–263. doi:http://doi.org/10.2224/sbp.2003.31.3.253

Grant, A. M. (2006). A personal perspective on professional coaching and the development of coaching psychology. *International Coaching Psychology Review, 1*(1), 12–22. Retrieved from http://groups.psychology.org.au

Grant, A. M. (2008). Personal life coaching for coaches-in-training enhances goal attainment, insight and learning. *Coaching: An International Journal of Theory, Research and Practice, 1*(1), 54–70. doi:http://doi.org/10.1080/17521880701878141

Grant, A. M. (2012). An integrated model of goal-focused coaching: An evidence-based framework for teaching and practice. *International Coaching Psychology Review,* 7(2), 146–165. doi:http://doi.org/10.1080/17521880903102308

Grant, A. M. (2013). The efficacy of coaching. In J. Passmore, D. B. Peterson, & T. Freire (Eds.), *The Wiley-Blackwell handbook of the psychology of coaching and mentoring* (1st ed., pp. 15–39). West-Sussex: Wiley-Blackwell. doi:http://doi.org/10.1002/9781118326459

Grant, A. M., Curtayne, L., & Burton, G. (2009). Executive coaching enhances goal attainment, resilience and workplace wellbeing: A randomised controlled study. *The Journal of Positive Psychology, 4*(5), 396–407. doi:http://doi.org/10.1080/17439760902992456

Grant, A. M., Green, L. S., & Rynsaardt, J. (2010). Developmental coaching for high school teachers: Executive coaching goes to school. *Consulting Psychology Journal: Practice and Research, 62*(3), 151–168. doi:http://doi.org/10.1037/a0019212

Hackman, J. R., & Wageman, R. (2005). A theory of team coaching. *Academy of Management Review, 30*(2), 269–287. doi:http://doi.org/10.5465/AMR.2005.16387885

International Coach Federation. (2012). Retrieved from www.coachfederation.org

Jackson, K. M., & Trochim, W. M. K. (2002). Concept mapping as an alternative approach for the analysis of open-ended survey responses. *Organizational Research Methods, 5*(4), 307–336. doi:http://doi.org/10.1177/109442802237114

Jones, R. J., Woods, S. A., & Guillaume, Y. R. F. (2016). The effectiveness of workplace coaching: A meta-analysis of learning and performance outcomes from coaching. *Journal of Occupational and Organizational Psychology, 89*(2), 249–277. doi:http://doi.org/10.1111/joop.12119

Joo, Y. J., Joung, S., & Sim, W. J. (2011). Structural relationships among internal locus of control, institutional support, flow, and learner persistence in cyber universities. *Computers in Human Behavior, 27*(2), 714–722. doi:http://doi.org/10.1016/j.chb.2010.09.007

Kets de Vries, M. F. R. (2011). The leader on the couch: A clinical approach to changing people and organizations. West-Sussex: John Wiley & Sons.

Kirkpatrick, D. L. (1979). Techniques for evaluating training programs. *Training and Development Journal, 76*(4), 604–620.

Kochanowski, S., Seifert, C. F., & Yukl, G. (2010). Using coaching to enhance the effects of behavioral feedback to managers. *Journal of Leadership & Organizational Studies,* 17(4), 363–369. doi:http://doi.org/10.1177/1548051809352663

Kraiger, K., Ford, J. K., & Salas, E. (1993). Application of cognitive, skill-based, and affective theories of learning outcomes to new methods of training evaluation. *Journal of Applied Psychology, 78*, 311–328. doi:http://doi.org/10.1037/0021-9010.78.2.311

Kruskal, J. B., & Whish, M. (1978). *Multidimensional scaling.* Thousand Oaks, CA: Sage Publications, Inc.

Le, H., Oh, I. S., Robbins, S. B., Ilies, R., Holland, E., & Westrick, P. (2011). Too much of a good thing: Curvilinear relationships between personality traits and job performance. *Journal of Applied Psychology, 96*(1), 113–133. doi:http://doi.org/10.1037/a0021016

Lepine, J. A., Colquitt, J. A., & Erez, A. (2000). Adaptability to changing task contexts: Effects of general cognitive ability, conscientiousness, and openness to experience. *Personnel Psychology, 53*(3), 563–593. doi:http://doi.org/10.1111/j.1744-6570.2000.tb00214.x

Moen, F., & Federici, R. A. (2012). The effect from external executive coaching. *Coaching: An International Journal of Theory, Research and Practice, 5*(2), 113–131. doi:http://doi.org/10.1080/17521882.2012.708355

Moen, F., & Skaalvik, E. (2009). The effect from executive coaching on performance psychology. *International Journal of Evidence Based Coaching and Mentoring*, 7(2), 31–49.

Mount, M. K., Oh, I. S., & Burns, M. (2008). Incremental validity of perceptual speed and accuracy over general mental ability. *Personnel Psychology, 61*(1), 113–139. dpo:http://doi.org/10.1111/j.1744-6570.2008.00107.x

Oades, L. G., & Spence, G. B. (2011). Coaching with self-determination in mind: Using theory to advance evidence-based coaching practice. *International Journal of Evidence Based Coaching and Mentoring, 9*(2), 37–55.

Peterson, D. B. (2011). Good to great coaching. In G. Hernez-Broome & L. A. Boyce, (Eds.), *Advancing executive coaching: Setting the course of successful leadership coaching* (pp. 83–102). San Francisco, CA: John Wiley & Sons.

Prochaska, J. O., & Velicer, W. F. (1997). The transtheoretical model of health behavior change. *American Journal of Health Promotion, 12*(1), 38–48. doi:http://doi.org/10.4278/0890-1171-12.1.38

R Core Team. (2013). *R: A language and environment for statistical computing*. Vienna, Austria: R Foundation for Statistical Computing. Retrieved from www.r-project.org

Rotter, J. B. (1966). Generalized expectancies for internal versus external control of reinforcement. *Psychological Monographs: General and Applied, 80*(1), 1–28. doi:http://doi.org/10.1037/h0092976

Sheldon, K. M., & Houser-Marko, L. (2001). Self-concordance, goal attainment, and the pursuit of happiness: Can there be an upward spiral? *Journal of Personality and Social Psychology, 80*, 152–162. doi:http://dx.doi.org/10.1037/0022-3514.80.1.152

Smither, J. W., London, M., Flautt, R., Vargas, Y., & Kucine, I. (2003). Can working with an executive coach improve multisource feedback ratings over time? A quasi-experimental field study. *Personnel Psychology, 56*(1), 23–44. doi:http://doi.org/10.1111/j.1744-6570.2003.tb00142.x

Sonesh, S. C., Coultas, C. W., Lacerenza, C. N., Marlow, S. L., Benishek, L. E., & Salas, E. (2015). The power of coaching: A meta-analytic investigation. *Coaching: An International Journal of Theory, Research and Practice, 8*, 1–23. doi:http://doi.org/10.1080/17521882.2015.1071418

Theeboom, T., Beersma, B., & van Vianen, A. E. M. (2014). Does coaching work? A meta-analysis on the effects of coaching on individual level outcomes in an organizational context. *The Journal of Positive Psychology, 9*, 1–18. doi:http://doi.org/10.1080/17439760.2013.837499

Tracey, T. J. G., Lichtenberg, J. W., Goodyear, R. K., Claiborn, C. D., & Wampold, B. E. (2003). Concept mapping of therapeutic common factors. *Psychotherapy Research, 13*(4), 401–413. doi:http://doi.org/10.1093/ptr/kpg041

Trochim, W. M. K. (1989). Outcome pattern matching and program theory. *Evaluation and Program Planning, 12*(4), 355–366. doi:http://doi.org/10.1016/0149-7189(89)90052-9

Van Blankenstein, F. M., Dolmans, D. H. J. M., Van der Vleuten, C. P. M., & Schmidt, H. G. (2011). Which cognitive processes support learning during small-group discussion? The role of providing explanations and listening to others. *Instructional Science, 39*(2), 189–204. doi:http://doi.org/10.1007/s11251-009-9124-7

Vansteenkiste, M., Neyrinck, B., Niemiec, C. P., Soenens, B., Witte, H., & Broeck, A. (2007). On the relations among work value orientations, psychological need satisfaction and job outcomes: A self-determination theory approach. *Journal of Occupational and Organizational Psychology, 80*(2), 251–277. doi:http://doi.org/10.1348/096317906X11102

Part II

Career counseling and counseling for professional life

Increased levels of uncertainty and insecurity, reduced linearity in the construction of professional pathways, and increasing inequality in the distribution of wealth tend to depress hope for the future and weaken the belief that we can still think of the future in personal as well as professional planning terms.

Career counseling and career coaching are called upon to do their part and show that, with renewed sensitivity and up-to-date instrumentation and notwithstanding what was said earlier, they can still help people, organizations and contexts identify objectives to pursue, opportunities to seize, strategies and conditions to propose and implement.

Their actions must aim to promote and foster the abilities and competences that each individual needs to take on an agentic role, become the "designer" of their professional pathways and, in general, of their own life. In the construction of a professional life, increasing importance is being given to new dimensions and abilities, such as career adaptability, hope, optimism, resilience, time perspective, career preparedness, etc. There is the need to aim at the development of a series of individual resources that people should be able to use to cope with our current times and to construct their professional life.

The second part of this volume gathers together some of the contributions that career counseling and career coaching can bring to professional planning, on the one hand to help diminish the gap still existing in this domain between theory and practice and, on the other hand, to stimulate fresh awareness and new reflections.

In Chapter 5, *Maria Eduarda Duarte* underlines the need for new models, tools and methods prompted from the diverse questions posed by society, and maintains that career coaching can accompany career counseling in these intervention actions. These two approaches lead to the assumption that both can emerge as global projects, with the common mission of helping workers manage and adapt to the psychosocial and cultural demands of their working lives. Besides being considered in their differences and similarities, the two approaches are examined also from the perspective of the Life Design approach, which emphasizes the role of narrative thought in explanation and intervention in the process of career construction, where a career is viewed as the macro-narrative of an individual's path, navigating multiple roles throughout their lifespan.

In Chapter 6, *Robert W. Lent* and *Steven D. Brown* describe the Social Cognitive Career Theory self-management model and draw implications for career counseling and coaching. They seek to explain and predict the conditions under which people will engage in a variety of adaptive career behaviors such as regulating affect, adapting to changing work and educational circumstances, exploring career options, managing work-family conflict, and engaging in job search behavior. They provide suggestions to counselors and coaches to help people navigate the expected and unexpected career and educational challenges that they may face over the course of their lives.

In Chapter 7, *Michael L. Wehmeyer* and *Karrie A. Shogren* propose the Causal Agency Theory – outlining its relationships with the Life Design Approach and with self-determination theory – and the idea that young people will need to be autonomously and intrinsically motivated. The chapter examines the role of autonomous motivation, action-control beliefs, hope, and causal action in the development and emergence of self-determination and overviews autonomy supportive strategies that can be implemented by counselors and coaches to promote self-determination and self-regulated goal attainment and enable young people to engage in causal action to achieve more positive life and career outcomes.

Some of these aspects are also emphasized by *Laura Aleni Sestito, Luigia Simona Sica* and *Tiziana Di Palma* in the Chapter 4. They underline that establishing life goals, making plans for the future and developing identity are seen as intertwined developmental tasks that actively involve young people. The authors, in accordance with the narrative identity approach, describe the narrative *career counseling model* in its theoretical and empirical aspects within the lifespan developmental psychology. They present activities useful to support positive identity development during the transition from late adolescence to young adulthood, from high school to university or work, to develop agentive resources that young people could invest in identity-related work.

Elisabetta Camussi, Chiara Annovazzi, Lorenzo Montali and *Maria Cristina Ginevra* focus the reader's attention on gender-sensitive counseling, by emphasizing that career counselors help both women and men realize their potential, by identifying possible career paths and showing how to achieve career goals, and by considering the gender aspects that may characterize career construction. They encourage public engagement and social behavioral changes on gender issues in young adults and society adopting a "bottom up" and "participatory" approach, offering suggestions on how to favor awareness, activation and participation to facilitate the ability to recognize stereotypes in everyday language, behaviors and practices.

Chapter 10, written by *Terence J. G. Tracey*, concludes the section by placing emphasis on the role of a reflective examination of outcome information using a disconfirmatory hypothesis testing approach to increase the expertise of counselors and coaches. The author describes the actions that practitioners should take starting from the observation that the key issue is that they have little basis to know what worked or not with whom. This posited lack of expertise is argued to be alterable, making reference to (a) the provision of quality feedback information regarding outcomes, (b) focused, deliberate practice, avoidance of hindsight bias, and (c) explicit testing of hypotheses in a disconfirmatory manner.

Chapter 5

Career counseling and career coaching in working contexts

Learning from each other

Maria Eduarda Duarte

Introduction

Economic globalization and the way the modern world works contribute to growing instability in our lives and our occupations are no exception. That same instability is what triggers a key question: How can we help individuals better cope with the transitions that they will face over the course of their working lives? In response, counseling practices in a broad sense are adjusting to better assist the world's workforce in adapting and surpassing new and often very different situations. However, career counseling in its current state does not appear to be efficient enough. A need for new models, tools and methods originates from the diversity of questions posed by society, creating a space for career coaching rooted in epistemic issues. This is essentially a new way of looking at the same problem. The present-day consideration of career counseling as part of Life Design counseling (LDC, Savickas, 2011, 2015a) helps individuals to design their own lives, in a society that no longer provides for the easy choice of a stable trajectory. This chapter will look at the contributions made by career counseling, with the goal of providing for a better understanding of the career counseling process as a whole. Career coaching does, of course, have its similarities in comparison to career counseling, but several differences with both theoretical and practical implications can also be unearthed. This chapter will discuss these similarities and differences, in the process offering a consideration of some of the key milestones of counseling and coaching.

Having set the stage, an identification of the main issues and themes which can be found in the discourses of career counseling and career coaching follows. The hypothetical middle ground to be found between these two approaches leads to an assumption that both have emerged as global projects, with a common mission of helping workers manage and adapt to the psychosocial and cultural demands of their working lives.

A third section on common concerns and prospects follows, providing a brief analysis over three distinct domains: counselors and coaches training; delivery practices; and tools and techniques.

In conclusion, an emphasis is shaped around a spirit of openness and the future possibilities of common learning, thereby taking lessons from the long history of career counseling and from the still relatively short history of career coaching. Both forms of intervention and practice are, of course, radically human and look to share a common project and, to a certain extent, common models, methods, tools and materials.

The key milestones of career counseling and career coaching

With the expression of career coaching absolutely bursting onto the scene towards the later stages of the 20th century, in particular as part of the world of organization, attention is easily diverted from what was essentially the movement's first "business partner", whose origins stretch a lot further back in time: career counseling. To understand how we arrived at where we are now, we must of course look back, briefly, at the course of history.

Literature on career issues tells us that we cannot understand the meaning of career counseling and, consequently, career coaching, without first having a grasp of the different meanings of *career*, shifting since the beginning of the industrial revolution right through to present day. It was from this concept and its spinoffs that the contours of career work were first traced, before further integrating into the procedures of so-called career practitioners those who, in today's jargon, are called career counselors or career coaches.

The body of knowledge that makes up our understanding of the career "issue" has long been the object of scientific study, production and case studies geared around employment and companies, bringing together researchers from various social sciences. Peiperl and Arthur (2000) identify four main areas of research into career theory (psychology, sociology, education and management), feeding into other's fields of study such as psychology/personality, sociology/structure, education/vocation and management/work organization. However, the existence of this compartmentalization (Schein, 2007), as well as a general lack of interaction between the various fields that report on the same theme, has brought about its fair share of problems. It would appear that all of these separate disciplines follow down parallel paths, where the inexistence of any form of crossroad or bridge between them prevents the finding of any common scientific ground and, consequently, stands in the way of a much desired interdisciplinary perspective, not to mention the balkanization of these fields (Gottfredson, 2001), or the disciplinary provincialism (Leong, 1996) within the psychology of careers, responsible for a sort of impoverishment of the science.

From here we can ask ourselves the big question on which the remainder of this chapter sits: is the disintegration – or lack of integration – of the field of career studies within a comprehensive intellectual framework of practice, application and evaluation at the heart of the emergence of career coaching, and the expansion of interventions in work contexts, excluding any expression of career counseling in the process? Are we not, even at the end of the second decade of the 21st century, still suffering from the consequences of the gradual disconnection started in the 1930s (Erdheim, Zickar, & Yankelevich, 2007) with the cracking of vocational psychology into two groups: one vocational and the other the industrial/organizational (I/O)? Of course, the goal here is not to find some kind of cure-all elixir, but instead to seek out a more comprehensive framework, where the meaning or meanings of contexts can be considered and where counseling/coaching can serve the needs of the work/employment market and its workers.

Although some authors have made a conscious effort for "unification" (e.g., Collin & Patton, 2009), studies on career theories are still largely built into two subfields and guided by two different perspectives. The first of these subfields is vocational psychology, shaped as the study of vocational behavior and development, concerned with career choice and work adjustment, career decision making and the influence of context upon choice. We could also refer to this as career psychology, in that its field of practice can be found in career counseling and guidance, career education and the provision of career information. The second is more based on organizational psychology, associated with human resources management and developments that are responsible for career interventions in organizations (Collin, 2009), with a growing field of practice referred to as career coaching.

Both perspectives share the same concerns, including the individual motivation and needs that are common to individuals and organizations, and both seek to promote the development of initiatives which achieve common objectives. What we are talking about here is essentially the same field of study.

The career as a concept is at the root of career counseling and can take on a wide range of meanings and find itself applicable in very different realities and contexts. In relation to the notion of the career in adults, the available literature shows us that the expression of "careers in organizations" varies from author to author. For example, Hall (1976), with his protean career construct, attributes the responsibility of making and transforming one's own career to the individual; a protean career resembles the concept of career resilience (Waterman, Waterman, & Collard, 1994), in that it emphasizes self-knowledge, flexibility, information seeking and the prioritization of career objectives (both mid-and long-term), independent of the employing organization (Duarte, 2009a). The intelligent career concept defined by Arthur, Claman, and DeFilipi (1995) suggests the requirement of new career competencies, opening new horizons to the career and to its importance in the world of organizations. The notion of the boundaryless career (Arthur, 1994) is also of significance: along with the necessity of understanding the nature of careers and how to integrate them into the spectrum of life, the internal career, in the definition of Baruch (2004), designates the perceptions which each person has of the development and management of his/her own life.

In contrast to career choice or career development, the Life Design (LD) paradigm (Savickas et al., 2009), with its wider approach and deeper integration into the time and space of our lives (including our working lives), has recently allowed for an examination of career counseling that moves away from the restrictions brought on by the choice of profession and decisions which are taken in relation to nothing but our occupations. Also, constructivist career counseling (Peavy, 1998), or my system of career influences (McMahon, Patton, & Watson, 2005), or my career chapter (McIlveen, 2007), all these specific instances of the LD paradigm share the same goal: to prompt meaningful activities that further self-making, identity shaping and career constructing (Savickas, 2012). These new generations of theories are good examples to support counselors and/ or coaches, and all of them incorporate the activities of career practitioners; it is sure about different designations, but the diversity of names appear because the career counselor/career coach profession(s) had not, for the moment, determined a global name for the same activities.

So where then are the relationships, the connections, between career counseling and the notions of career that are touched on in this chapter? The answer to that question can be found in social imposition, in the changes in the organization of the workplace, in technological evolution, in the models which are developing to give better answers to our individual needs (Duarte, 2009b).

At the beginning of the 21st century, or perhaps even a little earlier, the introduction of the concept of employability into the notion of career, in consequence of a change and implementation of a new social order in the workplace, opened up fertile terrain for alternative interventions geared around the preparation, update and development of competencies (particularly executive and management competencies). To cope with this development, high impact counseling/coaching processes were drafted and experimented with, focusing on results and a compatibility with the modern world and built with the aim of strengthening an individual's lesser developed aspects and optimizing his/ her competencies. It is into this scenario and through a varied conjunction of individuals that coaching moves into organizations, as "an industry, and not a profession, there are no barriers to entry, no regulation, no government sanctioned accreditation or qualification process and no clear authority to be a coach" (Grant, 2008, p. 27). As a consequence, the challenges "for the emerging sub-discipline of coaching psychology will be to develop coaching interventions that utilize existing theory and technique" (Grant, 2008, p. 36). This affirmation, if considered valid for coaching in general, can also be applied to the *momentum* of career coaching, whether that be when drinking from the theoretical fountains of career counseling and when built around the specificity of career issues, or in the refinement or contextualization of the techniques used in career counseling.

Throughout its history, career counseling has sought to respond to the challenges that society has thrown at it, the first expression of which is associated with the origins of vocational psychology in the United States in the second half of the 19th century (Savickas, 2008), progressively extending out to other countries at the beginning of the 20th century. The main goal was to respond to a collection of social needs stemming from the transformations that were taking place on pretty much every level in what was a dramatically shifting world. At the time, the more industrialized countries experienced a transition from the agricultural to the industrial age, resulting in a transformation of the social organization in the workplace. Crafts/trades gave way to jobs and to salaried work, encouraging simplification and demanding rapid specialization in a factory environment (Blustein, 2006).

It was in this social environment that Parsons launched that which was/is considered to be the first model of career counseling (Parsons, 1909), designated as the matching of individuals and work. In this model, the work of the counselor consists of analyzing the capacities of the individual, thereby comparing them to the demands of a particular profession and assisting in the choice of a profession which would best suit those capacities. When looking back at that model from today's perspective, we see a classic model that was adequate for the demands of the rational organization of work.

The development of the various fields of humanities, the appearance of large-scale companies and the intensification of industrialization was at the heart of the creation of new jobs and new professions. The big employment sectors which had dominated, such as agriculture, commerce and factory work, began to cede space to the big corporations characterized by rigid pyramid structures, establishing boundaries among departments and defining the upward climb that everybody wanted to scale to earn greater responsibility and prestige. In response to this evolution, new alternative theories began to appear in the area of vocational guidance, leading to important conceptual changes. One such change was the move from professional models to career models, with the work of Ginzberg, Ginsburg, Axelrad, and Herma (1951) and of Donald Super (1957, 1990) certainly noteworthy for positioning counseling in a dynamic process that focused on professional choice as a developmentalist process beginning in infancy and extending into adult life.

These movements develop the concept of career (Super, 1990), or career education, and mark out learning and highlight the understanding and involvement of the individual in the performance of roles. From here, we can trace a second transition: career exists because it is possible to "go up in life" and to break out from the masses rolling off the production line (Savickas et al., 2009 In this context, the role of the counselor is extremely pedagogical and, to quote Savickas (2015b): "Career educators in the schools, and career coaches in organizations taught students and coach clients in making decisions, seeking information, managing time, overcoming barriers, and solving problems." (p. 136). While considering the designations used by Savickas, namely career educators and career coaches, it becomes clear that they essentially do the same job, use similar methodologies and have the same aims, although they work with different populations. What we are dealing with then are professional designations and not theoretical conceptualizations or differentiated interventions that use different models. Career educators and career coaches have the same mission: to help the individual climb up the career ladder.

What we see today is a move from the age of big corporations to the age of information, coming about because of a transition imposed on us by globalized economies, urbanization for globalization and the migration of the workforce around the planet. Organizations are becoming smaller, more intelligent and more agile. The workplace now demands, on top of specific skills, a set of generic competencies that allow for a swift adaptation to change. The sheer speed of that change makes it so that the paths to be taken by people become more and more unpredictable. The new metaphor of career is not climbing up the ladder, but rather jumping from one project to the next, taking on different attributes in different contents and acquiring a multitude of competencies in the process (Savickas et al., 2009).

Within this socio-economic framework, the theory and practice of counseling has also been modified to support people in light of the new demands of work and careers (Duarte, 2015). The focus is now more on the promotion of employability rather than on employment itself, thereby looking to help people develop general skills (e.g., communication, mathematics, foreign language skills, decision making/problem resolution) as well as specific competencies that allow them to take on a wide range of tasks.

The practical elements of these developments are holistic, considering the individual within the life cycle that he/she is in and the various roles that he/she plays. Career counseling integrates methods found in other psychological practices (e.g., technical narratives, experiential, genograms) and takes into account the role of emotions and/or interpersonal interaction to understand and intervene in the difficulties of career construction (Niles & Karajic, 2008). Counseling is more than just the simple application of evidence to psychological evaluation; it is more than using an individual profile to inform results or schooling/professional opportunities. Supporting development in one area is fundamentally supporting personal development across the multitude of roles played by each individual, helping people to give order and continuity to their existence and helping them to manage without losing their own sense of self and identity (Guichard, 2005; Savickas, 2012). Approaches built on psychological constructivism (Gergen, 2001; Neimeyer, 1992; Peavy, 1998), as well as ecological, systematic and contextualized approaches (Cook, Heppner, & O'Brien, 2004; Patton & McMahon, 2006; Young, Valach, & Collin, 2002) and narratives (Brott, 2001; Cochran, 1997; Guichard, 2009; Savickas, 2011) are illustrative of this idea.

The flexibility of these models is what has allowed for the appearance of new responses to the challenges that adults now face.

Initially, counseling sought to help the individual adapt to his/her particular position, before then transitioning through a period focused on preparation for career development until we reach the present day, where the role of the counselor or coach generically consists of promoting the necessary flexibility and autonomy to manage change and unpredictability. The focus on the individual and his/her adaptation tends to emphasize the psychological dimensions of career construction and its complementarity with contextual dimensions.

Looking at the world of work, rather than at the job market, we see transformation taking place at an almost dizzying speed, morphing the market into one that now focuses on competencies. The notion of the worker now belongs to the past, either we treat employees as a kind of business partner, or precariousness is sure to follow. It is here that we can really point to the ever increasing importance of contexts: aspects of a cultural nature (Duarte & Rossier, 2008); the impact of new technologies; a view of projects as being part of our professional paths within the notion of a career; employment in new areas; the evolution of the concept of work; and the promotion of success which depends on the management of human resources all make up an innovative push that interacts, integrates and sustains the working life of each employee in each particular context.

So how can organizations work together with individuals in the current setting? In this new post-capitalist society, the web of relationships between the individual and organizations gives the management of human resources a fundamental role in the jigsaw which helps organizations reach their objectives (Drucker, 1993). This management must have a collection of scientific tools at its disposal and must serve to understand the construction of the individual.

It was in the second half of the 20th century and at the beginning of the 21st century that career counseling interventions took a practice designed to help self-knowledge, and also the awareness of the various ecological variables (facilitators or inhibitors in the decision-making process), and in the application of strategies, including feedback practices (e.g., give feedback to the worker about performance evaluation results). This intervention has taken on a bi-directional system that allows the individual to craft realistic plans which are adapted to changing situations and which enables organizations to establish career plans in line with strategies that can be defined beforehand. However, it is also no less true that career counseling, namely in the context of the workplace, does not clearly distinguish itself from the practices of career coaching, with the exception of its focus on organizational consulting. Although career coaching has gained a tremendous amount of ground, indeed almost claiming a sort of popularity or fashion, the truth is that career coaching does not have a technical makeup that could be considered as "independent" or "autonomous" from career counseling, nor does it consider a classification that distinguishes theories of vocational guidance and development from theories of career counseling (Savickas & Lent, 1994; Savickas & Walsh, 1996). In the 1990s, emergent career development theories, including social-cognitive theory (Lent, Brown, & Hackett, 1994) and career construction theory (Savickas, 2012, 2015c), saw the integration of a series of psychological variables and dimensions into career counseling which had until that time been considered as the "property" of other fields of psychology such as, for example, narrative and psychotherapy, *stress* and work and occupational psychology. To put it another way, career counseling, generically speaking, has opened itself up to other *psychologies*. However, if we are to consider that the focus of career coaching is usually strictly internal in nature – i.e. "the goal of coaching is to modify employees' behaviors to better fit their present positions within the firm rather than helping employees to reposition themselves for better positions outside the firm" (Feldman, 2004, p. 29) – then it has arguably neglected the organizational dimension. Although that could be considered as a somewhat narrow affirmation, it does not change the fact that career coaching firmly depends on organizational context.

Not to overlook other translations of career counseling and indeed career coaching, let us drill down into two definitions in particular: career counseling is defined as the process in which a counselor works collaboratively to help counselees/students clarify, specify, implement and adjust to work-related decisions (Amundson, Harris-Bowlsbey, & Niles, 2005, pp. 6–7); another, according to Savickas, "to provide counseling to individuals that moves them from finding one's life work to constructing how to make one's life work requires a science of intervention that deals with designing a life and deciding how to use work in that life" (Savickas, 2011, p. 15). Career coaching may be defined as a means by which the coach can guide the individual in exploring work-related concerns, leading to personal development and, therefore, organizational change (Bench, 2008); or "career coaching as one of the most focused, result oriented forms of coaching" (Hazen & Steckler, 2010, p. 311). While these four definitions are not particularly contradictory, they cannot differentiate coaching from counseling, except in what is related to organizational change and only if the counselee is looking for a positive, action-oriented, future-focused interaction (Yates, 2014). If we accept the more generic definitions sometimes applied to counseling and coaching, with the exception of those that reduce counseling to a therapeutic process and interventions with clinical populations, then it becomes all the more difficult to understand these differences. For example, the proposal made by the International Coaching Federation (ICF, 2008) sustains that coaching is partnering with clients in a thought-provoking and creative process that inspires them to maximize their personal and professional potential. According to the International Association of Applied Psychology (IAAP, 2016), counseling psychology aims to help individuals, families, groups and organizations with their educational, development and adjustment issues and in so doing employs a wide range of assessment and intervention strategies. It seems obvious then that more similarities than differences exist, across all definitions.

Maybe in the history of career counseling and career coaching we can find a few more reasons for this alleged difference between the two practices. While research into career counseling has a long history that stretches back to the beginning of the 20th century, the discipline of coaching psychology finds its roots in the 1920s (for more details, see Grant & Cavanagh, 2004; Palmer & Whybrow, 2008), while research into career coaching as an academic discipline only began to find its footing in the 1960s (Yates, 2014). It is perhaps indicative that in an index search on coaching-related journals (*International Coaching Psychology Review, International Journal of Evidence Based Coaching and Mentoring, The Coaching Psychologist*, and *Coaching:An International journal of Theory, Research and Practice*), we could not find articles that have the expression "career coaching" in their title.

Another reason to be taken into account is the wide scope of the word "coaching", often serving as a catch-all umbrella to gather a diverse range of professions and training. A kind of purification now sees more and more coaching courses include psychology-based subjects in their programs, with coaching psychology taking on a more influential role as a result (Cavanagh & Palmer, 2006).

However, we have still not reached a theorization and practice (and change of mentalities?) that allows for the identification of a theoretical footing for career coaching. While being a field that integrates psychological processes and organizational and business issues, counseling can also integrate therapeutic processes (Cardoso, 2016). Likewise, it can choose not to integrate these processes, as can be seen in the executive coaching model developed by Augustijnen, Schnitzer, and Van Esbroeck (2011) that "sheds new light on how coaching can be situated in the broader framework of career interventions" (Van Esbroeck & Augustijnen, 2015, p. 171). Coaching can sit on the fence that separates career education from counseling, or it can work as a bridge between career education and counseling. It can make use of theoretical scopes and practices that break down that same fence, thereby permitting the development and progress of career interventions and career work.

In their meta-analysis, Brown and his colleagues (2003) explore the specific ingredients in career interventions that contribute to specific outcomes. The conclusion they reach is that many of those ingredients can be found at the core of career coaching. The work developed in career counseling is barely known by career coaches and vice versa. As such, it would appear that both are missing out on opportunities to lay the foundations of a more holistic school of thought geared around career issues, so needed as part of interventions and practice.

The bottom line is that career counseling and career coaching come out of the same common matrix of any counseling or psychotherapy system: "accurate listening, concern, caring, acceptance and understanding of the client as a unique person" (James & Gilliland, 2003, p. 172).

Whitworth, Kimsey-House, Kimsey-House, and Sandahl (2007) also suggest that a coaching conversation is mainly about discovery, awareness and choice. It is a way of effectively empowering people to find their own answers, encouraging and supporting them on the path as they continue to make important choices.

The discourse of career counseling and career coaching

In looking to systematize their similarities and differences, career counselors and career coaches actually share a similar vocabulary (Reid, 2016). In their identifications we can find identical concerns, including career planning, career adjustment, implementation of career choices and the relationship between personal (other domains of life) and career issues. Both practices follow common procedures, such as the establishment of a work alliance, confidentiality and the setting of the number of sessions (although career coaching tends to last longer). There are, however, a few peculiarities specific to career counselors, for example the fact that career counselors help clients to find success in their life/careers, but do not generally work with clients as if running a business. On the flip side of the coin, coaches hone in on job performance and productivity through focus and strategy. The context for coaching interventions is usually specified by a contract, according to the specific request of the client, the particular coach's area of expertise and the assignment of the organization (if) involved (Bachkirova, 2008).

In terms of differentiation, it is actually remarkably difficult to put up any sort of barrier between those considered as experts and others. What really matters here is to sift and separate what is good counseling/good coaching from what is not good counseling/not good coaching. To quote the literature:

> Coaching psychology should develop a competent adaptation of **existing counseling theories**, [bold placed by author] methods and ideas for the practice of coaching. . . . The use of such theories by coaches could give an opportunity to communicate with colleagues in their own fields of work and in the counseling field about developmental phenomena and so would enrich both practices by providing the framework for shared understanding and mutually beneficial research.
>
> (Bachkirova, 2008, p. 363)

Although this quotation does not specifically refer to career work, it arguably fits like a glove to the notion. Perhaps the big difference between career counseling and career coaching is not actually in a framework for interventions, but rather in the existing differences between the theories specifically developed in the field of career issues, and other theories that were not developed being as a target career issues. Career counselors and/or career coaches need to understand how this new world affects workers and, consequently, career issues. A wide array of theoretical approaches and the use of appropriate tools could sustain counseling and coaching practices and allow for discernment between good and bad practices, between those who are specialists and those who are simply just curious and between scientific method and amateurism.

Hazen and Steckler (2010) refer to a blend of different theoretical approaches within the framework of career coaching and offer an overview of those that are arguably the most relevant: cognitive behavioral approaches, narrative approaches, positive psychology approaches and person-centered approaches. Likewise, Yates (2014) notes a wide range of theoretic approaches, giving a particular emphasis to career decision-making, humanistic coaching, the GROW model, motivational interviewing, positive approaches, the cognitive behavioral approach and transactional analysis. These are, of course, all approaches built on models found in psychology.

Common concerns and prospects

It simply would not be possible to analyze every single issue related to training, delivery practices and the wealth of tools and techniques (for more details, see Segers, Dries, & Versées, 2015) used in career counseling/coaching. Without forgetting the other approaches useful in the process of narrative career counseling (e.g., Cochran, 1997; McMahon, 2006; Patton & McMahon, 2006), for simplicity's sake let us use career construction theory (Savickas, 2005) and its basic assumptions as an example and from there reflect on the three main components underlying this section.

Although neither the career coaching nor career counseling narrative has yet accumulated a solid collection of irrefutable evidence (McIlveen & Patton, 2007) or a strong body of literature, this apparent absence of "norms" does make both potentially useful for practitioners looking to invest in less classical approaches.

Narrative career counseling is one of the most predominant approaches within the constructivist school of career counseling and, as such, exemplifies the constructivist approach to careers. This approach takes the form of a counseling process in which the counselee is supported in creating a personal story (or stories) that holistically account(s) for his or her life and career and enables the making of meaningfully informed career decisions and actions (McIlveen & Patton, 2007).

The theory of Career Construction (Savickas, 2005) explains "the interpretive and interpersonal processes through which individuals impose meaning and direction on their vocational behavior" (p. 42) and integrates three psychological pillars: individual differences, lifespan development and narrative. These three pillars, in turn, define the three main components mentioned earlier: vocational personality, career adaptability and life themes (which are of course the focus of narrative career counseling). The vocational personality of an individual corresponds to his/her capacities, needs, values and interests in relation to his/her career. Savickas (2005) gives credence to Holland's (1997) typology embodied by the RIASEC hexagonal models which act as a practical structure for identifying personality types in relation to vocational choice. Another component which must be given a mention is career "adaptability, whether in adolescents or in adults, involves playful attitudes, self and environment exploration, and informed decision making" (Savickas, 1997, p. 254).

The third component, being life themes, extends beyond behavior, giving significance and distinctive character. These themes give us a form of consistency and, therefore, make us understandable to ourselves and recognizable to others. An understanding of the narrative is therefore a fundamental element for the understanding of both career and individual identity, giving unity and significance to the story underlying these identifies. Career stories "tell how the self of yesterday became the self of today and will become the self of tomorrow" (Savickas, 2005, p. 58).

Life Design counseling (LDC; Savickas, 2011, 2015a) is a meaning-making approach to career intervention. Substantiated in social constructivism, LDC emphasizes the role of narrative thought in explanation and intervention in the process of career construction. Within this particular perspective, a career is viewed as the macro-narrative of an individual's path, navigating multiple roles throughout his/her lifespan. To support career construction, LDC aims to help clients to re-author their narrative identity and to project new possibilities of self-construction into career roles.

The intervention itself is organized into three instances, usually corresponding to three sessions. In the first, the client introduces him/herself and touches on various episodes of their particular story through a semi-structured interview, taking the form of the Career Construction Interview (CCI; Savickas, 2011, 2015a). The counselor enquires into five topics: (1) role models for self-construction; (2) magazines, television shows or websites for manifest interests, (3) favorite story from a book or movie for the script for the next episode; (4) sayings or mottos for advice to self; and (5) early recollections for the perspective on the present problem or transition.

In the second session, the client is helped to give coherence to the episodes of his/her life, told in the previous session. Through this process of co-construction of meaning, the client and the counselor explore the meanings contained in the five topics discussed, with the goal of helping the client to identify a life theme that gives coherence and continuity to the episodes of his/her life which were previously told.

In the third session, the client elaborates realistic career plans, rooted in the reorganization of his/her narrative identity. In this way, the process of career construction is integrated into the dynamic of the client's particular psychosocial functioning and the career plans drafted take into account the multiple roles played in his/her particular life (Cardoso, Silva, Gonçalves, & Duarte, 2014).

In that sense, career counseling is based on a collaborative process between the counselor and the client in the promotion of change. It is a space for dialogue that permits a mutual reflection that should drive the transformation of the client, thereby helping to rewrite a narrative identity in a way that opens up new possibilities for the reconstruction of the *self* as part of working life.

Considering that the narrative coaching approach focuses on enhancing the wellbeing and performance of individuals or groups within an organizational or community settings through storytelling (Law, 2008, p. 174) and noting that as a genre this approach can help clients to clarify their life stories and write their next chapter (Drake, 2007), it seems obvious that the resulting epistemological matrix is characterized more by similarities than differences.

Although not referring to the specifics of career coaching, Law (2008) suggests that the combined narrative approach consists of techniques such as externalizing conversations, re-authoring/remembering, outsider witness retelling and retellings of retellings.

Interestingly, Yates (2016) recently affirmed that the Life Design model (Savickas et al., 2009) offers a framework for career development and proposes that career coaching should respond to the challenges of contemporary working life, using this model. In truth, we have not really referred specifically to career coaching. However, not doing so is perhaps one of the best ways to tackle the questions raised at the beginning of this chapter. Perhaps the best way is to encourage/recognize the integration of career counseling and career coaching, using the same theoretical framework and building on a generation of new theories for supporting coaches and/or counselors. At the end of the day, both approaches are there to support the workforce.

The issue of training has in some form surfaced throughout this chapter with the study and re-study of theories, looking for ways to fit them into specific areas of intervention, to use specific techniques and ways to guide interventions without straying outside the limits which a sense of ethics defines for us. We must try and establish at least some form of systemization.

Looking specifically at the construction of models that focus in on training (or the self-co-construction of the counselor), the reflections herein presented would appear to sustain a set of variables that should be constantly kept in mind. Any potential new model design should consider who the particular actors are, what structure to adopt, which strategy to define, which process to develop and what results to obtain. In order to give body to these attributes, we must of course identify obstacles, formulate a training agreement and interrogate the detail (Duarte, 2012).

One can never lose sight of the context of existing structures, local cultures, strategies and processes. Sitting at the center is the individual and we must not forget the importance of cognitive, conative and cultural influences.

A model can be used as an instrument of study, but also as a diagnostic tool. In contemporary society, the suitability of a model depends on context. For example, for collaborator-workers who are habitually designated as *core employees*, coaching-career counseling (or training) would have to focus on learning as a personal investment and the development of other competencies to survive in a market with no set boundaries. For those habitually referred to as *peripheral* or temporary workers, coaching/career counseling (or training) should focus in on learning cycles and the ability to deal with transition, as well as the promotion of employability (responses consolidated by new competencies and the acquisition of new responsibilities). In order to assist those considered as *marginalized*, namely those who currently rely on precarious work, investment should be put into preparation for a state of flexibility, thereby allowing for short term projects. Investment for this particular group could also look to guide individuals in the use of social frameworks or perhaps even support these individuals in the re-invention of other forms of work that could potentially determine their employability (Savickas et al., 2009).

The force and success of any training activity lie more within the possibility of responding to a set of different questions rather than those that are considered as the classic/traditional approaches to training. The key issue here is an understanding of the construction processes of the self. The process of how each person constructs his/her life, namely his/her working life, in a society of individuals who each independently act and develop (Duarte, 2012).

Finding a way of fusing together career work training (career counselors and career coaches) will play a crucial role in the future, equipping counselors with wider competencies for interventions that use different paradigms. This approach will allow for interventions specifically focused on the issues raised by the counselee, thereby seeing the counseling/coaching process as an enabler of the counselee as his/her own author. The range of competencies listed by international associations can serve as guidelines for the training of career counselors/career coaches.

Conclusions

New paths for careers are opening in career counseling theories, both from the theoretical point of view, as well as from the point of view of the actual intervention. This allows for counseling to be understood as an interrogative process of critical thinking. This includes career coaching and career counseling and will likely be the start of a new study of new problems that counseling/coaching will bring about.

Career counseling denotes a multifaceted discipline with three major paradigms. The first paradigm is logical positivism and its intervention practices of vocational guidance and academic advising. The second paradigm is humanism with its intervention practices of career education and career coaching. And the third paradigm is social constructionism with its practices of self-construction and life-designing dialogues. I view the practices as verbs not nouns. Career counselors can guide, coach and dialogue. Career coaches can guide, coach and dialogue. Psychotherapists can guide, coach and dialogue. Distinguishing between nouns and verbs may help to temper the disciplinary wars by asserting that the professional group does not own the practices.

There is no such thing as a universally accepted theory. What is taken to be counseling or coaching is diluted through a considerable number of theories. We can always identify a terminology that in some way reveals a determined theoretical perspective relative to counseling or to coaching, even in a critical analysis that does not make an explicit use of any particular theory. This happens because any analysis comes about from a learning process, a learning process comes about through understanding and understanding comes about through an empirical contact that can be used as theory. An understanding through analysis that only a theory is capable of facilitating and, for this reason, and contrary to a definition, theory can also take into account intersections with social manifestations, thereby generating the possibility of self-reflective thought that allows for a capacity of self-regeneration.

The merging of career counseling and career coaching is tracing new paths that cross a holistic perspective with the inter-link of cognition/emotion and an interdisciplinary and multi-methodological approach. From this interjector emerges the structure of a bridge, capable of taking us across the divide to where idiographic principle is not hindered by methodological limitations.

In what concerns career coaching, in a modern-day approach, it seems it is coherent to consider that career coaching (as a verb) does not have a theoretical body which could be autonomous or independent from career counseling in its broader sense as a general rubric subsuming diverse intervention practices. We may say that career coaches (as a noun) utilize the modern generation of psychological practices, including Life Design. The core requirement of these interventions as verbs is about the competencies that are required to do such work functions. The core requirement of the professions is the way that they certify the competencies of counselors, coaches and psychologists (as nouns).

Perhaps in a not too distant future something which we consider to be a given fact will be systematically revitalized. Perhaps that something will be the mutual estrangement that exists between discourses (the false dichotomy between theory and practice, between career counseling and personal counseling, or career counseling and career coaching, to give just three examples) that have different methods of considering the same objects and relationships and that both unite and distinguish those discourses.

A lot of work is still to be done in setting the roots of coaching (management consulting, leadership training and organizational development) and it must be career issues that feed any approach. We must take a wider look at all of the discourses and perspectives that are involved. In doing so, we might promote a multiplicity of perspectives and possibly even the emergence of something new. Maybe that something new could be (1) a counsellogical (Kargulowa, 2013) way of thinking, "a dialogue-sensitive anthropocentric thinking" (Podgórna, 2013, p. 189); (2) an ongoing questioning of one's assumptions and opening up to the world of the other through dialogue; (3) a critical examination of the role of power/power differentials in counseling work; (4) an immersion experience for advanced students, so as to promote a practical, rather than detached, theoretical, and often stereotyped view, of the other; or (5) training in the theoretical and practical aspects of counseling/coaching.

One of the best ways to put career counseling/career coaching at the service of the people, thereby bringing them hope, is to "feed" counseling with new perspectives, transforming a merely professional act into a personal and accessible project with an added value that integrates the strengths of science, the arts and the humanities into a single imaginative way to promote personal gratification.

Everyday life practice needs to face career counseling/coaching as a process of continuous interactions, which helps in the resolution of problems, which allows the conjunction of the necessities of individuals with those of the contexts they act, develop and live, including the organization. An integrative background and the development of a process of learning which specifies the components of knowledge acquisition and the level of experience needed for this knowledge to be applied seems to be the future. From the theoretical will arise the use of common intervention methods and techniques, as well as new methodology for research, new practice-based research networks, such as different groups, national and /or international, of practitioners who have agreed to implement research statements, collected data and examine common (or not) counseling/coaching problems. The advantage will open several possibilities, such as the development of an international network with the aim of analyzing career counseling/career coaching problems and interventions, create the possibility of emerging areas of interest, the identification of compelling research issues.

In summary, practitioners, career counselors or career coaches must consider that from the theoretical will arise the use of intervention methods and techniques; training programs focus on reading and research to provide scientifically supported interventions (instead of insisting on "old" theories, try new ones like the development of theory around Life Design, for example). At the end, practitioners need to make an effort to study and re-study "good" theories.

The starting gun for the agglutination of the knowledge which has been developed since the start of the 20th century could well be the massively intriguing issue of our social nature and how it influences our behavior in the workplace, our employability, our development and our wellbeing.

References

Amundson, N., Harris-Bowlsbey, H., & Niles, S. (2005). *Essential elements of career counseling*. Upper Saddle River, NJ: Pearson.

Arthur, M. (1994). The boundaryless career: A new perspective for organizational inquiry. *Journal of Organizational Behavior, 15*(4), 295–306.

Arthur, M., Claman, P., & DeFilippi, R. (1995). Intelligent enterprise, intelligent careers. *Academy of Management Executive, 9*(4), 7–22.

Augustijnen, M-T., Schnitzer, G., & Van Esbroeck, R. (2011). A model of executive coaching: A qualitative study. *International Coaching Psychology Review, 6*, 150–164.

Bachkirova, T. (2008). Role of coaching psychology in defining boundaries between counselling and coaching. In S. Palmer & A. Whybrow (Eds.), *Handbook of coaching psychology* (pp. 351–366). London, UK: Routledge.

Baruch, Y. (2004). *Managing careers*. London, UK: Prentice-Hall.

Bench, M. (2008). *Career coaching: An insider's guide* (2nd ed.). Portland, OR: High Flight Press.

Blustein, D. (2006). The psychology of working: A new perspective for career development, counselling and public policy. Mahwah, NJ: Erlbaum.

Brott, P. (2001). The storied approach: A postmodern perspective for career counselling. *The Career Development Quarterly, 49*, 304–313. doi:10.1002/j.2161-0045.2001.tb00958.x

Brown, S., Ryan-Krane, N., Brecheisen, J., Castelino, P., Budisin, I., & Miller, M. (2003). Critical ingredients of career choice interventions: More analyses and new hypothesis. *Journal of Vocational Behavior, 62*, 411–428. doi:http://doi:10.1016/S0001-879(02)00052-0

Cardoso, P. (2016). Integrating Life Design counseling and psychotherapy: Possibilities and practices. *Career Development Quarterly, 64*, 49–65. doi:http://doi:10.1002/cdq.12040

Cardoso, P., Silva, J., Gonçalves, M., & Duarte, M. E. (2014). Narrative innovation in life design counseling: The case of Ryan. *Journal of Vocational Behavior, 85*, 276–286. doi:http://doi:10.1016/j.jvb2014.o8.001

Cavanagh, M., & Palmer, S. (2006). Editorial – The theory, practice and research base of coaching psychology is developing at a fast pace. *International Coaching Psychology Review, 1*(1), 5–7.

Cochran, L. (1997). *Career counseling: A narrative approach*. Thousand Oaks, CA: Sage.

Collin, A. (2009). One step towards realising the multidisciplinarity of career studies. In A. Collin & W. Patton (Eds.), *Vocational psychological and organisational perspectives on career* (pp. 3–18). Rotterdam, The Netherlands: Sense Publishers.

Collin, A., & Patton, W. (Eds.). (2009). *Vocational psychological and organisational perspectives on career*. Rotterdam, The Netherlands: Sense Publishers.

Cook, E., Heppner, M., & O'Brien, K. (2004). An ecological model of career development. In R. Conyne & E. Cook (Eds.), *Ecological counselling: An innovative approach to conceptualizing person-environment interaction* (pp. 219–242). Alexandria, VA: American Counseling Association.

Drake, D. (2007). The art of thinking narratively: Implications for coaching psychology and practice. *Australian Psychologist, 42*(4), 283–294. doi:http://doi:10.1080/00050060701648159

Drucker, P. (1993). La fin de l'autorité hiérarchique [The end of hierarchical authority]. *Harvard- L'Expansion, Automne 1993*, 33–44.

Duarte, M. E. (2009a). Um século depois de Parsons: escolher uma profissão ou apostar na psicologia da construção da vida? [One century after Parsons: Choose an occupation or a bet on the psychology of life construction?]. *Revista Brasileira de Orientação Profissional, 10*(2), 5–14.

Duarte, M. E. (2009b). The psychology of life construction. *Journal of Vocational Behavior, 75*, 259–266. doi:http://doi:10.1016/j.jvb.2009.06.009

Duarte, M. E. (2012). Reflections on the training of career counselors. *Cypriot Journal of Educational Sciences*, 7(4), 265–275. Retrieved from www.awer-center.org/cjes/

Duarte, M. E. (2015). Some reflections on guidance and career counselling in the 21st century. In A. di Fabio & J-L. Bernaud (Eds.), *The construction of the identity in 21st century* (pp. 59–72). New York, NY: Nova Science Publishers.

Duarte, M. E., & Rossier, J. (2008). Testing and assessment in an international context: Cross- and multi-cultural issues. In J. Athanasou & R. Van Esbroeck (Eds.), *International handbook of career guidance* (pp. 489–510). New York/Heidelberg: Springer Science.

Erdheim, J., Zickar, M. J., & Yankelevich, M. (2007). Remembering Donald G. Paterson: Before the separation of industrial-organizational and vocational psychology. *Journal of Vocational Behavior, 70*, 205–221. doi:http://doi:10.1016/j.jvb.2006.09.001

Feldman, D. (2004). Career coaching: What HR professionals and managers need to know. *Human Resources Planning, 24*, 26–35.

Gergen, K. (2001). Psychological science in a postmodern context. *American Psychologist, 56*, 803–813.

Ginzberg, E., Ginsburg, S., Axelrad, S., & Herma, J. (1951). *Occupational choice: An approach to a general theory*. New York: Columbia University Press.

Gottfredson, L. (2001). Fostering the scientific practice of vocational psychology. *Journal of Vocational Behavior, 59*, 192–202. doi:http://doi:10.1006/jvbe.2001.1825

Grant, A. (2008). Past, present and future: The evolution of professional coaching and coaching psychology. In In S. Palmer & A. Whybrow (Eds.), *Handbook of coaching psychology* (pp. 23–39). London, UK: Routledge.

Grant, A., & Cavanagh, M. (2004). Toward a profession of coaching: Sixty-five years of progress and challenges for the future. *International Journal of Evidence Based Coaching and Mentoring, 2*(1), 1–16.

Guichard, J. (2005). Life-long self-construction. *International Journal for Educational and Vocational Guidance, 5*, 111–124. doi:http://doi:10.1007/s10775-005-8789-y

Guichard, J. (2009). Self-constructing. *Journal of Vocational Behavior, 75*, 251–258. doi:http://doi:10.1016/j.jvb.2009.06.009

Hall, D. (1976). *Careers in organizations*. Glenview, IL: Scott Foresman.

Hazen, B., & Steckler, N. (2010). Career coaching. In E. Cox, T. Bachkirova, & D. Clutterbuck (Eds.), *The complete handbook of coaching* (pp. 311–323). London, UK: Sage.

Holland, J. (1997). Making vocational choices: A theory of vocational personalities and work environments (3rd ed.). Odessa, FL: Psychological Assessment Resources.

International Association of Applied Psychology (IAAP). (2016). Retrieved April 15, 2016, from www.iaapsy.org/divisions

International Coaching Federation (ICF). (2008). Retrieved April 15, 2016, from www.coachfereration.org/ICF

James, R., & Gilliland, B. (2003). *Theories and strategies in counselling & psychotherapy* (5th ed.). Boston, MA: Allyn and Bacon.

Kargulowa, A. (2013). Why we need counsellogical research: Towards an anthropology of counselling. *Journal of Counsellogy, 2,* 258–276. ISSN: 2299-4971

Law, H. (2008). Narrative coaching and psychology of learning from multicultural perspectives. In S. Palmer & A. Whybrow (Eds.), *Handbook of coaching psychology* (pp. 174–192). London, UK: Routledge.

Lent, R., Brown, S., & Hackett, G. (1994). Toward a unifying social cognitive theory of career and academic interest, choice, and performance [Monograph]. *Journal of Vocational Behavior, 45*, 79–122. doi:http://doi:10.1006/jvbe.1994.1027

Leong, F. (1996). Challenges to career counseling: Boundaries, cultures, and complexity. In M. Savickas & B. Walsh (Eds.), *Handbook of career counseling theory and practice* (pp. 333–345). Palo Alto, CA: Davies-Black.

McIlveen, P. (2007). Counsellor's personal experience and appraisal of my career chapter. *Australian Journal of Career Development, 16*, 12–19. doi:http://doi:10.1177/103841620701600204

McIlveen, P., & Patton, W. (2007). Narrative career counselling: Theory and exemplars of practice. *Australian Psychologist, 42*(3), 226–235. doi:http://doi.org/10.1080/00050060701405592

McMahon, M. (2006). Working with storytellers: A metaphor for career counselling. In M. McMahon & W. Patton (Eds.), *Career counselling: Constructivist approaches* (pp. 16–29). London, UK: Routledge.

McMahon, M., Patton, W., & Watson, M. (2005). *My system of career influences*. Cumberwell, Victoria, Australia: ACER Press.

Neimeyer, G. (1992). Personal constructs in career counselling and development. *Journal of Career Development, 18*, 163–173. doi:http://doi:10.1007/BF01321709

Niles, S., & Karajic, A. (2008). Training career practitioners in the 21st century. In J. Athanasou & R. Van Esbroeck (Eds.), *International handbook of career guidance* (pp. 355–372). New York, NY/Heidelberg: Springer Science.

Palmer, J., & Whybrow, A. (2008). Coaching psychology: An introduction. In S. Palmer & A. Whybrow (Eds.), *Handbook of coaching psychology* (pp. 1–20). London, UK: Routledge.

Parsons, F. (1909). *Choosing a vocation*. Boston, MA: Houghton-Mifflin.

Patton, W., & McMahon, M. (2006). Constructivism: What does it mean for career counselling? In M. McMahon & W. Patton (Eds.), *Career counselling: Constructivist approaches* (pp. 3–15). Abingdon, UK: Routledge.

Peavy, R. (1998). Socio-dynamic counseling: A constructivist perspective. Victoria, BC: Trafford.

Peiperl, M., & Arthur, M. (2000). Topics for conversation: Career themes old and new. In M. Peiperl, M. Arthur, R. Goffee, & T. Morris (Eds.), *Career frontiers: New conceptions of working lives* (pp. 1–19). Oxford, UK: Oxford University Press.

Podgórna, V. (2013). Thinking like a counsellogist. *Journal of Counsellogy, 1,* 187–190. ISSN: 2299-4971

Reid, H. (2016). Introduction to career counselling and coaching. Abington, Oxon, UK: Sage.

Savickas, M. (1997). Adaptability: An integrative construct for lifespan, life-space theory. *Career Development Quarterly, 45,* 247–259. doi:http://doi:10.1002/j.2161-0045.1997.tb00469.x

Savickas, M. (2005). The theory and practice of career construction. In S. D. Brown & R. W. Lent (Eds.), *Career development and counseling: Putting theory and research to work* (pp. 42–70). Hoboken, NJ: John Wiley & Sons.

Savickas, M. (2008). History of the guidance profession. In J. Athanasou & R. Van Esbroeck (Eds.), *International handbook of career guidance* (pp. 97–113). New York, NY/Heidelberg: Springer Science.

Savickas, M. L. (2011). *Career counseling*. Washington, DC: APA Books.

Savickas, M. L. (2012). Life design: A paradigm for intervention in the 21st century. *Journal of Counseling and Development, 90,* 13–19. doi:http://doi:10.1111/j.1556-6676.2012.00002.x

Savickas, M. (2015a). *Life design counseling manual*. Retrieved from www.Vocopher.com

Savickas, M. (2015b). Life designing with adults: Developmental individualization using biographical bricolage. In L. Nota & J. Rossier (Eds.), *Handbook of life design: From practice to theory and from theory to practice* (pp. 135–149). Gottingen, Germany: Hogrefe Publishing.

Savickas, M. L. (2015c). Career counseling paradigms: Guiding, developing, and designing. In P. Hartung, M. Savickas, & B. Walsh (Eds.), *The APA handbook of career intervention* (Vol. 1, pp. 129–143). Washington, DC: APA Books.

Savickas, M., & Lent, R. (Eds.). (1994). *Convergence in theories of career development: Implications for science and practice*. Palo Alto, CA: Consulting Psychologists Press.

Savickas, M., Nota, L., Rossier, J., Dauwalder, J-P., Duarte, M. E., Guichard, J., Soresi, S., Van Esbroeck, R., & Van Vianen, A. (2009). Life designing: A paradigm for career construction in the 21st century. *Journal of Vocational Behavior, 75*(3), 239–250. doi:10:1016/j.jvb.2009.04.004.

Savickas, M., & Walsh, B. (1996). *Handbook of career counseling theory and practice*. Palo Alto, CA: Davies-Black.

Schein, E. (2007). Afterword: Career research: Some issues and dilemmas. In H. Gunz & M. Peiperl (Eds.), *Handbook of career studies* (pp. 573–576). Thousand Oaks, CA: Sage.

Segers, J., Dries, N., & Versées, D. (2015). Coaching. In P. Hartung, M. Savickas, & B. Walsh (Eds.), *The APA handbook of career intervention* (vol. 2, pp. 397–411). Washington, DC: APA Books.

Super, D. E. (1957). The psychology of careers: An introduction to vocational development. New York, NY: Harper & Row.

Super, D. E. (1990). A lifespan, life-space approach to career development. In D. Brown & L. Brooks (Eds.), *Career choice and development* (2nd ed., pp. 197–261). San Francisco, CA: Jossey-Bass.

Van Esbroeck, R., & Augustijnen, M-T. (2015). Coaching: A career intervention model within life design. In L. Nota & J. Rossier (Eds.), *Handbook of life design: From practice to theory and from theory to practice* (pp. 169–182). Gottingen, Germany: Hogrefe Publishing.

Waterman, R., Waterman, J., & Collard, B. (1994). Toward a career resilient workforce. *Harvard Business Review, 1*, 87–95.

Whitworth, L., Kimsey-House, K., Kimsey-House., H., & Sandahl, P. (2007). *Co-active coaching* (2nd ed.). Mountain View, CA: Davies Black Publishing.

Yates, J. (2014). *The career coaching handbook.* Abingdon, Oxon, UK: Routledge.

Yates, J. (2016). Coaching for career and professional development. In C. van Nieuwerburgh (Ed.), *Coaching in professional contexts* (pp. 41–54). London, UK: Sage.

Young, R., Valach, L., & Collin, A. (2002). A contextual explanation of career. In D. Brown & Associates (Eds.), *Career choice and development* (4th ed., pp. 206–252). San Francisco, CA: Jossey-Bass.

Chapter 6

Promoting adaptive career behavior

A Social Cognitive Career Theory perspective

Steven D. Brown and Robert W. Lent

Social Cognitive Career Theory (SCCT), first introduced by Lent, Brown, and Hackett (1994), was developed to address important aspects of career and educational development across the lifespan. The theory (Lent et al., 1994) originally consisted of three inter-locking models designed to explain how people (a) develop career and educational interests, (b) make and revise career and educational choices, and (c) achieve varying levels of career and educational performance and stability. Anchored in Bandura's (1986) general social cognitive theory, the original models relied on three central social cognitive constructs (self-efficacy beliefs, outcome expectations, and goals) to explain how educational and vocational interests are developed, choice goals are formulated and enacted, and performance is attained in educational and work settings.

Self-efficacy refers to people's confidence in their abilities to engage in occupationally or educationally relevant behaviors (e.g., confidence in successfully completing math or social tasks). Outcome expectations are individuals' expectations about the likely outcomes (positive and negative) of task engagement (e.g., expected outcomes for engaging in math-related or socially-related tasks). These can take several forms, including physical (e.g., monetary gains and losses), social (e.g., social approval or disapproval), and self-evaluative (e.g., esteem enhancing or deflating) expectations (Bandura, 1986). Together, self-efficacy beliefs and outcome expectations give rise to interests. For example, persons with strong math self-efficacy and who anticipate positive consequences associated with engaging in math tasks (e.g., parental approval) will be more likely to develop interests in math-related activities, math majors, and careers involving math than will those with weaker self-efficacy beliefs or less positive outcome expectations. Interests then give rise to goals to further pursue interest-related activities, which, in turn promote active engagement in these activities. Contextual (e.g., environmental supports and barriers) and other person (e.g., gender) variables, act distally to inform self-efficacy beliefs and outcome expectations (via learning experiences) and proximally to facilitate or hinder the translations of interests into goals and goals into actions.

Two additional models, one focused on work and educational satisfaction (Lent & Brown, 2006, 2008) and the other on the process of career self-management (Lent & Brown, 2013) subsequently appeared in the literature. The initial interest, choice, and performance models have generated a great deal of research since their publication. The satisfaction model, although more recently developed, has also sustained inquiry over the past 10 years (see Brown & Lent, 2016; Lent, 2013 for reviews of research on the first four models). These models and their applications are probably also somewhat familiar to the readers of this volume. Thus, the purpose of this chapter is to introduce readers to the newest SCCT career self-management model (CSM; Lent & Brown, 2013). We will start by briefly describing the self-management model and then review extant research on the model. We will conclude by providing suggestions about how counselors and coaches can use the model to help people navigate the expected and unexpected career and educational challenges that they may face over the course of their lives.

SCCT career self-management model

The original three SCCT models of interest, choice, and performance emphasized important *content* aspects of career development; namely, predicting the types of educational and occupational activities toward which individuals gravitate (e.g., nuclear physics or house painting) and in which they will perform well and persist. The CSM model, on the other hand, focuses on *process* aspects of career and educational development by addressing the ways in which people adapt both to routine career tasks and unusual career challenges. The model is primarily concerned with whether and how people will, under varying environmental conditions, engage in adaptive behaviors that can be employed to help direct their career and educational development under ordinary circumstances and when confronted with stressful conditions. Lent and Brown's (2013) Table 1 (p. 559) provides a selective list of adaptive career behaviors across the life cycle and include, for example, engaging in career exploration, making career-related decisions, negotiating the transitions from school to work, finding jobs, balancing work and other life roles, responding to work setbacks, and planning for retirement. Thus, the CSM model is designed to be applicable to a wide array of adaptive tasks and offers predictions about the conditions under which people will be motivated to engage in adaptive career behaviors under normal conditions and at times of career or educational challenge.

Figure 6.1 presents the self-management model. It looks similar to the prior SCCT content models because it represents an extension of these models, though it defines and contextualizes the core SCCT variables in somewhat novel ways. According to the CSM model, engagement in adaptive career behaviors (e.g., career exploration, job finding) is assumed to be affected by self-efficacy beliefs, outcome expectations, goals, environmental supports and barriers, and personality and other personal factors. In the context of career self-management, self-efficacy reflects individuals' confidence in their abilities to enact adaptive career behaviors (e.g., behaviors associated with career

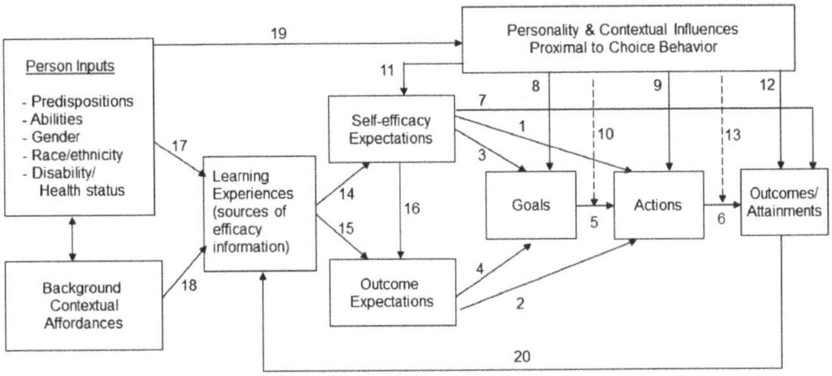

Figure 6.1 Model of career self-management

exploration or the job search process), while outcome expectations refer to the positive and negative outcomes that individuals expect to encounter during the process (e.g., while exploring careers or engaging in the job search). Together, robust self-efficacy beliefs and positive outcome expectations directly increase the likelihood that people will actively engage in the adaptive career behavior (e.g., engage in career exploration or the job search – see paths 1 and 2 in Figure 6.1). Self-efficacy beliefs and outcome expectations also indirectly influence actions via goal setting (paths 3 and 4). That is, self-efficacy beliefs and outcome expectations prompt the setting of goals which, in turn, are likely to lead to actions (path 5). Goal-directed actions will increase the likelihood (but do not ensure) that people will attain the outcomes they desire (e.g., to identify career options or find a job – path 6). Self-efficacy is also seen as having a direct influence on outcomes (path 7).

Supports and barriers and other contextual influences act on the engagement in adaptive career barriers in three primary ways. First, they may promote or hinder goals setting and actions directly (paths 8 and 9). For example, in the case of job finding, active engagement in the job search process is facilitated by a supportive network that offers advice, encouragement, and the emotional sustenance necessary to maintain search efforts in the face of obstacles. On the other hand, non-supportive networks or the presence of barriers (e.g., lack of transportation) will make it more difficult to initiate and sustain job search efforts.

Second, supports and barriers may moderate the relationships between goals and actions and between actions and outcomes by making it harder (or easier) to turn goals into actions (dotted path 10) and actions into desired outcomes (dotted path 13). For example, supportive environments facilitate an individual's ability to translate job search goals into actions, while non-supportive environments hinder this process. Similarly, prevailing economic conditions may make it more or less likely that an individual's efforts will pay off.

Third, contextual variables may also act more distally as sources of self-efficacy beliefs and outcome expectations – supportive environments foster more robust self-efficacy beliefs and more positive outcome expectations than do less supportive ones via the types of learning experiences fostered by supportive environments (paths 18, 14, and 15). Personality and other person variables can operate in much the same way as contextual variables – as direct facilitators of or obstacles to goals and actions (paths 8 and 9), as moderators of goal-action (dotted path 10) and action-outcome relationships (dotted path 13), and as distal influences on the development of self-efficacy beliefs and outcome expectations via learning experiences (paths 17, 14, and 15). The effects of person inputs, such as gender and race/ethnicity, can also be mediated by more proximal contextual variables (path 19; e.g., differential supports and barriers provided to certain persons based on cultural norms). In addition, the outcomes of one's actions (e.g., success and failure experiences) are envisioned as comprising a feedback loop that informs subsequent self-efficacy beliefs and outcome expectations (path 20).

Research on the SCCT self-management model

Although a number of studies that pre-dated the formal introduction of the CSM model have explored bivariate and multivariate relations among selected CSM variables (see Lent & Brown, 2013 for a review), the model has only recently begun to receive formal empirical testing. In this section, we present the results of six studies that tested the CSM model in relation to four different adaptive career behaviors: (a) career exploration and decision-making, (b) job finding intentions and actions, (c) multiple role planning, (d) workplace sexual identity management.

Lent, Ezeofor, Morrison, Penn, and Ireland (2016) tested the CSM model in the context of career exploration and decision-making among university undergraduates in two studies. After collecting and presenting psychometric data on a new measure of career exploration and decision-making self-efficacy beliefs (CEDSE) in the first study, Lent et al. employed this measure in the second study along with extant measures of career exploration outcome expectations, career exploration support, and trait conscientiousness in a path model predicting exploration goals, decisional anxiety, and career decidedness. Results generally supported CSM model predictions. Specifically, both self-efficacy and outcome expectations (which were significantly related) produced significant paths to career exploration goals. Self-efficacy, but not outcome expectations, also yielded significant paths to decisional anxiety and levels of decidedness in expected directions. Social support along with self-efficacy predicted outcome expectations and goals. The effect of conscientiousness on goals was fully mediated by self-efficacy and via the self-efficacy to outcome expectations path.

In summary, the results suggested, consistent with the CSM model, that college students' intentions to engage in career exploration activities (goals) was facilitated by strong and robust career exploration and decision-making self-efficacy and positive outcome expectations. Support, also as predicted by the CSM, influenced intentions in two ways – by directly facilitating goal-setting efforts and via its relationship to self-efficacy beliefs and outcome expectations (the moderator hypothesis about the effect of support was not tested). The relationship of conscientiousness to goal setting was fully mediated by self-efficacy beliefs and outcome expectations.

Lim, Lent, and Penn (2016) predicted job search intentions and behaviors via the CSM model among unemployed job seekers (study 1) and college seniors (study 2). Both studies employed the same CSM variables as in Lent, Ezeofor, Morrison, Penn, and Ireland (2016), but within the job search context – job search self-efficacy beliefs and outcome expectations, job search support, and conscientiousness. In addition, a measure of volition (perceived control over the outcome of the job search process) was added to test assumptions of the psychology of working perspective (Blustein, 2006) that the relation of self-efficacy to goals and intentions would be stronger for those with higher rather than lower perceived control over the process. While study 1 predicted job search goals, study 2 predicted job search goals as well as subsequent actions (three months later).

In study 1, self-efficacy beliefs and outcome expectations (though not support) were found to produce significant paths to intentions. Self-efficacy also produced significant paths to outcome expectations, and support showed direct paths to self-efficacy and outcome expectations. The effect of conscientiousness on intentions was again fully mediated by self-efficacy and outcome expectations. Contrary to assumptions of the psychology of working perspective, perceived outcome control did not produce a direct path to intentions nor moderate the self-efficacy to intentions path among the unemployed.

Study 2 produced similar findings regarding the role of self-efficacy, support, and conscientiousness to job search goals. Outcome expectations were, however, not found to uniquely predict goals, as was the case in study 1. Goals mediated the relation of self-efficacy to job search actions. Interestingly, among college seniors, perceived outcome control moderated the relationships between self-efficacy and intentions, but in a direction opposite to what would be predicted by the psychology of working perspective. That is, job search self-efficacy was more predictive of job search intentions under low rather than high levels of perceived outcome control.

Roche, Daskalova, and Brown (2017) tested the ability of the CSM model to predict multiple role balance goals (intentions) among emerging adults. Included in the model test were measures of role balance self-efficacy beliefs and outcome expectations and trait conscientiousness. Gender was also included as a person input. Results indicated that self-efficacy beliefs were significantly related to role balance intentions, while the path between outcome expectations and intentions was marginally significant ($p < .06$). Self-efficacy and outcome expectations were related and the conscientiousness to intentions path was once again fully mediated by self-efficacy. Gender had only a direct effect on intentions, suggesting that young women had stronger intentions to balance multiple roles in the future than did young men, regardless of their feelings of efficacy or anticipated outcomes.

Tatum, Formica, and Brown (2017) tested the CSM model in the context of workplace sexual identity management, specifically in the degree to which LGBTQ participants had revealed their sexual identities at work – an important career challenge for sexual minority workers. Included along with measures of sexual identity management self-efficacy beliefs and outcome expectation were measures of workplace climate and concealment motivation – two variables that had previously been found to relate (in opposite directions) to workplace sexual identity disclosure (Button, 2001; Chrobot-Mason, Button, & Diclementi, 2001). Results revealed that the paths from sexual identity management self-efficacy beliefs and outcome expectations to sexual identity disclosure were significant and that the relations of concealment motivation and workplace climate to disclosure were partially mediated by self-efficacy beliefs and outcome expectations. There is a wealth of prior research linking positive workplace climates to increased sexual identity disclosure (see Button, 2001). The results of this investigation suggest that the CSM model may provide a partial explanation for this link – that positive workplace climates foster stronger self-efficacy beliefs and positive outcome expectations regarding disclosure behaviors than do less LGBTQ-supportive environments.

In summary, the CSM model has been shown to fit the data well in six studies that focused on career exploration and decision-making, job search, multiple role balance intentions, and sexual identity disclosure at work. Each study found significant links between self-efficacy beliefs and outcome expectations and between self-efficacy beliefs and intentions or actions. Outcome expectations also showed significant paths with intentions in all but the study of multiple role balance intentions and the study of college students' job search intentions. Thus, it seems that strong self-efficacy beliefs are reliably (and positive outcome expectations are somewhat less reliably) predictive of intentions to engage in career exploration, job search, and multiple role balance efforts. Self-efficacy beliefs and outcome expectations may also facilitate the coming-out process at work and may help explain why supportive workplace climates are associated with increased workplace sexual identity disclosure. Trait conscientiousness was included as a person input in four studies and consistently showed that its relationship to career exploration, job search, and multiple role management intentions was fully mediated by self-efficacy beliefs and, somewhat less consistently, via the self-efficacy to outcome expectations path.

Implications for career counselors and coaches

The findings of six studies suggest that the CSM model offers a plausible account of the ways in which social cognitive, contextual, and personality variables work together to promote intentions to engage in at least three adaptive career behaviors (career exploration, job searching, and multiple role balance) and to facilitate two types of adaptive behaviors, job-seeking and sexual identity disclosure at work. Given the early stage of research on the CSM model, implications for career counselors and coaches must be considered as tentative. However, the following suggestions may be offered, pending continued research support for the model.

First, the results of all six studies suggest that interventions designed to boost self-efficacy beliefs may be particularly effective in fostering intentions to engage in career exploration, job finding, and multiple role balance activities. Exposing clients to gender and ethnically similar models, helping them to build encouraging social networks and to manage their anxiety, and fostering incrementally graded success experiences are theoretically important sources of self-efficacy information that could be incorporated into efficacy-building interventions (Bandura, 1997; Lent, 2013; Lent & Brown, 2013).

Second, although our data suggest that efficacy-building efforts should also lead to more positive outcome expectations, it may often be necessary to focus on helping clients build more positive outcome expectations for enacting adaptive behaviors. For example, it may be unlikely to expect that adolescents living in poverty will see that engaging in career exploration will lead to many positive work-related outcomes, regardless of the strength of their career exploration self-efficacy beliefs. Similarly, older job seekers, especially in today's economy, may have little hope that their efforts will lead to satisfying work no matter how efficacious they may feel about their job search skills. Lim et al. (2016) suggested that job seekers should be helped to focus on outcomes that they can control (e.g., the effort that one puts into the job search process) rather than outcomes that they cannot control (e.g., getting an acceptable job offer). The positive potential outcomes of putting effort into activities that can be controlled in the job search process may be particularly motivating. Similar strategies might also be useful in motivating the career exploration behavior of marginalized youth and in promoting a variety of other adaptive career behaviors. In most cases, the ultimate outcomes associated with engaging in adaptive career behaviors (e.g., retirement planning, multiple role planning) are not entirely under the individual's control but are, rather, influenced by a variety of non-agentic factors. Thus, helping clients to focus on what they can control may be a useful intervention strategy.

Third, the finding that the relation of trait conscientiousness to intentions is fully mediated by self-efficacy beliefs and outcome expectations suggests that career exploration, job finding, and multiple role balance interventions may be particularly valuable for those who are not naturally high in trait conscientiousness. Such individuals may benefit from assistance with time management and organization behaviors. Interventions that also break conscientiousness into its constituent components by fostering and reinforcing (for example) goal setting and planning efforts in a supportive and challenging environment may help less conscientious individuals experience the type of performance accomplishments that are necessary to build more robust self-efficacy beliefs about their abilities to engage in adaptive career behaviors.

Fourth, the findings also suggest that efforts to bolster support for career exploration and job-finding activities may be another route to boosting both self-efficacy and intentions for career exploration, job finding, and multiple role balance efforts. The findings concerning the importance of an affirming and supportive workplace climate on the sexual identity disclosure process suggest that such climates foster stronger and more robust disclosure self-efficacy beliefs and more positive outcome expectations about sexual identity disclosure. This finding not only provides one explanation for why supportive workplace climates foster sexual identity disclosure (e.g., Button, 2001), but also advocates for providing more affirmative workplace environments for sexual minority employees.

Conclusion

The Social Cognitive Career Self-Management (CSM) model was developed to explain and predict the conditions under which individuals will engage in a variety of adaptive career behaviors across the lifespan to deal with both expected and unexpected career events and challenges. Practically, the model is intended to outline mechanisms of personal agency – to suggest ways that people, regardless of their current circumstances, can take part in their own career development, adaptation, and renewal.

We have presented the results of six studies that largely supported the CSM model with four different adaptive career tasks – career exploration and decision-making, job searching, multiple role planning, and sexual identity disclosure at work. These studies also suggest how widely studied person (conscientiousness) and contextual (social and workplace support) variables may operate in tandem with CSM's core cognitive variables to (a) foster more robust intentions to engage in career exploration, job-seeking, and multiple role management behaviors; and (b) promote feelings of safety to disclose one's sexual identity at work. Our findings are also consistent with meta-analytic evidence showing that job search self-efficacy, goal setting, social support, and trait conscientiousness are important correlates of job finding success (Kanfer, Wanberg, & Kantrowitz, 2001) and that self-efficacy, goal setting, and support are critical ingredients of job search interventions (Liu, Huang, & Wang, 2014). The CSM model provides a framework for understanding the interrelations among these variables and for directing practical efforts to refine job search interventions.

We also suggested how the results of our studies could be used to inform counseling and coaching interventions to promote career exploration, job search, and multiple role planning goals, and to create safe workplace environments for sexual minority employees. Although our suggestions are offered tentatively, we hope that readers find them useful and that counseling and coaching researchers use them to design and test CSM-derived remedial and preventive interventions. The existing findings also suggest the potential value of extending study of the CSM model to other types of adaptive career behaviors, such as the negotiation of the job loss process and the retirement planning and adjustment process.

References

Bandura, A. (1986). *Social foundations of thought and action: A social cognitive theory.* Englewood Cliffs, NJ: Prentice Hall.

Bandura, A. (1997). *Self-efficacy: The exercise of control.* New York, NY: W. H. Freeman.

Blustein, D. L. (2006). The psychology of working: A new perspective for career development, counseling, and public policy. Mahwah, NJ: Erlbaum.

Brown, S. D., & Lent, R. W. (2016). Vocational psychology: Agency, equity, and wellbeing. *Annual Review of Psychology, 67*, 541–566.

Button, S. B. (2001). Organizational efforts to affirm sexual diversity: A cross-level examination. *Journal of Applied Psychology, 86*, 17–28.

Chrobot-Mason, D., Button, S. B., & Diclementi, J. D. (2001). Sexual identify management strategies: An exploration of antecedents and consequences. *Sex Roles, 45*, 321–336.

Kanfer, R., Wanberg, C. R., & Kantrowitz, T. M. (2001). Job search and employment: A personality-motivational analysis and meta-analytic review. *Journal of Applied Psychology, 86*, 837–855.

Lent, R. W. (2013). Social cognitive career theory. In S. D. Brown & R. W. Lent (Eds.), *Career development and counseling: Putting theory and research to work* (2nd ed., pp. 115–146). Hoboken, NJ: Wiley.

Lent, R. W., & Brown, S. D. (2006). Integrating person and situation perspectives on work satisfaction: A social-cognitive view. *Journal of Vocational Behavior, 69*, 236–247.

Lent, R. W., & Brown, S. D. (2008). Social cognitive career theory and subjective wellbeing in the context of work. *Journal of Career Assessment, 16*, 6–21.

Lent, R. W., & Brown, S. D. (2013). Social cognitive model of career self-management: Toward a unifying view of adaptive career behavior across the lifespan. *Journal of Counseling Psychology, 60*, 557–568.

Lent, R. W., Brown, S. D., & Hackett, G. (1994). Toward a unifying social cognitive theory o career and academic interest, choice, and performance [Monograph]. *Journal of Vocational Behavior, 45*, 79–122.

Lent, R. W., Ezeofor, I., Morrison, M. A., Penn, L. T., & Ireland, G. W. (2016). Applying the social cognitive model of career self-management to career exploration and decision-making. *Journal of Vocational Behavior, 93*, 47–57.

Lim, R. H., Lent, R. W., & Penn, L. T. (2016). Prediction of job search intentions and behaviors: Testing the social cognitive model of career self-management. *Journal of Counseling Psychology, 63*(5), 594–603.

Liu, S., Huang, J. L., & Wang, M. (2014). Effectiveness of job search interventions: A meta-analytic review. *Psychological Bulletin, 140*, 1009–1041.

Roche, M. K., Daskalova, P., & Brown, S. D. (in pres2017). Anticipated multiple role management in emerging adults: A test of the social cognitive career theory self-management model. *Journal of Career Assessment, 25*(1), 121–134.

Tatum, A. K., Formica, L. J., & Brown, S. D. (in press2017). Testing a social cognitive model of workplace sexual identity management. *Journal of Career Assessment, 25*(1), 107–120.

Chapter 7

Life design and career counseling

Self-determination and autonomous motivation

Michael L. Wehmeyer and Karrie A. Shogren

The Life Design paradigm emphasizes that "career theories and vocational guidance techniques must be reformulated to fit the post-modern economy" (Savickas et al., 2009, p. 240) and that "theoretical models are needed that emphasize human flexibility, adaptability, and life-long learning" (Savickas et al, 2009, p. 240). Life-designing emphasizes enabling young people to become experts in "constructing" their own career paths, taking on transitions, addressing threats and opportunities, and designing a better life (Nota & Rossier, 2015). What, in essence, the Life Design paradigm requires is that young people become self-determined and act autonomously to be causal agents in their own lives (Wehmeyer & Shogren, 2017). This chapter introduces a theoretical model of the development of self-determination that explains how autonomously motivated young people engage in causal action to become more self-determined and to make or cause things to happen in their own lives. The model provides a theoretical foundation for autonomy-supportive interventions that can provide career and vocational counselors and coaches with research-based means to promote self-directed goal setting and attainment pertaining to career and vocational outcomes and to enhance self-determination and effective life designing.

Self-determination

In modern psychology, self-determination is conceptualized under the organizing structure of theories of human agentic action or human agency (Wehmeyer, Shogren, Little, & Lopez, 2017). An agentic person is someone who is the "origin of his or her actions, perseveres in the face of obstacles, sees more and varied options for action, learns from failures, and overall, has a greater sense of well-being" (Little, Hawley, Henrich, & Marsland, 2002, p. 390). Human agentic theories "share the meta-theoretical view that organismic aspirations drive human behaviors" (Little, Snyder, & Wehmeyer, 2006, p. 61). An organismic approach views people as active contributors to, or "authors" of, their behavior and action. Organismic approaches see behavior as self-regulated and goal-directed action. Unlike stimulus-response accounts of behavior, actions are defined as purposive and self-initiated activities (Wehmeyer & Little, 2013).

Self-determination, as a psychological construct, refers to self- (vs. other-) caused action – to people acting volitionally, based on their own will (Wehmeyer & Shogren, 2017). The construct is derived from the philosophical doctrine of determinism, which is the idea that every event or action, including human action, is an effect of preceding causes. Andras Angyal, an early theorist in personality psychology, posited that human action can be viewed as reflecting two sources of causation: autonomous determinism (self-caused or internally governed action), and heteronomous determinism (other caused or externally governed action) (Angyal, 1941).

Two theoretical approaches to self-determination, self-determination theory and causal agency theory, provide foundations for developing, evaluating, and implementing approaches to promoting self-determination and enabling young people to construct their own career paths and be the actors in their own lives.

Self-determination theory

Self-determination theory (SDT) is a comprehensive macro-theory of human motivation that provides a framework to understand the origins and outcomes of human agentic action (Vansteenkiste, Niemiec, & Soenens, 2010). Self-determination theory divides motivation into autonomous and controlled types (Deci & Ryan, 2008). According to SDT, there are three basic psychological needs – competence, autonomy, and relatedness – that must be met to support healthy psychological development (Deci & Ryan, 2012). The need for *competence* reflects humans' desires to effectively master their environment and experience a sense of competence in it. The need for autonomy is satisfied when a person experiences choice and volition in their actions, and perceives themselves to be the origin of their actions. The need for relatedness is associated with social belonging; a satisfaction derived from a sense of connectedness with others; to care and be cared for by others (Adams, Little, & Ryan, 2017).

Self-determination theory is composed of six mini-theories, posited to address specific problems of motivation theory and that, together, explain how SDT operates (Adams et al., 2017). A comprehensive examination of these mini-theories is beyond the scope of this chapter, but in the context of implementing autonomy-motivating interventions to promote Life Design activities, it is worth detailing two of the mini-theories: causality orientations theory (COT) and organismic integration theory (OIT). The former (COT) proposes three types of general motivational orientations – autonomous, controlled, or impersonal (Deci & Ryan, 1985). As one would suspect, autonomously oriented people orient to the environment and regulate their behavior in intrinsically motivated, self-initiated ways that support their autonomy. Controlled orientation reflects a general motivational orientation toward extrinsic motivators, including rewards, directives of others, and so forth. An impersonal orientation reflects someone whose general orientation is one of amotivation and feelings of ineffectiveness (Deci & Ryan, 1985).

The second mini-theory, organismic integration theory, addresses the fact that despite one's general motivational orientation, most common day-to-day activities are not, in fact, intrinsically motivated. Organismic integration theory posits that extrinsically motivated actions can be either controlled or autonomous, and proposes six types of motivations that exist along a continuum from extrinsic to intrinsic (amotivation, external regulation, introjected regulation, identified regulation, integrated regulation, and intrinsic motivation) (Deci & Ryan, 2012). This continuum reflects a movement from non-self-determined behavior (motivation type amotivation) to extrinsically motivated action that is not internalized (external regulation, introjected regulation) to more self-determined, though still extrinsically motivated, action (identified regulation, integrated regulation) and, finally, to self-determined action (intrinsic motivation).

To be life designers, young people need to be autonomously and intrinsically motivated. Such motivation, in turn, leads to causal action, as described by causal agency theory.

Causal agency theory

Shogren et al. (2015) proposed causal agency theory to explain how people become self-determined; that is, how they identify and implement the actions and beliefs necessary to engage in self-caused, autonomous action that addresses basic psychological needs. Self-determination is defined as a

> dispositional characteristic manifested as acting as the causal agent in one's life. Self-determined people (i.e., causal agents) act in service to freely chosen goals. Self-determined actions function to enable a person to be the causal agent is his or her life.
>
> (p. 258)

A dispositional characteristic is an enduring tendency used to characterize and describe differences between people; a tendency to act or think in a particular way, but presumes contextual variance (i.e., socio-contextual supports and opportunities and threats and impediments). Broadly defined, causal agency implies that it is the person who makes or causes things to happen in his or her life; that the person acts to accomplish a specific end or to cause or create change. Self-determined actions enable a person to act as a causal agent.

Within causal agency theory, self-determined action is characterized by three essential characteristics – volitional action, causal action, and action-control beliefs. These essential characteristics refer not to specific actions performed or the beliefs that drive action, but to the function the action serves for the individual; that is, whether the action enabled the person to act as a causal agent.

Volitional action

Self-determined people act volitionally. Volition refers to making a conscious choice based on one's preferences. Conscious choice implies intentionality; self-determined actions are intentionally conceived, deliberate acts that occur without direct external influence. As such, volitional actions are self-initiated and function to enable a person to act autonomously (i.e., engage in self-governed action). Volitional actions involve the initiation and activation of causal capabilities – the capacity to cause something to happen – and something to happen in one's life.

Agentic action

An agent is someone who acts; a means by which something is done or achieved. Agency refers to action in the service of a goal. Self-determined people act to identify pathways that lead to a specific end or cause or create change. The identification of pathways is a proactive, purposive process. As such, agentic actions are self-regulated and self-directed. Such actions function to enable a person to make progress toward freely chosen goals and respond to opportunities and challenges in their environments. Such actions involve agentic capabilities; the capacity to direct it to achieve an outcome.

Action-control beliefs

Self-determined people have a sense of personal empowerment; they believe they have what it takes to achieve freely chosen goals. There are three types of action-control beliefs: beliefs about the link between the self and the goal (control expectancy; "When I want to do, I can"); beliefs about the link between the self and the means for achieving the goal (capacity beliefs; "I have the capabilities to do ______"); and beliefs about the utility or usefulness of a given means for attaining a goal (causality beliefs; "I believe my effort will lead to goal achievement" vs. "I believe other factors – luck, access to teachers or social capital – will lead to goal achievement"). Positive action-control beliefs function to enable a person to act with self-awareness and self-knowledge in an empowered, goal-directed manner.

The development of self-determination

As noted previously, SDT posits three basic psychological needs for autonomy, competence, and relatedness. Satisfaction of these basic needs facilitates autonomous motivation, defined as intrinsic motivation and well-internalized extrinsic motivation (Deci & Ryan, 2012, p. 88). Consistent with self-determination as situated within organismic theories, the interplay between the context and the individual's psychological needs satisfaction is complex and reciprocal. When a motive or motives are salient, people are in a position to select goals based on their expectations about the satisfaction of these motives (Deci & Ryan, 1985, p. 235). These psychological needs initiate a causal action sequence that, through interaction with environmental supports and opportunities, enables the development of a "synergistic set of action-control beliefs and behaviors that provide the self-regulatory foundation that is called upon to negotiate the various tasks and challenges of the life course" (Little et al., 2002, p. 396). Action-control beliefs about the link between the self and the goal (control expectancy beliefs), the links between the self and the means that are available for use to address a challenge (agency beliefs), and about which specific means are most effective for reaching one's goals (causality beliefs) (Little et al., 2002, p. 396) interact with and mediate volitional and agentic actions (as described in causal agency theory, previously), resulting in experiences of causal agency. Repeated experiences with the causal action sequence leads to multiple experiences with causal agency and, as a result, enhanced self-determination.

Autonomy-supportive strategies for counseling and coaching

So, what can counselors and coaches do to enable young people to engage in causal action to achieve more positive life and career outcomes? Research on autonomy-supportive classrooms and on interventions to promote self-determination are directly applicable to this situation, and this chapter concludes with an overview of these strategies.

Strategies to promote autonomous motivation

Research on autonomy-supportive conversational actions can be applied to the counseling and coaching situations. De Naeghel and colleagues (2014) identified strategies linked to each of the basic psychological needs identified by SDT: autonomy, competence, and relatedness.

Autonomy support strategies, linked to the basic need for autonomy, include:

- giving young people options from which to choose;
- identifying and basing instruction on young people's preferences and interests;
- promoting self-initiation of actions.

Strategies linked to the young person's need for competence involve practices that

- provide optimal challenges for young people;
- clearly communicate expectations,
- provide consistent and positive feedback.

Strategies that are linked to young people's need for relatedness include strategies that

- emphasize relationship-building;
- promote positive social interactions.

Research generally shows that motivation supports cognitive ability, rather than operates independent from it (Schunk & Zimmerman, 2011). For example, highly motivated students demonstrate increased effort, perseverance, help-seeking (e.g., asking questions or seeking assistance), and active engagement (Vansteenkiste, Lens, & Deci, 2006) and show continued persistence in the face of obstacles and adversity (Multon, Brown, & Lent, 1991; Schunk, 1991). As such, for Life Design purposes, promoting student autonomous motivation is important, and can be accomplished by implementing autonomy-supportive interventions and self-determination.

Autonomy-supportive interventions to promote self-determination

Promoting self-determination involves enabling young people to acquire and practice skills enabling them to act as causal agents in their lives – skills such as goal-setting, problem-solving, decision-making, self-advocacy, and others. Since counselors and coaches are not always (or even primarily) in roles of direct instruction, it is important for them to employ strategies that maximize the involvement of the young person in the processes leading to goal-setting and attainment. This can be done by implementing self-regulation or self-management strategies and by engaging young people in goal-setting and attainment using strategies that maximize:

Self-regulation or self-management strategies. Self-regulation or self-management strategies involve enabling young people modify to regulate their own behavior. There are numerous such strategies, but several that are of particular importance (self-instruction, self-monitoring, and self-evaluation) are highlighted here, although these components are usually bundled together and paired with other strategies, such as goal-setting.

- *Self-instruction* involves supporting young people to provide their own verbal cues prior to the execution of target behaviors. Self-instruction allows students to provide themselves with sufficient verbal information to cue a response, information that might otherwise not be provided or be provided by an adult.
- *Self-monitoring* involves enabling students to observe whether they have performed a targeted behavior and whether the response met whatever existing criteria present. Self-monitoring and self-recording procedures have been shown to improve the motivation and performance of students.

- *Self-evaluation* involves enabling a young person to compare his or her performance (as tracked through self-monitoring) and comparing that performance with a desired goal or outcome.

The most frequently studied self-management strategy is the use of self-monitoring. Generally, some sort of checklist or tally device is used in self-monitoring. Self-monitoring usually focuses on tasks, behaviors, or processes that a student already knows how to do, a behavior that a student is already aware that he or she does, or as a way for the student to monitor progress toward a goal. Self-evaluation is an extension of self-monitoring, enabling young people to determine if their performance, as recorded through self-monitoring, meets a standard. This can be done through a rating scale, charting, graphing, or other means of summarizing the self-monitoring information.

Self-determined career development model

The primary process we have developed and evaluated to enable young people to self-regulate the goal-setting process to set and attain job- and career-related goals has been the Self-Determined Career Development Model (SDCDM, Wehmeyer et al., 2003), designed to enable youth and young adults to self-regulate decision-making pertaining to career and job-related outcomes (see Tables 7.1–7.3). Because career coaches and counselors often provide guidance and support to youth and young adults in making decisions about and planning for desired adult and life outcomes, the SDCDM is a model of support that would provide coaches and counselors the means to support young people both to become more self-determined and to assume greater responsibility for setting goals pertaining to employment, creating action plans to achieve those goals, and evaluating their progress toward those goals, modifying the goal or plan as needed.

The SDCDM was developed to enable vocational rehabilitation counselors and others to support adolescents and young adults with disabilities to self-direct goal-setting and attainment processes related to job and career goals, but is just as suitable for use by adolescents and young adults without disabilities. With this model, facilitators implement a three-phase process, depicted in Tables 7.1–7.3, that enables youth or adults with disabilities to select goals on which they want to work. Youth and young adults are supported through each of the three phases, answering four questions that reflect steps in the problem-solving process. As movement through the phases continues, participants are required to reflect on their goals (through their own question answering) and goal attainment. If youth or young adults identify barriers that might prevent them from reaching their goals, they are encouraged to develop solutions to these barriers. Through this entire process, participants monitor and regulate their target goals and make adaptations (problem solve) as they deem fit. The model also contains objectives that serve as steps in generating information

Table 7.1 Phase 1, self-determined career development model

Problem to Solve: What are my career and job goals?	
Question 1: **What career and job do I want?** Objectives: • Enable person to identify career/job preferences/interests/beliefs/values. • Enable person to identify strengths and needs related to jobs/careers. • Enable and support person to prioritize career and jobs options and select preferred option(s). Question 2: **What do I know about it now?** Objectives: • Enable person to identify his or her current status in relation to prioritized job and career option(s). • Enable person to identify knowledge/skills/needs of job/career option. • Assist person to gather information about opportunities and barriers in their environments pertaining to prioritized job and career option(s). Question 3: **What must change for me to get the job and career I want?** Objectives: • Support person to prioritize needs related to job/career preference(s). • Enable person to choose primary need and decide if action needs to be focused toward capacity building, modifying the environment or both. Question 4: **What can I do to make this happen?** Objectives: • Teach person to state career/employment goals/objectives.	**Employment Supports** • Awareness Training • Self-Assess job or career preferences/abilities. • Career and job exploration. • Job Shadowing and Sampling. • Organizational Skills Training • Problem Solving Instruction • Choice-Making Instruction • Decision-Making Instruction • Goal-Setting Instruction

on skills, interests, and abilities. The objectives assist the facilitator (coach or counselor) in working through the questions with participants by scaffolding support, directly instructing, or collaborating with participants.

The four questions within each phase are different but represent identical steps in the problem-solving process. In essence, as youth or young adults are

Table 7.2 Phase 2, self-determined career development model

Problem to Solve: What is my plan?	
Question 1: **What actions can I take to reach my career or employment goal?** Objectives: • Enable person identify alternatives to achieve career/employment goal. • Assist person to gather information on consequences of alternatives. • Enable person to select best action alternatives. Question 2: **What could keep me from taking action?** Objectives: • Support person to identify barriers to implementing action alternatives. • Support person to identify actions to remove barriers. Question 3: **What can I do to remove these barriers?** Objectives: • Assist person in identifying appropriate employment supports to implement selected action alternative. • Teach person knowledge/skills needed to implement selected supports. Question 4: **When will I take action?** Objectives: • Enable person to determine schedule for action plan to remove barriers and implement supports. • Support and enable person to implement the action plan. • Enable person to self-monitor their progress.	**Employment Supports** • Exploration of community resource/support • Problem-solving instruction • Self-scheduling training • Self-instruction training • Picture-cue training • Decision-Making Instruction • Self-Advocacy Instruction • Assertiveness training • Self-Monitoring Instruction

answering the questions in each phase, they must: (a) identify the problem, (b) identify potential solutions to the problem, (c) identify barriers to solving the problem, and (d) identify the consequences of each solution.

In essence, the SDCDM provides a process that youth and young adults can learn to self-regulate problem-solving leading to goal setting and attainment and, essentially, engage in "life designing" to set goals related to their career outcomes. Research in disability supports using the SDCDM and a companion process, the Self-Determined Learning Model of Instruction, which is intended

Table 7.3 Phase 3, self-determined career development model

Problem to Solve: What have I achieved?	
Question 1: **What actions have I taken?** Objectives: • Enable person to self-evaluate and articulate progress toward goal. Question 2: **What barriers have been removed?** Objectives: • Assist person to compare progress with their desired outcomes. Question 3: **What has changed to enable me to get the job and career I want?** Objectives: • Support person to reevaluate goal if progress is insufficient. • Assist person to decide if goal remains the same or changes. • Collaborate with person to identify if the action plan is adequate or inadequate given revised or retained goal. • Assist person to change action plan if necessary. Question 4: **Have I achieved what I want to achieve?** Objectives: • Enable person to decide if progress is adequate, inadequate, or if goal has been achieved. • If this goal has been achieved, enable person to decide if a different goal is needed to achieve their employment or career goals.	**Employment Supports** Self-Evaluation Instruction

to enable students to self-regulate school and other domain-related goal-setting and attainment, that (1) if provided opportunities to learn processes, like the SDCDM/SDLMI, and to acquire skills pertaining to goal-setting, problem-solving, decision-making, and so forth, young people become more self-determined (Wehmeyer, Palmer, Shogren, Williams-Diehm, & Soukup, 2012); and (2) that young people who are more self-determined achieve more positive transition, employment, and community access outcomes as young adults (Shogren, Palmer, Wehmeyer, Williams-Diehm, & Little, 2012; Shogren, Wehmeyer, Palmer, Rifenbark, & Little, 2015).

Conclusion

Promoting self-determination is at the heart of the process that will be necessary to enable youth and young adults to learn to self-regulate learning, planning, goal-setting and attainment, and to achieve the life and career outcomes that reflect their preferences, interests, abilities, and values. By enabling youth and young adults to self-regulate and self-manage their actions and to apply self-regulated problem-solving processes to set and attain goals through supports like the SDCDM, coaches and counselors can enable them to become actors in their own lives, and to design the lives and the careers they want.

References

Adams, N., Little, T., & Ryan, R. (2017). Self-determination theory. In M. L. Wehmeyer, K. A. Shogren, T. D. Little, & S. Lopez (Eds.), *Handbook on the development of self-determination* (pp. 47–54). New York: Springer.

Angyal, A. (1941). *Foundations for a science of personality*. Cambridge, MA: Harvard University Press.

De Naeghel, J., Van Keer, H., & Vanderlinde, R. (2014). Strategies for promoting autonomous reading motivation: A multiple case study research in primary education. *Frontline Learning Research, 3*, 83–101.

Deci, E. L., & Ryan, R. M. (1985). Intrinsic motivation and self-determination in human behavior. New York: Plenum Press.

Deci, E. L., & Ryan, R. M. (2008). Facilitating optimal motivation and psychological wellbeing across life's domains. *Canadian Psychology, 49*, 14–23.

Deci, E. L., & Ryan, R. M. (2012). Motivation, personality, and development within embedded social contexts: An overview of self-determination theory. In R. M. Ryan (Ed.), *Oxford handbook of human motivation* (pp. 85–107). Oxford, UK: Oxford University Press.

Little, T. D., Hawley, P. H., Henrich, C. C., & Marsland, K. (2002). Three views of the agentic self: A developmental synthesis. In E. L. Deci & R. M. Ryan (Eds.), *Handbook of self-determination research* (pp. 389–404). Rochester, NY: University of Rochester Press.

Little, T. D., Snyder, C. R., & Wehmeyer, M. (2006). The agentic self: On the nature and origins of personal agency across the lifespan. In D. K. Mroczek & T. D. Little (Eds.), *Handbook of personality development* (pp. 61–80). Mahwah, NJ: LEA.

Multon, K. D., Brown, S. D., & Lent, R. W. (1991). Relation of self-efficacy beliefs to academic outcomes: A meta-analytic investigation. *Journal of Counseling Psychology, 38*, 30–38.

Nota, L., & Rossier, J. (Eds.). (2015). Handbook of life design: From practice to theory and from theory to practice. Göttingen: Hogrefe Publishing.

Savickas, M. L., Nota, L., Rossier, J., Dauwalder, J-P., Duarte, M. E., Guichard, J., . . . van Vianen, A. E. M. (2009). Life designing: A paradigm for career construction in the 21st century. *Journal of Vocational Behavior, 75*(3), 239–250.

Schunk, D. H. (1991). Self-efficacy and academic motivation. *Educational Psychologist, 26*, 207–231.

Schunk, D. H., & Zimmerman, B. J. (2011). *Handbook of self-regulation of learning and performance*. New York, NY: Routledge.

Shogren, K. A., Palmer, S., Wehmeyer, M. L., Williams-Diehm, K., & Little, T. (2012). Effect of intervention with the self-determined learning model of instruction on access and goal attainment. *Remedial and Special Education, 33*(5), 320–330.

Shogren, K. A., Wehmeyer, M. L., Palmer, S. B., Forber-Pratt, A., Little, T., & Lopez, S. (2015). Causal agency theory: Reconceptualizing a functional model of self-determination. *Education and Training in Autism and Developmental Disabilities, 50*(3), 251–263.

Shogren, K. A., Wehmeyer, M. L., Palmer, S. B., Rifenbark, G., & Little, T. (2015). Relationships between self-determination and postschool outcomes for youth with disabilities. *Journal of Special Education, 48*(4), 256–267.

Vansteenkiste, M., Lens, W., & Deci, E. L. (2006). Intrinsic versus extrinsic goal contents in self-determination theory: Another look at the quality of academic motivation. *Educational Psychologist, 41*, 19–31.

Vansteenkiste, M., Niemiec, C., & Soenens, B. (2010). The development of the five mini-theories of self-determination theory: An historical overview, emerging trends, and future directions. In T. Urdan & S. Karabenick (Eds.), *Advances in motivation and achievement, vol. 16: The decade ahead*. Bingley, UK: Emerald Publishing.

Wehmeyer, M., Lattimore, J., Jorgensen, J., Palmer, S., Thompson, E., & Schumaker, K. M. (2003). The self-determined career development model: A pilot study. *Journal of Vocational Rehabilitation, 19*, 79–87.

Wehmeyer, M. L., & Little, T. (2013). Self-determination, positive psychology, and disability. In M. L. Wehmeyer (Ed.), *Handbook of positive psychology and disability* (pp. 116–136). Oxford, UK: Oxford University Press.

Wehmeyer, M. L., Palmer, S., Shogren, K., Williams-Diehm, K., & Soukup, J. (2012). Establishing a causal relationship between interventions to promote self-determination and enhanced student self-determination. *Journal of Special Education, 46*(4), 195–210.

Wehmeyer, M. L., & Shogren, K. A. (in press 2017). The development of self-determination in adolescence. In M. L. Wehmeyer, K. A. Shogren, T. D. Little, & S. Lopez (Eds.), *Handbook on the development of self-determination* (pp. 89–98). New York, NY: Springer.

Wehmeyer, M. L., Shogren, K. A., Little, T. D., & Lopez, S. J. (Eds.). (in pres2017). *Handbook of the development of self-determination*. New York, NY: Springer.

Wehmeyer, M. L., Shogren, K. A., Palmer, S., Williams-Diehm, K., Little, T., & Boulton, A. (2012). The impact of the self-determined learning model of instruction on student self-determination. *Exceptional Children, 78*(2), 135–153.

Chapter 8

Narrative career counseling

Theoretical and application proposals within the narrative vocational identity

Laura Aleni Sestito, Luigia Simona Sica, and Tiziana Di Palma

According to lifespan developmental psychology, identifying adequate school and professional paths and developing projects consistent with one's own aspirations and motivations are crucial in the years of transition to adulthood. Indeed, in addition to satisfying the basic needs (Deci & Ryan, 2000) of self-actualization (Deci et al., 2001; Vansteenkiste, Zhou, Lens, & Soenens, 2005), young people have to cope with developmental tasks mainly to define and consolidate identity and to acquire fulfilling adult roles. Late adolescents and young people moving into adulthood have to make plans about family, education and work (Zarrett & Eccles, 2006), have to engage actively in goal setting and goal pursuit and have to adjust their goals contingent upon their perceived opportunities or contextual affordances (Vondracek & Schulenberg, 1986). In this perspective, future planning about working activities helps young people to define each one's own place in the social context, suggests styles and value models, induces and supports specific relational ways, and is a central reference for developmental paths and identity processes (Niemiec, Ryan, & Deci, 2009).

Despite this, the contemporary post-industrial society – complex, fluid and unstable – has also produced significant changes in the labour market (Buchmann & Kriesi, 2011); for example, the diffusion of precarious jobs, short contracts, freelance collaborations, self-employed, atypical contracts that may involve the end of a stable and predictable work organization. Due to this, planning for the future and resolving vocational identity for contemporary young people seems to have become a more complex task, with broader and deeper dimensions that are harder to solve (Sica, Crocetti, Ragozini, Aleni Sestito, & Serafini, 2016). The uncertainty, the lack of future orientation, overcoming identity moratorium and identity diffusion linked to identity distress, which characterize young people of industrialized societies, could be enhanced by new elements of unpredictability deriving from the characteristics that the world of work took over in the 21st century (Savickas, 2012). In many countries of Southern Europe, such as Italy, the economic crisis associated with changes in the labour market mostly characterized by lack of opportunity, insecurity and instability seem to have discouraged young people on the threshold of university from making long-term decisions and developing a self-image that integrates dimensions of personal and professional projects. Main problems that affect Southern European youth include high rates of unemployment (ranging approximately from 35% to 55% in the last quarter of 2012; Eurostat, 2014); a large number of youth being "Not in Education, Employment, or Training" (NEET; Bynner, 2012; Bynner & Parson, 2002); widespread job insecurity; and a deep-rooted crisis of confidence in educational institutions and employers. In fact, in Italy there is also a high rate of youth unemployment (36.4% of young people from 15 to 24 years are unemployed, ISTAT, 2016). Furthermore, Italian young people, even after concluding their prolonged courses of study have to experience additional periods of instability, insecurity and economic uncertainty. This occurrence, defined as "delay syndrome" (Livi Bacci, 2008), is considered a "transitional stressor" (Sica, Sestito, & Ragozini, 2014) that increases identity instability in late adolescence and could be a determining factor in postponing the achievement of important commitments in multiple life domains and especially occupational ones (Crocetti, Rabaglietti, & Sica, 2012). Thus, all the evidence gives rise to a problematic area for young people's future orientation, for their definition of career identity projects and for the realization of their career projects. In order to identify solutions for the highlighted problems, the present work reviews the theoretical approach and application models of narrative vocational identity that focus on identity development processes, self-reflection and self-construction activity (Savickas, 2005), and it proposes an application model of career counseling that seems more culturally and contextually sensitive, and inclusive of qualitative and subjective processes.

Theoretical framework for narrative vocational identity

Vocational identity is a core construct in career and lifespan development. A number of studies have repeatedly shown that vocational identity achievement relates positively to psychological adjustment, career success and life satisfaction (see Skorikov & Vondracek, 2007 for a review). Vocational identity, as well as occupational, work, professional or career identity, refers to the *conscious awareness of oneself as a worker* (Skorikov & Vondracek, 2007, p. 694). It has been conceptualized as a domain-specific aspect of overall identity and as a major component of one's overall sense of identity (Skorikov & Vondracek, 2011), providing young people with a framework to regulate the pursuit of their academic and career objectives (Hirschi, 2012). People exhibiting an advanced identity status show greater career planning and decidedness (Wallace-Broscious, Serafica, & Osipio, 1994) and more advanced identity. Numerous studies also confirm the positive association between vocational and overall identity (Aleni et al., 2015; Nauta & Kahn, 2007) demonstrating that engaging in occupational exploration and making occupational commitments promote identity development from childhood through adulthood. Although the literature emphasizes that identity develops and operates differently in different life domains in the sense that "most adolescents are in different identity statuses in different domains" (Goossens, 2001, p. 696), Erikson (1959) even assigned a leading role to vocational identity development in the overall process of identity formation, because a positive occupational identity enables an adaptive ego identity to be established. In contrast to Erikson (1959), Skorikov and Vondracek (2011) suggest that identity development is an asynchronous process in which vocational identity develops earlier and becomes a driving force behind identity formation in others' domains.

Recently, Porfeli, Lee, Vondracek, and Weigold (2011) proposed a model of vocational identity based on three processes: exploration of possible vocational identity choices, commitment in a given vocational identity related to decisions and choices and, finally, reconsideration of career alternatives characterized by a review of the commitments made. This model identify six statuses supporting the previously established achievement, moratorium, foreclosed and diffused statuses along with two additional statuses termed searching moratorium (individuals seeking a new commitment suited to their aspirations, and are thus characterized by high levels of commitment, in-depth exploration and reconsideration of commitment) and undifferentiated (individuals who reflect moderate levels of all six constructs and are conceptually situated in the centre of a two- dimensional space defined by commitment and exploration).

Findings from a recent Italian study (Aleni et al., 2015), confirming Goossens' (2001) the assumption that identity can develop and operate differently in different life domains, shows that the vocational identity appears particularly sensitive to labour context and especially to the extremely distressed economic situation in Italy. In this perspective, the delay syndrome and delayed normative overall identity development (Crocetti et al., 2012) ascribed to Italian young people in transition, could specifically impact on vocational identity processes and career plans.

Within the developmental contextual perspective on career development, recently Skorikov and Vondracek (2011) proposed that the expansion of the identity status paradigm is a step in the right direction but still does not capture the complex and evolving structure of meanings in which individuals link their motivations and competencies to acceptable career roles. They focus on occupational identity as a dynamic organization of occupational self-perception, shaped by "qualitative and quantitative changes in the structure and form of identification with the role of worker as a result of the interaction between the epigenetic unfolding of the person's capabilities and learning through self-chosen and socially assigned vocational, educational and leisure activities" (Skorikov & Vondracek, 2007, p. 146).

More recently, the new approaches to vocational identity that have emerged within the field of career counseling appear most suited to evaluating the complexity of individuals' lives through dynamic, recursively connected individual, social and environmental-societal systems of influence. In this respect, many scholars have pointed out that a career identity that is suitable for navigating the world of the boundary less (Arthur, Khapova, & Wilderom, 2005) and protean career in an ever more uncertain economy is a well-structured story, based on life themes, that explains "how the self of yesterday became the self of today and will become the self of tomorrow" (Savickas, 2005, p. 58). The starting point is that "narration can be used to form a subjective construction of meaning that employs self as a main character in a career-defining story" (Cochran, 1997, p. 55). This focus on subjective construction of meanings, and self-reflection and self-construction processes, finds its best expression in the approach of narrative identity that places specific emphasis on individuals' subjective assessment of their personal experiences and the stories that they tell about themselves (McAdams, 2011). In this sense, McAdams regards identity as "an internalized and evolving life story", subsequently called "narrative identity" (McAdams, 2011).

The narrative identity approach is based on the narrative self-conceptualization according to which, alongside a self that can be directly observed and cognized by means of self-reporting instruments, there is another self that can be cognized through narratives, and studying narrative accounts provides insights into personal interpretations of experiences that are not accessible through questionnaire measures alone. So, this narrative approach can be understood as the most suitable avenue for examining identity and focusing on domain contents that are actually important (such the vocational) to young people in the years of transition to work. The main assumption of narrative research is that the impact of experiences on individuals' identity development depends not only on what happens to people, but most of all on the meanings they give to the narrated events. Thus, meaning-making has been proposed as one of the major processes by which identity is constructed and as behaviour that reflects the current state of an individual's identity (McLean, Pasupathi, & Pals, 2007). From a narrative perspective, a coherent sense of identity is created through the construction of a life story that connects individuals' memories of past experiences with their present and with their imagined future in meaningful ways and, in turn, with their future work plans. Individuals need to update their life stories by adding new episodes and by reworking old ones in relation to new experiences. Assuming that narratives are the key schemes by which human beings make their experiences meaningful and understand temporality, a number of authors suggest that career identity could express itself in a story told by a person, showing his/her life theme(s) (Savickas, 2005, 2011) and the way she/he identifies herself/himself based on these life theme(s) with a specific occupation or career.

Narrative career counseling: approaches and practices

In line with the described theoretical approaches based on the constructivist model to career development, a large body of practices were proposed in the field of narrative career counseling in the last decades. McIlveen and Patton

(2007) reviewed theory and exemplars of practice of narrative career counseling until 2007. The approaches identified as prevailing were the *systems theory framework* (STF; Patton & McMahon, 2006) and the *theory of career construction* (Savickas, 2005). Both propose narrative approaches to career counseling practices. The STF, which emphasizes the conception of the individual as active, participative and central, has the concept of "story" as a key feature for counseling. The theory of career construction to which we referred theoretically in the previous section of this chapter identifies in the *life themes* component the primary focus of its counseling practice. The Savickas' approach for life-theme counseling proposes the *Career Style Interview* that is technically structured and embedded in client-centred conversation. As well as for this latter approach, even for the STF, the interview is a privileged instrument for counseling. McIlveen and Patton (2007) propose the *Career Systems Interview*, a process in which the counselor facilitates a free-flowing discussion with the client.

Overall, the principal forms of narrative counseling procedures identified by Patton and McMahon are all qualitative, idiographic, spoken (Campbell & Ungar, 2004; Savickas, 2005) or written (Cochran, 1997), and client-counselor dialogued. A number of visual and spatial forms of counseling were also identified – e.g. goal maps (Brott, 2004), guided fantasy (Cochran, 1997) and collage.

More recently, new approaches have been developed to address the career challenges of our era and are commonly aimed at helping individuals to develop a career/vocational identity. The current section introduces one of these approaches that uses written and dialogical narrative-based counseling to promote career identity for students, namely the *career writing model* (Lengelle & Meijers, 2014; Meijers & Lengelle, 2012). In the consecutive section, we introduce a proposal of narrative vocational identity counseling for high school students (Kuijpers, Meijers, & Gundy, 2011). These authors propose that creative, expressive and reflective writing can offer ways for students to construct work-life stories that provide both personal meaning and societal direction (Meijers & Lengelle, 2012). In this context, meaning refers to the necessity of exploring and constructing what is individually important in relation to existing work roles and highlights the importance of a dialogue with oneself and the role of emotions in work-life choices (Meijers & Wardekker, 2002). In other words, the central elements identified are the concepts of "meaning" and "direction". As for the latter term, the authors cited refer to the ability to make a choice, articulate a preference, and take action based on what an individual deems to be his/her contribution to community and society. The career counselor supports the clients (in many cases, students) to create a career narrative, which identifies and expresses the individual's contribution to society in ways that are personally meaningful.

To summarise, narrative approaches to career counseling enlist storytelling processes to assist individuals to construct their current and future identities. They also focus on narrative meaning making to support people in developing their career identity.

Promoting vocational identity and career planning: a proposal for high school students

In the present section, we discuss a proposal of a narrative training program for vocational identity that could be applied by counselors in school contexts. Previously (Sica, Di Palma, & Aleni Sestito, 2016), the training program was tested and implemented for Italian high school students to promote a narrative construction of vocational identity and career planning during their school years (through activation and enhancement of agentive resources and self-reflection capacities).

Theoretical assumptions and aims

In light of theoretical approaches and practices described and of critical features of the Italian context outlined (see introduction), our training program focuses especially on young people's developmental tasks inherent to exploring, defining and consolidating identity, and mainly exploring and committing vocational identity (Porfeli et al., 2011). From this perspective, our training program takes the form of a program that helps young people to construct their career identity (Meijers & Lengelle, 2012). Our option was driven by the fact that in Italian high school career counselling, orientation founded on the narrative counseling approach is still rare and not included in the educational curriculum. Guidance and counseling provided by Italian high schools are mostly informative, and they are proposed only in favour of small numbers of students attending the last year of school. Therefore, frequently the students are expected to make important decisions about their career future with negligible educational training.

For these reasons, it was conducted for high school students over two school years (the last two) but in extra-curricular time, and was conceived as primarily focused on activities useful to support positive identity development (Tsang, Hui, & Law, 2012) during the transition from late adolescence to young adulthood, from high school to university or work. Recently Coté (1996, 1997, 2016) developed a theoretical model that seeks to characterize the essential issues associated with prolonged identity formation in societies characterized by this prolonged transition into adulthood, based on a neo-Eriksonian model. This socio-developmental Identity Capital Model (ICM) gives a framework for understanding how young people develop and use the resources necessary to function effectively within a prolonged-formation/schooling context, such university, and respond in an active way being involved in their own personal growth in an agentic way (Côté, 2000, 2002). According to the literature on the ICM (Coté, 1997, 2016), our starting assumption is that this specific training program is the most effective means to promote and foster a proactive and agentive way with which young people manage to navigate into the modern and unstable labour market to define their overall and vocational identity.

Our proposal, therefore, aims to develop agentive resources that young people could invest in identity-related work and with which they could understand and negotiate the various obstacles and opportunities commonly encountered throughout late-modern life. According to Schwartz, Côté, and Arnett (2005), the features of personal agency that we consider critical for developing a vocational identity include the sense of responsibility for one's life course, the belief that one is in control of one's decisions and is responsible for their outcomes, and the confidence that one will be able to overcome obstacles that impede one's progress along one's chosen life course.

Furthermore, our proposal matches the narrative approach both in terms of identity construction processes and career counseling. As previously highlighted, we understand identity development as

> the internalized and evolving story of the self that a person constructs to make sense and meaning out of his or her life, as a selective reconstruction of the autobiographical past and a narrative anticipation of the imagined future that serves to explain, for the self and others, how the person came to be and where his or her life may be going.
>
> (McAdams, 2012, p. 99)

In particular, the previously cited developmental theorists emphasize that narrative implies a connection between past events and the present or future events and asserts the importance of striving to make sense of past experience in the identity formation process. Especially during the transition periods (such as from school to university or work), young people have to make a sense of their life changes and cope with difficulties related to the psychological dimension of uncertainty, as evidenced by the literature on processes of decision-making, problem-solving, and related to difficulties in overcoming the moratorium and identity crisis. The narrative-identity processes allow young people to connect their own past story to the present, plan the future in light of the internal and external changes, pinpoint personal and work projects and integrate internal instances with the resources and opportunities offered by the context through self-reflection and meaning-making processes, as well as autobiographical reasoning. From this perspective, basing our argument on the belief that individuals attach meanings to events in their lives by constructing storied accounts of them, recently some scholars have argued explicitly that narratives are also important for individuals in the construction of their career. Alongside the heuristic functions of the narrative to collect research data information, they pointed out the narrative "possibilities" for the development, adjustment and wellbeing, namely the transformative power of storytelling and writing about themselves and about their own experiences. Focusing on narrative as a transformative learning process, our assumption is that the career narrative especially enables young people to take up a self-reflection and self-construction process. Consistent with this, a career story that is encouraged by the instructor or counselor's specific questions helps young people to define who he/she is and how he/she should act in the changing career context, by giving meaning and direction, and can serve as a sort of "black box" useful to promote the processing of personal experiences, even emotionally dense experiences, to plan for their future working life (as outlined by the *Transformative Through Writing Model* of Lengelle and Meijers, 2009).

Strategies, paths and tools for intervention

Our proposal suggests that in the course of the two final years of high school, a team of counselors with specialist expertise in the field of vocational identity and narrative career counseling could conduct the training program cited previously, consisting of a range of actions in three different stages for years. (a) First year of the program. At the *starting stage*, the counselors explain the overall goals and methods of the program to students attending the penultimate year of high school, inviting them to participate. Voluntary participation involves the commitment of each student for the full duration of the program. All students who choose to participate are asked to produce a written autobiographical narrative answering the following prompt: *Write down at what point of your story you are and how you have arrived there.... Start from wherever you like.... In your story, recall the turning points or changes, say how you dealt with them . . . remember any specific events or times in your life during which you feel your parents have influenced you* (Pizzorno, Benozzo, & Carey, 2015; Sankey & Young, 1996). In previous research conducted with Italian students from high school and university (Sica et al., 2016), we experienced that this narrative prompt was a useful tool to bring out autobiographical accounts and to foster the meaning-making processes, in which everyone reconstructs their personal life story, through the perceived parental influence, turning points, changes and coping strategies. This first narrative enables young people to explore their vocational identity development when they are still far from making choices and expressing commitment for their future such as the last year of school. In the *subsequent stage*, all students, in small groups (6–8), are involved in a monthly series of six audio and videotaped focus group discussions, conducted by a psychologist counselor, to analyse and explore life themes and critical features of vocational identity emerging from their narrative. The focus group discussions in the first year could be devoted particularly to students' past experiences and their autobiographical reasoning, supporting them in their in-depth exploration of identity and encouraging them to reconsider their commitments in terms of self-doubt and flexibility (Porfeli et al., 2011). In our training program, these focus group discussions are conceived as a narrative tool that is designed to enable each individual to continue their self-reflection process in depth through the sharing, the self-disclosure, the participation in experiences and difficulties narrated by peers. In the *final stage*, at the end of the series of six focus group discussions, the participants are asked to complete individually a graphical map of their vocational identity development, highlighting their life paths from the past to the present. This map (*Identity Map*) is an adapted version of Shepard's graphical approach (Shepard & Marshall, 1999). In designing this map, participants can figure out the components of their identity that have emerged through their written narratives and the focus groups. (b) Second year of the program. At the *starting stage*, the participants are asked to produce once again a written autobiographical narrative answering a prompt quite similar to the previous one but containing special reference to future plans: *Write down at what point of your story you are and how you have arrived there. . . . Start from wherever you like . . . In your story, recall the turning points or changes, relate how you dealt with them . . . and now, and what your plans for the future are* (Pizzorno et al., 2015; Sankey & Young, 1996). Also, the second narrative aims to bring out autobiographical accounts and foster the meaning making processes about the participant's vocational identity but this stage focuses particularly on a narrative anticipation of the imagined future that serves to explain how the person came to be and where his or her life may be going, on the future possible selves that describe who everyone is and how he/she should act in the changing career context. During this second year the participants, in small groups (6–8), are involved in a monthly series of six audio and videotaped focus group discussions, conducted by a psychologist counselor. Here, the focus group discussions aim to analyse and explore especially critical features of vocational identity, namely beliefs about who everyone hopes or expects to become, as well as who everyone fears to become, that have emerged from the new narrative. In the *final stage*, in other words at the end of this new series of six focus group discussions, the participants are asked to complete individually a graphical map of vocational identity in which they can define a goal (expected or feared vocational possible selves) and a starting point (actual self). The route from the start to the end could be represented by a drawing illustrating possible selves, internal resources, external resources, obstacles (internal and external), coping strategies and concrete steps. The pictorial tool enables each participant to visualize a goal (in terms of vocational projects) and to plan an integrated itinerary to achieve it. Thus, the Possible Selves Map constitutes a useful tool for the conclusion of the entire training program, supporting participants in the future orientation of their vocational identity, in their career projects and in their school/work choices.

The proposed training program was tested and validated through a pilot study designed during a university course about Life Design counseling titled Methods and Techniques of Life-designing Counseling. During the course, students were trained to conduct the described training program in the school context, then the course's students (trainees) conducted the pilot study with 20 Italian high school students at their last two years, age 17 to 19 years (M_{age} = 17,55 years, *SD* = 1,61). The effectiveness of the pilot study was verified through assessment at the beginning and at the end of the training program using the same instruments to evaluate its effectiveness to explore and compare both possible selves and future orientation dimensions. The measures were

(a) Possible Selves Questionnaire (Oyserman, Bybee, Terry, & Hart-Johnson, 2004) for the assessment of"individuals' ideas of what they might become, what they would like to become, and what they are afraid of becoming as cognitive components of hopes, fears, goals, and threats, and they give the specific self-relevant form, meaning, organization, and direction to these dynamics" (the opened answers were analysed as narratives using thematic analysis of content in terms of exploration in order to pinpoint the future-oriented selves of the participants in terms of change) and (b) Design my Future (Santilli et al., 2017) for the assessment of future orientation. The results of the assessments showed that the intervention had effects in terms of: increasing congruence between expected and feared selves; activation of future-oriented and planning processes (both comparing T1 and T2 and the "experimental" group and control group). Furthermore, these results allowed us to identify three different types of change (change as activation of exploration in depth processes; change as activation of exploration in breadth processes; change as activation of commitment processes) and two modalities of no-change (without planning for the future and with planning for the future).

Conclusion

In this chapter, we described the narrative *career counseling model* in its theoretical and empirical aspects within the lifespan developmental psychology, because it appears as a congruent and promising approach for supporting the vocational identity formation processes of high school students. Consistent with these assumptions, we have proposed a training program for high school students who have successfully tested. Our belief (denoted as the "take-home message" of this chapter) is that the orientation to the future and the vocational identity formation of students especially of high school can be supported with actual effectiveness through training program including instruments that promote self-reflection processes, exploration of desires and fears for the future, as well as the identification of individual internal resources (agency) that help to move from vague and abstract projects to concrete and realistic projects.

According to this vision, we suggest a few practical considerations to promote the effectiveness of narrative training programs. In overall terms, career counselors need to convey a non-judgmental attitude when working with young people and to promote personal reflection on all of the lifeline (past, present and future) and not only on one temporal segment. With regard to the use of individual measures (as the narrative one), career counselors are encouraged to support self-reflection processes; with regard to the collective measures (as the focus group discussion), career counselors could support both self-reflection processes and self-disclosure processes. All of these suggestions are to promote the co-construction of meanings for the career projects and to improve flexibility in the meaning-making processes and in the ability to generate multiple ideas and solutions to problems. These skills are valued more than ever before for the current societies and the current labour market context.

References

Aleni Sestito, L., Sica, L. S., Ragozini, G., Porfeli, E., Weisblat, G., & Di Palma, T. (2015). Vocational and overall identity: A person-centered approach in Italian university students. *Journal of Vocational Behavior, 91*, 157–169. doi:10.1016/j.jvb.2015.10.001

Arthur, M. B., Khapova, S. N., & Wilderom, C. P. (2005). Career success in a boundary less career world. *Journal of Organizational Behavior, 26*(2), 177–202. doi:10.1177/0018726710393537

Brott, P. (2004). Constructivist assessment in career counseling. *Journal of Career Development, 30*, 189–200. doi:10.1177/089484530403000302

Buchmann, M. C., & Kriesi, I. (2011). Transition to adulthood in Europe. *Annual Review of Sociology, 37*(1), 481–503. doi:10.1146/annurev-soc-081309–150212.

Bynner, J. (2012). Policy reflections guided by longitudinal study, youth training, social exclusion, and more recently NEET. *British Journal of Educational Studies, 60*(1), 39–52. doi:http://dx.doi.org/10.1080/00071005.2011.650943

Bynner, J., & Parsons, S. (2002). Social exclusion and the transition from school to work: The case of young people not in education, employment, or training (NEET). *Journal of Vocational Behavior, 60*(2), 289–309. doi:http://dx.doi.org/10.1006/jvbe.2001.1868

Campbell, C., & Ungar, M. (2004). Constructing a life that works: Part 2, an approach to practice. *Career Development Quarterly, 53*, 28–40. doi:10.1002/j.2161-0045.2004.tb00653.x

Cochran, L. (1997). *Career counseling: A narrative approach.* Thousand Oaks, CA: Sage Publications.

Côté, J. E. (1996). Sociological perspectives on identity formation: The culture-identity link and identity capital. *Journal of Adolescence, 19*, 417–428. doi:10.1006/jado.1996.0040.

Côté, J. E. (1997). An empirical test of the identity capital model. *Journal of Adolescence, 20*, 421–437. doi:10.1006/jado.1997.0111

Côté, J. E. (2000). Arrested adulthood: The changing nature of maturity and identity. New York, NY: New York University Press.

Côté, J. E. (2002). The role of identity capital in the transition to adulthood: The individualization tesi examined. *Journal of Youth Studies, 5*, 117–134. doi:10.1080/13676260220134403

Côté, J. E. (2016). *The identity capital model: A handbook of theory, methods, and findings.* Unpublished manuscript, Department of Sociology, The University of Western Ontario, Ontario.

Crocetti, E., Rabaglietti, E., & Sica, L. S. (2012). Personal identity in Italy. *New Directions for Child and Adolescent Development, 138*, 87–102. doi:10.1002/cad.20023

Crocetti, E., Scrignaro, M., Sica, L., & Magrin, M. (2012). Correlates of identity configurations: three studies with adolescent and emerging adult cohorts. *Journal of Youth and Adolescence, 41*(6), 732–748.

Deci, E. L., & Ryan, R. M. (2000). The 'What' and 'Why' of goal pursuits: Human need and the self-determination of behavior. *Psychological Inquiry, 11*, 227–268.

Deci, E. L., Ryan, R. M., Gagne´, M., Leone, D. R., Usunov, J., & Kornazheva, B. P. (2001). Need satisfaction, motivation, and wellbeing in the work organizations of a former Eastern Bloc country. *Personality and Social Psychology Bulletin, 27*, 930–942.

Erikson, E. H. (1959). Identity and the life cycle: Selected papers. *Psychological issues, 1*, 1–171.

Eurostat. (2014). *Unemployment statistics.* Retrieved from http://ec.europa.eu/eurostat/statistics-explained/index.php/Unemployment_statistics

Goossens, L. (2001). Global versus domain-specific statuses in identity research: A comparison of two self-report measures. *Journal of Adolescence, 24*(6), 681–699. doi:10.1006/jado.2001.0438

Hirschi, A. (2012). Vocational identity trajectories: Difference in personality and development of wellbeing. *European Journal of Personality, 26*(2), 2–12. doi:10.1002/per.812

ISTAT. (2016). *Unemployment*. Retrieved from http://dati.istat.it/Index.aspx?DataSetCode=DCCV_TAXDISOCCU

Kuijpers, M., Meijers, F., & Gundy, C. (2011). The relationship between learning environment and career competencies of students in vocational education. *Journal of Vocational Behavior, 78*, 21–30. doi:10.1016/j.jvb.2010.05.005

Lengelle, R., & Meijers, F. (2009). Mystery to mastery: An exploration of what happens in the black box of writing and healing. *Journal of Poetry Therapy, 22*(2), 57–75. doi:10.1080/08893670903072935

Lengelle, R., & Meijers, F. (2014). Narrative Identity: Writing the self in career learning. *British Journal of Guidance and Counselling, 42*, 52–72. doi:10.1080/03069885.2013.816837

Livi Bacci, M. (2008). *Avanti giovani, alla riscossa*! [Full steam ahead youth, to get the rescue!]. Bologna, Italy: il Mulino.

Luyckx, K., Schwartz, S. J., Goossens, L., Soenens, B., & Beyers, W. (2008). Developmental typologies of identity formation and adjustment in female emerging adults: A latent class growth analysis approach. *Journal of Research on Adolescence, 18*, 595–619. doi: 10.1111/j.1532-7795.2008.00573.x.

McAdams, D. P. (2008). Personal narratives and the life story. In O. P. John, R. W. Robins, & L. A. Pervin (Eds.), *Handbook of personality: Theory and research* (3rd ed., pp. 242–262). New York, NY: Guilford Press.

McAdams, D. P. (2011). Narrative identity. In S. J. Schwartz, K. Luyckx, & V. L. Vignoles, (Eds.), *Handbook of identity theory and research* (pp. 99–115). New York, NY: Springer. doi:10.1007/978-1-4419-7988-9_5

McAdams, D. P. (2012). Exploring psychological themes through life-narrative accounts. In J. A. Holstein & J. F. Gubrium (Eds.), *Varieties of narrative analysis* (pp. 15–32). Thousand Oaks, CA: Sage Publications.

McAdams, D. P. (2014). The life narrative at midlife. *New Directions for Child and Adolescent Development, 145*, 57–69.

McIlveen, P. F., & Patton, W. A. (2007). Narrative career counselling: Theory and exemplars of practice. *Australian Psychologist, 42*, 226–235.

McLean, K. C., Pasupathi, M., & Pals, J. L. (2007). Selves creating stories creating selves: A process model of narrative self development in adolescence and adulthood. *Personality and Social Psychology Review, 11*, 262–278. doi:10.1177/1088868307301034

Meijers, F., & Lengelle, R. (2012). Narratives at work: The development of a career identity. *British Journal of Guidance and Counselling, 40*, 157–177. doi:10.1080/03069885.2012.665159

Meijers, F., & Wardekker, W. (2002). Career learning in a changing world: The role of emotions. *International Journal for the Advancement of Counselling, 24*, 149–167. doi:10.1023/A:1022970404517

Nauta, N. M., & Kahn, J. H. (2007). Identity status, consistency and differentiation of interest and career decision self-efficacy. *Journal of Career Assessment, 15*(1), 55–65. doi:10.1177/1069072705283786

Niemiec, C. P., Ryan, R. M., & Deci, E. L. (2009). The path taken: Consequences of attaining intrinsic and extrinsic aspirations in post-college life. *Journal of Research in Personality, 43*(3), 291–306. doi:10.1016/j.jrp.2008.09.001

Oyserman, D., Bybee, D., Terry, K., & Hart-Johnson, T. (2004). Possible selves as roadmaps. *Journal of Research in Personality, 38*(2), 130–149. doi:10.1016/S0092-6566(03)00057-6

Patton, W., & McMahon, M. (2006). Career development and systems theory: Connecting theory and practice. Rotterdam: Sense Publishers.

Pizzorno, M. C., Benozzo, A., & Carey, N. (2015). Narrating career, positioning identity and constructing gender in an Italian adolescent's personal narratives. *Journal of Vocational Behavior, 88*, 195–204. doi:10.1016/j.jvb.2015.03.002

Porfeli, E. J., Lee, B., Vondracek, F., W., & Weigold, I., K. (2011). A Multidimensional measure of vocational identity status. *Journal of Adolescence, 34*, 853–871. doi:10.1016/j.adolescence.2011.02.001

Ryan, R. M. (1995). Psychological needs and the facilitation of integrative processes. *Journal of Personality, 63*, 397–427.

Sankey, A. M., & Young, R. A. (1996). Ego-identity status and narrative structure in retrospective accounts of parental career influence. *Journal of Adolescence, 19*, 141–153. doi.org/10.14288/1.0054090

Santilli, S., Ginevra, M. C., Sgaramella, T. M., Nota, L., Ferrari, L., & Soresi, S. (2017). Design my future an instrument to assess future orientation and resilience. *Journal of Career Assessment, 25*(2), 281–295 doi:10.1177/1069072715621524

Savickas, M. L. (2005). The theory and practice of career construction. In S. D. Brown & R. W. Lent (Eds.), *Career development and counseling: Putting theory and research to work* (pp. 42–70). Hoboken, NJ: John Wiley & Sons.

Savickas, M. L. (2011). Constructing careers: Actors, agents, and authors. *The Counseling Psychologist, XX*(X), 1–15.

Savickas, M. L. (2012). Life design: A paradigm for career intervention in the 21st century. *Journal of Counseling and Development, 90*, 13–19. doi:10.1111/j.1556-6676.2012.00002.x

Savickas, M. L., Nota, L., Rossier, J., Dauwalder, J. P., Duarte, M. E., Guichard, J., . . . & Van Vianen, A. E. (2009). Life designing: A paradigm for career construction in the 21st century. *Journal of Vocational Behavior, 75*, 239–250. doi:10.1016/j.jvb.2009.04.004

Schwartz, S. J., Côté, J. E., & Arnett, J. J. (2005). Identity and agency in emerging adulthood two developmental routes in the individualization process. *Youth & Society, 37*(2), 201–229. doi:10.1177/0044118X0527596

Sheldon, K. M., & Elliot, A. J. (1999). Goal striving, need satisfaction, and longitudinal well-being: The self-concordance model. *Journal of Personality and Social Psychology, 76*, 482-497.

Shepard, B., & Marshall, A. (1999). Possible selves mapping: Life-career exploration with young adolescents. *Canadian Journal of Counselling, 33*(1), 37–54. ISSN: ISSN-0828-3893

Sica, L. S., Crocetti, E., Ragozini, G., Aleni Sestito, L., & Serafini, T. (2016). Future-oriented or present-focused? The role of social support and identity styles on 'futuring'in Italian late adolescents and emerging adults. *Journal ofYouth Studies, 19*(2), 183–203. doi:10.1080/13676261.2015.1059925

Sica, L. S., Di Palma, T., & Aleni Sestito, L. (2016, September). *Narrative vocational identity: Mapping possible selves.* Poster presented to the 15th Biennial Conference of the European Association for Research on Adolescence, Spain.

Sica, L. S., Sestito, L. A., & Ragozini, G. (2014). Identity coping in the first years of university: Identity diffusion, adjustment and identity distress. *Journal of Adult Development, 21*(3), 159–172. doi:10.1007/s10804-014-9188-8

Skorikov, V. B., & Vondracek, F. W. (2007). Vocational identity. In V. B. Skorikov & W. Patton (Eds.), *Career development in childhood and adolescence* (pp. 143–168). Rotterdam: Sense Publishers.

Skorikov, V. B., & Vondracek, F. W. (2011). Occupational identity. In S. J. Schwartz, K. Luyckx, & V. L. Vignoles (Eds.), *Handbook of identity theory and research* (pp. 693–714). New York, NY: Springer. doi: 10.1007/978-1-4419-7988-9_29

Tsang, S. K., Hui, E. K., & Law, B. (2012). Positive identity as a positive youth development construct: A conceptual review. *The Scientific World Journal, 1*, 1–8. doi:10.1100/2012/529691

Vansteenkiste, M., Zhou, M., Lens, W., & Soenens, B. (2005). Experiences of autonomy and control among Chinese learners: Vitalizing or immobilizing? *Journal of Educational Psychology, 97*, 468–483.

Vondracek, F. W., & Schulenberg, J. E. (1986). Career development in adolescence: Some conceptual and intervention issues. *Vocational Guidance Quarterly, 34*(4), 247–254. doi:10.1002/j.2164-585X.1986.tb00860.x

Wallace-Broscious, A., Serafica, F. C., & Osipio, S. H. (1994). Adolescent career development: Relationship to self-concept and identity status. *Journal of Research on Adolescence, 4*(1), 127–149. doi:10.1207/s15327795jra0401_7

Zarrett, N., & Eccles, J. (2006). The passage to adulthood: Challenges of late adolescence. *New Directions for Youth Development, 111*, 13–28. doi:10.1002/yd.179

Chapter 9

Gender-sensitive career counseling

An innovative approach

Elisabetta Camussi, Chiara Annovazzi, Lorenzo Montali, and Maria Cristina Ginevra

Equality and inequality between men and women in Western countries

Significant social changes and affirmative action policies that have occurred in the last three decades in the Western world have still not reduced status differences and inequalities between men and women (Camussi, Annovazzi, & Montali, 2016). According to the European Institute for Gender Equality (2015), the mean Gender Equality Index in European countries on a scale from 0 (total inequality) to 100 (total equality) is 54.0.

Although the gap between male and female employment rates has declined since early 2008 (given that the economic crisis in Europe had a greater impact on men), the employment rate for women in 2014 (59.5%) remained lower than that for men (70.1%; EUROSTAT, 2015).

Women are still significantly underrepresented in traditionally male fields of employment, such as science, technology, engineering, and mathematics (STEM), as revealed in the European Commission's "She figures 2015" report (2016) showing that across the EU-28 countries, women constitute only 40.58% of the labor force in STEM. In addition, women are still underrepresented in top academic decision-making positions, suggesting a gender inequality in research and innovation, an area that is crucial for economic growth.

Furthermore, young women are at a greater disadvantage in the current job landscape marked by precariousness, globalization, unpredictability, and economic recession (Savickas et al., 2009), experiencing greater difficulty in accessing the labor market (horizontal segregation), gender inequality in promotions and salary (vertical segregation), as well as career barriers such as work/life (im) balance and double burden (Camussi & Annovazzi, 2016).

Therefore, as the EU Research and Innovation program "Horizon 2020" has specified, realization of gender equity remains a major challenge. This question seems particularly important, as young European adults are unprepared to recognize and contrast gender stereotypes and discriminations because of the widespread presence of the "free to choose" rhetoric – i.e. the common, but incorrect, belief that gender inequalities no longer exist (Andersen & Collins, 2015).

Given these premises, the present chapter examines the effect of gender stereotypes on occupational choices and discusses intervention strategies that counselors can use to address such stereotypes. In addition, we propose a new methodological and conceptual approach to overcoming gender stereotypes that involves career counselors in a wider process of public engagement. This approach aims to promote social behavioral changes regarding gender issues in large numbers of people at affordable costs.

Gender stereotypes and occupational choices

Gender differences observed in occupational choices may be due to occupational gender stereotypes that are internalized by individuals (Camussi, Montali, Colombo, Pirovano, & Grosso Gonçalves, 2009). These gender stereotypes concern beliefs regarding occupational roles and the types of training men and women should take on. These stereotypes act in two main ways: first, they describe expectations with respect to men's and women's occupational roles so as to promote a "lack of fit" between stereotypical attributes that women/men are thought to possess and the characteristics considered essential to succeed in typical gender-typed jobs (Burgess & Borgida, 1999). Second, stereotypes are prescriptive: they establish expectations of men's and women's occupational roles, causing a devaluation in those who do not respect these gender norms (Burgess & Borgida, 1999).

As a result, occupational gender stereotypes can significantly affect career choices by promoting distorted beliefs about education, training, and the labor market, thus influencing perceptions of viable occupational options and discouraging individuals from enterprising educational and occupational pathways considered unsuitable for their gender (Eccles, 2011). However, as shown by statistics on employment rates (EUROSTAT, 2015), these cognitive and social processes penalize women more than men (Caleo & Heilman, 2013).

Research carried out since 1970 in Western countries has found that as a result of descriptive gender stereotypes, adolescents and young adults prefer and tend to opt for occupations they perceive as being most suitable to their own gender (Gadassi & Gati, 2009). For example, Ji, Lapan, and Tate (2004) found that adolescents perceived realistic, investigative and enterprising occupations as more suited to the male gender, while, conversely, social, artistic, and enterprising occupations were seen as more appropriate for the female gender. In line with their stereotypes, boys and girls preferred and had perceived abilities (self-efficacy beliefs) for traditionally male and female occupations.

In a more recent study involving Italian adolescents, Ginevra and Nota (2015) found that given a list of 23 emerging jobs in the area of the "new economy" (e.g. software engineer and webmaster) and traditional jobs in the health and education sectors (e.g. nurse, occupational therapist), both girls and boys perceived almost 60% of the jobs as gender-stereotyped and gender-segregated. Specifically, adolescents saw emerging professions, which are generally characterized by the lowest unemployment rates, the highest social prestige, the greatest career prospects, and the best salaries, as male-stereotyped and male-segregated jobs. On the other hand, traditional jobs were perceived as female gender-stereotyped and female-segregated. Consequently, adolescents expressed career interests in line with the degree to which an occupation was perceived as appropriately gender-stereotyped and congruently gender-segregated.

Given prescriptive occupational gender stereotypes, research has further found that men and women who engage in counter-stereotypical occupations tend to face personal derogation in terms of a devaluation of their characteristics and performance (Heilman, Wallen, Fuchs, & Tamkins, 2004). For example, studies have shown that women in masculine occupations tend to experience penalties that endanger their career progress, such as reduced salary, less intention to hire and promote, and fewer references for organizational rewards (Caleo & Heilman, 2013). Similarly, men in female-typed jobs, such as teachers working in kindergarten and primary school, incur professional devaluation, resulting in penalties and disapproval (Erden, Ozgun, & Ciftci, 2011).

Approaches and interventions in gender-sensitive counseling to overcome gender stereotypes

Gender-sensitive counseling is not a theory of counseling but rather a conceptualizing perspective when working with clients that is valid in different theoretical approaches and emphasizes the need to examine gender issues in counseling.

Two different issues are at stake in gender-specific counseling. The first concerns a counselor's beliefs about the roles men and women have to play in the educational and labor markets, and how these beliefs could impact the counselor's everyday practice (Bhargava & Sriram, 2016); the second involves clients' stereotyped beliefs and, consequently, strategies and suggestions that counselors could use in their activities to support their clients' occupational choices.

Counselor's perspective

Fretz (1981) was the first to point out the need for the counselor to develop her/his gender awareness, given the relevance of gender in occupational and career choices. In this respect, Romano, Goh, and Wahl (2005) argued that counselors should reach a full understanding of the cultural context in which they operate by analyzing the social expectations for boys and girls and by focalizing on individuals' belief about gender. However, despite these suggestions, the importance of gender in career counseling still has to be fully recognized (Swanson & O'Brien, 2002).

Three kind of counselor style regarding gender issues can be identified (Equal Success Stories, 2009):

- Gender blindness: Counselors tend to act with cultural preconceptions and biases about the roles of men and women and do not consider the gender issue in their counseling practice. This occurs, for example, when counselors, albeit inadvertently, encourage acceptance of the status quo, fail to discuss gender roles, and miss issues of gender discrimination. As Lonborg and Hackett (2006) stated, counselors who treat clients in a gender-blind way often contribute to maintaining and reinforcing gender stereotypes.

- Gender neutrality: Gender is not considered a resource and clients (both girls and boys) receive the same consulting. In this approach, counselors observe the principle of equal treatment of men and women very strictly and provide career counseling to individuals without considering their gender. They work only on the client's ideas and projects – often influenced by gender stereotypes – without introducing any new non-stereotyped ideas.
- Gender consciousness: Counselors consider gender as a fundamental factor in occupational choices and are aware of gender barriers to individuals' occupational choices. They believe it is possible to modify the social and work environment rather than merely adapting their clients to the environment. Counselors do not limit themselves to stereotypical choices, but discuss multiple options and possible alternatives with their clients. Moreover, as suggested by Good, Gilbert, and Scher (1990), counselors sensitive to gender consider client problems within their social context, actively addressing gender injustices and respecting clients' freedom of career choice.

In this third case, counselors must become aware of their gender expectations and assumptions, as gender stereotypes are implicit. To this end, counselors should engage in a process of self-reflection regarding their own gender prejudices, so that they can offer ethical and appropriate counseling to both women and men, especially to those clients whose perspectives and career decisions significantly differ from those of the counselor (Kocet & Herlihy, 2014). Once the counselors have focused on this self-reflection process, they can genuinely help their clients to question their own gender expectations and to explore occupational representations and roles beyond gender stereotypes (Lonborg & Hackett, 2006).

Clients' perspective

Several suggestions and strategies can be found in the literature and used by career counselors to modify and restructure their clients' gender-stereotyped beliefs. In an experimental setting, a meta-analysis by Lenton, Bruder, and Sedikides (2009) suggested three categories of interventions to reduce clients' gender stereotypes. The first category involves interventions that inhibit stereotype activation, promoting a higher level of engagement with the stimulus category before a task/activity. For example, Johns, Schmader, and Martens (2005) found that informing women before a difficult math test about a stereotype threat and providing a means to explain the anxiety that might be experienced allows candidates to improve their performance. The second category of interventions activates the gender stereotype, emphasizing individuals' attention toward the counter-stereotypical aspect or subtype and, in this way, highlighting the inconsistency of the stereotypical representation. For example, Lenton, Sedikides, and Bruder (2009) asked individuals to think of a counter-stereotypical image of the woman (a strong woman) before an implicit assessment of gender stereotypes. The third category of interventions seeks to train individuals so that stereotype expression, but not necessarily stereotype activation, can be prevented or inhibited. For example, Boccato, Corneille, and Yzerbyt (2006) trained participants to "just say no" when they were presented in a gender-stereotypical way.

This meta-analysis provides several useful practical implications that can be used in career counseling activities aimed at restructuring and modifying individuals' gender stereotypical beliefs. Regarding the first category of interventions, counselors could inform individuals of the negative consequences of gender stereotypes, stimulating their awareness of social and cultural factors that can influence their occupational decisions before they make career decisions.

For the second category, clients can be provided with counter-stereotypical information, using movies, stories, and pictures stimulating exposure to non-traditional models, and can be encouraged to reflect on different occupational roles that do not inevitably overlap "stereotyped patterns" (Ginevra & Nota, 2017). In several studies (e.g. Abedi, Noorbala, & Saeedi, 2010), this latter strategy has been found useful in reducing gender-stereotyped beliefs in the labor market.

Last, with the third category, counselors can help clients to avoid stereotypical self-presentations in the workplace and recognize stereotypic associations between personal attributes and occupational characteristics by training them to analyze occupations through accurate job analyses rather than basing their assessments on stereotypical traits.

Additionally, Romano et al. (2005) argued that a career counselor should not only encourage non-stereotyped beliefs and behaviors, but that he/she should also provide specific strategies to support non-stereotyped choices. For example, it is useful to train individuals to defend their rights in an assertive way, to clarify the pros and cons of their choice, and to seek social support to reach their career goals. Betz (2008) stated that this is particularly important for young people who experience gender discrimination. They should be helped to seek supporters (e.g. family members, peers, mentors, and teachers) who do not adhere to stereotyped visions of the labor market.

A new approach: implementing widespread gender-sensitive methods

As highlighted in the previous paragraph, even when counselors are aware of the need to hinder gender stereotypes, they still need to support their clients' new perspectives and help them to realize their goals (Liotard, 2012; Morgan,

2017). Specifically, career interventions on gender stereotypes generally operate only individually or on small groups and therefore do not influence the overall social context, which unknowingly tends to reproduce stereotyped beliefs, rather than deconstruct them (Heilman & Eagly, 2008).

Hence, there is a strong need for an innovative, interdisciplinary, and more effective, but still economically viable, approach to gender issues that can promote a change in attitudes and behaviors (Joshi, 2015). In order to exert a systematic influence on large groups of young adults and, ultimately, on society overall, interventions must operate on several levels with synergistic actions that along with career counselors also include parents, teachers, and mentors.

Unlike interventions for the general public – e.g. experts' conferences or public communication campaigns – public engagement actions that promote involvement are useful to change individuals' and groups' attitudes and behaviors (Simon & Klandermans, 2001).

To encourage public engagement and social behavioral changes on gender issues in young adults and society, a "bottom up" and "participatory" approach acting through the three fundamental dimensions of public engagement – awareness, activation, and participation – can be implemented (Camussi & Gangemi, 2016). This conceptual and methodological approach has already been applied in the healthcare sector by the international Hacking Health network (Camussi & Gangemi, 2016). This network has involved professionals with different expertise (e.g. doctors, designers, developers, engineers, and psychologists) and has obtained realistic and human-centric technological solutions to frontline healthcare problems (www.hackinghealthmilano.it).

The promotion of social innovation via technology is based on theoretical and methodological assumptions that may make the approach useful in different processes of social change, such as those to tackle gender stereotypes and to promote solutions and tools to handle gender biases and constraints. Specifically, it is an interdisciplinary approach, bringing together the general public, researchers, and experts from different disciplines to address a complex social problem, such as the gender issue, from different perspectives, therefore advancing the knowledge base and suggesting solutions (Bruce, Lyall, Tait, & Williams, 2004). As in the case of the healthcare project, tools and methods from other research areas, such as *World Cafés* (Brown & Isaacs, 2005), *Service Design Thinking* (Brown, 2009), and *Hackathons* (Briscoe, 2014) can also be exploited in gender questions, to obtain greater public awareness of gender stereotypes in education, training, and the workplace through bottom-up solutions and participatory activities to create "devices" that are easily reusable on a large scale and effectively address critical issues in people's real lives. Furthermore, the proposed approach makes massive use of group interventions, bringing people together via group discussion (Cafés) and group decisions (Barcamps, Generative Laboratories). This methodology is more effective than public campaigns and conferences in ensuring not only greater awareness but making behavioral changes durable (Simon & Klandermans, 2001). In fact, when people are involved in groups led by an experienced guide, they generate the motivation to act and to change attitudes and behaviors. As already mentioned, the psychosocial "bottom up" and "participative" approaches are two key features of the public engagement framework, which starts from participants' everyday experiences so as to be certain that group members become active, committed, and motivated participants. Rather than receiving standard solutions, participants become both change-actors and recipients by building meanings and solutions together (Cohn & Fredrickson, 2010).

Another key element in the approach is the Design Thinking method (Brown & Wyatt, 2015), on which the approach is based. This method can be considered as a process to address open and complex innovation problems in many professions, most notably information technology (IT) and business, and more recently also the social field (Brown & Wyatt, 2015). It is conceptualized as a system of three overlapping spaces, rather than a sequence of fixed steps: *inspiration*, i.e. the motivation to find solutions to a problem; *ideation*, i.e. the process of producing, developing, and examining ideas; and *implementation* of the identified solution into people's lives (Brown & Wyatt, 2015).

Here, the Design Thinking method is further combined with psychosocial qualitative methodologies (e.g. ethnographic observations, narrative interviews; Smith, 2015), as this "mixed" perspective is considered ideal to address complex, multifactorial, and ill-defined problems, such as gender stereotypes, which need to be "shaped" by involving people who experience such obstacles (visible and invisible) directly in their real lives. Based on these assumptions, specific activities on gender issues could be organized around the three main objectives of public engagement: awareness, activation, and participation (see Figure 9.1).

As this approach to gender issues has not yet been applied, the timeline (about 10 months) and the number of people involved in each phase is derived from similar projects that use public engagement to address social issues and

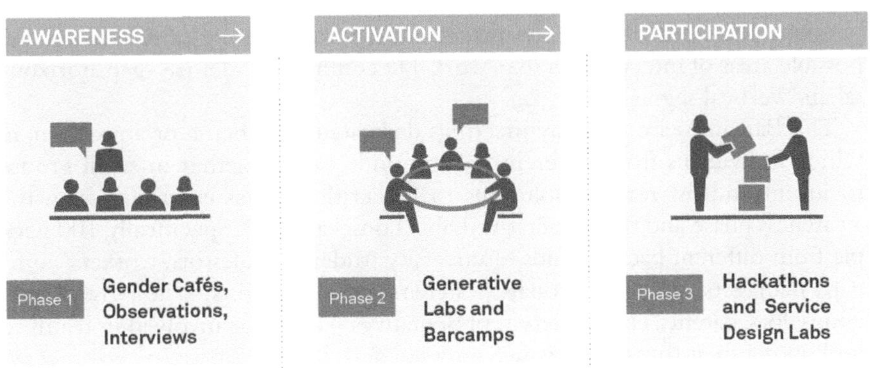

Figure 9.1 Overview of the conceptual and methodological approach to public engagement on gender issues

generate long-lasting innovation (Camussi & Gangemi, 2016; www.hacking healthmilano.it).

The first phase would seek to increase public *awareness* regarding gender stereotypes in education, training, and the workplace through debates held in Gender Cafés and participatory activities, such as ethnographic observations and interviews to present, discuss, and re-shape the state-of-the-art directly with the target groups. Specifically, Gender Cafés, derived from the World Café Method (Brown & Isaacs, 2005), constitute a means to encourage participation from a broad range of persons in collecting and sharing information, comparing stories and experiences, or imaging scenarios for a different future. For the issue of gender, three or four Gender Cafés supervised by career counselors could be promoted for groups of 40–50 participants (e.g. young people, practitioners, parents, workers, company managers, and the general public). In addition, career counselors could conduct interviews and observations with participants in educational and work contexts, as this can constitute an "ecological" method to understand both the implicit and explicit meanings of the actions (interview; Bates, 2005) and to observe actions and behaviors within the natural contexts in which these actions take place day-by-day (observations; Smith, 2015).

The second phase would focus on the *activation* of targets by encouraging reflection and ideas through the implementation of group interventions to identify ways to recognize and reduce gender stereotypes and discrimination within everyday life. Three Generative Laboratories and one Barcamp could be proposed under the supervision of career counselors in the role of facilitators. The Generative Laboratories are discussion/decision groups that seek to analyze, interpret, and elaborate on the information collected from the Cafés, interviews and ethnographic observations, and aggregate the identified critical elements into major clusters (relatively homogeneous macro-areas of critical issues and possibilities for intervention) (Pallot, Trousse, Senach, & Scapin, 2010). Using this methodology, about 100 young people could be involved in multidisciplinary teams, and invited to analyze the stimuli elaborated in the previous phase and to generate macro-clusters representing critical issues and possible areas of intervention (e.g. work-life conflicts, gender pay-gap, horizontal and vertical segregation, etc.).

The Barcamps are one-day meetings dedicated to a theme or a problem, in which individuals from different backgrounds work together in small groups to invent and list realistic solutions to the critical issues emerging from the awareness phase and the Generative Labs (Fonseca, 2011). Specifically, 100 people from different backgrounds – university students, professors, workers, company managers, HR professionals, designers, anthropologists, sociologists, career counselors, parents, civil society representatives – could be involved in teams to look in depth at the gender issue.

Last, the third phase would be dedicated to the promotion of *participation* in the planning of realizable solutions and tools to address concrete problems in gender issues through Hackathon events and Service Design Labs that aim to implement and distribute potential (technological) solutions at a collective level.

A Hackathon is a problem-focused programming experience, as well as a tournament to program and provide examples of prototype digital innovations. Programmers and other professionals (e.g. interface designers, graphic designers) collaborate intensively over a short period of time to produce valid and concrete solutions (artifacts and prototypes) to a crucial social problem (Richard, Kafai, Adleberg, & Telhan, 2015). Hackathons are increasingly emerging in the literature as an effective method to promote innovation through digital technologies in a large range of different fields, while offering professionals an opportunity to collaborate and create new medium- to long-term professional relations (Briscoe, 2014). Therefore, a multidisciplinary environment involving individuals with different expertise (e.g. computer programmers, interface designers, project managers, psychologists, company managers, career counselors, researchers, etc.) could be proposed to promote intense collaboration over a short period (two days) and develop innovative ideas on gender issues. Service Design Labs, on the other hand, are participatory design labs in which a number of Hackathon prototypes are further developed into working products and services in real-life contexts (Björgvinsson, Ehn, & Hillgren, 2010). Here, the solutions proposed in the earlier stages can be seen as a process for change in developing services, systems, and environments that can support social behavioral changes. Those projects from the Hackathons that career counselors involved in gender issues consider the most promising could be further developed (e.g. new career guidance tools, e-learning devices) and made accessible to virtually unlimited numbers of recipients (e.g. university students, teachers, educators, employers, managers, career guidance professionals, the general public). Specifically, a "collection of training pills" (e.g. new Career Guidance services and tools, e-learning materials, physical products with gender implications) could be designed for university students, which would also be valuable for teachers, educators, workers, company managers, trade unions and, ultimately, the general public.

Conclusion

This chapter has analyzed the effect of gender stereotypes on young adults' occupational choices, and intervention strategies to address this issue. We have also presented a methodological and conceptual approach to promote among young adults, and in society as a whole, public engagement and social behavioral changes regarding gender issues that will hopefully encourage a democratic environment for both genders.

During all three phases of the proposed approach, career counselors play a key role as agents of change seeking to promote greater social equity and sustainable and productive employment opportunities for both men and women. In this respect, it is particularly important that career counselors should be prepared to use multiple strategies and approaches in setting up small and group activities and interventions to supervise, train, and sensitize other professionals. They should be able to collaborate with researchers and practitioners from social, political, and STEM fields, and share the respective scientific language, to increase the probability of achieving specific results, producing *artifacts* and proposing concrete responses to important gender issues in people's lives. Counselors should have a good understanding (not necessarily an in-depth knowledge) of the various discipline domains involved in the phases, a wide-ranging career trajectory, and a broad range of interests, flexibility and creativity, an open mind to ideas from other disciplines and experiences, social and team-building skills, and a proactive approach to other professionals (Bruce et al., 2004).

References

Abedi, F. H., Noorbala, F., & Saeedi, Z. (2010). Stereotypical beliefs about sex role-typed occupations and the mediating effect of exposure to counterstereotypic examples in Iranian students. *Procedia-Social and Behavioral Sciences, 5*, 1425–1428.

Andersen, M., & Collins, P. H. (2015). *Race, class, & gender: An anthology*. Scarborough, North Yorkshire, Canada: Nelson Education.

Bates, J. A. (2005). Use of narrative interviewing in everyday information behavior research. *Library & Information Science Research, 26*(1), 15–28.

Betz, N. E. (2008). Women's career development. In S. D. Brown & R. W. Lent (Eds.), *Career development and counseling: Putting theory and research to work* (pp. 253–277). Hoboken, NJ: John Wiley.

Bhargava, S., & Sriram, S. (2016). Counselor characteristics and the counseling experience. In S. Sriram (Ed.), *Counseling in India: Reflections on the process* (pp. 13–33). New York, NY: Springer.

Björgvinsson, E., Ehn, P., & Hillgren, P. A. (2010, November). Participatory design and democratizing innovation. In T. Robertson (Ed.), *Proceedings of the 11th Biennial participatory design conference* (pp. 41–50). New York, NY: ACM.

Boccato, G., Corneille, O., & Yzerbyt, V. (2006). *Just say no: Effects of training in the negation of non-stereotypic associations on stereotype activation*. Unpublished manuscript, Universitè Catholique de Louvain, Belgium.

Briscoe, G. (2014). *Digital innovation: The hackathon phenomenon*. Retrieved from http://qmro.qmul.ac.uk/xmlui/handle/123456789/11418

Brown, J., & Isaacs, D. (2005). *The world Café: Shaping our futures through conversation that matter.* San Francisco, CA: Berreth-Koelher.

Brown, T. (2009). Change by design: How design thinking transforms organizations and inspires innovation. New York, NY: HarperCollins Publishers.

Brown, T., & Wyatt, J. (2015). Design thinking for social innovation. *Annual Review of Policy Design, 3*(1), 1–10.

Bruce, A., Lyall, C., Tait, J., & Williams, R. (2004). Interdisciplinary integration in Europe: The case of the Fifth Framework programme. *Futures, 36*(4), 457–470.

Burgess, D., & Borgida, E. (1999). Who women are, who women should be: Descriptive and prescriptive gender stereotyping in sex discrimination. *Psychology, Public Policy, and Law, 5*(3), 665–692.

Caleo, S., & Heilman, M. E. (2013). Gender stereotypes and their implications for women's career progress. In S.Vinnicombe, R. J. Burke, S. Blake-Beard, & L. L. Moore (Eds.), *Handbook of research on promoting women's careers* (pp. 143–161). Camberley, Surrey, UK: Edward Elgar Publishing.

Camussi, E., & Annovazzi, C. (2016). A proposito di (im)pari opportunità tra uomini e donne: la questione del "Gender Pay Gap" [About (un)equal opportunities between men and women: The "Gender Pay Gap" issue. In A. Quadrio & D. Pajardi (Eds.), *La Società ri-pensata* [The re-thought Society] (pp. 41–60). Milano: EDRA.

Camussi, E., Annovazzi, C., & Montali, L. (2016). Coraggio, futuro e differenze di genere [Courage, future and gender differences]. In S. Soresi, L. Nota, & M. C. Ginevra (Eds.), *Le funzioni del counseling: criticità, prospettive ed applicazioni [The function of counseling: Critical issues, perspectives and applications]* (pp. 157–166). Firenze, IT: Hoegrefe Editore.

Camussi, E., & Gangemi, S. (2016, October). *Orientamento e innovazione: l'esperienza di Hacking Health [Vocational guidance and innovation: The Hacking Health experience].* Symposium conducted at the XVI Congress of SIO-Italian Society of Career Guidance, University of Milano-Bicocca, Milano, IT.

Camussi, E., Montali, L., Colombo, C., Pirovano, A., & Grosso Gonçalves, V. E. S. (2009). Masculinity and femininity in gender-specific professions: A social representation perspective study. In P. Gaborit (Ed.), *Les stéréotypes de genre* (pp. 129–162). Paris: L'Harmattan.

Cohn, M. A., & Fredrickson, B. L. (2010). In search of durable positive psychology interventions: Predictors and consequences of long-term positive behavior change. *The Journal of Positive Psychology, 5*(5), 355–366.

Eccles, J. S. (2011). Understanding women's achievement choices looking back and looking forward. *Psychology of Women Quarterly, 35*(3), 510–516.

Equal Success Stories. (2009). *Report: Overcoming gender blindness in career guidance.* Roskilde: Research Centre on Gender Equality.

Erden, S., Ozgun, O., & Ciftci, M. A. (2011). "I am a man, but I am a pre-school education teacher": Self-and social-perception of male pre-school teachers. *Procedia-Social and Behavioral Sciences, 15*, 3199–3204.

European Commission. (2016). *She figures 2015 report. Gender in research and innovation.* Luxembourg: Publications Office of the European Union.

European Institute for Gender Equality-EIGE. (2015). *Gender equality index: Measuring gender equality in the European Union* 2005–2012. Luxemburg: Publications Office of the European Union.

Eurostat – Statistical Office of the European Communities. (2015). *Regional statistics: Reference guide.* Luxembourg: Eurostat.

Fonseca, D. E. L. (2011). EduCamp Colombia: Social networked learning for teacher training. *The International Review of Research in Open and Distributed Learning, 12*(3), 60–79.

Fretz, B. R. (1981). Evaluating the effectiveness of career interventions. *Journal of Counseling Psychology, 28*(1), 77–90.

Gadassi, R., & Gati, I. (2009). The effect of gender stereotypes on explicit and implicit career preferences. *The Counseling Psychologist, 37*(6), 902–922.

Ginevra, M. C., & Nota, L. (2017). Occupational gender stereotypes and problem-solving in Italian adolescents. *British Journal of Guidance & Counseling, 45*(3), 312–327. 6.

Good, G. E., Gilbert, L. A., & Scher, M. (1990). Gender aware therapy: A synthesis of feminist therapy and knowledge about gender. *Journal of Counseling Development, 68*, 376–380.

Heilman, M. E., & Eagly, A. H. (2008). Gender stereotypes are alive, well, and busy producing workplace discrimination. *Industrial and Organizational Psychology, 1*(4), 393–398.

Heilman, M. E., Wallen, A. S., Fuchs, D., & Tamkins, M. M. (2004). Penalties for success: Reactions to women who succeed at male gender-typed tasks. *Journal of Applied Psychology, 89*(3), 416–427.

Ji, P.Y., Lapan, R. T., & Tate, K. (2004). Vocational interests and career efficacy expectations in relation to occupational sex-typing beliefs for eighth grade students. *Journal of Career Development, 31*(2), 143–154.

Johns, M., Schmader, T., & Martens, A. (2005). Knowing is half the battle: Teaching stereotype threat as a means of improving women's math performance. *Psychological Science, 16*, 175–179.

Joshi, A. (2015). Need for gender sensitive counseling interventions in India. *Psychological Studies, 60*(3), 346–355.

Kocet, M. M., & Herlihy, B. J. (2014). Addressing value-based conflicts within the counseling relationship: A decision-making model. *Journal of Counseling & Development, 92*(2), 180–186.

Lenton, A. P., Bruder, M., & Sedikides, C. (2009). A meta-analysis on the malleability of automatic gender stereotypes. *Psychology of Women Quarterly, 33*(2), 183–196.

Lenton, A. P., Sedikides, C., & Bruder, M. (2009). A latent semantic analysis of gender stereotype-consistency and narrowness in American English. *Sex Roles, 60*, 269–278.

Liotard, K. T. (2012). *On eliminating gender stereotypes in the EU.* Report of the Committee on Women's Rights and Gender Equality. Retrieved from www.europarl.europa.eu/sides/get

Lonborg, S. D., & Hackett, G. (2006). Career assessment and counseling for women. In W. B. Walsh & M. J. Heppner (Eds.), *Handbook of career counseling for women* (2nd ed., pp. 103–116). Hillsdale, NJ: Lawrence Erlbaum.

Morgan, M. S. (2017). Glass ceilings and sticky floors: Drawing new ontologies. In K. Chemla & E. Fox Keller (Eds.), *Cultures without culturalism in the making of scientific knowledge.* Durham, NC: Duke University Press.

Pallot, M., Trousse, B., Senach, B., & Scapin, D. (2010). *Living lab research landscape: From user centred design and user experience towards user cocreation.* Retrieved from https://hal.inria.fr/inria-00612632/document

Richard, G. T., Kafai, Y. B., Adleberg, B., & Telhan, O. (2015, February). StitchFest: Diversifying a College Hackathon to broaden participation and perceptions in computing. In *Proceedings of the 46th ACM Technical Symposium on Computer Science Education* (pp. 114–119). ACM.

Romano, J. L., Goh, M., & Wahl, K. H. (2005). School counseling in the United States: Implications for the Asia-Pacific region. *Asia Pacific Education Review, 6*(2), 113–123.

Savickas, M. L., Nota, L., Rossier, J., Dauwalder, J. P., Duarte, M. E., Guichard, J., . . . Van Vianen, A. E. (2009). Life designing: A paradigm for career construction in the 21st century. *Journal of Vocational Behaviour, 75*(3), 239–250.

Simon, B., & Klandermans, B. (2001). Politicized collective identity: A social psychological analysis. *American Psychologist, 56*(4), 319–331.

Smith, J. A. (Ed.). (2015). Qualitative psychology: A practical guide to research methods. London: Sage.

Swanson, J. L., & O'Brien, K. M. (2002). Training career counselors: Meeting the challenges of clients in the 21st century. In S. G. Niles (Ed.), *Adult career development: Concepts, issues and practices* (3rd ed., pp. 354–369). Washington, DC: National Career Development Association.

Chapter 10

Improving expertise in career counseling and coaching

Terence J. G. Tracey

There is a growing literature demonstrating that career counseling and coaching are effective. Career counseling interventions have been demonstrated to be effective in several literature reviews (Flynn, 1994; Fretz, 1981; Holland, Magoon, & Spokane, 1981; Myers, 1986; Swanson, 1995) and meta-analyses (Brown & Ryan Krane, 2000; Oliver & Spokane, 1988; Spokane & Oliver, 1983; Whiston, Brecheisen, & Stephens, 2003; Whiston, Sexton, & Lasoff, 1998). Although there is less of a history of examining the effectiveness of coaching, a recent meta-analysis has demonstrated that it too is effective on a variety of outcomes (Theeboom, Beersma, & van Vianen, 2014).

There is a wide variety of career interventions that have been used and Whiston et al. (2003) found that those interventions that involved counselors were the most effective. Counselors, thus, are a key element in the provision of career interventions. Given this centrality of counselors in the interventions, an examination of what makes counselors skilled is warranted. Of specific interest is Whiston et al.'s (1998) finding that counselors in training had better outcomes than experienced counselors, which runs counter to the expectation that those more experienced should demonstrate better outcomes. So it appears that while our interventions are successful, especially those involving counselors, the most effective counselors appear to be those with less experience. This outcome superiority of those less experienced mirrors similar results from the psychotherapeutic literature (e.g., Budge et al., 2013). Given the similarity of tasks and processes among career counseling, coaching and psychotherapy, it is not surprising that there are similar results with respect to the failure of more experienced practitioners to have better outcomes.

Within the psychotherapy literature, there has been recent attention (Tracey, Wampold, Lichtenberg, & Goodyear, 2014; Tracey, Wampold, Goodyear, & Lichtenberg, 2015) on the lack of expertise for the profession of psychotherapy. This conclusion is based on the work of Shanteau (1992; Shanteau & Weiss, 2014) who defined expertise at the professional level as performance improvement with experience. While his analysis did not include career counseling or coaching, many professions did not demonstrate expertise using this definition, clinical psychology among them. The key defining issue involved in this assessment of expertise is demonstrated outcomes. Do outcomes improve with greater experience? With regard to psychotherapy, the literature indicates that they do not (Budge et al., 2013; Goldberg et al., 2016). Like the literature in career counseling and coaching, the literature on psychotherapeutic effectiveness is strong (Lambert & Ogles, 2004; Smith & Glass, 1977; Wampold, 2001a, 2001b) so there is not a concern with the quality of interventions themselves. The focus rests on the increase in performance among practitioners with experience.

Shanteau's (1992) focus is on the profession as a whole. Certainly, it is possible, or even probable, that there are individuals who have achieved expertise in career counseling and coaching. However, this attainment of expertise does not appear to be related to experience as a rule. Those with more experience do not have demonstrated superiority in performance and within individuals, increased experience over time is not associated with gains in performance. Shanteau and Weiss (2014) note that performance can be defined either internally to the profession as in acting according to accepted protocols, or externally via evidence of effectiveness. In professions without the ability to demonstrate effectiveness, adherence to internal protocol can be used as a definition of professional performance, but this is a much weaker criterion. The example they give is astrology where one can be viewed as having high performance by adhering to certain behaviors in generating predictions; however, the external criterion of accuracy is lacking. So the best means of establishing expertise is via demonstrated performance on key aspects of practice and outcomes. Expertise is thus evident when increased professional experience results in increased quality of professional performance as indicated by demonstrated performance outcomes.

It would be expected that increased practice would result in increased performance. Indeed, this is a general assumption in learning. Interacting with more and different clients should provide a fuller knowledge base, added learning, and opportunity to develop added skills. Yet this does not occur. With respect to clinical decision making (the ability of clinicians to make accurate diagnoses and treatment prognostications), the literature has demonstrated that those with more experience are not any better than novices (and in some cases worse) (Dawes, 1994). How more experienced clinicians differ from less experienced ones is that they are more certain of their accuracy even though in actuality they are not more accurate (Ægisdóttir et al., 2006; Dawes, 1994; Garb, 1989, 2005; Goldberg, 1968; Spengler et al., 2009; Strasser & Gruber, 2004; Witteman & Van den Bercken, 2007; Witterman, Weiss, & Metzmacher, 2012). Clinicians do not have an accurate assessment of their ability. Walfish, McAlister, O'Donnell, and Lambert (2012) asked clinicians to rate anonymously where they stood relative to other clinicians with respect to skill and outcome and everyone rated themselves as above average with 25% viewing themselves in the top 10%. So not only are those more experienced not better in professional performance, they are also less perceptive of their overall performance. This overconfidence has the less desirable effect of decreasing motivation to improve (Pintrich, 2003). Given the many similarities within psychotherapy, career counseling and coaching, it is probable that a similar state of affairs exits within career counseling and coaching.

Tracey et al. (2014) argue that this pattern of not being able to benefit from experience is the norm as indicted in the literature but that it is attributable in part to a lack of quality feedback of outcomes. Counselors get little quality feedback on their interventions. There is a dearth of reliable and valid instruments used to assess interventions. Measures, when used, are often homemade, narrow in scope, and not well validated. Quality information on effectiveness would entail obtaining information at termination and also later to assess the stability of effects. This is rarely done and almost never to provide feedback to individual practitioners. The key issue is that practitioners thus have little basis to know what worked or not with whom. There are three key types of feedback that are needed: across clients, across time and across practitioners.

Feedback across clients

At the simplest level, practitioners need to know the degree of effectiveness of their intervention. This would involve an assessment of gains in key variables between starting and ending the intervention. Are there gains demonstrated at the end of the intervention? Even better would be an assessment of long-term gains, say six months after the intervention was complete. Only by having such data can any practitioner know if indeed the intervention was successful.

There are two important aspects involved in this assessment of client gain: the specific variables examined and the determination of gain. If assessments are made, they often involve satisfaction measures (i.e., the extent to which an individual found the experience valuable). While these satisfaction measures are valuable, they tend to be skewed with most responses being very favorable. An additional measure would involve actual gains obtained in key outcomes, such as increased career choice certainty. To assess such outcomes would require the use of standardized measures that have norms that would provide information on the amount of gain. However, even these narrowly defined assessments could be inadequate because they provide a limited picture. Career counseling and coaching are viewed as encompassing interventions that can have broad effects. As such, the assessment should also incorporate several measures that capture an individual's functioning beyond just a narrow, specific outcome measure. For example, it is also important to assess overall functions by including both positive (e.g., satisfaction with life) and negative (symptomology). Did the intervention affect the client's quality of life? Being able to know general satisfaction, focused intervention effects and general functioning provides a complete assessment and crucial information to enable the practitioner to know the extent to which and where the intervention was helpful.

One problem of providing pre/post scores changes from clients to practitioners is that it is difficult to evaluate the magnitude or importance of the scores. How big a difference is needed for it to represent an important gain or important deleterious effect? To assist in this endeavor, it is desirable to use the clinically significant change score formula developed by Jacobson and Truax (1991). This formula provides an easy to calculate and use index to know when one has had a successful outcome. Adopting this clinically significant change definition for the various assessments (i.e., intervention specific, positive function and negative functioning indicators) enables accurate information on the extent to which any client changed, how much that client changed and the extent to which that client changed relative to other clients. All of these are essential pieces of information that facilitate altering behavior in the future to better adapt to and assist other clients.

Feedback over time

The assessment of final effectiveness is essential, but it is limited in that it is only based on final outcome assessments. It provides information on adjusting behavior for future clients but is limited in that it cannot be used with current clients. An important added source of outcome information is more formative assessments that involve periodic (e.g., daily or weekly) measurement where the practitioner can see the relative gains or losses in key outcomes over time and then make alterations in behavior to better achieve desired gains. Administering brief scales focused on key functioning (e.g., specific focus of the work, overall functioning) a symptomology instrument (e.g., Outcome Questionnaire, Vermeersch et al., 2004), and a process instrument such as the Working Alliance Inventory-Short (Tracey & Kokotovic, 1989) would yield information on the progress or lack thereof as it is transpiring. Changes in these measures over time would provide stimulus to alter behavior with the client. The benefits of providing periodic information on general functioning to psychotherapists have been supported (Duncan, Miller, Wampold, & Hubble, 2010; Lambert, Harmon, Slade, Whipple, & Hawkins, 2005; Lambert & Shimokawa, 2011; Miller, Duncan, & Hubble, 2005; Reese, Norsworthy, & Rowlands, 2009). A similar procedure where brief assessments of specific aspects of the intervention and overall functioning would prove of great assistance. Without such longitudinal information, the practitioner has little basis for deciding what is working well and what is not.

Feedback across practitioners

One reason that practitioners may overevaluate their own effectiveness is that it is relatively rare to obtain normative information on how well each practitioner does relative to others. It is rare for practitioners to get any information on the overall effectiveness of their work with any specific client but to get information regarding how well one's outcomes across clients compare to theirs is almost never done. Such information appears crucial in assisting the practitioner to know if indeed major alterations are needed. Without such feedback, practitioners can easily maintain inaccurate, and therefore unhelpful, assessments of their effectiveness. If I find that I am at the lower end of effectiveness relative to other career counselors, I will then become motivated to obtain new skills to enable better outcomes.

Deliberate practice

The overall point is that quality outcome information is required for any expertise to occur. Without quality information on effectiveness across clients, across time, and across practitioners, there will be no gain in expertise. Thus, quality effectiveness feedback is a necessary condition for the attainment of expertise. However, while such information is necessary, it is not sufficient. The research in expertise has demonstrated that deliberate practice is required (Ellis, Carette, Anseel, & Lievens, 2014; Ericsson, 2006, 2009). But it also is not simply the amount of time practicing but that the time needs to be spent in a reflective manner targeted at improving skills (Chow, Miller, Seidel, Kane, & Thornton, 2015). A recent study found that therapist perceptions of professional self-doubt were positively related to therapy outcome (Nissen-Lie, Monsen, Ulleberg, & Rønnestad, 2012) indicating that a self-critical approach to practice is beneficial. Tracey et al. (2014) argued that this deliberate, reflective practice that accompanies clinical work should manifest explicit hypothesis testing in a disconfirmatory manner, whereby common heuristics are minimized.

There is extensive literature on the use of heuristics (logical shortcuts) by clinicians and the relation of these to poor clinical decision making (e.g., Arkes, 1981; Dumont, 1991; Faust, 1991; Garb, 1998; Garb & Boyle, 2003; Goldberg, 1991; Salovey & Turk, 1991; Tracey & Rounds, 1999; Wierzbicki, 1993). The use of such shortcuts are human nature but care needs to be taken to limit their use in professional contexts. Tracey et al. (2014) noted the common recommendations to minimize these heuristics: (a) adopting a Bayesian approach by looking at base rates and the predictability of behavior, (b) obtaining quality information (e.g., relying on valid measures rather than clinical impressions), (c) relying less on memory, (d) recognizing personal biases and their effects, (e) being aware of regression to the mean where less extreme behavior follows extreme behavior, and (f) adopting a disconfirming, scientific approach to practice. Of these general recommendations, they highlighted the last, that of adopting a scientific, disconfirmatory approach to practice.

This disconfirmatory scientific approach incorporates three steps. First there should be explicit hypotheses generated. The practitioner has a conception of how the intervention is going and should make explicit predictions of client behavior based on such an understanding. Only by making explicit hypotheses can the practitioner know whether the conception of how the intervention is progressing is accurate or not. If one makes an explicit hypothesis and then gathers information on whether it is met or not, then the practitioner has information on the "correctness" of the hypothesis and the underlying theory used in deriving the hypothesis. For example, in the previous case where the practitioner gathers outcome information about the general effectiveness of an intervention by collecting measures at termination and then again six months later, seeing this information would certainly help the practitioner understand how the treatment went and perhaps validate his or her clinical impressions. However, in cases like this, the practitioner is prone to use the hindsight bias (Wedding & Faust, 1989) where after the "facts" are seen, people are prone to think that they knew all along. Such post-hoc bias does not lead to learning. For this outcome information to be more usable, an a priori approach is needed where the practitioner makes specific hypotheses about the amount of gain (or loss) on each measure at termination. The practitioner uses his or her understanding of the client and the work together to derive these hypotheses. Then these specific hypotheses can be examined when the data come in. Only by making explicit predictions will the practitioner avoid hindsight bias, where he or she knew all along how it would go, and get accurate information on the accuracy of his or her understanding of the client.

The second aspect is that the means of testing should be disconfirmatory in nature. People tend to seek confirmatory evidence for hypotheses or what they believe to be true (Kahneman, 2013). While it is commendable that individuals seek to confirm their beliefs, this confirmatory approach tends to be relatively ineffective as there often is a wealth of evidence for our beliefs but that such evidence could also be indicative of many other beliefs. In other words, confirmatory approaches often seek nondistinctive information. If I wish to believe that astrology is valid, I will look for aspects where it fits. I tend to not notice aspects where it does not, nor do I attend to predictions that are not distinctive (i.e., they apply to most everyone). A disconfirmatory approach requires that the individual specify how one's belief could be disproved and then tries to gather such information. This results in far better information and decision making. In the case of my belief in the merits of astrology, a disconfirmatory approach would be to specify what evidence would be needed to disprove my belief. This would focus on instances where the predictions do not fit and also examination of the distinctiveness of any prediction. Only predictions that are very distinctive for me and not others would be the best material for examination. If these distinctive predictions could not be disproven, then there is greater support for my belief in astrology. So to adopt a disconfirmatory approach, the practitioner would need to specify in advance what specific information would prove him or her wrong. If this information is found, then the practitioner has a strong basis to modify his or her approach to treatment. The merits of individuals using a disconfirmatory approach has strong support in the research (Aldashev, Carletti, & Righi, 2011; Davies, 2003).

Collecting process information over time can prove very helpful in honing practice when used in this disconfirmatory, hypothesis examination manner.

One of the key issues in working with any client or group is the relative balance of positive and negative information. Sanford (1962) noted long ago that there is an optimal balance of challenge and support needed to help individuals develop. But being able to know this balance is difficult to determine. If the practitioner has a good understanding of the client, then the practitioner can specify the appropriate balance of challenge and support and also what specifically the client finds challenging and supporting. If the practitioner is correct, then the process scales that are given daily or weekly will show improvement. However if the amount is off or if the wrong aspects are hypothesized to be supportive, then the progress could stagnate or even there could be worsening. In such cases, a different balance, say more support, or looking for different things that are supportive for this individual client could be chosen. Some individuals may need frequent reassurance, while for others this is not supportive. By having frequent feedback, the practitioner has information to use with respect to altering current work.

Summary

Tracey et al. (2014, 2015) argue that there is no expertise for the profession of psychotherapy and that this is attributable to the lack of quality outcome information available to clinicians and further that even when such information is available, a reflective examination of this information using a disconfirmatory hypothesis testing approach is needed for expertise to result. The premise of this chapter is that a similar state of affairs exists with respect to the professions of career counseling and coaching given their high similarity with regard to practice. It is desirable that practitioners get better outcomes with experience and for this to occur there needs to be quality information relating to which clients benefit from the interventions, how these outcomes play out over time and the relative level of outcome across practitioner. When these data are available, reflective, deliberate examination will prove beneficial.

References

Ægisdóttir, S., White, M. J., Spengler, P. M., Maugherman, A. S., Anderson, L. A., Cook, R. S., & Nichols, C. S. (2006). The meta-analysis of clinical judgment project: Fifty-six years of accumulated research on clinical versus statistical prediction. *The Counseling Psychologist, 34*, 341–382. doi:10.1177/0011000005285875

Aldashev, G., Carletti, T., & Righi, S. (2011). Follies subdued: Informational efficiency under adaptive expectations and confirmatory bias. *Journal of Economic Behavior & Organization, 80*, 110–121.

Arkes, H. R. (1981). Impediments to accurate clinical judgment and possible ways to minimize their impact. *Journal of Consulting and Clinical Psychology, 49*, 323–330.

Brown, S. D., & Ryan Krane, N. E. (2000). Four (or five) sessions and a cloud of dust: Old assumptions and new observations about career counseling. In S. D. Brown & R. W. Lent (Eds.), *Handbook of counseling psychology* (3rd ed., pp. 740–766). New York, NY: Wiley.

Budge, S. L., Owen, J. J., Kopta, S. M., Minami, T., Hansen, M. R., & Hirsch, G. (2013). Differences among trainees in client outcomes associated with the phase model of change. *Psychotherapy, 50*, 150–157. doi:10.1037/a0029565

Chow, D. L., Miller, S. D., Seidel, J. A., Kane, R. T., & Thornton, J. A. (2015). The role of deliberate practice in the development of highly effective psychotherapists. *Psychotherapy, 52*(3), 337–345

Davies, M. F. (2003). Confirmatory bias in the evaluation of personality descriptions: Positive test strategies and output interference. *Journal of Personality and Social Psychology, 85*, 736–744.

Dawes, R. M. (1994). House of cards: Psychology and psychiatry built on myth. New York, NY: Free Press.

Dumont, F. (1991). Expertise in psychotherapy: Inherent liabilities of becoming experienced. *Psychotherapy, 28*, 422–428.

Duncan, B. L., Miller, S. D., Wampold, B. E., & Hubble, M. A. (2010). *The heart and soul of change: Delivering what works in therapy* (2nd ed.). Washington, DC: American Psychological Association.

Ellis, S., Carette, B., Anseel, F., & Lievens, F. (2014). Systematic reflection: Implications for learning from failures and successes. *Current Directions in Psychological Science, 23*, 67–72. doi:10.1177/0963721413504106

Ericsson, K. A. (2006). The Influence of experience and deliberate practice on the development of superior expert performance. In K. A. Ericsson, N. Charness, P. J. Feltovich, & R. R. Hoffman (Eds.), *The Cambridge handbook of expertise and expert performance* (pp. 683–703). Cambridge: Cambridge University Press. doi:10.1017/CBO9780511816796.038

Ericsson, K. A. (2009). Enhancing the development of professional performance: Implications from the study of deliberate practice. In K. A. Ericsson (Ed.), *Development of professional expertise: Toward measurement of expert performance and design of optimal learning environments* (pp. 405–431). New York, NY: Cambridge University Press.

Faust, D. (1991). What if we had really listened? Present reflections on altered pasts. In D. Cicchetti & W. M. Grove (Eds.), *Thinking clearly about psychology: Vol. 1. Matters of public interest* (pp. 185–216). Minneapolis, MN: University of Minnesota Press.

Flynn, R. (1994). Evaluating the effectiveness of career counselling: Recent evidence and recommended strategies. *Canadian Journal of Counseling, 28*, 270–280.

Fretz, B. R. (1981). Evaluating the effectiveness of career interventions. *Journal of Counseling (Monograph), 28*, 77–90.

Garb, H. N. (1989). Clinical judgment, clinical training, and professional experience. *Psychological Bulletin, 105*, 387–392.

Garb, H. N. (1998). *Studying the clinician: Judgment research and psychological assessment.* Washington, DC: American Psychological Association.

Garb, H. N. (2005). Clinical judgment and decision-making. *Annual Review of Clinical Psychology, 1*, 67–89. doi:10.1146/annurev.clinpsy.1.102803.143810

Garb, H. N., & Boyle, P. A. (2003). Understanding why some clinicians use pseudoscientific methods: Findings from research on clinical judgment. In S. O. Lilienfeld, S. J. Lynn, & J. M. Lohr (Eds.), *Science and pseudoscience in clinical psychology* (pp. 17–38). New York, NY: Guilford.

Goldberg, L. R. (1968). Simple models or simple processes? Some research on clinical judgment. *American Psychologist, 23*, 483–496.

Goldberg, L. R. (1991). Human mind versus regression equation: Five contrasts. In D. Cicchetti & W. M. Grove (Eds.), *Thinking clearly about psychology; Vol. 1: Matters of public interest* (pp. 173–184). Minneapolis, MN: University of Minnesota Press.

Goldberg, S., Rousmaniere, T. G., Miller, S. D., Whipple, J. L., Nielsen, S. L., & Wampold, B. E. (2016). Do psychotherapists improve with time and experience? A longitudinal analysis of real world outcome data. *Journal of Counseling Psychology, 63*, 1–11. doi:10.1037/cou0000131.

Holland, J. L., Magoon, T. M., & Spokane, A. R. (1981). Counseling psychology: Career interventions, research, and theory. *Annual Review of Psychology, 32*, 279–305.

Jacobson, N. S., & Truax, P. (1991). Clinical significance: A statistical approach to defining meaningful change in psychotherapy research. *Journal of Consulting and Clinical Psychology, 59*, 12–19.

Kahneman, D. (2013). *Thinking fast and slow*. New York, NY: Macmillan.

Lambert, M. J., Harmon, C., Slade, K., Whipple, J. L., & Hawkins, E. J. (2005). Providing feedback to psychotherapists on their patients' progress: Clinical results and practice suggestions. *Journal of Clinical Psychology, 61*(2), 165–174.

Lambert, M. J., & Ogles, B. M. (2004). The efficacy and effectiveness of psychotherapy. In M. J. Lambert (Ed.), *Bergin and Garfield's handbook of psychotherapy and behavior change* (5th ed., pp. 139–193). New York, NY: Wiley.

Lambert, M. J., & Shimokawa, K. (2011). Collecting client feedback. In J. C. Norcross & J. C. Norcross (Eds.), *Psychotherapy relationships that work: Evidence-based responsiveness* (2nd ed., pp. 203–223). New York, NY: Oxford University Press.

Miller, S. D., Duncan, B. L., & Hubble, M. A. (2005). Outcome-informed clinical work. In J. C. Norcross & M. R. Goldfried (Eds.), *Handbook of psychotherapy integration* (2nd ed., pp. 84–102). New York, NY: Oxford University Press.

Myers, R. A. (1986). Research on educational and vocational counseling. In A. E. Bergin & S. L. Garfield (Eds.), *Handbook of psychotherapy and behavior change: An empirical analysis* (3rd ed., pp. 72 98). New York, NY: Wiley.

Nissen-Lie, H. A., Monsen, J. T., Ulleberg, P., & Rønnestad, M. H. (2012). Psychotherapists' self-reports of their interpersonal functioning and difficulties in practice as predictors of patient outcome. *Psychotherapy Research, 22*, 1–19.

Oliver, L. W., & Spokane, A. R. (1988). Career-intervention outcome: What contributes to client gain? *Journal of Counseling Psychology, 35*, 447–462.

Pintrich, P. R. (2003). A motivational science perspective on the role of student motivation in learning and teaching contexts. *Journal of Educational Psychology, 95*, 667–686.

Reese, R. J., Norsworthy, L. A., & Rowlands, S. R. (2009). Does a continuous feedback system improve psychotherapy outcome? *Psychotherapy: Theory, Research, Practice, Training, 46*, 418–431. doi:10.1037/a0017901

Salovey, P., & Turk, D. C. (1991). Clinical judgment and decision-making. In C. R. Snyder & D. R. Forsyth (Eds.), *Handbook of social and clinical psychology: The health perspective* (pp. 416–437). New York, NY: Pergamon.

Sanford, N. (1962). The American college: A psychological and social interpretation of the higher learning. Hoboken, NJ: Wiley.

Shanteau, J. (1992). Competence in experts: The role of task characteristics. *Organizational Behavior and Human Decision Processes, 53*, 252–266.

Shanteau, J., & Weiss, D. J. (2014). Individual expertise versus domain expertise. *American Psychologist, 69*, 711–712. doi:10.1037/a0037874

Smith, M. L., & Glass, G.V. (1977). Meta-analysis of psychotherapy outcome studies. *American Psychologist, 32*, 752–777.

Spengler, P. M., White, M. J., Ægisdóttir, S., Maugherman, A. S., Anderson, L. A., Cook, R. S., Nichols, C. N., Lampropoulos, G. K., Walker, B. S., Cohen, G. R., & Rush, J. D. (2009). The meta-analysis of clinical judgment project: Effects of experience on judgment accuracy. *The Counseling Psychologist, 37*, 350–399.

Spokane, A. R., & Oliver, L. W. (1983). The outcomes of vocational interventions. In W. B. Walsh & S. H. Osipow (Eds.), *Handbook of vocational psychology* (pp. 99–116). Hillsdale, NJ: Erlbaum.

Strasser, J., & Gruber, H. (2004). The role of experience in professional training and development of psychological counsellors. In H. P. A. Boshuizen, R. Bromme, & H. Gruber (Eds.), *Professional learning: Gaps and transitions on the way from novice to expert* (pp. 11–28). Dordrecht, The Netherlands: Kluwer Academic.

Swanson, J. L. (1995). The process and outcome of career counseling. In W. B. Walsh & S. H. Osipow (Eds.), *The handbook of vocational psychology* (pp. 217–259). Mahwah, NJ: Erlbaum.

Theeboom, T., Beersma, B., & van Vianen, A. E. M. (2014). Does coaching work? A meta-analysis on the effects of coaching on individual level outcomes in an organizational context. *Journal of Positive Psychology, 9*, 1–18. doi:10.1080/17439760.2013.837499

Tracey, T. J. G., & Rounds, J. (1999). Inference and attribution errors in test interpretation. In R. K. Goodyear & J. W. Lichtenberg (Eds.), *Test interpretation: Integrating science and practice* (pp. 113–131). Boston, MA: Allyn & Bacon.

Tracey, T. J. G., Wampold, B. E., Goodyear, R. K., & Lichtenberg, J. W. (2015). Improving expertise in psychotherapy. *Psychotherapy Bulletin, 50*(1), 7–13.

Tracey, T. J., & Kokotovic, A. M. (1989). Factor structure of the working alliance inventory. *Psychological Assessment: A Journal of Consulting and Clinical Psychology, 1*, 207–210. doi:10.1037//1040-3590.1.3.207

Tracey, T. J. G., Wampold, B. E., Lichtenberg, J. W., & Goodyear, R. K. (2014). Expertise in psychotherapy: An elusive goal? *American Psychologist, 69*, 218–229. doi:10.1037/a0035099

Vermeersch, D A., Whipple, J. L., Lambert, M. J., Hawkins, E. J., Burchfield, C. M., & Okiishi, J. C. (2004). Outcome Questionnaire: Item sensitivity to changes in counseling center clients. *Journal of Counseling Psychology, 51*, 38–49.

Walfish, S., McAlister, B., O'Donnell, P., & Lambert, M. J. (2012). An investigation of self-assessment bias in mental health providers. *Psychological Reports, 110*, 639–644. doi:10.2466/02.07.17.PR0.110.2.639-644 ISSN: 0033-2941

Wampold, B. E. (2001a). *The great psychotherapy debate: Models, methods, and findings*. Mahwah, NJ: Lawrence Erlbaum Associates.

Wampold, B. E. (2001b). Contextualizing psychotherapy as a healing practice: Culture, history, and methods. *Applied and Preventative Psychology, 10*, 69–86.

Wedding, D., & Faust, D. (1989). Clinical judgment and decision making in neuropsychology. *Archives of Clinical Neuropsychology, 4*, 233–265.

Whiston, S. C., Brecheisen, B. K., & Stephens, J. 2003). Does treatment modality affect career counseling effectiveness? *Journal of Vocational Behavior, 62*, 390–410. doi:10.1016/S0001-8791(02)00050-7

Whiston, S. C., Sexton, T. L., & Lasoff, D. L. (1998). Career-intervention outcome: A replication and extension of Olive and Spokane (1988). *Journal of Counseling Psychology, 45*, 150–165.

Wierzbicki, M. (1993). Issues in clinical psychology: Subjective versus objective approaches. Boston, MA: Allyn & Bacon.

Witteman, C. L. M., & Van den Bercken, J. H. L. (2007). Intermediate effects in psychodiagnostic classification. *European Journal of Psychological Assessment, 23*, 56–61. DOI:10.1027/1015-5759.23.1.56

Witterman, C. L. M., Weiss, D. J., & Metzmacher, M. (2012). Assessing diagnostic expertise of counselors using the Cochran-Weiss-Shanteau (CWS) index. *Journal of Counseling and Development, 90*, 30–34.

Part III

Counseling and coaching actions for wellbeing and inclusion

This third part focuses on the contributions that different counseling and coaching actions could give in favor, above all, of the disadvantaged segments of the population and of the promotion of greater social justice.

To pursue this aim, counseling and coaching professionals should first of all take inspiration from the most credited models of interpretation and analysis of the themes associated with vulnerability and disability. They should also be guided by the conviction that all individuals, including those with disabilities and vulnerabilities, desire happiness, wish to live a meaningful life, to have a decent and satisfying job, to be able to make decisions and choose how to realize themselves, and how to purse their own wellbeing. Achieving wellbeing and increased quality of life cannot happen unless we hold markedly inclusive views of society. Inclusion does not concern this or that category of citizens; it no longer makes sense to talk about individuals with disabilities or with psychiatric problems, about immigrants and so on. This perhaps might have been correct when we used to refer to concepts like integration, or maybe when, in the second half of the last century, the movements advocating inclusion and integration were just at their beginning. Today, inclusion is considered a prevalently contextual issue that refers to the ability of educational, working and social contexts to respect everybody's needs, expectations and requests regardless of their specific characteristics. In this, as we have already said, the counseling and coaching of the present and of the near future should help set *homo economicus* against *homo empaticus*, who promotes solidarity, inclusion and civil responsibility at the same time suggesting that there is a moral obligation to safeguard and take care of the environment in which we live.

In line with that, Chapter 11, written by John L. Romano, examines preventive interventions that can be carried out by counselors and coaches. He maintains that preventive interventions are critically important and necessary to educate and help individuals and community groups, especially those who have not been well served by traditional crisis-oriented services. In addition, prevention interventions have been shown to be cost effective compared to remedial approaches after problems are manifested. Prevention in the 21st century aims to (1) influence social and political actions and policies promoting the health and wellbeing of an entire community, and (2) support social justice initiatives since the goals of prevention interventions empower individuals and foster health and wellbeing across the lifecycle.

In Chapter 12, contributions by Teresa Maria Sgaramella, Lea Ferrari and Ilaria di Maggio focus on parents, especially of children with disability, emphasizing their crucial role in supporting the social and personal adjustment of children and in developing inclusive contexts. The authors examine main interventions focused on parents to support and empower parenting skills coping with their educational role and to train them to be engaged in the diffusion and promotion of inclusion. They address parent counseling, parent training, and the most recently developed parent coaching, both for their effectiveness and for the preventive value towards inclusion, and provide for each of them suggestions and examples.

In Chapter 13, Rachel Gali Cinamon examines career development of Israeli Arab adolescents and young adults as a case study to discuss career counseling for minorities in multicultural societies. The author proposes three conceptual frameworks – i.e. career construction theory, psychology of working theory, and perspective about the interplay between citizenship, identity, culture and career – that could be useful to guide career counselors who work with minorities in general and with Israeli Arab young adults in particular. For each of these perspectives, she provides examples and suggestions for career counselors to enable young people to construct their individual identity.

In Chapter 14, Valentina Di Mattei, Martina Bernardi and Letizia Carnelli examine the discomfort associated with serious illnesses. Such situations are complex and the involvement of the patient is important in the healing process. Starting from the current literature, the authors outline a reference framework to describe an intervention with a preventive role, to inform patients, or a more supportive role in assisting patients and their families across the various phases from diagnosis, to treatment, to follow-up or, in some cases, to the end of life. Counseling must help patients and caregivers in healthcare settings share worries, fears, uncertainties, and expectations to try to experience the illness with the least possible distress.

In Chapter 15, Kate Scorgie and Sarah Scorgie focus on students with disability and underline the importance of counseling in favoring access and continuation of university students to the advantage for their future. They underscore that many persons with disabilities are reluctant to disclose in post-secondary and workplace settings, resulting in limited access to resources needed for success. With this chapter, they explore the complex dialogue surrounding the disclosure of disability in post-secondary and workplace settings and offer counselors a template to guide understanding and engage in collaborative solution-building and strategies to favor advocacy, self-advocacy, negotiation and equity accommodation.

Last, special consideration is reserved to children, the adults of the future. In Chapter 16 by Maria Cristina Ginevra and Sara Santilli, the readers are encouraged to reflect, within the strength-building approach, on the importance of investing in personal strengths such as courage, future-mindedness, hope, optimism, resilience, interpersonal skills and flourishing. Particular attention is given to courage and to how it can favor development in a context characterized by globalization, uncertainty about the future, and insecurity, and to the actions that can be implemented to support it. Assessment instruments and suggestions for coaches interested in promoting this personal resource in childhood are described.

Chapter 11

Prevention psychology

Interventions to promote health and wellbeing

John L. Romano

Counseling, psychology, and other mental health professions have emphasized for many years interventions and processes that react to problems well after they have manifested themselves and become serious problems. This orientation has focused on individuals with emotional and behavioral problems, and supported one-on-one and small group crisis interventions. The mental health professions have been dominated in service delivery, training, and research on treatments to correct dysfunctional behavior rather than on prevention interventions to reduce problems. In contrast, the relatively new specialty of personal or life-skills coaching focuses on the enhancement of personal and professional potential as defined by the International Coaching Federation (ICF; www.coachingfederation.org). ICF was established in 1995 and currently has a robust international membership, according to its website. Therefore, prevention science with its proactive, growth-enhancing emphasis is strongly aligned with personal coaching. However, personal coaching and traditional counseling and psychotherapy are not distinctly separate specialties and they can be integrated within professional mental health areas of practice (Biswas-Diener, 2009; Popovic & Jinks, 2014). As examples, personal coaching interventions have been implemented to increase college student retention and success (Dalton & Crosby, 2014) and to enhance vocational guidance of secondary school students (Jordan, Gessnitzer, & Kauffeld, 2016). However, personal coaching is a much newer specialty and it has not advanced to the level of an agreed upon education and curriculum of training, and the practice of coaching is not as regulated as other mental health disciplines (Copper, Newman, & Fuqua, 2012). Nevertheless, the topics addressed in this chapter and their relevance to prevention science apply to both traditional mental health professions and professional coaching. Coaching is often referred to by various types of coaching in the literature – e.g. lifestyle coaching, personal coaching, executive coaching, etc. In this chapter, these references to coaching will be used interchangeably.

The chapter will argue for greater attention to prevention applications, research, and training within traditional mental health professions and coaching. As the chapter unfolds, advocacy for prevention science will articulate several critically important arguments for prevention: (a) prevention interventions have the potential to serve many more people who can benefit from preventive mental health interventions, educational services, and coaching, especially those who are currently underserved; (b) prevention offers cost-benefit advantages by addressing individual and societal needs through prevention science rather than waiting until crises occur; and (c) prevention supports the importance of addressing institutional and public policy changes that promote personal and social wellbeing across the lifespan.

The chapter will begin with a definition of prevention psychology, including other conceptualizations of prevention. Next, the importance of prevention to increase access to mental health and life skills services and promote social justice will be discussed. The next section will present possibilities for prevention applications and research across different settings and population groups. Finally, examples of activities and tools that can be used in prevention research, practice, and professional training will be provided.

Prevention psychology

Romano (2015) has advanced a conceptualization of prevention that incorporates other definitions of the term used since the last half of the 20th century. Prevention psychology highlights prevention as an important specialty within psychology and other mental health professions. The emphasis of prevention psychology is the promotion of evidence-based interventions that promote individual, institutional, and community wellbeing through programs and activities designed to reduce risk factors and strengthen protective factors among a population or group targeted for a prevention intervention. Prevention psychology promotes theoretically and empirically supported interventions designed to improve the health and wellbeing of people across the life cycle, in settings where they live (communities), where they are educated (schools and universities), and at their workplaces. The goal of prevention psychology is to reduce incidences of emotional and behavioral dysfunction that are related to any number of problem areas, including school failure, career dissatisfaction, depression, physical health problems, addictions, and community and domestic violence. Prevention psychology adheres to the belief that correcting problem behaviors once they become fully manifested will be more difficult to correct and costly to the individual and society, compared to the prevention of the problem.

While prevention psychology conceptualizes prevention as discussed above, others have defined prevention more specifically. For example, Caplan (1964) offered three types of prevention interventions: primary (interventions to prevent problems from ever occurring), secondary (interventions for those at-risk), and tertiary (interventions to reduce the impact of an existing problem, e.g. rehabilitation programs). However, several years later the United States' Institute of Medicine Committee on the Prevention of Mental Disorders: Division of Biobehavioral Sciences and Mental Disorders (Mrazek & Haggerty, 1994) adopted Gordon's (1987) classification as more applicable to prevention. Gordon's classification of prevention interventions are: universal prevention interventions (for an entire population or entity), selected (interventions for those at risk for developing a problem), and indicated (interventions for those at high risk and exhibiting symptoms of a problem). The committee argued that tertiary interventions are not preventive since the disorder already exists. Romano and Hage (2000) expanded Caplan's conceptualization through a five-part definition. The first three parts are similar to Caplan, but they also added prevention interventions that promote protective factors and institutional and public policy initiatives as important prevention activities. Finally, Conyne (2015) offers the perspective of prevention and wellness as interrelated and viable across the lifespan at individual and community levels.

Therefore, the conceptualization of prevention has evolved in recent years. Prevention interventions not only include the prevention of harmful behaviors, but also the promotion of protective behaviors and actions. These conceptualizations also address the importance of developing and strengthening policies at the institutional (e.g. school and workplace) and public policy (e.g. laws and regulations) levels to improve the health and wellbeing of individuals and groups. An example of the former are clearly defined school policies related to drug and alcohol use; broader public policies for communities or larger areas might include laws governing cigarette smoking (e.g. prohibitions on smoking in public places) and penalties for underage alcohol use.

Prevention is essential to increase mental health access and promote social justice

There has long been ample evidence demonstrating that many people who could benefit from counseling and other psychological services never receive the help they need. For example, the World Health Organization (WHO, 2003) estimated that in higher income countries 40%–70% of people with mental health disorders do not receive treatment, and the percentage increases to nearly 90% of those not receiving treatment in lower-income countries. In the United States, 14%–20% of children and adolescents experience a mental or behavioral disorders each year, and many of these youth do not receive treatment (O'Connell, Boat, & Warner, 2009; Ringel & Sturm, 2001). There are several reasons for people not receiving needed treatment, including the lack of professionals to deliver the services, lack of resources, and social stigma associated with mental illness and receiving psychological services (Corrigan & Watson, 2002; WHO, 2013). These reasons are compounded greatly by major inequities across the globe. For example, in higher income countries, the median number of mental health workers is over 50 per 100,000, while in lower income countries the median number is less than 1 per 100,000 (WHO, 2015). Furthermore, in many lower and middle income countries, health budgets allocate less than 2% to the treatment and prevention of mental disorders, and even in higher income countries the percentage of the overall health budget dedicated to mental health treatment and prevention is relatively low at 5.1% (WHO, 2013). In terms of stigma, social and cultural variables impact the strength of stigma associated with receiving mental health care, and negative attitudes toward mental health, emotional, and behavioral problems will impact utilization of services (WHO, 2015). However, coaching services (e.g. executive coaching, life-skills coaching) are typically less stigmatized than psychological services. In addition, an increase in coaching services can reduce the discrepancy between those needing to enhance their lives and the availability of helpers. One caveat, however, is that due to the lack of standardization of training and credentialing of coaches, there are risks associated with receiving assistance from coaches who are not adequately trained.

Preventive services are critically important as avenues to increase access to mental health services, to enhance personal development, and to promote equity and social justice among population groups. Even in the most industrialized countries, use of mental health services by those in need once problems become acute can be problematic because of the lack of available services, stigma associated with receiving services, and costs to the person receiving the service. In addition, by failing to reduce the incidence of problems or reduce their impact at early stages, family and friends of the afflicted person suffer emotional and financial consequences, and the community and society in which the problems occur also realize increased financial burdens. A World Economic Forum study, reported by WHO (2013), estimated that the economic impact of mental disorders worldwide will result in a loss of $16 trillion US dollars over the next 20 years.

The specialty of prevention science offers many opportunities for professionals from various disciplines and specialties to reduce problems and mitigate their impact if identified and treated at early stages. Prevention interventions are relevant across disciplines and specialties, and often are more effective if conducted within interdisciplinary collaborations. Giving greater attention to preventive interventions in schools, communities, and workplaces across the lifespan will enrich the lives and wellbeing of people across the globe. Through education and preventive interventions, prevention science offers the potential for improved access to mental health and other specialists, reduce stigma, and reduce costs associated with crisis intervention treatments.

Prevention applications

In recent decades, an increasing number of evidence-supported prevention applications have been developed for implementation in different settings and across the life cycle. These applications have been developed and implemented in educational institutions, medical settings, and community-based organizations (Romano, 2015). For several years, the US government's *National Registry of Evidence-Based Prevention Programs and Practices* has catalogued evidenced-based prevention applications after substantive reviews of their efficacy (www.nrepp.samhsa.gov). On a global level, the United Nations Office on Drugs and Crime has disseminated *International Standards on Drug Use Prevention* to support evidence-based prevention initiatives across the globe (Campello, Heikkila, & Maalouf, 2017). In addition, country-specific (e. g. Israel) prevention standards have been developed in recent years (Israelashvili, 2017). Prevention applications have been developed worldwide across a range of topical areas and strategies, with the majority of them being implemented in more resource-rich countries (Romano & Israelashvili, 2017).

Historically, many programs, focusing on the prevention of tobacco, alcohol, and drug use, were implemented in schools with children and adolescents. However, prevention interventions with this population have expanded greatly, including prevention of major educational, emotional, and social issues confronting youth – e.g. bullying, poor academic achievement, premature sexual activity and pregnancy, and depression. Many of these same behaviors have been targeted for prevention activities at colleges and universities, including prevention of alcohol and drug abuse and sexual assault. Beyond the traditional years of schooling, prevention initiatives have been implemented with adults, including senior populations. These interventions might include smoking cessation programs, stress reduction programs in the workplace, and prevention activities for elder populations. The latter may include social networking activities to combat senior loneliness and to promote senior community engagement.

While describing even briefly the range of prevention initiatives across the globe is beyond the scope of this chapter [the reader is encouraged to review the US National Registry and Standards discussed above for specific prevention programs and *The Cambridge Handbook of International Prevention Science* (Israelashvili & Romano, 2017), as well as other resources germane to their location], there are several guidelines that are important with respect to developing prevention programs. First, if a given school, medical center, community, or workplace recognizes that there are areas that demand a preventive response, a group of stakeholders from the locale should meet to address the problem. Second, a needs assessment should be undertaken to help determine behaviors to be prevented or behaviors to be promoted. Third, prevention activities are selected and implemented. Fourth, evaluation data are collected to assess the outcomes of the initial intervention, and data collection continues to assess the impact of the intervention. Fifth, evaluation data are shared regularly with major stakeholders as the prevention program is refined as needed.

Prevention interventions are opportunities for educators, mental health professionals, and life coaches to deliver cost-effective services to individuals who might not otherwise voluntarily seek out services, or only seek them out after a crisis or problem develops and becomes a major problem for them. Prevention interventions can be population specific, as, for example, a school-based bullying prevention program, or they can be broader in scope such as universal prevention messages that are delivered through mass media and social media outlets (Cugelman, Thelwall, & Dawes, 2011). In many locations, a combination of approaches is recommended. For example, a university may send social media messages about problems associated with alcohol use to students prior to a major celebration weekend, and also provide individual and small group prevention intervention sessions for students who are cited for alcohol intoxication on campus (selective and indicated prevention interventions).

It is critically important that regardless of the prevention intervention and activities selected for implementation, they must be culturally specific to the targeted population. It should not be assumed that a prevention program and intervention that has been successful with one cultural group will also be successful with a different cultural group. Therefore, the prevention specialist should take care to conduct pilot projects, focus groups, or elicitation research [Theory of Reasoned Action and Planned Behavior (Ajzen & Fishbein, 1980; Romano & Netland, 2008)]. These methods will provide the prevention specialist greater understanding of the most salient variables that motivate a specific group to engage in behaviors that the specialist wants to promote. From this understanding, prevention activities can be tailored to the group targeted for a prevention intervention. For example, it should not be assumed that safe-sex prevention activities delivered to adolescents will be equally effective for all students in a school. Sub-sets of students (e.g. girls/boys, ethnic groups) may respond differently to any given activity. Elicitation research helps to understand differences within the targeted population in terms of attitudes, social norms, and perceived control in carrying out new behaviors.

In summary, there are any number of prevention activities and programs that can be undertaken within a smaller setting or larger community. In many cases, prevention specialists and others advocate for government policies and laws that impact an entire country's population such as laws governing access to alcohol and tobacco, government services for children with special needs, access to quality health care, laws against discrimination, and government funding to reduce poverty. Many of these broader-based prevention initiatives are usually controversial as people will differ based on their personal values and priorities, especially related to funding for services and the rights of individuals versus those of the larger group or society.

Prevention skills and activities

In countries across the globe people are regularly reminded, often through media campaigns, about behaviors and actions that can prevent problems. For example, various types of media messages alert users of public transportation to be aware of pickpockets, to avoid excessive alcohol use, and to eat healthy foods and participate in regular physical exercise. These universal messages are important to deliver, but generally they are insufficient to change behaviors, even though social media has greatly increased their use. Therefore, additional steps need to be taken by educators, coaches, and healthcare providers to engage people in behavioral change strategies and maintenance of positive behavioral changes. Several suggestions are offered to bring greater attention to preventive interventions to the public.

Professional commitment to prevention

One of the most critical components in promoting prevention and health promotion starts with professional organizations, educational institutions, and accrediting and licensing bodies. It is critically important that these entities give greater attention to prevention and health promotion. There needs to be more of a balance between correcting problems and preventing them. Currently, most of the training of students for the counseling and applied psychology professions emphasizes theories and practices that address crisis interventions, rather than prevention. It is not uncommon for students to enroll in these programs with a strong social service desire "to help people". This motivation is laudable, but we also need to educate students about the importance of developing expertise in prevention science and health promotion. Some education will be delivered didactically in classrooms, but students should also be expected to complete field placements in settings where prevention interventions are practiced (Conyne, Newmeyer, Kenny, Romano, & Matthews, 2008). Prevention interventions usually require an activist approach to helping others. For example, instead of waiting for a client with a problem to find a counselor's office, the counselor develops programs, activities, and interventions that attempt to help people before behaviors or emotions become problematic. In this regard, schools have developed programs designed to prevent the use of alcohol and other risk behaviors. Psychologists and counselors can also use their expertise to train teachers and other providers about how to identify risks that they observe in their students and clients, and how they may assist that person through direct interventions or referrals. A similar commitment to prevention must also be made by those who aspire to be or are currently engaged in professional coaching.

Basically, the helping professions and educators need to develop a greater commitment to prevention, and learn how they can intervene. The American Psychological Association (APA) has developed Guidelines for Prevention in Psychology (APA, 2014) which provide a set of aspirations for psychologists in relation to prevention. Among the nine guidelines are those that focus on evidence-based interventions, socially and culturally relevant prevention practices, ethics in prevention, and the development of public policies that promote health and wellbeing. These are the first set of guidelines on prevention promulgated by the APA. While these guidelines were developed by psychologists, they can also apply to other human development specialists, such as counselors and coaches.

In addition to increased training in prevention, there is a great need to adjust credentialing requirements to include knowledge and skills related to prevention. For example, psychology licensing boards in the United States that I am familiar with require licensees to demonstrate knowledge and skills in psychotherapy theory and practices, but none in prevention science. Likewise, organizations that accredit training programs should require prevention science as a visible part of the training of future mental health professionals. Similarly, prevention science should be included in the training curriculum of coaches.

In summary, the healthcare and human development professions need to give greater attention to prevention science in training and practices. Students need to be exposed to models of interventions that are preventive and that promote health and wellbeing. Currently, much of the training emphasizes remediation, with little attention to prevention.

Group skills

Generally, the work of prevention is initiated, developed, and implemented within various types of groups. Therefore, it is important that prevention specialists be knowledgeable about and skilled in leading groups. The group work may involve leading task groups, psycho-educational groups, and prevention intervention groups. Each of these will be discussed.

Task groups are important during the process of designing, implementing, and evaluating a prevention initiative. Generally, the task group will be composed of major stakeholders who have an interest in the prevention project, and these stakeholders are brought together by the prevention project leader or leaders. The process may be advanced by identifying co-leaders for the group, one being a prevention specialist and the other a major stakeholder. The prevention specialist must be able to identify, often through appropriate networks, major stakeholders and invite them to participate. For example, in a school setting a stakeholder task group may include administrators, teachers, community leaders, and students. Of course, students will be selected as appropriate to their age. A stakeholder group comes together for several reasons: (a) to reach agreement on the importance of addressing the problem that merits preventive action, (b) to offer suggestions about what needs to be prevented or promoted to reduce the problem, (c) to make recommendations about activities and procedures to implement the prevention project, (d) to give support during implementation of the project, (e) to review project evaluation procedures, (f) to receive evaluation data and help to disseminate evaluative data to important constituent groups, (g) develop strategies to strengthen the project based on evaluation data and plan for the continuation of the prevention project, as needed. Thus, a continuous cycle of tasks are conducted. It is important that the prevention specialist be knowledgeable about task group process dynamics, as there likely will be differences among stakeholders. Therefore, managing conflicts and differences of opinions within the group are important. It is also necessary for the group leader or leaders to be respectful of members by setting up convenient meeting times, developing meeting agendas, and managing time during the meeting. Over the life of a stakeholder task group, it may be necessary to replace members for various reasons, and new members should be identified and invited to join the group as soon as possible.

Psycho-educational group skills are important in prevention. Psych-educational groups offer opportunities to communicate with larger groups of people for a variety of reasons. For example, a community-based psycho-educational group could be formed to educate expectant parents about postpartum depression. A university psycho-educational group could be developed to help students manage stress during examination periods. In the workplace, an executive coach could offer a psycho-educational group to managers on identifying employees who would benefit from coaching. Psycho-educational groups can be designed for one or more sessions, and can be considered universal, selective, or indicated prevention. However, it is important that the leader of these groups be skilled in leading them. Perhaps the most common mistake made by leaders is that most of the scheduled time is taken up by lecturing about the topic by the leader, and very little time is given to group interactions and dialogue. In the recruitment of participants to psycho-educational groups, leaders should develop clear goals and objectives of the group, and state specific information about the group (e.g. topic, length of time, location, etc.). It is important that leaders schedule the group time so that there is sufficient time for discussion, questions, and follow-up information. Leaders should avoid dominating group sessions with lectures imparting information, and give priority to group discussion and questions. Information about the topic can be distributed prior to the group meeting so that more discussion time is available during the session. If the group is large (e.g. more than 20–30 members), leaders may want to use breakout groups for discussion to help ensure that people have sufficient time for discussion. Small breakout groups also have the advantage of increasing the comfort level of participants who may hesitate talking in a larger group.

Social advocacy through political action

Prevention activity also occurs at macro-levels of communities, institutions, workplaces, and governments to bring about change to enhance the health and wellbeing of a given population group. Countries across the globe enlist varying levels of government actions to promote health and prevent disease and behavioral problems. Some examples include laws governing the sale and purchase of tobacco and alcohol to youth, automobile seatbelt use, sale and possession of guns and other weapons, immunization programs for children, and many others. At local and institutional levels, communities may enact youth curfews, and schools may enact nutrition standards for school lunches. Some universities regularly offer to students "screening for depression" and refer to mental health services those at risk for depression, thus promoting positive mental health on campus. Companies may offer benefits to employees who participate in physical exercise programs. Prevention specialists can become informed about policy and government actions that are being debated within their context and offer evidence-based information and data to decision-makers about the policy debate. These debates are often contentious, as individual freedoms sometimes conflict with collective wisdom and the common good. People may also enter the debate with differing values associated with the topic. Some examples of proposals that have yielded mixed opinions and strong debates in the United States include cigarette smoking in restaurants, sex education in the schools, availability of free birth control products on college campuses, and legislation to control the purchase and use of guns. The potential for involvement in public policy debates was well stated in Guidelines 8 and 9 of the APA Guidelines for Prevention in Psychology (APA, 2014). Guideline 8 encourages psychologists to engage in systemic and institutional change interventions to strengthen health and prevent psychological and physical problems; Guideline 9 states, "Psychologists are encouraged to inform the deliberation of public policies that promote health and wellbeing when relevant prevention science findings are available" (p. 292). In order for prevention specialists to offer their expertise, they must become aware of the policies being debated, and then find ways to offer their expertise to influence decision-makers.

Referral skills

Once prevention specialists and other professionals become aware of individuals and groups who might need more intensive interventions to correct potentially problematic behaviors, then they must be ready to initiate appropriate referrals to professionals who can assist them. This skill is especially important for coaches, as their clients may deny more serious problems that are interfering with their development. Unfortunately, too often individuals with risk behaviors identified through routine screenings are simply directed to change that behavior but are not referred to services or given specific instructions on how to change the behavior. Some examples of adult chronic lifestyle behaviors to reduce disease and dysfunction include directives to stop smoking, get more physical exercise, eat more nutritionally and lose weight, reduce verbally aggressive workplace behaviors, etc. For youth, they may be informed about risks associated with excessive use of the internet and electronic devices, cigarette smoking, alcohol and drug use, sexual behaviors and unprotected sex, etc. However, without addressing specific adult and youth motivations that support these risk behaviors, and without specific interventions to change behaviors, many are unable to make needed changes. Several theories have been advanced over many years of research to assist the prevention specialist in helping individuals with risk behaviors to make changes. These theories include: motivational interviewing (Miller & Rose, 2009), Transtheoretical Model of Change (Prochaska, Johnson, & Lee, 2009), and cognitive behavioral theories (Bandura, 1986; Beck, 1976). It behooves behavioral change specialists to become familiar with these and other theories that can guide them in helping their clientele reduce risk behaviors and promote health-enhancing behaviors.

Conclusion

This chapter has provided background, interventions, and skills related to prevention science. Within a prevention psychology framework, the chapter advocates for strengthening the goals of prevention science through the prevention of problem behaviors, the promotion of protective behaviors, and advocacy at macro-levels of society to enhance health and wellbeing across the lifespan. Prevention applications and interventions have the potential to reach many more people in need of assistance, compared to more crisis-intervention approaches. Prevention psychology also offers the potential to empower large groups of people through legislative actions that promote health. Thus, this chapter recommends the involvement of prevention specialists and other professionals in matters of public policy that relate to health and wellbeing by sharing their relevant knowledge and expertise with decision-makers about topics that relate to improving health and wellbeing. Examples of topics of expertise may include the health risks associated with secondhand cigarette smoke, inclusion of special needs children in schools, preparing high school students for postsecondary education and careers, laws to reduce educational and health disparities in communities, and violence reduction in schools, workplaces, and communities.

It is critically important that prevention specialists and other professionals carefully assess cultural and normative dynamics associated with a given locale, country, or region when designing a prevention intervention. It cannot be assumed that a prevention intervention designed and evaluated within one context will be equally successful within a different context. Even within any given context, for example in a high school, it should not be assumed that girls and boys will respond similarly to a prevention intervention. Therefore, conducting research to assess differences among subgroups of a given population is important prior to initiating a major prevention intervention to maximize the impact of the intervention.

It is important that prevention interventions use empirically supported interventions and a variety of methods to inform and teach the clientele targeted for a prevention intervention. As discussed in this chapter, there are several resources that can be accessed to identify empirically supported interventions. In addition, many people across the globe have access to the internet and social media, and therefore, technology can be used to educate, teach, and collect data on topics important to prevention. Creative and technologically enhanced approaches are likely to attract the attention of more people, especially younger clientele.

Finally, prevention science offers the potential to empower people and improve their health and wellbeing across the lifespan, but prevention must become more prominent in the training and education of professionals across disciplines. Integrating prevention science knowledge and skills more fully throughout the professions offers challenges, but the rewards of doing so will benefit many, especially less powerful and disenfranchised members of society who are more vulnerable to crisis situations.

References

Ajzen, I., & Fishbein, M. (1980). *Understanding attitudes and predicting social behavior*. Englewood Cliffs, NJ: Prentice-Hall.

APA. (2014). Guidelines for prevention in psychology. *American Psychologist, 69*, 285–296.

Bandura, A. (1986). Social foundations of thought and action: A social cognitive theory. Englewood Cliffs, NJ: Prentice-Hall.

Beck, A. T. (1976). *Cognitive therapy and the emotional disorders*. New York, NY: International Universities Press.

Biswas-Diener, R. (2009). Personal coaching as a positive intervention. *Journal of Clinical Psychology, 65*, 544–553.

Campello, G., Heikkila, H., & Maalouf, W. (2017). International standards on drug use prevention: Tool to support policy makers globally to implement an evidence-based prevention response. In M. Israelashvili & J. L. Romano (Eds.), *The Cambridge handbook of international prevention science* (pp. 134–159). New York, NY: Cambridge University Press.

Caplan, G. (1964). *Principles of preventive psychiatry*. New York, NY: Basic Books.

Conyne, R. K. (2015). Counseling for wellness and prevention: Helping people become empowered in systems and settings (3rd ed.). New York, NY: Routledge.

Conyne, R. K., Newmeyer, M. D., Kenny, M., Romano, J. L., & Matthews, C. R. (2008). Two key strategies for teaching prevention: Specialized course and infusion. *Journal of Primary Prevention, 29*, 375–401. doi:10.1007/s10935-008-0146-8

Cooper, S. E., Newman, J. L., & Fuqua, D. R. (2012). Counseling psychologists as consultants. In N. A. Fouad, J. A. Carter, & L. M. Subich (Eds.), *APA handbook of counseling psychology-vol 2* (pp. 515–539). Washington, DC: American Psychological Association.

Corrigan, P. W., & Watson, A. C. (2002). Understanding the impact of stigma on people with mental illness. *World Psychiatry, 1*, 16–20.

Cugelman, B., Thelwall, M., & Dawes, P. (2011). Online interventions for social marketing health behavior change campaigns: A meta-analysis of psychological architectures and adherence factors. *Journal of Medical Internet Research, 13*, e17. doi:10.2196/jmir.1367.

Dalton, J. C., & Crosby, P. C. (2014). The power of personal coaching: Helping first-year students to connect and commit in college. *Journal of College and Character, 15*, 59–66. doi:10.1515/jcc-2014-0010.

Gordon, R. (1987). An operational definition of disease prevention. In J. A. Sternberg & M. M. Silverman (Eds.), *Preventing mental disorders* (pp. 20–26). Rockville, MD: U.S. Department of Health and Human Services.

Israelashvili, M., & Romano, J. L. (Eds.). (2017). *The Cambridge handbook of international prevention science*. New York, NY: Cambridge University Press.

Israelashvili, M. (2017). What intensifies government support of prevention? Lessons from Israel. In M. Israelashvili & J. L. Romano (Eds.), *The Cambridge handbook of international prevention science* (pp. 978–997). New York, NY: Cambridge University Press.

Jordan, S, Gessnitzer, S., & Kauffeld, S. (2016). Effects of group coaching for the vocational orientation of secondary school pupils. *Coaching: An International Journal of Theory, Research, and Practice, 9*, 143–157.

Miller, W. R., & Rose, G. S. (2009). Toward a theory of motivational interviewing. *American Psychologist, 64*, 527–537. doi:10.1037/a0016830

Mrazek, P. J., & Haggerty, R. J. (Eds.). (1994). Committee on the prevention of mental disorders: Division of biobehavioral sciences and mental disorders: Reducing risks for mental disorders: Frontiers for preventive intervention research. Washington, DC: National Academy Press.

O'Connell, M. E., Boat, T., & Warner, K. E. (Eds.). (2009). *Preventing mental, emotional, and behavioral disorders among young people: Progress and possibilities*. Washington, DC: National Academies Press.

Popovic, N., & Jinks, D. (2014). Personal consultancy: A model for integrating counselling and coaching. New York, NY and London: Routledge.

Prochaska, J. O., Johnson, S., & Lee, P. (2009). The transtheoretical model of behavior change. In S. A. Shumaker, J. K. Ockene, & K. A. Riekert (Eds.), *The handbook of behavior change* (3rd ed., pp. 59–83). New York, NY: Springer.

Ringel, J., & Sturm, R. (2001). National estimates of mental health utilization and expenditures for children in 1998. *Journal of Behavioral Health Services and Research, 28*, 319–332.

Romano, J. L. (2015). *Prevention psychology: Enhancing personal and social well-being*. Washington, DC: American Psychological Association.

Romano, J. L., & Hage, S. M. (2000). Prevention and counseling psychology revitalizing commitments for the 21st century. *The Counseling Psychologist, 28*(6), 733–763.

Romano, J. L., & Israelashvili, M. (2017). Prevention science: A call for global action. In M. Israelashvili & J. L. Romano (Eds.), *The Cambridge handbook of international prevention science* (pp. 1021–1036). New York, NY: Cambridge University Press.

Romano, J. L., & Netland, J. D. (2008). The application of the theory of reasoned action and planned behavior to prevention science in counseling psychology. *The Counseling Psychologist, 36*, 777–806. doi:10.1177/0011000007301670

WHO. (2003). *Investing in mental health*. Geneva, Switzerland: Department of Mental Health and Substance Dependence, World Health Organization.

WHO. (2013). *Investing in mental health: Evidence for action*. Geneva, Switzerland: Department of Mental Health and Substance Dependence, World Health Organization.

WHO. (2015). *Mental health atlas 2014*. Geneva, Switzerland: World Health Organization.

Chapter 12

Counseling, training and coaching with mothers and fathers

Pathways for promoting inclusion

Lea Ferrari, Teresa Maria Sgaramella, and Ilaria Di Maggio

We can say without a doubt that the complex society we live in – characterized by globalization, multi-diversity, rapid technological advancement, financial crises, just to mention a few aspects – impinges also on the challenges that parents have to face every day to provide a living for their families while trying to assure them a decent present and future.

Parents have not only been recognized as having a crucial role in preventing possible issues in the social and personal adjustment of their children but also a social role as agents able to act in their life contexts to prompt change and improvement. Within this perspective, supporting parents in carrying out their duties seems nowadays inevitable if we want to guarantee acceptable quality of life and achieve the flourishing of family resources that can be exploited at best for them, their children and their life contexts.

Parental involvement is today considered crucial also in the realization of a more inclusive society in which attention is paid to doing together and co-constructing contexts that value everybody's uniqueness. Parents can not only be models for their children and foster tolerant attitudes toward diversity in them, but can also contribute to create welcoming supportive contexts that promote everybody's inclusion and participation (Ferrari & Nota, 2015).

This chapter will focus in particular on parents of children with disability who, just because of their children, find themselves on the frontline when facing the issue of inclusion. Research studies on parents of children with disability are certainly not a novelty and those carried out in the past have not been very fair about parents' characteristics, thus contributing, just as has happened for their children, to spread negative views of the conditions and prospects of these persons.

Also prompted by the advent of positive psychology, the latest models have instead focused attention on the resources and strengths of these parents, underlined and, albeit slowly, diminished stereotypical and negative visions of them. For example, Blacher, Baker, and Berkovits' (2013) model reminds us that bringing up a child implies joys and satisfactions regardless of the child's specific issues and of the difficulties experienced by the family. Naturally, parents of children with disability have negative and positive characteristics similar to those of other parents, but they also have specific experiences coming from having a child with impairment. For instance, parents able to revise their objectives are the ones who report "growing" more from living with their children's disability and also becoming better able to cope with stressful situations. These parents seem to see themselves as more sensitive to and tolerant of diversity, better able to understand others, to open toward new life perspectives and life experiences, which include also taking up an active role in the community as regards disability and inclusion (King, Zwaignebaum, Bates, Baxter, & Rosenbaum, 2012).

This suggests that people engaged in the services, counselors and coaches should certainly take into account parents' difficulties and long-term levels of stress, but also exploit the potentials that accompany the life stories of these persons and the resources they have used to favor everybody's inclusion. Therefore, in this chapter we have chosen to propose some suggestions that could be used to promote counseling actions that help parents develop a constructive mindset characterized by optimism and positive views of disability because of the role they can play in maintaining their quality of life and in adopting inclusive actions.

Main interventions centered on parents, as proposed in the international literature, will be described namely parent counseling, parent training, and the most recently developed parent coaching essentially addressed to individual families, both for the proved effectiveness and for the preventive value that make these as necessary steps toward the inclusion and participation of children and their families to the normal contexts of people's lives.

Parent counseling: a positive approach to complex issues

If we made a summary of what already exists in the literature, it would seem clear that many parents consider raising a child with a disability an enriching and positive experience, which, albeit alongside continuous commitment and stress, has allowed them to redefine their role and discover new and unexpected strengths and meanings (Hastings & Taunt, 2002). The research studies that give voice to these parents list among the issues dear to them aspects such as the strengthening of their sensitivity and tolerance, understanding and emotional maturity, new life perspectives, improved family cohesion and dynamics, an opportunity to learn new things and take up an active role to the advantage of society as concerns the issues of disability and inclusion (Bayat, 2007; Myers, Mackintosh, & Goin-Kochel, 2009; Hastings & Taunt, 2002; King et al., 2012). When the positive aspects are examined, such as the pleasantness of the time spent with their children or the energy that their children make them feel, differences between parents of children with or without disability are seldom marked (Blacher & Baker, 2007). Similar results were obtained also in a series of studies carried out in the Italian context (Nota, Soresi, Ferrari, Wilgosh, & Scorgie, 2005; Wilgosh, Nota, Scorgie, & Soresi, 2004), where the Life Management Survey (Scorgie, Wilgosh, & McDonald, 1997) was used to compare parents of children with autism, Down's syndrome, growth hormone deficit, reduced visual ability, and without disability.

What was said previously should urge counselors to revise their ideas on parents of children with disabilities and look at them as individuals whose life has been enriched by the experience of raising their children. They should then transfer this new vision to the contexts they are working in and become counselors engaged in the diffusion of inclusion with actions tailored to develop awareness on these issues, both with teachers and with parents of children without disability. In their interactions with the world of education and the services advocating inclusion, they should promote constructive ideas on the structure of the family of children with disability, for instance by supporting the positivity of these parents and preparing informative materials on them and on the importance given to them by the school and the services.

Focusing on the work that can be done with parents, and also in line with De Boer, Pijl, and Minnaert's (2010) meta-analysis, one of the elements on which counselors advocating inclusion in the 21st century should take action is the development and maintenance of positive attitudes toward diversities. Counselors could work with all parents on the way they explicitly talk about disability, narrate and comment on stories about inclusion to children and within their networks, as that affects other people's ideas and behaviors. At the same time, they could stimulate the description of ways to relate to schoolmates and offer help, collaboration and solidarity to them, and how to choose those to interact with, or to exclude, or to be friends with affect children's attitudes with the aim of facilitating positive attitudes (Bigler & Liben, 2007). Research carried out in the Italian context by Nota, Ferrari, Ginevra, and Soresi (2015), involving more than 1,000 parents showed that attitudes toward inclusion are more positive when the descriptions of students with disability to be included in the class are positive rather than neutral. And this is true regardless of their specific impairment. In this research, parents were asked to answer some questions after the presentation of a vignette about a child with physical, intellectual or behavioral disability. These descriptions differed when presented with a sentence where (the positive condition) some strengths of the child were emphasized.

All of this suggests to counselors the need to encourage parents to acquire a vocabulary of inclusion, in which the linguistic labels that convey stereotypes and negative visions are substituted with the description of abilities and strengths of children with disability, and space is given to what they can do and to what they are appreciated for by schoolmates and teachers (Siperstein, Parker, Bardon, & Widaman, 2007). In the worksheet called "Vocabulary of Inclusion" (see Table 12.1), examples of sentences are given that could be useful to encourage especially the parents of children with disabilities to use a language centered

Table 12.1 Example of worksheet

"The vocabulary of inclusion"
Positive description Mary, my little lady, has a visual impairment that makes it difficult for her to move quickly because she can't see very well. She is a lovely little girl who likes mixing with others and joins in the school activities, doing her bit, often in an original way.
Positive description with a suggestion My son has some language difficulties, but he's working hard and is learning fast. Whispering the right words and waiting for him to finish the sentence without substituting for him is helpful.
Wish with a description I really would like peers to invite Jin to play with them during playtime. Even if he can't run very fast, he can do other things, and they could all together find games to play that they never even thought of before.
Positive description with a positive reinforcement Yesterday again, John fulfilled his homework with one of his classmates. He has really applied himself, he wants so much to learn and he likes when working in small groups. When his mind wanders, he could really do with someone next to him that helps him concentrate. I'm very grateful that you planned activities so that peers could help John at home, too.

on strengths in situations where diversity is involved. After reading an example, parents can be invited to reflect on the elements of the sentence that actually point to strengths and then are encouraged to produce similar descriptions associated with their school and daily life and identify the advantages of speaking of inclusion in those terms.

A second point that counselors should consider is the need to support a positive view of the future by stimulating optimism (Nota, Ginevra, Di Maggio, & Soresi, 2017; Peer & Hillman, 2014). Defined as a generalized positive expectation of the future (Carver, Scheier, & Segerstrom, 2010), optimism is associated with several advantageous outcomes.

From a personal viewpoint, optimistic parents engage more in the problem-solving process, resort more frequently to coping, and they are more inclined to invest in the future (Dougall, Hyman, Hayward, McFeeley, & Baum, 2001; Hastings, Allen, McDermott, & Still, 2002). Also, they can establish more successful relationships with their children, regardless of their cultural background or whether the children are with or without disability, by adopting more adaptive parenting practices (Ellingsen, Baker, Blacher, & Crnic, 2013; Kao & Tienda, 1995; Koenig, Barry, & Kochanska, 2010).

To encourage parents to be optimistic, counselors should help them focus attention on their own abilities and on their opportunities rather than on their problems and difficulties; they should take an interest in people's lives and employ co-construction strategies such as reinforcements to underline successes achieved and barriers overcome by highlighting their strengths and resources. They should also present role models that have already handled similar situations, thus making the possibility to overcome problems more realistic and feasible for parents, by resorting to reformulation to facilitate revisiting of events and attribution of new meanings. Parents should be encouraged to reflect on their child's strengths, abilities and achievements by recognizing and focusing on the positive events that occur every day to their child and to their family and on the observation and identification of improvements, albeit small, and should also be taught reformulation strategies. For instance, what one cannot do and is described as an unsurmountable limit can be presented as something that can be learned by identifying the right supports. The aim is to favor re-examination of one's own life stories and reformulation of goals, instill hope and determination in looking for and finding resources and solutions to best respond to a child's needs, favor the identification of strategies to the advantage of inclusion (Kausar, Jevne, & Sobsey, 2003).

A third element counselors should work on with parents to the favor inclusion is the strengthening of parental advocacy, understood as a form of participation based on the realization of parental rights and responsibilities, whose main object is the safeguard of one's own rights and those of one's children, the solution of problems, and the particularly significant acquisition of services to support inclusion and promote a tolerant culture. Parents can resort to their advocacy abilities when they feel the need to apply for and obtain information and supports from the school; when they feel they must defend their educational ways and their children's care; when they feel they have to justify the participation or non-participation of their children in school activities or the frequency of the services; when they have to support learning activities (Brolan et al., 2012).

Making reference to Trainor's (2010) work, counselors could stimulate all that by helping parents reflect on the ways they present themselves and put forward their requests, by identifying more efficacious formulations that can best exploit their experiences and knowledge, and providing examples when necessary. They should be able to use the knowledge they have of their children by saying for example: "I know my child well enough to be able to say that . . ."; "I know that my child . . .", or the knowledge they have derived from specialists, books, websites and use specific terms by saying, for example, "Based on what I have read in the book by . . ."; "Prof. So-and-so maintains . . .". They could also use their knowledge to monitor situations and make decisions on how to go about applying for what they think is necessary by saying, for example, "As happened in the case of G., we think we could . . ."; "From previous experiences we had, it would be better to . . ." and to respond to the need of acquiring greater knowledge and stimulate the construction of a support network to produce change at systemic level by involving teachers, school personnel and also other parents. For instance, they could say, "We could ask So-and-so, who is an expert in this field, to explain to us . . ." or "To go on with this, we could ask So-and-so's support; this could facilitate . . .".

Working with parents to support inclusion requires counselors to continuously work on their *forma mentis* by introducing new constructs they refer to and update their *modus operandi* by innovating their practices. Assuming the role of active agents and inclusion promoters, counselors can also propose activities in the environment for the benefit of parents and more generally of the community, thus encouraging the dissemination of inclusive ideas and behaviors. One way for persecuting this is delivering parent-training activities based on themes and goals, such as those addressed in the following examples.

Parent training

There is a more general consensus on benefits derived from involving mothers and fathers in parent trainings and on the effectiveness of these activities in reducing behavioral problems while at the same time increasing parenting skills, their self-efficacy beliefs and satisfaction (Pfiffner et al., 2014). Among the most famous evidence-based programs there are trainings involving parents of children and adolescents of different ages, with eating disorders, behavioral problems or impairments, and also parents who are separating or divorcing. The Parent Plus Program (Sharry & Fitzpatrick, 1998), for instance, was developed for parents of typically developing children who show behavioral problems. Its effectiveness was evidenced in reducing problematic behaviors (Wynne et al., 2016) as well as levels of stress in parents but also in increasing confidence in their parenting skills and their life satisfaction (Hand, Raghallaigh, Cuppage, Coyle, & Sharry, 2013).

A program based on social learning theory and on positive reinforcement is the Stepping Stones Triple P (SSTP; Connell, Sanders, & Markie-Dadds, 1997) which aims at teaching a number of strategies for developing a positive relationship between parents and children. Its effectiveness was evidenced in families having children with developmental disabilities (Tellegen & Sanders, 2013). Similarly, Incredible Years (Webster-Stratton & Reid, 2010) has been successfully proposed to parents of typically developing children and of children with intellectual disabilities. Efficacy of the training has been described in reducing maladaptive behaviors of children as well as on parents' dysfunctional educational practices (McIntyre, 2008). However, these programs can be proposed to all parents regardless of their children's difficulties. This offers great opportunities in terms of inclusion. Additionally, it is important to involve heterogeneous groups in which space to build solidarity and tolerant networks exists and to make their voices heard in various life contexts, thus nurturing a culture of inclusion and participation in their communities.

Regarding the Italian context, the experiences conducted since the 1980s by Soresi and collaborators in this field have assumed a leading role. In one of the last editions, participants were parents of children with ADHD and parents of typical development children. They benefited from eight weekly, two-hour meetings whose themes are reported in Table 12.2 (Ferrari, Pagliai, Benincà, Soresi, & Concato, 2013).

In implementing the program, the active participation of parents was emphasized by asking them to describe their experiences, strategies employed and difficulties encountered in implementing target strategies outlined during the meetings. The heightened realism was also promoted through examples representative of reality and through the analysis of what parents themselves suggested and described. The careful designing, through the operational description and, from time to time, publicizing the goal to be achieved in each meeting, is another founding element of this training (Nota & Soresi, 2004).

Taking into account the complexity of our times, these parent trainings assume a significant role for inclusion in the 21st century. They often have been proposed to heterogeneous groups, simultaneously attended by parents of children with or without disabilities, by parents of different ethnic backgrounds and socioeconomic status. Their aim has always been increasing the

Table 12.2 An example of parent training (adapted from Ferrari et al., 2013)

Meeting themes	*Content and goals addressed*
How behaviors are learned	Defining behaviors and learning and the laws that regulate them; distinguishing behavior from other descriptions such as opinions or judgments
When children's behaviors are a problem	What is an inappropriate behavior, how inappropriate behaviors persist and how to distinguish those from the appropriate ones
Does the punishment really work	Defining punishment, the rules to follow to ensure that the punishment produces the expected results and disadvantages of this approach
How to observe children's behavior	A functional analysis of a problematic behavior, its antecedents and consequents, the operational language
Alternatives to punishment: preventing inappropriate behaviors	Acting on antecedents through reduction of discriminatory stimuli and of exposure to inappropriate behavior
Alternatives to punishment: increasing appropriate behaviors	Increasing appropriate behaviors without resorting to punishment, by adopting reinforcement and extinction of inappropriate behavior
Alternatives to punishment: reducing inappropriate behaviors	Acting on consequences to reduce unwanted behaviors through differential reinforcement and time-out
Parents as problem-solvers	Parents' ability to solve educational problems by promoting appropriate behaviors in children through skills developed during the program

ability of mothers and fathers to create supportive and positive relationships among them and among their children, hence emphasizing the respect of diversity and development of solidarity. Parents are invited to act as models for other parents and stimulate thoughts and actions promoting *inclusion for all*. Moreover, interventions encouraged partnerships among universities, health services and schools to give life to an "inclusive community hug", to facilitate the perception of a common effort and to reduce feelings of isolation and abandon.

An attempt to stimulate parents' advocacy and disseminate an inclusive culture was carried out by Carter, Swedeen, Walter, and Moss (2012) who involved mothers and fathers in organizing and implementing community conversations. Parents attended five training days run by the project staff and by two parents who had previous experiences in the field of disability and worked as facilitators.

The analysis of the concept of inclusion and of barriers that might be encountered in the community was a central theme as well as strategies parents can use to encourage inclusion in community and school settings. Ways and suggestions giving rise to new opportunities for inclusion were also explored by taking advantage of community resources. Parents were also given information and tips on how to organize and manage community conversations. Specifically, the World Café methodology was introduced (Brown & Isaacs, 2005; www.theworldcafe.com) and set up to facilitate dialogue in fairly large groups on specific topics. This method requires preparing the environment; welcoming participants and introducing the topic under discussion; exploring selected topics by working in sub-groups, encouraging the contribution of all, finding points of contact between different perspectives, listening carefully for better understanding of key elements, generating ideas and sharing results with the group.

Cummings, Sills-Busio, Barker, and Dobbins (2015), on the other hand, involved parents in three days of training on inclusive practices. They were engaged in general and small-group discussions, creating make-and-take materials, writing individualized lists of strategies and resources, and demonstrating how to perform activities. Moreover, between two training sessions, participants continued working on goals developed in the previous sessions and received feedback and suggestions via an online blog community. Procedures adopted fostered an effective understanding of children and learning strategies useful to cope with their difficulties as well as to better communicate, collaborate and decide together with professionals. What seems important to emphasize at this point is that giving value to parents and supporting the development of skills and actions in favor of inclusion within their families and their networks is mandatory for counselors. They cannot abdicate if their goal is to positively influence people's lives they are dealing with and to introduce a change in their living contexts. Moreover, these parents could become cornerstones to reach those parents who find it difficult to interface with these issues and services dealing with these needs.

Parent coaching

Besides more well-established procedures and actions, recent years have seen the rise of interest in parent coaching activities. The work of Rush and colleagues (Rush, Sheldon, & Hanft, 2003) has underscored the need to carry out coaching actions with families. Coaches, in fact, using a conversational approach based on listening and questioning, can cooperate with families and focus their actions on family-specific routines in everyday life rather than present themselves as experts providing suggestions in a top-down hierarchical approach. Coach actions are, in fact, tailored to enable parents as those who produce ideas fostering changes and define personal goals thus differentiating their actions from other types of interventions where professionals provide suggestions or ideas on the most appropriate way to follow or reach a given goal (Rush & Shelden, 2011).

Several methodologies are available to coaches interested in working with parents. Rush and Shelden (2011) and also Foster, Dunn, and Lawson (2013) provide some examples of these methodologies:

(a) *Sharing a project.* Parents and coaches together decide the issues to be addressed, either the general goal of the action or the goal of a specific activity.
(b) *Observing the target individual* while adopting routine or newly acquired strategies. Coaches can help parents in a task analysis by formulating reflexive questions or behaving as a model. Similarly, parents after observing a coach can behave as models or observe children's behaviors.
(c) *Acting between sessions.* Parents practice in everyday context what they have learned during coaching sessions and describe what happens.
(d) *Reflecting.* By asking questions, the coach facilitates parents' reflection on what is going on, on what they already tried to carry out and on resources they might refer to, thus facilitating the awareness and development of strengths.
(e) *Providing feedback on the coaching process.* Based on the behavior observed and on thoughts shared, the coach provides information on resources or strategies being developed to foster the emerging of new strategies and ideas.

Dunn, Cox, Foster, Mische-Lawson, and Tanquary (2012) provide a useful example of this process in a 10-hour intervention they carried out with 20 parents of children with autism whose ages ranged from 3 to 10 years old. The actions took place in their living environments – i.e. at home (bedroom, bathroom and transition between rooms) and in the community (church, public gardens and shop). During the first session, the coach and parents set goals and decided the activities to be fostered according to their relevance and interest (i.e. home, public garden and a shop). They also agreed on the specific target routines on which they were going to focus in each week and on related goals. During the sessions, coaches used Rush and Shelden (2011) suggestions, namely using reflexive sentences and questions encouraging parents to discuss ways to reach goals they already decided and avoiding yes/no questions, thus promoting the emerging of new ideas. For instance, they asked, "How is he used to washing the face now? (Awareness), "List other occasions in which he threw things on his face. What did happen?" (Analysis); "I wonder how we can use strategies which were already successful in the past to change this routine?" (Alternative); "Which supports are useful in order to reach the goal?" (Action). Analyses conducted at the end of the intervention showed parents considering themselves more competent and children participating more actively in their everyday life.

Although definitions and efficacy analysis still need more studies (Kemp & Turnbull, 2014) the use of technology in coaching actions with parents receives increasing attention. One of the most important motivations supporting internet interventions is the goal of helping a higher number of individuals with a low amount of professional involvement, saving time and reducing costs. Moreover, it means providing support available to parents who for diverse circumstances have difficulties in accessing professional help (Nieuwboer, Fukkink, & Hermanns, 2013). An example is provided by Wade, Oberjohn, Conaway, Osinska, and Bangert (2011) who developed a web-coaching intervention for parents of children who suffered from head trauma. InTERACT consists in a first session at home followed by 10–14 self-directed web sessions and 10–14 online synchronic coaching sessions where participants in real time communicate with their coach. With the first session, coaches have the opportunity to know the family and their challenges, describe the program together with providing all the information needed to use the web by also providing them an instruction manual. Self-directed weekly sessions last 25 minutes and are focused on parenting skills. Each session includes information on target skills, video clips showing parents and children performing the target activity and interactive exercises to strengthen learning. An online coaching session follows that includes three parts: 15–20 minutes for analyzing the self-directed session and are aimed at increasing understanding of the situation; 5 minutes to observing parent-child interaction; 20–30 minutes for analyzing the specific parenting skills implemented. Preliminary results support the usefulness of technology in coaching actions. Nine of the 13 parents participating in the activity, additionally, affirmed they preferred this type of activity to the more traditional ones.

These studies underline the agentic role coaches can play in promoting inclusion in the 21st century, which consists in stimulating parent's reflexivity on the advantages deriving from sharing goals and efforts and on promoting the development of partnerships advantageous for all. In order to foster this attitude and their role parents should, for instance, ask themselves what kind of actions tailored to inclusion is the school promoting (Awareness); what goals have already been reached or are still lacking in school (Analysis); if the school has already and successfully undertaken strategies to foster inclusion, which of them can be implemented also for future goals (Alternatives); what possible actions can be carried out to reach these goals (Actions). Additionally, information gathered and situations directly experienced in working with families can help coaches to develop and actively co-construct services more appropriately answering the needs of families they are working with.

Conclusion

Studies described in this analysis pictured parents as a valuable resource in developing inclusive contexts. Counselors and coach interested in the future of our society are strongly invited to not only support and empower parenting skills useful in more successfully dealing with their educational role but also to value and flourish the efforts fathers and mothers can provide in the contexts where they live, to the benefit of inclusion. More particularly, parents of children with disabilities represent a unique point of reference for the community.

Inclusion is a challenge. It requires coaches and counselors to make a systematic effort in updating their theoretical and applied knowledge but also in suggesting ideas and innovations. It is worth then mentioning at this point that the assessment of efficacy is crucial for advancing research but also for high-quality professional standards. It also makes explicit some grey areas and suggests new possible pathways.

Readers might have also realized that distinguishing between coaching and counseling is not an easy task. But following Kemp and Turnbull (2014), we might refer to coaching as to the process of listening and learning focused on a relationship where the *what*, the *how* and the *when* are the consequences of sharing a specific type of feedback given to parents when they try to use target strategies. Coaching strategies and procedures can then be used in several different situations, including parent training.

Finally, there is *a scarlet thread* that runs through counseling and coaching of the future which is increasingly strengthened in on-the-move-actions which go beyond the professional setting and opens to parents in different everyday life settings often mediated by technology (Sools & Schuhmann, 2014). This takes on a preventive value, as a background for professionals interested in promoting inclusion.

References

Bayat, M. (2007). Evidence of resilience in families of children with autism. *Journal of Intellectual Disability Research, 51*(9), 702–714.

Bigler, R. S., & Liben, L. S. (2007). Developmental intergroup theory: Explaining and reducing children's social stereotyping and prejudice. *Current Directions in Psychological Science, 16*(3), 162–166.

Blacher, J., & Baker, B. L. (2007). Positive impact of intellectual disability on families. *American Journal on Mental Retardation, 112*(5), 330–348.

Blacher, J., Baker, B. L., & Berkovits, L. (2013). Family perspectives on child disability: Views from the sunny side of the street. In M. L. Wehmeyer (Ed.), *Oxford handbook of positive psychology and disability* (pp. 164–181). New York, NY: Oxford University Press.

Brolan, C. E., Boyle, F. M., Dean, J. H., Taylor Gomez, M., Ware, R. S., & Lennox, N. G. (2012). Health advocacy: A vital step in attaining human rights for adults with intellectual disability. *Journal of Intellectual Disability Research*, *56*(11), 1087–1097.

Brown, J., & Isaacs, D. (2005). *The world cafe*. San Francisco, CA: Berrett-Koehler Publishers.

Carter, E., Swedeen, B., Walter, M. C. M., & Moss, C. K. (2012). "I don't have to do this by myself?" Parent-led community conversations to promote inclusion. *Research and Practice for Persons with Severe Disabilities*, *37*(1), 9–23.

Carver, C. S., Scheier, M. F., & Segerstrom, S. C. (2010). Optimism. *Clinical Psychology Review*, *30*(7), 879–889.

Connell, S., Sanders, M. R., & Markie-Dadds, C. (1997). Self-directed behavioral family intervention for parents of oppositional children in rural and remote areas. *Behavior Modification*, *21*(4), 379–408.

Cummings, K. P., Sills-Busio, D., Barker, A. F., & Dobbins, N. (2015). Parent – professional partnerships in early education: Relationships for effective inclusion of students with disabilities. *Journal of Early Childhood Teacher Education*, *36*(4), 309–323.

De Boer, A., Pijl, S. J., & Minnaert, A. (2010). Attitudes of parents towards inclusive education: A review of the literature. *European Journal of Special Needs Education*, *25*(2), 165–181.

Dougall, A. L., Hyman, K. B., Hayward, M. C., McFeeley, S., & Baum, A. (2001). Optimism and traumatic stress: The importance of social support and coping. *Journal of Applied Social Psychology*, *31*(2), 223–245.

Dunn, W., Cox, J., Foster, L., Mische-Lawson, L., & Tanquary, J. (2012). Impact of a contextual intervention on child participation and parent competence among children with autism spectrum disorders: A pretest/posttest repeated-measures design. *American Journal of Occupational Therapy*, *66*(5), 520–528.

Ellingsen, R., Baker, B. L., Blacher, J., & Crnic, K. (2014). Resilient parenting of children at developmental risk across middle childhood. *Research in Developmental Disabilities*, *35*(6), 1364–1374.

Ferrari, L., & Nota, L. (2015). Il coinvolgimento e il ruolo dei genitori per una scuola inclusiva [The involvement and the role of parents for the school inlcusion]. In L. Nota, M. C. Ginevra, & S. Soresi (Eds.), *L'inclusione scolastica nel 21° secolo: Programmi per favorirla e sostenerla*. Padova: Cleup.

Ferrari, L., Pagliai, M., Benincà, A. C., Soresi, S., & Concato, F., (2013). Support parents of children with disabilities through parent training. *Life Span and Disability*, *16*, 61–78.

Foster, L., Dunn, W., & Lawson, L. M. (2013). Coaching mothers of children with autism: A qualitative study for occupational therapy practice. *Physical & Occupational Therapy in Pediatrics*, *33*(2), 253–263.

Hand, A., Raghallaigh, C. N., Cuppage, J., Coyle, S., & Sharry, J. (2013). A controlled clinical evaluation of the Parents Plus Children's Programme for parents of children aged 6–12 with mild intellectual disability in a school setting. *Clinical Child Psychology and Psychiatry*, *18*(4), 536–555.

Hastings, R. P., Allen, R., McDermott, K., & Still, D. (2002). Factors related to positive perceptions in mothers of children with intellectual disabilities. *Journal of Applied Research in Intellectual Disabilities*, *15*(3), 269–275.

Hastings, R. P., & Taunt, H. M. (2002). Positive perceptions in families of children with developmental disabilities. *American Journal on Mental Retardation*, *107*(2), 116–127.

Kao, G., & Tienda, M. (1995). Optimism and achievement: The educational performance of immigrant youth. *Social Science Quarterly*, *76*(1), 1–19.

Kausar, S., Jevne, R. F., & Sobsey, D. (2003). Hope in families of children with developmental disabilities. *Journal on Developmental Disabilities, 10*(1), 35–46.

Kemp, P., & Turnbull, A. P. (2014). Coaching with parents in early intervention: An interdisciplinary research synthesis. *Infants & Young Children, 27*(4), 305–324.

King, G., Zwaigenbaum, L., Bates, A., Baxter, D., & Rosenbaum, P. (2012). Parent views of the positive contributions of elementary and high school-aged children with autism spectrum disorders and Down syndrome. *Child: Care, Health and Development, 38*(6), 817–828.

Koenig, J. L., Barry, R. A., & Kochanska, G. (2010). Rearing difficult children: Parents' personality and children's proneness to anger as predictors of future parenting. *Parenting: Science and Practice, 10*(4), 258–273.

McIntyre, L. L. (2008). Adapting Webster-Stratton's incredible years parent training for children with developmental delay: Findings from a treatment group only study. *Journal of Intellectual Disability Research, 52*(12), 1176–1192.

Myers, B. J., Mackintosh, V. H., & Goin-Kochel, R. P. (2009). "My greatest joy and my greatest heart ache:" Parents' own words on how having a child in the autism spectrum has affected their lives and their families' lives. *Research in Autism Spectrum Disorders, 3*(3), 670–684.

Nieuwboer, C. C., Fukkink, R. G., & Hermanns, J. M. (2013). Online programs as tools to improve parenting: A meta-analytic review. *Children and Youth Services Review, 35*(11), 1823–1829.

Nota, L., Ferrari, L., Ginevra, M. C., & Soresi, S. (2015, April). *Le minacce all 'inclusione: Etichette, aspettative ed atteggiamenti* [Threat to inclusion: Labels, expectations and attitudes]. Paper presented at seminar "Inclusione "senza se e senza ma", Padova.

Nota, L., Ginevra, M. C., Di Maggio, & I., Soresi, S. (2017). Engaging Parent Strengths for Inclusion: The Power of Optimism, Hope, and Courage. In K. Scorgie, & D. Sobsey (Eds.), *Working with families for inclusive education. International Perspectives on Inclusive Education* (pp. 209 - 224). Bingley: Emerald.

Nota, L., & Soresi, S. (2004). Improving the problem-solving and decision-making skills of a high indecision group of young adolescents: A test of the "difficult: No problem!" training. *International Journal for Educational and Vocational Guidance, 4*(1), 3–21.

Nota, L., Soresi, S., Ferrari, L., Wilgosh, L., & Scorgie, K. (2005). Life Management and quality of life of parents of children with diverse disabilities. *Developmental Disabilities Bulletin, 31*, 155–181.

Peer, J. W., & Hillman, S. B. (2014). Stress and resilience for parents of children with intellectual and developmental disabilities: A review of key factors and recommendations for practitioners. *Journal of Policy and Practice in Intellectual Disabilities, 11*(2), 92–98.

Pfiffner, L. J., Hinshaw, S. P., Owens, E., Zalecki, C., Kaiser, N. M., Villodas, M., & McBurnett, K. (2014). A two-site randomized clinical trial of integrated psychosocial treatment for ADHD-inattentive type. *Journal of Consulting and Clinical Psychology, 82*(6), 1115–1127.

Rush, D. D., & Shelden, M. L. L. (2011). *The early childhood coaching handbook*. Baltimore, MD: Brookes Publishing Company.

Rush, D., Sheldon, M. L. L., & Hanft, B. (2003). Coaching families and colleagues: A process for collaboration in natural settings. *Infants & Young Children, 16*(1), 33–47.

Scorgie, K., Wilgosh, L., & McDonald, L. (1997). A survey follow-up on managing life when a child has a disability. *Developmental Disabilities Bulletin, 25*, 65–69.

Sharry, J., & Fitzpatrick, C. (1998). Parents plus programme: A practical and positive video-based course for managing and solving discipline problems in children. *Manual and videos*. Dublin: Mater Hospital.

Siperstein, G. N., Parker, R. C., Bardon, J. N., & Widaman, K. F. (2007). A national study of youth attitudes toward the inclusion of students with intellectual disabilities. *Exceptional Children, 73*(4), 435–455.

Sools, A., & Schuhmann, C. (2014). Theorizing the narrative dimension of psychotherapy and counseling: A big and small story approach. *Journal of Contemporary Psychotherapy, 44*(3), 191–200.

Tellegen, C. L., & Sanders, M. R. (2013). Stepping-stones triple P-positive parenting program for children with disability: A systematic review and meta-analysis. *Research in Developmental Disabilities, 34*(5), 1556–1571.

Trainor, A. A. (2010). Diverse approaches to parent advocacy during special education home – school interactions identification and use of cultural and social capital. *Remedial and Special Education, 31*(1), 34–47.

Wade, S. L., Oberjohn, K., Conaway, K., Osinska, P., & Bangert, L. (2011). Live coaching of parenting skills using the internet: Implications for clinical practice. *Professional Psychology: Research and Practice, 42*(6), 487–493.

Webster-Stratton, C., & Reid, M. (2010). Adapting the Incredible Years, an evidence-based parenting programme, for families involved in the child welfare system. *Journal of Children's Services, 5*(1), 25–42.

Wilgosh, L., Nota, L., Scorgie, K., & Soresi, S. (2004). Effective life management in parents of children with disabilities: A cross-national extension. *International Journal for the Advancement of Counselling, 26*(3), 301–312.

Wynne, C., Doyle, C., Kenny, R., Brosnan, E. & Sharry, J. (2016). A first-level evaluation of a family intervention for adolescent social, emotional and behavioural difficulties in child and adolescent mental health services. *Journal of Child and Adolescent Mental Health*, 28, 33–46.

Chapter 13

The challenge of career counseling and guidance for adolescents and young adults in areas of global migration and multicultural societies

The case of Israeli Arabs

Rachel Gali Cinamon

Along with global social reforms, dramatic technological developments have changed the nature of the world of work. Stability, security and belonging are no longer integral elements of being an employed person. Experiencing insecurity, hectic changes and alienation have become more common among many workers in our global economy (Blustein, 2013; Savickas, 2012). The challenge of having to manage and succeed with regard to current employment demands is more difficult and sometimes even impossible to achieve by at-risk populations such as immigrants, minorities, poor people and people with special needs (e.g., Cinamon, Habayib, & Ziv, 2016; Michael, Most, & Cinamon, 2013). These people are usually marginalized and lack essential resources such as different types of social capital (Bourdieu, 1986), access to information, access to resources and career sponsorship. These types of social capital are essential for career success (Seibert, Kraimer, & Liden, 2001). Therefore, the lifelong journey of finding an occupation and managing work and other life roles is much more complicated for these people.

Different forms of marginalization patterns documented in the literature differ according to group characteristics (e.g., women, people with disabilities, ethnic or political minorities) and contextual factors, economic conditions and political circumstances (e.g., Abrams, Hogg, & Marques, 2004; Barnes & Mercer, 2005; Enosh & Ben-Ari, 2013; Gor Ziv, 2015; Gorodzeisky, 2013; Hindman, 2011; Martell, Emrich, & Robison-Cox, 2012). These studies, along with the understanding that each culture has unique and specific values and traditions that shape it, highlight the importance of understanding marginalization in the concept of career development within the specific context in which they are taking place. The current chapter focuses on career development of Israeli Arab adolescents and young adults as a case study to address challenges and dilemmas faced by career counselors who work with minorities in multicultural societies. After describing the Israeli Arab context, I will address the questions that emerge from the complexity I described, as follows: What are the major issues faced by young Israeli Arabs after high school? What are the best theoretical foundations that can serve career counselors and career guidance who work with these young people? What are the issues and skills that should be addressed in career counseling and career guidance with these populations? And what training is required for counselors who work with these groups?

Emerging adulthood in a multicultural society – the Israeli Arab context

Two interrelated contextual factors should be considered when studying the period of adolescence and emerging adulthood in Israel: the diverse cultural makeup of the country and the security-political situation in the region (Enosh & Ben-Ari, 2013). Following massive waves of Jewish immigration from more than 70 countries, Israel is characterized by a mixture of countries of origin, religions, traditions and heritages. Traditional patterns exist alongside modern lifestyles, Western culture coexists with Middle-Eastern heritage, and religious values and practices range from secular to highly orthodox (Lavee & Katz, 2003). As a result, there are numerous cultural cleavages in Israeli society. One important cultural divide relates to Jewish citizens, who comprise about 80% of the population, and Arab citizens, who constitute 20.7% of the general population (Central Bureau of Statistics, 2016). The majority of Arab society (83%) is Moslem and 39% live in Arab villages or Arab cities in Israel's northern region. They have an independent educational system and Arabic is their official language (Golan-Agnon, 2006). As a result, social interaction between young Israeli Arabs and Jews is relatively limited.

These two cultural groups have different qualities that shape their young people's development. Most Jews are characterized as having individualistic values and adhering to a modern, Western way of life (Schwartz, 1994). This Western culture emphasizes the importance of achieving personal goals, individual development, competition and economic success. In contrast, many Israeli Arabs, especially those coming from rural areas, have been characterized as having collectivistic values, as having strong ties to extended families and maintaining traditional cultural norms (Abu-Baker, 2002; Herzog & Singer-Avitz, 2004). Arab culture is considered to be traditional, homogenous, patriarchal-hierarchical and collective-oriented (Barakat, 1985; Hassan, 1999). Arab collectivistic culture is associated with an emphasis on interdependence, family security, social hierarchy and a low level of competition. Arab society's collectivism focuses mostly on ethnic-religious elements (Oyserman, 1993).

Collectivism underscores the roles of its members in maintaining social norms and performing social duties as defined by the in-group. The male's primary role in this society is that of the breadwinner, while women in this society usually carry the heaviest burden when it comes to domestic duties, and they have less access to resources than do the men (Cinamon et al., 2016). This even holds true in dual-career Moslem families, where both members of the couple are educated and working (Kulik & Rayyan, 2003). Such cultural codes tend to censure men's, and especially women's, aspirations with regard to individual and career development in general (Abu-Rabia-Queder, 2007)

Furthermore, the Arab-Israel conflict creates differential political and social experiences and opportunities for the two groups of citizen of the Israeli state. Israeli Arabs are a national minority in Israel, while the other members of their Palestinian nationality are spread throughout Gaza, the West Bank, Jordan and Lebanon. This situation led Rabinowitz (2001) to call Israeli Arabs a "trapped minority". They have formal citizenship in the State of Israel, including the right to vote and to be elected, while the majority of Palestinians living outside the borders of Israel are engaged in an ongoing and violent conflict with Israel. In his article, Rabinowitz (2001) cites a Palestinian member of Israel's Knesset (Parliament) who describes this complication: "I am in a tragic situation, whereby my country is at war with my people". As a result, due to their citizenship and acculturation in Israel, they are being marginalized twice over by two political entities: Israeli Jewish society and Palestinians and Arabs abroad (Rabinowitz, 2001).

The Israeli Arab population is usually less educated than the Jewish population (median years of study of 12 versus 12.9) and earns only 61% of the average salary of Jewish employees (Central Bureau of Statistics, 2014). Just like other minorities around the globe, the Israeli Arab participation in the Israeli labor market is characterized by a relatively low rate of participants (41% compared to 60% among Israeli Jews), a relatively high rate of unemployment (8.5% vs. 7.4% among Israeli Jews), and a high rate of workers in fields which pay low wages and do not require high skills (43% of the Arab working males work in construction and 60% of the females, in health and education). Furthermore, they earn less: Arab males earn 60% less per hour than Jewish males, and Arab women earn 75% less per hour than Jewish women (Yashiv, 2012; Yashiv & Kasir, 2014).

Just as with minorities in many other countries, Israeli Arabs also consider higher education to be a top priority (Seginer & Mahajna, 2016). Unfortunately, they constitute only 13.1% of the undergraduate students, 10.1% of the graduate students and approximately 5.4% of the doctoral students (Central Bureau of Statistics, 2014). The Arabs' path to higher education might be considered to be overcoming an obstacle that consists of systemic educational, as well as social, cultural and institutional challenges. The obstacles include a lack of interest in school, language difficulties (the majority of higher education institutions in Israel use Hebrew as the major language of study, while most Israeli Arabs students, until reaching high school, studied in the Arab education system that uses Arabic as the major language of study) and a lack of learning skills and difficulties in graduating from institutions of higher education (Ali, 2013; Shaviv, Binstein, Stone, & Fudem, 2013).

Since Israeli Arab adolescents usually study in Arab education systems in Arab towns or villages, the transition to academia is a huge one for them. For most of them, it is the first time that they find themselves studying with the Jewish majority and in Hebrew. Indeed, compared to Jewish students, Arab university students report more career barriers than Jewish university students, barriers that involve ethnic and gender discrimination, childcare and family issues, and a lower sense of efficacy for coping with career barriers (Lipshits-Braziler & Tatar, 2012). Furthermore, they also perceive that strong connections, support and obligations from and toward families are simultaneously both a resource and a barrier (Mansour, 2005; Massalha, 2008). It should be mentioned that since 1995, several Arab colleges have been established, mainly Arab colleges of education, and these were certified by the Israel Council for Higher Education, and teach only in Arabic.

The student body consists only of Israeli Arab students and almost all the teachers are Israeli Arabs, as well. Israeli Arab students studying in these institutions are not exposed to, and therefore do not experience, all the previously mentioned obstacles (Cinamon et al., 2016).

Higher education is widely recognized by Israeli Arabs as being the most important factor in determining one's occupational class and one's chances for upward mobility in modern society (Khattab & Miaari, 2013). Those who overcome these obstacles usually prefer careers that make it more likely that they will secure employment and a higher income, as well as careers that are perceived by their social environment as being prestigious (Sharabi, 2013; Shaviv et al., 2013). For example, Arab students' preferred occupations are medicine, paramedical professions (mainly pharmacology, nursing and optometry) and teaching (Shaviv et al., 2013). Their representation in computer science studies, the field that is considered to be the field of future employment (Brynjolfsson & McAfee, 2014; Frey & Osborne, 2013; Kaczmarczyk & Dopplick, 2014) is very low – only 7% of computer science students in universities are Israeli Arabs, while only 1.8% of all hi-tech employees are Arabs males (Central Bureau of Statistics, 2014). However, attaining higher education does not ensure equality of opportunity, and the jobs actually obtained by many Israeli Arabs who have graduated from college do not match their levels of education (Ali, 2013; Gera & Cohen, 2005; Khattab & Miaari, 2013).

The career situation is even more challenging for Israeli Arab women. While Arab women in Israel have increased their rate of enrollment in higher education and participation in the workforce, there still exists a disparity between Israeli Arab and Jewish women (Arar & Abu-Rabia-Queder, 2011). Israeli Arab women achieve an average of 11.3 years of schooling compared to 14.1 years among Jewish women. Twenty-five percent (25.1%) of all Arab women work (compared to 72.4% of all Jewish women), while 43.9% of them only work part-time (compared to 32.4% among employed Jewish women). Forty-two percent (42.8%) of Arab working women are employed in education, while the disparity in salary levels between them and Jewish women in education stands at 30% (Central Bureau of Statistics, 2011).

These disparities can be explained by two factors: (a) traditional Arab sociocultural norms for gender roles that emphasize the role of women in the household or in stereotypical female professions (e.g., social work, teaching, nursing), or jobs that allow them to combine work and family obligations (e.g., part-time jobs, working at home) (Abu-Baker, 2002; Arar & Mustafa, 2009; Cinamon et al., 2016); and (b) structural factors such as a lack of employment opportunities in the Arab sector, the problematic attitudes of Jewish employers (i.e., discrimination and stereotyping) and government policies toward the Arab population regarding infrastructure, education, training and employment assistance, including childcare arrangements (e.g., Khattab, 2002).

The Arab family plays a major role in young people's decisions regarding education, employment and even romantic relations. A study of the exploration process among young Israeli adults (Cinamon, Rich, & Spector, 2012) found that Israeli Arab young adults consult their parents and other extended family members about their higher education and other career plans. They also mentioned difficulties when consulting with members of the older generation who live in a more collectivistic environment and have traditional values regarding an occupational future in a more modern and individualistic society. In a recently published previous study that I conducted with colleges on conceptions of work and higher education among Israeli Arab female students (Cinamon et al., 2016), we found the important role of family members, especially parents and spouses, in young Arab women's career development. Some of the women participants in this study had to struggle to be allowed to study in the Israeli higher education system. The relatively new Islamic colleges near their Arab cities and villages helped them convince their fathers or spouses to allow them to study, since they would continue to live with their families while pursuing their studies and would only interact with Israeli Arab students and teachers. Family members were also mentioned as an important resource in their studies, by encouraging, taking care of young children and helping them with housework.

Israeli Arab young adults are also occupied with political and religious issues. They explore political relations and issues in Israel and abroad, and speculate about political issues more than do Israeli Jewish young adults (Cinamon et al., 2012). They are also more engaged in religious issues than Jewish young adult (Cinamon et al., 2012), and perceive religion and faith as being major resources in their career development (Cinamon et al., 2016).

The previous description highlights several unique challenges faced by young Israeli Arabs throughout their career development journey, challenges such as the need to overcome marginalization and discrimination, the need to construct a notional identity that will enable them to be part of the Palestinian nation but at the same time be integral contributing citizens of the Israeli state, the importance of overcoming traditional gender role separation and division of labor, and the need to manage work and family obligations as members of a society in transition (transition from tradition to modernity, from collectivism values to more individualistic values, from villages to cities, etc.). These challenges and missions are in addition to those faced by all young people in our changing world of work. Furthermore, it is clear that the parents, and even other members of the extended family, should be part of these interventions because of the important role of relations and family in Arab culture.

Because of these issues and missions, career counselors must use specific conceptual and theoretical approaches as guiding principles to be able to address the unique needs of Israeli Arab young adults. The following paragraph expands upon relevant theoretical frameworks that can guide career counselors, along with practical suggestions that result from these conceptions.

Theoretical and conceptual frameworks that are highly relevant for career counselors of Israeli Arab young adults

The importance of acknowledging the changing nature of the world of work, the crucial role of social conditions and social relations in the course of an individual's career development are reflected in several career theories and conceptual frameworks. Career construction theory (Savickas, 2005) emphasizes the actively ongoing role a person must adopt to manage one's career and adapt it to economic and social changes. The psychology of working theory (Blustein, 2013; Duffy, Blustein, Diemer, & Autin, 2016) (PWT) underscores marginalization and social conditions as initial antecedents that shape important vocational constructs such as work volition and the ability to acquire decent work. Flum and Cinamon (2011) discuss the interplay between citizenship, identity and career in the context of immigration, and mark the potential of active citizenship and identity for performing a meaningful career.

The conceptual model of work and family interface (Frone, 2003) and the accumulative empirical studies that support it (for review see Whiston and Cinamon, 2015) suggest specific individual and environmental variables that contribute to a person's ability to manage work and family effectively.

As I will elaborate next, these conceptions can serve career counselors who work with young adults from minorities in general and with Israeli Arab young adults in particular. Since I previously wrote about the work-family interface in the life of Israeli Arab women (Cinamon, 2009), and I also suggested several intervention models to prepare minority adolescents and young adults for managing work and family effectively (Cinamon, 2006, 2016), I will not expand on this important subject in this chapter. Rather, I refer the readers to these resources and emphasize the importance of this subject in career counseling for any group of young people, and in particular, for young people from collectivistic societies.

Savickas's career construction theory (2005) focuses on people's need to adapt to social life implications and changes. This theory perceives human development as being driven by adaptation to social environment to enable the person and the environment to become integrated, a process of matching and finding meaning, and making it all matter to oneself and to society. This comprehensive theory integrates four elements of vocational behavior: life structure, strategies, stories and style. Life structure includes work and other life roles that shape and construct our life. Strategies include coping behaviors that people use to manage and come to terms with developmental tasks, transitions and changes. Narrative, the third component, involves narrative stories that can teach and point to motivational patterns and themes in a person's life. The last element refers to self-concept in terms of individual characteristics, abilities, interests and personality. Based on the narrative paradigm, career construction counseling prompts clients to design their lives and author their own life-career stories in a way that enhances their experience of work as a meaningful context for development and an endeavor that matters both personally and socially.

This conceptual framework is especially relevant for career counselors who work with minorities, especially with minorities from traditional societies. As was described previously, the need to adapt to changes is an important challenge among young Israeli Arabs, especially during the transition from high school to higher education, or from high school or higher education to the world of work. For most of them, it will be the first time that they meet and study or work with Israeli Jews, using a different language, Hebrew; the first time that they socialize and interact with "others" who hold more individualistic values and live a more modern way of life compared to their own traditional lifestyle. Therefore, it is crucial that they be prepared for this change, and acquire information about new social rules and behaviors that are acceptable in the new situation (work or university). This does not mean they must behave like the others, but it is important that they know and understand the new social codes. This recommendation is based on the assumption that individuals can adapt more effectively when provided with awareness and information (Savickas & Porfeli, 2012).

Since adaptability is considered by Savickas to be a psychosocial construct, it is recommended that these young people be guided so that they can identify resources in their own homes and their old social environments that could prove to be useful during the process of adapting to the new role or environment. Resource-identification can be done through the structure task of identifying and writing different sorts of resources that are available for the clients: emotional, spiritual, physical, social and financial resources. Writing and describing these resources and how they were useful in previous transitions can be a valuable preparation tool for the next transition. Based upon the work of Brown and Ryane Krane (2000), I recommend writing and not merely talking.

Imagining life after the period of adaptation to the new place or role can be another helpful technique. The counselor can invite the client to imagine and write about a day in his/her life after the process of adaptation. Writing at least two versions of how life can be after adapting to the needed change while relating to various life roles during the day (e.g., also writing about family, community and leisure activities) can facilitate and accelerate the adaptation process by constructing possible preferred narratives that not focus only on the worker role.

The psychology of working theory (PWT) can be another appropriate conceptual framework for career counseling and guidance of Israeli Arab young adults. This theory was designed as an ecosystem model that is particularly relevant for individuals from non-dominant groups who have been ignored in prior theories. This framework accounts for external factors as well as for individual differences that impact career development and decision-making.

Two key contextual factors central to the PWT are: marginalization and economic constraints, both of which play a crucial role in shaping access to decent work. Marginalization takes many forms and has been demonstrated to have a major impact on career development of women, people of color, the poor and minorities such as Israeli Arabs, as was described earlier in this chapter. The role of economic constraints is another key PWT variable associated with the pursuit of and persistence in higher education (e.g., Cinamon, 2016; Li, Wu, Zhang, Wang, & Sun, 2013). The PWT proposes that economic constraints and experiences of marginalization limit career options, often because these contextual factors hamper the development of self-perceptions of being able to choose desired careers (work volition) and/or skills in being able to adapt in the world of work (career adaptability). Since it is not easy to change contextual variables, certain flexible variables are presented in this model as mediators: proactive personality, social support and critical consciousness. These variables can attenuate the effects that constraints and marginalization have on feeling volitional and adaptable and, in turn, entering work fields that offer the opportunity of decent work.

Following the concept of the PWT, career counselors can work with their minority clients, such as Israeli Arab young adults, regarding understanding the process of marginalization. Since marginalization is not always familiar or recognized by those who are being marginalized, and they perceive their current situation as being an indication of their abilities and efforts, it is important to discuss this process and encourage the young clients not to take all the responsibility for their current career situation upon themselves. Developing critical consciousness can increase an understanding of marginalization. Providing updated statistics data regarding gaps between sub-groups in Israeli society can be a good start (e.g., differences in working rates between males and females in Israel and around the globe, or between people with and without disabilities). Discussions about several possible explanations for these gaps and describing the marginalization process as another powerful process that explains these differences might help young members of minorities to understand this mechanism. After discussing other marginalized groups, it will also be possible to discuss the marginalization of Israeli Arabs more easily and in more depth. I recommend that one start with examples regarding other marginalized groups and only later discuss the Israeli Arab situation, since it easier and less emotional to start learning about this phenomenon by first concentrating on other groups. It is important that they understand their limits and the boundaries of responsibility for their current situation.

At the same time, as presented in the PWT, practicing proactive behavior can be very useful. Identifying a client's previous proactive behavior can be a good place to start to work. Providing examples about proactive behavior from other narratives can be very helpful. Another possible option is to provide the client with short stories about other marginalized groups that are facing obstacles, and invite then to suggest activities and behaviors for these people that could enable them to change or improve their situation. If it is difficult for them to think or describe these proactive activities, the counselors can suggest some and invite their reactions to them. I also recommend that the client be invited to choose a proactive behavior to practice between sessions and to discuss his/her feelings about this action and its results.

Due to the importance of the role of social support in the individual's development in general, in the PWT, and as was reflected in studies mentioned earlier about Israeli Arabs, it is crucial to acknowledge social support as an important resource and to develop the skill of asking for and providing help and support. Identifying the list of people who can possibly provide support and important resources is a good start. Furthermore, classifying different types of support the client receives (e.g., emotional, financial, practical) can be very useful. Role-playing asking for support is another technique that may prove to be useful.

The last conceptual framework I would like to offer is Flum and Cinamon's (2011) perspective about the interplay among citizenship, identity, culture and career. In this article, we discussed several approaches to citizenship and their theoretical derivatives and branches (see also Janoski & Gran, 2002) and the common assumption that social, participation and economic citizenship rights include the rights to education and employment. A more detailed account might include an opportunity to be involved in education from pre-primary to higher education, vocational training, educational and vocational counseling, labor market information, job placement and job security. At the same time, we suggest that an obligation (in relation to work) might include not only sharing income by paying taxes, but also social involvement and contribution to society through work and "active citizenship".

This concept of active citizenship as pivotal proactive behavior of citizenship that can also foster the career development of marginalized groups can be very useful for counselors working with Israeli Arab young adults. To be active citizens who are involved in their own communities in various areas (e.g., formal and non-formal educational activities, initiatives to improve their villages or neighborhood public gardens) as well as other volunteer activities in their own Arab communities, can increase their social involvement and their potential for influence. At the same time, it will enable them to gain and practice different types of skills, increase their social network and increase their knowledge about their own environments.

This suggestion can also be a type of solution for their feelings of tension as citizens of a state that is involved in a violent conflict with their own people, as I described at the beginning of this chapter. A similar idea was also proposed by Rabinowitz (2001) who claimed that the responsibility for change lies partially with those who are trapped, who themselves can become active political agents seeking change within political movements within the Palestinian community inside Israel. In any case, considerable weight is still given to the host state and the mother nation rather than to individuals. By offering and encouraging active citizenship among marginalized groups, I consider the important concept of adaptation to be the first step in the journey of career development. I encourage counselors to urge their clients not just to adapt to changes but also to create some changes themselves and to reject others' attempts at change. Active citizenship, as described here, is a powerful concept and can serve as a first step that can enable marginalized citizens to create a change in their own communities and in their lives by being involved and resourceful in their communities.

Closing remarks on training

In the current chapter, I propose three conceptual frameworks that could serve as a guide for career counselors working with Israeli Arab young adults. By using these interrelated concepts of career construction, PWT and active citizenship, the counselors can enable these young people to construct their identity in a way that can empower them. By discussing their national identity and encouraging active citizenship, they can help them practice proactive behaviors that not only help them to adapt themselves, but also to create a better society. This concept works on the interrelations between the individual and the society of which he/she is a part. Furthermore, this concept may foster the client's willingness and ability to create an individual as well as a group narrative that are characterized by optimism and hope. Practicing proactive behavior, learning and understanding social context and social processes such as marginalization can reduce self-blame and despair.

The use of these ideas requires more social and political perspectives from career counselors, who usually trained in a more individualistic perspective that normally focuses on individual differences. In order to be able to facilitate career development of vulnerable and marginalized groups, we should include more courses than usual in our training programs on social justice and social perspectives on human development. Furthermore, career counselors of marginalized groups need a deep and broad understanding about the culture of their clients and about their current educational and employment status. Relevant types of courses (e.g., courses about non-Western cultures and about the political and economic status of different groups) are important as well.

Since the family is an integral part of the individual identity of young people from collectivistic societies such as Israeli Arabs, career counselors who work with these young people need to involve family members in their counseling sessions. The common technique of working merely with one individual client may be less effective in this situation and we must create different forms of counseling (i.e., a few individual sessions, some sessions with parents and some that are joint sessions – parents and young adults together). A similar concept was presented by Richard Young in his Family Project model (Young et al., 2001). It is essential that career counselors be trained to be flexible and creative in developing different forms of guidance that are relevant to marginalized clients from collectivistic cultures.

Furthermore, focusing on marginalized groups requires more collaboration with other disciplines and professions such as social work, political science and education. We can train towards this collaboration through combined courses during the master's and PhD levels. In view of the important role of religion and faith in their lives, it is recommended that special attention be paid to the potential of collaborating with Muslim religious figures.

I cannot end this chapter without referring to important questions on identity and language. Can a Jewish career counselor who is part of the hegemonic majority work and promote the identity construction of Israeli Arab young adults as I just suggested? Can a female counselor promote more egalitarian perspectives among clients from collectivistic and traditional societies among Israeli Arab young adults? Answering these questions requires another chapter, but I will close this chapter with an initial response that "yes, we can!" We can be good and efficient career counselors for members of "other" groups if we never stop developing our own social consciousness and perspective of social justice and never stop searching for a moral and better society.

References

Abrams, D., Hogg, M. A., & Marques, J. M. (Eds.). (2004). *Social psychology of inclusion and exclusion*. New York, NY: Psychology Press.

Abu-Baker, K. (2002). Career women or working women? Change versus stability for young Palestinian women in Israel. *Journal of Israeli History, 21*, 85–109.

Abu-Rabia-Queder, S. (2007). The activism of Bedouin women: Social and political resistance. *HAGAR: Studies in Culture Polity and Identities*, 7, 67–85.

Ali, N. (2013). Representation of Arab citizens in the institutions of higher education in Israel. Haifa-Jerusalem: Sikkuy.

Arar, K. H., & Abu-Rabia-Queder, S. (2011). Turning points in the lives of two pioneer Arab women principals in Israel. *Gender and Education, 23*(4), 415–429.

Arar, K. H., & Mustafa, M. (2009). Higher education and occupations among Arab women in Israel: Barriers and changes. In A. Faisel & R. Hertz-Lazarovitch (Eds.), *Arab Women in Israel: Current Status and Future Prospects* (pp. 259–284). Tel Aviv: Ramot-Tel Aviv University.

Barakat, H. (1985). *Contemporary Arab society: An exploratory social study*. Beirut: Arab Unity Studies Centre.

Barnes, C., & Mercer, G. (2005). Disability, work, and welfare challenging the social exclusion of disabled people. *Work, Employment & Society, 19*(3), 527–545.

Blustein, D. (2013). The psychology of working: A new perspective for career development, counseling, and public policy. New York: NY: Routledge.

Bourdieu, P. (1984). *Distinction: A Social Critique of the Judgement of Taste*. London, UK: Routledge & Kegan Paul.

Brown, S. D., & Krane, N. E. R. (2000). Four (or five) sessions and a cloud of dust: Old assumptions and new observations about career counseling. In S. D. Brown & R. W. Lent (Eds.), *Handbook of counseling psychology* (3rd ed., pp. 740–766). New York, NY: Wiley.

Brynjolfsson, E., & McAfee, A. (2014). The second machine age: Work, progress, and prosperity in a time of brilliant technologies. London, UK: WW Norton & Company.

Central Bureau of Statistics. (2011). *Israel statistics monthly report*. Retrieved from www.cbs.gov.il/publications13/1504/pdf/h_print.pdf

Central Bureau of Statistics. (2014). *Israel statistics monthly report*. Retrieved from www.cbs.gov.il/reader/shnaton/templ_shnaton.html?num_tab=st08_53&CYear=2014

Central Bureau of Statistics. (2016). *Israel statistics monthly report*. Retrieved from www.cbs.gov.il/publications17/yarhon1216/pdf/b1.pdf

Cinamon, R. G. (2006). Anticipated work-family conflict: Effects of gender, self-efficacy, and family background. *The Career Development Quarterly*, *54*(3), 202–215.

Cinamon, R. G. (2009). Role salience, social support, and work-family conflict among Jewish and Arab Female Teachers in Israel. *Journal of Career Development*, *36*, 139–158.

Cinamon, R. G. (2016). Integrating work and study among young adults testing an empirical model. *Journal of Career Assessment*, *24*(3), 527–542.

Cinamon, R. G., Habayib, H., & Ziv, M. (2016). The conception of work and higher education among Israeli Arab women. *International Journal of Educational Research*, *76*, 129–140.

Cinamon, R. G., Rich, Y., & Spector, G. M. (2012, August). *What areas of life do Israeli Jewish and Arab young adults explore?* Paper presented at the meeting of the American Psychological Association, Orlando, FL.

Duffy, R. D., Blustein, D. L., Diemer, M. A., & Autin, K. L. (2016). The psychology of working theory. *Journal of Counseling Psychology*, *63*(2), 127–148.

Enosh, G., & Ben-Ari, A. (2013). Perceiving the other: Hostile and danger attributions among Jewish and Arab social work students in Israel. *European Journal of Social Work*, *16*(3), 427–442.

Flum, H., & Cinamon, R. G. (2011). Immigration and the interplay among citizenship, identity and career: The case of Ethiopian immigration to Israel. *Journal of Vocational Behavior*, *78*(3), 372–380.

Frey, C. B., & Osborne, M. A. (2013). *The future of employment: How susceptible are jobs to computerisation*. Retrieved from www.oxfordmartin.ox.ac.uk/downloads/academic/The_Future_of_Employment.pdf

Frone, M. F. (2003). Work-family balance. In J. C. Quick & L. E. Tetrick (Eds.), *Handbook of occupational health psychology* (pp. 143–162). Washington, DC: American Psychological Association.

Gera, R., & Cohen, R. (2005). Occupational Inequality between educated Arabs and Jews in the Israeli labor market. In A. Haider (Ed.), *The Arab community in Israel: Population, society, economy*. Jerusalem: The Van Leer Jerusalem Institute. [in Hebrew].

Golan-Agnon, D. (2006). Separate but not equal discrimination against Palestinian Arab students in Israel. *American Behavioral Scientist*, *49*(8), 1075–1084.

Gor Ziv, H. (2015). Education of deaf children in Israel: A case of marginalizing a minority group. *Journal for Critical Education Policy Studies*, *13*(1), 268–290.

Gorodzeisky, A. (2013). Mechanisms of exclusion: Attitudes toward allocation of social rights to out-group population. *Ethnic and Racial Studies, 36*(5), 795–817.

Hassan, E. (1999). Epidemiological study of scholastic underachievement among primary school children in Alexandria: Prevalence and causes (Doctoral dissertation). Faculty of Nursing, University of Alexandria.

Herzog, Z. E., & Singer-Avitz, L. (2004). Redefining the centre: The emergence of state in Judah. *Tel Aviv, 31*(2), 209–244.

Hindman, M. D. (2011). Rethinking intersectionality: Towards an understanding of discursive marginalization. *New Political Science, 33*(2), 189–210.

Janoski, T., & Gran, B. (2002). Political citizenship: Foundations of rights. In E. F. Isin & B. S. Turner (Eds.), *Handbook of citizenship studies* (pp. 13–52). London, UK: Sage.

Kaczmarczyk, L., & Dopplick, R. (2014). ACM report: Preparing students for computing workforce needs in the US. *ACM SIGCSE Bulletin, 46*(2), 8.

Khattab, N. (2002). Ethnicity and female labour market participation: A new look at the Palestinian enclave in Israel. *Work, Employment & Society, 16*(1), 91–110.

Khattab, N., & Miaari, S. (2013). On the reserve bench: Palestinian employees in Israel. In N. Khattab & S. Miaari (Eds.), *Palestinians in the Israeli labor market: A multi-disciplinary approach* (pp. 11–36). New York, NY: Palgrave Macmillan.

Kulik, L., & Rayyan, F. (2003). Wage-earning patterns, perceived division of domestic labor, and social support: A comparative analysis of educated Jewish and Arab-Muslim Israelis. *Sex Roles, 48*(1–2), 53–66.

Lavee, Y., & Katz, R. (2003). The family in Israel: Between tradition and modernity. *Marriage & Family Review, 35*(1–2), 193–217.

Li, Z., Wu, W., Zhang, B., Wang, B., & Sun, H. (2013, July). Dynamic economic dispatch with spinning reserve constraints considering wind power integration. In *2013 IEEE Power & Energy Society General Meeting* (pp. 1–5).

Lipshits-Braziler, Y., & Tatar, M. (2012). Perceived career barriers and coping among youth in Israel: Ethnic and gender differences. *Journal of Vocational Behavior, 80*(2), 545–554.

Mansour, F. (2005). *Barriers and resources in the career development of Israeli Arabs adolescents* (Unpublished master's thesis). Tel Aviv University, Tel-Aviv. [in Hebrew].

Martell, R. F., Emrich, C. G., & Robison-Cox, J. (2012). From bias to exclusion: A multilevel emergent theory of gender segregation in organizations. *Research in Organizational Behavior, 32*, 137–162.

Massalha, W. (2008). *Perception of work-family relations among Arab students with respect to gender and culture* (Unpublished master's thesis). Tel Aviv University: Tel-Aviv. [in Hebrew].

Michael, R., Most, T., & Cinamon, R. G. (2013). The contribution of perceived parental support to the career self-efficacy of deaf, hard-of-hearing, and hearing adolescents. *Journal of Deaf Studies and Deaf Education, 18*(3), 329–343.

Oyserman, D. (1993). The lens of personhood: Viewing the self and others in a multicultural society. *Journal of Personality and Social Psychology, 65*(5), 993.

Rabinowitz, D. (2001). The Palestinian citizens of Israel, the concept of trapped minority and the discourse of transnationalism in anthropology. *Ethnic and Racial Studies, 24*(1), 64–85.

Savickas, M. L. (2005). The theory and practice of career construction. *Career Development and Counseling: Putting Theory and Research to Work, 1*, 42–70.

Savickas, M. L. (2012). Life design: A paradigm for career intervention in the 21st century. *Journal of Counseling & Development, 90*(1), 13–19.

Savickas, M. L., & Porfeli, E. J. (2012). Career adaptabilities scale: Construction, reliability, and measurement equivalence across 13 countries. *Journal of Vocational Behavior, 80*, 661–673.

Schwartz, S. H. (1994). Are there universal aspects in the structure and contents of human values? *Journal of Social Issues*, *50*(4), 19–45.

Seginer, R., & Mahajna, S. (2016). On the meaning of higher education for transition to modernity youth: Lessons from future orientation research of Muslim girls in Israel. *International Journal of Educational Research*, *76*, 112–119.

Seibert, S. E., Kraimer, M. L., & Liden, R. C. (2001). A social capital theory of career success. *Academy of Management Journal*, *44*(2), 219–237.

Sharabi, M. (2013). Managing and improving service quality in higher education. *International journal of Quality and Service Sciences*, *5*(3), 309–320.

Shaviv, M., Binstein, N., Stone, A., & Fudem, O. (2013). *Pluralism and equal opportunity in higher education expanding access for Arabs, Druze and Circassians in Israel*. Report by the Planning and Budgeting Committee of the Council for Higher Education.

Whiston, S. C., & Cinamon, R. G. (2015). The work – family interface: Integrating research and career counseling practice. *The Career Development Quarterly*, *63*(1), 44–56.

Yashiv, E. (2012). *The Arabs in the Israeli labor market*. The Program for Economy and Society, Van Leer Jerusalem Institute.

Yashiv, E., & Kasir, N. (2014). *The labor market of Israeli Arabs: Key features and policy solutions*. Unpublished working paper, Tel Aviv University.

Young, R. A., Valach, L., Ball, J., Paseluikho, M., Wong, Y., DeVries, R. J., McLean, H., & Turkel, H. (2001). Career development in adolescence as a family project. *Journal of Counseling Psychology*, *48*, 190–202.

Chapter 14

Psychological distress and other aspects regarding cancer genetic testing

Valentina Di Mattei, Martina Bernardi, and Letizia Carnelli

Introduction

The word "counseling" is often thought of as simply "having a chat", however, counseling is a major field of psychology and has much to offer medical settings. It can be defined as a specific helping relationship, offered by a professional to a client who is in a situation of difficulty. It is the skilled use of the relationship that helps the client develop self-awareness, acceptance, and growth so that he/she can live more fully. Counseling can also be used to address issues such as decision-making, coping in crises, and helping with inner conflicts. A counselor's main duty is to help clients, but at the same time respect their ideas, values, and resources (Corney & Jenkins, 2005).

Counseling is widely used in many situations, in different settings, and professions. In healthcare settings, counseling is applied to situations that are often complex and where the involvement of the patient is important in the healing process. The intervention can have a preventive role, to inform patients, or a more supportive role in assisting patients and their families in the various phases from diagnosis, treatment, follow-up or, in some cases, to end-of-life. Counseling can help patients and caregivers in healthcare settings share worries, fears, uncertainties, and expectations to try to experience illness with the least possible distress.

Counseling psychologists evaluate patients' psychological functioning, act as consultants for medical staff, provide training, organize research, provide counseling, and other psychosocial interventions for both patients and caregivers (Karademas, 2009). In this chapter, we look specifically at genetic counseling and its effects.

Genetic counseling

Genetic counselors are trained healthcare professionals whose knowledge of genetics, epidemiology, and counseling allows them to provide patients with individualized help. They allow patients to *"understand and adapt to the medical, psychological and familial implications of genetic contributions to disease"* (National Society of Genetic Counselors' Definition Task Force, 2006, p. 77). Many genetic counselors work in hospitals or clinics alongside healthcare workers.

Genetic counselors work in different fields and offer varying services, including: cancer genetics, reproductive genetics, pediatric genetics, neurogenetics, and cardiovascular genetics.

Genetic counseling is an intervention aimed at informing and supporting individuals who must undertake a medical path that searches for and manages genetic defects or pathologies (NHS Choices, 2016). The intervention takes on two dimensions:

- the first is the educational dimension, which provides knowledge about the genetic pathology. This includes genetic transmission information, risk factors, and discussing and accepting its implications.
- the second concerns the facilitation and support of the individual's ensuing decisions, once the results of the genetic test have been communicated.

One must note that screening has increasingly become an important facet of biomedicine, as a form of secondary prevention. The drive to detect an illness at an asymptomatic phase of development is now an important objective. Carrier testing involves genetic tests that identify mutations for a recessive condition. Predictive testing, however, identifies people who are at risk of developing a disease in the future. For many conditions, such as cancer, a positive predictive test result only illustrates a high risk of it developing.

We have chosen to focus on Hereditary Breast and Ovarian Cancer syndrome (HBOC) as the genetic information acquired has relevance for those who undertake genetic testing and for their genetic relatives.

Hereditary breast and ovarian cancer syndrome

Among all the inheritable diseases, HBOC is perhaps the one that has recently caught the public eye. As around 1 in 500 women in the United States has either the BRCA1/2 (BReast CAncer susceptibility genes) gene mutation (NCI, 2015), it is understandable why this disease has attracted much attention. Medical research has focused on HBOC, but few studies have examined the psychological aspects of this disease and genetic counseling.

Most breast and ovarian cancers are sporadic, and not all women who have breast and ovarian cancer have HBOC. HBOC is caused by a specific germline mutation of BRCA1/2 genes (among others), which are found on chromosomes 17 and 13. There are several other gene mutations that are also associated with HBOC risk, but BRCA1/2 are the most common and indicate that a woman is at higher risk of developing breast or ovarian cancer (Carroll et al., 2008). A mutation in one of these genes indicates an incapacity to regulate cell death and the presence of uncontrolled cell growth, which both lead to cancer. The prevalence of HBOC is estimated at 1 in 400 (or 0.2–0.3%) in the general population (Moyer, 2014).

Diagnosis of HBOC is suspected based on a family history and then made following a molecular genetic test, usually carried out via a blood sample. Genetic testing is not usually offered to unaffected individuals, unless a mutation has been identified in the family. There is currently no test that detects all allelic variants of these two gene mutations. When investigating a patient's background, an increased risk of BRCA1/2 is suspected based on a family history of cancer. By examining an individual's clinical history, the geneticist takes into account: the age of onset of disease, the presence of bilateral breast and ovarian tumors, multiple ovarian or breast tumors, a diagnosis of triple negative breast cancer, as well as a diagnosis of male breast cancer. The probability of being a carrier of a genetic mutation increases in families with a pedigree characterized by multiple cases of breast cancer, which appear at a young age and in multiple generations, multiple tumors in the same individual, male breast cancer, and belonging to the Ashkenazi Hebrew population (American Society of Clinical Oncology-ASCO, 2015).

Treatment of breast and ovarian cancer in individuals with BRCA1/2-related tumors is similar to treatment for sporadic forms; however, new drugs targeting these tumors are being developed. Prevention or risk-reduction consists in prophylactic mastectomy or oophorectomy, which are both invasive and irreversible procedures, making the decision to endure such an intervention a personal and difficult decision. Chemoprevention using tamoxifen is also used as a risk-reducing intervention, whereby the individual is administered drugs to prevent cancer from developing. This option can be considered concurrently with screening techniques, which usually involve frequent clinical breast examinations, mammographies and breast Magnetic Resonance Imaging, pelvic examinations, trans-vaginal ultrasounds, and Cancer Antigen-125 blood testing (Petrucelli, Daly, & Feldman, 2013).

Once a BRCA1/2 mutation has been identified, at-risk relatives can be tested and thus increase surveillance and early intervention if cancer is identified. Women who have a BRCA1/2 mutation have approximately a 45–65% risk of developing breast cancer and an 11–39% risk of developing ovarian cancer in their lifetime (Antoniou et al., 2003; Chen & Parmigiani, 2007).

HBOC genetic testing and counseling

The ASCO (2015) upholds that genetic testing be presented to individuals with suspected inherited cancer risk where test results can be interpreted and when these can influence the medical management of the patient. Usually the genetic counseling and testing procedure unfolds as follows:

1 *Selection.* For a woman to take part in the genetic testing procedure there is usually a general practitioner's or oncologist's referral. These experts feel there is a necessity for the patient to undergo a genetic test because there are signs that the patient may have a hereditary form of cancer. Contrastingly, some patients feel they want to undertake the test themselves. Whether or not to subject the patient to the test is evaluated by a multidisciplinary team (a general practitioner, an oncologist, a geneticist, and a genetic counselor).

2 *Pre-testing stage*. If the multidisciplinary team agrees to the testing, the subject learns about the hereditary, familial, and sporadic forms of cancer and the methods available to identify the risk of developing these. The pedigree construction allows the geneticist to estimate the patient's risk profile; by examining an individual's clinical history, the geneticist considers all risk factors and the family history. The pre-test psychological interview aims at identifying users who experience cancer genetic counseling as stressful, assessing their coping strategies and psychological distress, and programming an intervention of personalized psychological support. There may be emotional reactions to the pre-test phase including anxiety and fear at having to answer personal questions and from the amount of information received.

3 *Testing stage*. In case of suspected inherited risk, a genetic test is offered; users then have to wait a variable amount of time for blood test results (a few weeks to a few months) depending on where and how the test is carried out.

4 *Post-test stage*. Once the test is complete, an interdisciplinary team usually communicates the test results to the patient: here the team helps the patient understand the results and also comprehend the implications these may have on the individual and his/her family. There are three possible results: positive, negative, or uncertain.

A positive test result indicates that the individual has a mutation that increases the likelihood of developing cancer. This means that a woman can try to improve clinical outcomes if she has not yet contracted cancer. If a woman has already had a tumor in the past, the test is carried out to identify whether the patient is at risk for other tumors and should undergo prophylactic interventions and stricter screening protocols. If the patient is currently undergoing therapy, then knowing whether the patient has a gene mutation can also help with therapeutic decisions. Family members who are at risk for developing the disease can be identified and positive health behaviors can be reinforced.

A negative test result can reassure an individual and his/her family that there is no BRCA1/2 mutation. However, this does not mean that they do not have other genetic mutations in less common genes. An inconclusive result indicates there are variants of unknown significance; further testing may be suggested in this case.

Psychological impact of test results

Various familial cancer syndromes that provide a high lifetime risk of cancer may be found with genetic testing, and progressively more women will contemplate testing as the availability and public awareness of genetic testing for HBOC susceptibility continues to develop. Research suggests that these individuals will have differing emotional responses to genetic testing and its results (Hirschberg, Chan-Smutko, & Pirl, 2015).

Prior to testing

Relevant psychological issues have been raised regarding HBOC and genetic testing. How a person reacts emotionally to this new situation can affect his/her quality of life and can interfere in some delicate family dynamics. Genetic testing can bring about an awareness of a state of increased health risk with possible fears about developing cancer attached to this and perhaps feelings of anger (towards relatives who have transmitted the disease) or guilt (about potentially transmitting the mutation to one's offspring) too.

It is, therefore, vital that prior to the genetic test, the patient be evaluated by a counselor in terms of decision-making abilities and psychological adaptation. Psychological issues may arise even *before testing* takes place, for instance, women with a higher perceived risk of cancer are more likely to be interested in genetic counseling (Bowen et al., 1999). Moreover, many women often overestimate their risk for breast cancer and the effectiveness of the screening procedures (Black, Nease, & Tosteson, 1995). There are factors that may influence risk perception: a family history of disease, beliefs about the disease and its risks, loss of a family member, and overidentification with a family member who has had the disease. Therefore, a balanced and accurate presentation of the information regarding cancer risk and screening effectiveness may help women during decision-making. Education allows the client to respond to the situation, but at the same time, too much new information/vocabulary can be a barrier to client understanding so the counselor must try to balance these aspects.

Positive test result

There are undoubtedly consequences that can also be negative to finding a gene mutation. There can be adverse psychological reactions that can lead to distress and family issues, especially as having the mutation does not equate to disease. Understandably, receiving a positive test result may increase worries regarding the development of cancer and women may assume illness is inevitable and untreatable. Studies have found that having relatives who have previously passed away from cancer is associated with more distress when confronting an affirmative result (van Oostrom et al., 2003). Once the positive result is communicated, patients are told about their medical risk-reducing options that can pose challenges including decisions regarding marriage, pregnancy, and medical interventions.

At the news of a positive test result, some women are inclined to undergo prophylactic surgery and screening measures. Those that choose to undergo such interventions often report less distress regarding cancer risk (Metcalfe, Esplen, Goel, & Narod, 2004) and feel like a weight has been lifted. However, there have been reports of effects on body image, sexual functioning, and self-concept, especially after surgical interventions. Contrastingly, learning about a genetic mutation can cause an emotional paralysis and some women do not know how to move on. The outcome of the test can have far-reaching implications for both the individual and their caregivers/family, and thus the individual must be conscious of the risks involved to be prepared. It is here that counseling is important; the communication of a positive result is a delicate moment and needs to be handled with care, by listening and providing the patient with the tools and knowledge to face this result. Counselors often use active listening and attending techniques and also promote a shared language when communicating results. The characteristics that a genetic counselor must employ when communicating the results include: clarity, expertise, and empathy.

Research has shown that although there were fears of how women with gene mutations would react to the news and to the management of disease, in fact women cope well and adapt to a stressful situation with the knowledge of their genetic condition (Pasacreta, 2003). Although rates of clinically significant psychological distress in samples who undergo cancer genetic testing are relatively low (around 6%), (Hirschberg et al., 2015) studies have shown that some women cope better than others.

Cancer survivors seem to have a higher risk of experiencing feelings and thoughts of a state of anger. The risk of re-acquiring the *status* of cancer patient, because of a relapse or for the possible preventative interventions, could make survivors feel as though they were re-living the negative experience of disease and treatment. As a consequence, it would be advisable to refer cancer survivors to genetic counseling at the beginning of the course of disease and treatment (Di Mattei, Bernardi, Madeddu, & Sarno, 2015). Furthermore, the same researchers showed that individuals who use avoidance coping strategies, measured via the COPE questionnaire (which assesses a broad variety of coping strategies and examines how people cope under stress (Carver, Scheier, & Weintraub, 1989), are more vulnerable to psychological distress compared to those who use problem-oriented ones, since they are hypothetically inclined to deny the mutation risk condition. Denial and mental detachment of the problem correlate with an increase of psycho-emotional distress, and constitute a psychological vulnerability factor as they predict an increase in depressive, anxious, and somatization symptoms. Genetic counseling should, therefore, be focused on evaluating and strengthening levels of awareness in patients with regard to the possibility of being a carrier of the gene mutation.

Negative test result

Receiving a negative test result may precipitate different emotional psychological reactions. This news is usually accompanied by a sense of relief and improved psychological functioning, but paradoxically individuals may experience difficulty in adjusting to their new risk status as they have integrated a sense of being at increased risk of cancer into their self-concept (van Oostrom et al., 2003). These patients may have problems integrating their new genetic status as they feel they are giving up a sense of inclusion to a group and feel distant from certain affected relatives (Esplen et al., 2004). Feelings of guilt may also arise after a negative test result. Perhaps other family members have tested positive and yet the individual is not a carrier. Smith, West, Croyle, and Botkin (2004) found that all non-carriers in their sample experienced survivor guilt toward their affected/at-risk siblings. Therefore, attention must still be paid to these patients and the barriers to client understanding including: fear, anxiety, depression, denial, anger, grief, and cultural beliefs must be considered.

Inconclusive test result

Inconclusive test results indicate that the individual does not carry a particular mutation but may be a carrier of other, rare chromosomal abnormalities that are not detectable during screening. Van Dijk, Otten, Tollenaar, van Asperen, and Tibben (2008) showed that personal beliefs and uncertainty about an inconclusive result were associated with cancer-related worry and distress and these beliefs were a predictor of whether women were able to leave the testing behind them. For women with uncertain results, levels of worry and distress were akin to those who tested positive. Individuals with these test results should be followed closely with regard to adhering to screening protocols and counselors must make sure that these patients have fully understood this test result so that they do not miscommunicate with family members. For counselors this may be the most emotionally difficult test result to communicate because one must make sure that the individual has understood all the implications, but at the same time one cannot give any assertive responses.

There are various interviewing techniques that a genetic counselor can use to see how a client is feeling and make sure a client has understood their situation, these include: questioning, rephrasing, reflecting, redirecting, and silence. During *questioning* the aim of the counselor is to use different types of questions (open-ended, closed-ended, and focused) to encourage the client to elaborate their emotions. By *rephrasing* the counselor states what the client just said but with different words and it shows that the counselor is listening and ensures that the counselor has understood the client. When a counselor repeats the last word of a client's statement in question form it encourages further exploration of a subject and encourages the client to provide more information without the counselor having to make assumptions, this is called *reflecting*. *Redirecting* is a technique used to pace the session and refocus the client on a particular topic. Last, silence can be used to allow the patient to reflect, to gain composure, and to think about what to say next (Uhlmann, Schuette, & Yashar, 2011).

Thus, different patients could react differently to the genetic testing procedure and to the communication of results, however, van Dijk and colleagues (2008) showed that in their sample, all three groups (positive, negative, and inconclusive) of women were less worried after the genetic test than before. Therefore, genetic testing can be beneficial, regardless of the result. If the result is positive, patients can prepare and start making decisions. The test result can also help with the prognosis and allows doctors to be specific in terms of the information they provide. The results can also allow treatment planning at an early stage, which has a positive effect on quality of life and life expectancy.

Counseling techniques and psychological approaches to support patients and caregivers

In order for patients and their families to adjust in the most optimal manner to genetic testing, psychological care approaches must be integrated into the standard genetic testing procedure. Counselors must take into account the patient's history and also the social and cultural contexts surrounding the patient.

Genetic counselors use the following techniques during the process: the first is risk estimation. This is when the counselor weighs the risks of possible outcomes with regard to disease; it can be objective, that is, numerical using percentages and fractions, or subjective. The word "risk estimation", which is one of the key elements that a counselor employs for HBOC on a hereditary-familial basis, may have a negative connotation, perhaps the words "chance" or "likelihood" could be used in its place when talking to the client.

The second is accompanying individuals and their relatives in understanding the disease, the risk of transmission, and the scientific basis for risk calculation. A counselor can help improve patient recall by organizing and categorizing all the information by using simple language and encouraging patients to repeat what they have understood. Third, the counselor employs educational processes to ensure informed consent and the will to participate in all phases of counseling are present on behalf of the client. Last, a psychological assessment can be undertaken together with the promotion of a safe space where the client can express emotional worries and the elaboration of experiences connected to HBOC. Examples include facilitating communication between the geneticist and the individual, carrying out psychological evaluations via a clinical session and the administration of questionnaires (National Society of Genetic Counselors, 2017).

Psychological screening tools are useful and can identify risk markers related to emotional distress. Once the history and the distress levels have been determined, interventions can be offered. Usually, for individuals with low levels of distress, psychoeducational interventions and materials suffice. For women with moderate levels of distress or family communication issues, sessions with a genetic counselor are suggested. For individuals with high levels of distress (e.g., suicidal ideation) more specialized services are indicated, such as individual psychotherapy sessions, psychotropic medication, longer follow-ups, and professionally led support groups (Esplen, 2006).

With regard to psychological and counseling interventions, once a genetic test has been communicated, cognitive behavioral therapy (CBT) and psychodynamic therapy approaches are often used. CBT is used for anxiety and stress management; these techniques can help with stress caused by medical and screening appointments. Decision aids (Wakefield et al., 2007) and distraction-based coping interventions have been used to manage anxiety and help in decision-making with both individuals and groups. For instance, women who have lost a mother to breast cancer can believe that it is inevitable that they will suffer the same fate (Wellisch, Gritz, Schain, Wang, & Siau, 1991). This "catastrophizing" mechanism should be identified and connected to a more objective risk to help facilitate adaptation.

Psychodynamic approaches have also been used although limited research has been conducted. This approach underscores emotions over cognitions and considers the relationship between therapist and client as a way of comprehending the client and creating an internal shift. The nature of these early relations or attachments can be reflective in adult expectations (Tassicker, 2005). Attachment style can allow the counselor to predict anxiety, fearfulness, trust, and uncertainty tolerance, which all pertain to the cancer genetic risk counseling. This approach could also be useful in understanding the processes of identification, fear of abandonment, and guilt that can be evident in genetic testing and are influenced by the client's experience of growing up with a parent affected by cancer. A counselor's recognition of these processes can illuminate practice and help understand an individual's motivations and behaviors. Via these approaches, women can come to terms with the issues they must face and find an adequate creative adjustment to both the testing procedure and the possible outcomes.

Cultural and social aspects of genetic testing

Genetic testing affects our beliefs about our nature and origins, as individuals and as a species. Therefore, the value of genetic information and testing depends on our culture's and society's perspective. Genetic information can trigger questions regarding personal responsibility, choice versus genetic determinism, and concepts of health/illness. Personal factors, family values, and religious and cultural beliefs will influence responses. These can in turn have an effect on the psychological balance of both patients and their relatives.

Ethical aspects of predictive testing are a concern. Themes in these discussions include: the right to know of one's disease status, the psychological impact of diagnosing certain disorders, and the possibility of encouraging suicidal thoughts. Furthermore, the idea of knowing that you will inherit a disease may lower your quality of life, which goes against screening ideals.

Genetic information may influence a person to change his/her behavior while others may choose to respond differently. Since there is no correct reaction, health professionals should be sensitive to cultural and societal values and work with patients to define the appropriate course of action to genetic testing and follow-up (Genetic Alliance, 2008).

Conclusion

Breast and ovarian cancer have been considered as examples of pathologies that can run in families. Cancer genetic counselors are healthcare providers with expertise in cancer genetics, and training in the use of specialized tools and statistical data to estimate individual risk. They will recommend appropriate options for screening and management of cancer risk and – when cancer is present – for treatment or follow-up care. They will also evaluate and help patients cope with this new and stressful situation.

In the future, genetic discoveries will most likely modify the way that disease and risk are conceptualized. Vig and Wang (2012) predict that guidance from genetic counselors and providers will be tailored to meet individual risk and needs; a new era of personalized medicine and counseling is taking shape. We foresee an expansion of expertise for many healthcare providers and underline the necessity for counseling practices to become more evidence-based and widespread, so that patients can confront genetic testing, its results, and the future in a more serene and supported manner.

References

American Society of Clinical Oncology. (2015). *Hereditary breast and ovarian cancer*. Retrieved from www.cancer.net/cancer-types/hereditary-breast-and-ovarian-cancer.

Antoniou, A., Pharoah, P. D., Narod, S., Risch, H. A., Eyfjord, J. E., Hopper, J. L., . . . Easton, D. F. (2003). Average risks of breast and ovarian cancer associated with BRCA1 or BRCA2 mutations detected in case series unselected for family history: A combined analysis of 22 studies. *American Journal of Human Genetics*, *72*(5), 1117–1130.

Black, W. C., Nease, R. F., Jr., & Tosteson, A. N. A. (1995). Perceptions of breast cancer risk and screening effectiveness in women younger than 50 years of age. *Journal of the National Cancer Institute*, *87*(10), 720–731.

Bowen, D., McTiernan, A., Burke, W., Powers, D., Pruski, J., Durfy, S., . . . Malone, K. (1999). Participation in breast cancer risk counseling among women with a family history. *Cancer Epidemiology Biomarkers & Prevention*, *8*(7), 581–585.

Carroll, J. C., Cremin, C., Allanson, J., Blaine, S. M., Dorman, H., Gibbons, C. A., . . . Wilson, B. J. (2008). Hereditary breast and ovarian cancers. *Canadian Family Physician*, *54*(12), 1691–1692.

Carver, C. S., Scheier, M. F., & Weintraub, J. K. (1989). Assessing coping strategies: A theoretically based approach. *Journal of Personality and Social Psychology*, *56*, 267–283.

Chen, S., & Parmigiani, G. (2007). Meta-analysis of BRCA1 and BRCA2 penetrance. *Journal of Clinical Oncology*, *25*(11), 1329–1333.

Corney, R., & Jenkins, R. (2005). *Counselling in general practice*. London: Routledge.

Di Mattei, V. E., Bernardi, M., Madeddu, F., & Sarno, L. (2015). Psychological distress and coping strategies among women who undergo cancer genetic testing. In C. Pracana (Ed.), *Psychology applications & developments II* (pp. 15–24). Lisbon: Science Press.

Esplen, M. J. (2006). Psychological aspects of genetic testing for adult-onset hereditary disorders. In N. Sharpe & R. Carter (Eds.), *Genetic testing: Care, consent, and liability* (pp. 61–77). Hoboken, NJ: John Wiley & Sons Inc.

Esplen, M. J., Hunter, J., Leszcz, M., Warner, E., Narod, S., Metcalfe, K., . . . Wong, J. (2004). A multicenter study of supportive-expressive group therapy for women with BRCA1/BRCA2 mutations. *Cancer, 101*(10), 2327–2340.

Genetic Alliance; the New York Mid-Atlantic Consortium for Genetic and Newborn Screening Services. (2008). *Understanding GENETICS: A New York, mid-atlantic guide for patients and health professionals* (Ch. 8). Washington DC: Genetic Alliance.

Hirschberg, A. M., Chan-Smutko, G., & Pirl, W. F. (2015). Psychiatric implications of cancer genetic testing. *Cancer, 121*(3), 341–360.

Karademas, E. C. (2009). Counselling psychology in medical settings: The promising role of counselling health psychology. *European Journal of Counselling Psychology, 1*(1), 18–37.

Metcalfe, K. A., Esplen, M. J., Goel, V., & Narod, S. A. (2004). Psychosocial functioning in women who have undergone bilateral prophylactic mastectomy. *Psychooncology, 13*(1), 14–25.

Moyer, V. A. (on behalf of the U.S. Preventive Services Task Force) (2014). Risk assessment, genetic counseling, and genetic testing for BRCA-related cancer in women: U.S. preventive services task force recommendation statement. *Annals of Internal Medicine, 160*, 271–281.

National Cancer Institute. (2015). *Genetics of breast and gynecologic cancers for health professionals (PDQ)*. Retrieved from www.cancer.gov/types/breast/hp/breast-ovarian-genetics-pdq#section/_88

National Society of Genetic Counselors. (2017). *How a genetic counselor could help you or your family*. Retrieved from www.nsgc.org/page/patients

National Society of Genetic Counselors' Definition Task Force. (2006). A new definition of genetic counselling: National society of genetic counselors' task force report. *Journal of Genetic Counselling, 15*(2), 77–83.

NHS Choices. (2016). *Genetics services*. Retrieved from www.nhs.uk/Conditions/Genetics/Pages/genetic-testing-and-counselling.aspx

Pasacreta, J. V. (2003). Psychosocial issues associated with genetic testing for breast and ovarian cancer risk: An integrative review. *Cancer Investigation, 21*(4), 588–623.

Petrucelli, N., Daly, M. B., & Feldman, G. L. (2013). BRCA1 and BRCA2 hereditary breast and ovarian cancer. In R. A. Pagon, M. P. Adam, H. H. Ardinger, S. E. Wallace, A. Amemiya, L. J. H. Bean, . . . Stephens, K. (Eds.), *Gene reviews* [Internet] (pp. 1993–2016). Seattle, WA: University of Washington.

Smith, K. R., West, J. A., Croyle, R. T., & Botkin, J. R. (2004). Familial context of genetic testing for cancer susceptibility: Moderating effect of siblings' test results on psychological distress one to two weeks after BRCA1 mutation testing. *Cancer Epidemiology, Biomarkers & Prevention, 8*(1), 385–392.

Tassicker, R. J. (2005). Psychodynamic theory and counseling in predictive testing for Huntington's disease. *Journal of Genetic Counselling, 14*(2), 99–107.

Uhlmann, W. R., Schuette, J. L., & Yashar, B. (2011). *A guide to genetic counselling*. Wiley-Blackwell: John Wiley & Sons Inc.

van Dijk, S., Otten, W., Tollenaar, R. A. E. M., van Asperen, C. J., & Tibben, A. (2008). Putting it all behind: Long-term psychological impact of an inconclusive DNA test result for breast cancer. *Genetics in Medicine, 10*, 745–750.

van Oostrom, I., Meijers-Heijboer, H., Lodder, L. N., Duivenvoorden, H. J., van Gool, A. R., Seynaeve, C., . . . Tibben, A. (2003). Long-term psychological impact of carrying a BRCA1/2 mutation and prophylactic surgery: A 5-year follow-up study. *Journal of Clinical Oncology, 21*(20), 3867–3874.

Vig, H. S., & Wang, C. (2012). The evolution of personalized cancer genetic counseling in the era of personalized medicine. *Familial Cancer, 11*, 539–544.

Wakefield, C. E., Meiser, B., Homewood, J., Peate, M., Kirk, J., Warner, . . . Tucker, K. (2007). Development and pilot testing of two decision aids for individuals considering genetic testing for cancer risk. *Journal of Genetic Counselling, 16*(3), 325–339.

Wellisch, D. K., Gritz, E. R., Schain, W., Wang, H. J., & Siau, J. (1991). Psychological functioning of daughters of breast cancer patients. Part I: Daughters and comparison subjects. *Psychosomatics, 32*(3), 324–336.

Chapter 15

The disclosure dilemma

Disability, identity and self-determination

Kate Scorgie and Sarah Scorgie

Research indicates that many persons with disability in postsecondary and workplace settings are reluctant to disclose their conditions to instructors, supervisors or coworkers resulting in limited access to services and accommodations that may be needed for success (Brock, 2007; Newman & Madaus, 2015). For example, citing data from the U.S. National Longitudinal Transition Study-2, which followed educational and vocational outcomes of over 10,000 students who received special education services in high school, Gil (2007) reported that two-thirds of students with disabilities did not have access to appropriate accommodation in postsecondary settings due to a lack of disclosure. In a continuation of the same study, Newman and Madaus (2015) found that only 35% of students who had received special education services in high school chose to disclose disability in a postsecondary setting.

This reluctance to disclose often extends into workplace settings. In a study of 500 persons diagnosed with learning disabilities, Madaus (2008) reported that although 73% indicated that their learning disability negatively affected their current employment, only 55% self-disclosed to their employer and even fewer, 12%, requested workplace accommodation. Similarly, Brock's (2007) study of educators with disability indicated that the majority chose to conceal their diagnosis as long as possible to preserve perceptions of competence and self-sufficiency. These findings seem surprising given the increased focus on self-determination within the disability population in general and in secondary transition programs in many countries.

Self-determination – defined as the ability to set and achieve personal goals, to be empowered to make choices in one's best interests to facilitate personal, social and vocational outcomes – has been shown to lead to higher quality of life across a range of domains for persons with complex learning and health needs (Carter, Lane, Pierson, & Stang, 2008; Jones, 2006; Palmer, 2010; Wehmeyer, 2004). One of the fundamental skills of self-determination is self-advocacy. According to Test and colleagues (2005), self-advocacy involves four competencies: knowledge of self, knowledge of rights, the ability to communicate, and leadership skills – that is, the ability to manage self and others. It has been suggested that skills for self-advocacy be embedded in educational programs for students with disability in primary and secondary grades to facilitate self-determination (Carter et al., 2013; Roberts, 2010; Trainor, 2010). The difficulty emerges, however, when the systems that shape higher education and the workplace are perceived to be at variance with disclosure that might result in doubts about competency, stigmatization, or discrimination.

Research suggests interconnection between deficit discourses associated with disability, disclosure of disability, and identity in persons with chronic illness and disability (Crooks, Chouinard, & Wilton, 2008; de Vet, Waitt, & Gorman-Murray, 2012; Riddell & Weedon, 2014). In order to engage in self-advocacy to secure self-chosen outcomes, it is essential to deconstruct the complex dialogue surrounding disclosure of disability and requests for appropriate services and accommodations in postsecondary and workplace environments. Counseling professionals often serve as a bridge during life transitions, providing safe space to navigate identity and choice during times of change. This chapter suggests a template that might serve as an additional tool for use by counselors in transition or vocational training programs, or postsecondary and workplace settings. The term *equity accommodation* is proposed to indicate the right of persons with disability to have access to services and environmental affordances that allow them to function with the same convenience and lack of obstruction as persons without disability to achieve desired education and vocational outcomes.

Disclosure, Identity, and Context

While many countries have regulations in place to protect the rights of persons with disabilities to secure needed or reasonable accommodation, many persons with disabilities are reluctant to disclose or to request services and accommodation – that is, to take advantage of their rights (Cohen & Avanzino, 2010; Dong, Oire, McDonald-Wilson, & Fabian, 2012; Madaus, 2008; Magnus & Tøssebro, 2014). A number of reasons have been cited for nondisclosure, such as concern about diminished perceptions of competence and employability, lowered expectations, and limited career choices or opportunities for advancement once employed (Brock, 2007; Dalgin & Gilbride, 2003; Evans, 2013; Madaus, 2008; Rocco, 2001; Roessler, Neath, McMahon, & Rumrill, 2007; Shaw, Chan, & McMahon, 2012). At a more fundamental level, however, issues surrounding nondisclosure are based in identity – that is, what it means to be a person with disability in a college or workplace setting. While it is true that individuals actively engage in constructing unique identities, they are also aware that they are situated within a larger society that ascribes identity to its members based on beliefs, values, group membership, roles, and status or position within the society (Brock, 2007; Crooks et al., 2008; Trainor, 2010).

Stentsenko and Arievitch (2004) suggest that identity is "simultaneously social and deeply individual," a continual interplay between one's internal construction of self and one's interaction in the world, situated in a specific time and place (p. 497). According to Bickenbach (2009) disability is socially constructed: "the outcome of, often extremely complex and little understood, interactive relationships between intrinsic features of the persons . . . and features of the overall context in which [the] person lives, works, and interacts with others. Environmental factors, the constituent elements of this context, are not only natural and physical, but also attitudinal, structural, political, social and cultural" (p. 1121).

Therefore, to be fully understood, disclosure must be situated within a specific context in which assumptions, values, beliefs, actions, and attitudes that determine who or what is valued and devalued, and what behaviors are acceptable, are embedded (Brock, 2007; Cloke & Goldsmith, 2011; Valle, Solis, Volpitta, & Connor, 2004). Educational and vocational settings are grounded in and value such personal attributes as ability, aptitude, competence, autonomy, efficiency, stamina, intelligence, and independence (Brislin, 2008; Hibbs & Pothier, 2006; Matthews, 2009). When disclosure involves risk to one's appearance as a capable student or employee, a person may choose to forgo access to the very affordances needed to achieve success (Cohen & Avanzino, 2010; Evans, 2013; Magnus & Tøssebro, 2014).

Bickenbach (2009) suggests that "what it means to be disabled fundamentally includes what it means to be viewed as disabled by others" (p. 1112). For the most part, disability continues to be depicted through a medical model or framework in which persons with disability are perceived as having deficits that require intervention or "cure" (Crooks et al., 2008; Matthews, 2009; Valle et al., 2004). Within academic and workplace settings, it is the responsibility of the person with disability to self-disclose their diagnosis, describe how it interferes with their ability to accomplish a task, and appeal for appropriate services and accommodation. This obligation further highlights deficit and difference (Beckett & Wrighton, 2000; Dong et al., 2012; Gold, Oire Fabian, & Wewiorski, 2012; Kelepouris, 2014; Worley & Cornett-DeVito, 2007). The burden of self-disclosure intensifies awareness for persons with disability that their identity is ascribed and evaluated by others, rather than being self-chosen, resulting in anxiety that one might be misrepresented, objectified, or stigmatized (Crooks et al., 2008; Lash, 2013; Magnus & Tøssebro, 2014; Valle et al., 2004; Wilgosh, Sobsey, Cey, & Scorgie, 2008). Additionally, there is awareness that the system or "able" are positioned to determine whether or not accommodations are justified or necessary, often based on their perception of need, what might constitute acceptable compensation, budgetary considerations, impact on others, and interpretation of the extent of legal responsibility to provide accommodation (Dong et al., 2012; Gold et al., 2012; Kelepouris, 2014).

Concern about confidentiality and access to information regarding disclosure can cause some people to fear loss of control and choice regarding who knows what, which is a violation of their right to autonomy and privacy (Beckett & Wrighton, 2000; Lash, 2013; Matthews, 2009). Even more difficult is the knowledge that disclosure does not always result in the intended outcome. Roessler et al. (2007) documented self-reports of discrimination from adults with multiple sclerosis following workplace disclosure, including lack of access to needed accommodation, poor performance reviews, limited access to training necessary for promotion, and disparities in compensation and benefits. Because of these realities, disclosure involves risk (Crooks et al., 2008; Valle et al., 2004). Therefore, understanding the processes surrounding decisions regarding when, how, or even if to disclose is essential to facilitating self-determination.

To tell or not to tell: the disclosure dilemma

For individuals with disabilities, disclosure is described as an ongoing and highly complex process that is strongly influenced by internal and external variables within a specific context or situation (Chaudoir & Fisher, 2010; Crooks et al., 2008; Evans, 2013; Lash, 2013; Magnus & Tøssebro, 2014; Riddell & Weedon, 2014). Persons with disabilities are aware that stigma and stereotyping are often associated with a disability (Cohen & Avanzino, 2010; Huws & Jones, 2008; Valle et al., 2004); that persons with disabilities are typically assigned lower status in school and society (Baglieri, Bejoian, Broderick, Conner, & Valle, 2011), have limited access to legal recourse, and are considerably "disadvantaged socially, vocationally, economically and educationally" (Shaw et al., 2012, pp. 82–83). Therefore, disclosure involves a cautious balance between potential risk and intended benefit, with awareness that the outcome might be quite different from that anticipated (Chaudoir & Fisher, 2010; Lash, 2013; Madaus, 2008; Rocco, 2001; Worley & Cornett-DiVito, 2007). For example, in their study of 55 women with fibromyalgia syndrome [FMS], Crooks et al. (2008) reported that to avoid labeling, some women distanced themselves from identification as a person with disability by "finding ways of describing the self that acknowledged impairment without understanding this as being disabled" (p. 1842). Others were able to view disability as existing within contextual spaces, thus defining themselves as disabled and therefore needing accommodation in one context or setting but non-disabled in another. This may suggest fluidity in disability as self-identity. Similarly, in their analysis of 45 autobiographies and written accounts by people with autism, Davidson and Henderson (2010) described four "sense-making disclosure clusters," one of which was a "keeping safe repertoire" in which individuals carefully determined when it was safe to disclose, or even if disclosure was necessary (p. 158). Some also turned to "qualified deception," attributing actions to other less stigmatizing causes, such as indicating that one needed to leave a noisy or busy environment to better hear a conversation partner.

It might be suggested that the more important a goal is to an individual, such as in this respect to graduate from a postsecondary program or secure employment, the more reluctant that person might be to take a risk that might call into question competence and ability. However, when education is related to higher employment prospects for individuals with disabilities, the lack of access to accommodation may have lasting implications.

Chaudoir and Fisher (2010) proposed a model, The Disclosure Process Model, based on a review of literature that explored the process of decision-making regarding disclosure in persons with "concealable stigmatized identity," such as HIV/AIDS and chronic mental or physical illness. In the majority of the literature surveyed, the reasons given for disclosure were socially determined, such as, to become more authentic or honest within an interpersonal relationship, to gain social support, or to educate others. According to Chaudoir and Fisher, decision-making regarding disclosure involves ongoing tension between goal attainment and "stigma management" (p. 249). Therefore, they suggested that two motivational goal orientations are used to negotiate most disclosure decision-making: (a) approach-oriented goals, or the desire to achieve a positive or hoped for outcome; and (b) avoidance-oriented goals, or the desire to avoid or prevent a negative or unwanted outcome. Disclosure, therefore, involves risk because it initiates "co-ownership" of potentially stigmatizing information between the discloser and confidant, which could set in motion the possibility of relational change.

While Chaudoir and Fisher's (2010) model depicts motivations that drive disclosure and factors important to the decision-making process within a social or interpersonal realm, there is need for greater understanding of the factors that influence disclosure in academic or vocational settings in which the goal is to attain services or accommodations to secure desired outcomes. The following section proposes a framework that might be used to deconstruct the dialogical discourse between student and professor, or employee and employer, to negotiate accommodation.

Negotiating accommodation: a template for self-advocacy

From an examination of the research, it is clear that many individuals with disability experience some difficulty with dialogue regarding disclosure or requests for needed accommodations and services. What seems to be needed is a method to deconstruct disclosure discourse to enable understanding of possible dialogical impasses and provide a tool to negotiate accommodation.

It might be argued at this point that access to necessary, or reasonable, services and accommodations is a "right" of persons with disability. Thought accurate in many situations, Bickenbach (2009) suggested, "one of the ironies of the theory and practice of human rights is that although, rhetorically, universal human rights are said to be 'non-negotiable,' in fact negotiation is the primary political mode of the realization of human rights" (p. 1122). In addition, defining reasonable accommodations in educational and workplace settings has been beset with differences of opinion and interpretation. Therefore, having a framework that counselors and coaches might use to enable persons with disability to understand and explore the various components intrinsic to dialogical difficulties might lead to a more collaborative means of negotiating outcome (Chaudoir & Fisher, 2010; Dong et al., 2012; Worley & Cornett-DeVito, 2007).

The review of literature supports a template that situates disclosure and dialogical dilemma as occurring in one or more of four domains within a specific context: People and Perceptions; Principles and Power; Pathways and Processes; and Product and Profit.

People and perceptions: the "who?" component

People and Perceptions has to do with the stakeholders involved in the conversation; their identities, assumptions, worldviews, needs, goals, responsibilities, and concerns (Cloke & Goldsmith, 2011). According to Stone, Patton, and Heen (2010), every conversation, at some level or another, is an "Identity Conversation."

"The Identity Conversation looks inward: it's all about who we are and how we see ourselves. How does what happened affect my self-esteem, my self-image, my sense of who I am in the world? What impact will it have on my future? What self-doubts do I harbor?" (p. 14).

Therefore, throughout a conversational exchange, each individual is closely attuned to the reactions of others, both verbal and non-verbal, and what those reactions imply about one's competence, trustworthiness, and worth. According to Stone et al. (2010), one's perceptions of being dismissed or devalued can produce "Identity Quake" – that is, doubts about one's ability or worth that can "knock [one] off balance" (p. 113).

It might be proposed that issues of identity may become more salient for those who enter dialogue with concerns about the potential of being labeled or having identity negatively ascribed by others (Cohen & Avanzino, 2010; Magnus & Tøssebro, 2014; Rocco, 2001; Worley & Cornett-DeVito, 2007). In addition, during conversational exchanges, participants are not simply reacting to perceived messages about themselves; they are also making inferences about the motives, trustworthiness, and intent of the conversational partner (Cloke & Goldsmith, 2011; Davidson, McElwee & Hannan, 2004). When responses fail to meet expectations, one might draw the conclusion that the other is insensitive, uncaring, or disinterested, reactions that can trigger dialogical impasse and the inability to consider alternate explanations (Beckett & Wrighton, 2000). For example, immediately ascribing negative intent to an instructor who opposes a request to allow an exam to be taken at a different time, in a different location, or in modified format might block the ability to consider that the instructor's response might be related to their understanding of departmental regulations regarding assessment, previous experiences with similar requests, or insufficient knowledge of the type of accommodation requested, rationale that might be open to negotiation. Therefore, the ability to understand how people and perceptions shape dialogue can enable students and employees to identify their own responses, recognize and suspend inferences that might impede dialogue, and focus on comprehending the perspective of another in a manner that would facilitate negotiation of a beneficial outcome.

Principles and power: the "why?" component

Principles are the criteria that serve as the basis for decision-making, or the rationale used to explain why a decision was made. Principles incorporate personal, organizational, and system-wide mission or vision statements, values, beliefs, ethics, morals, philosophies, opinions, rules, and norms that serve as the basis for defining conduct. Principles are used to determine what is acceptable, reasonable, or appropriate within a specific situation or context. Common considerations that guide decision-making include: What is correct and right? What is straightforward and typical? What serves the interests of the group? What has been used or viewed as successful in the past? and What is ethical or fair? For example, research indicates that persons with disability may forego disclosure due to concern for peers' or co-workers' perceptions of fairness (Dong et al., 2012; Scorgie, Kidal, & Wilgosh, 2010; Wilgosh et al., 2008). Fairness, in this case, might be repositioned to view accommodation as providing parity with others to attain a shared goal. Because principles are often rooted in tradition, change may be resisted – on principle.

Power refers to the persons or structures that are accorded authority to define a problem, set the rules, and decide what criteria will be applied to the decision-making processes. Power focuses on "who" gets to decide "what" (Baglieri et al., 2011). Power is both positional and contextual. For example, dialogue that occurs in a classroom or in the office of a supervisor or instructor may accentuate power differential for those who feel disempowered, affecting communicative exchange. Furthermore, in interactions between persons with unequal status and authority, dialogue may be impeded if the person with lower status views the other in a position of "gatekeeper" – that is, with the ability to influence, make decisions regarding, or control future or desired outcomes (Davidson et al., 2004). Power shapes what can be said and by whom. Responses associated with disappointment or frustration such as demanding, threatening, categorizing, and judging more often than not stall conversation and initiate an adversarial relationship (Cloke & Goldsmith, 2011). Rather than initiating a struggle for power, effective negotiators work to honor the authority and rights of each party while at the same time working for reciprocated empowerment to achieve optimal outcomes.

Pathways and processes: the "how?" component

The focus of Pathways and Processes is on how a task is accomplished – that is, what are considered acceptable methods and means to reach an outcome, and what resources and accommodations are appropriate. Traditionally in higher education, there has been the assumption that everyone should do the same thing, at the same time, in the same way. Newer conceptualizations of differentiation in teaching and learning are challenging these former assumptions, introducing multiple or alternative ways to complete a task. However, misunderstandings can still arise. For example, a student who has been allocated the right to audio record class sessions by the university department of disability services may encounter resistance from an instructor who utilizes a discussion-oriented or Socratic seminar method of teaching due to concern about the effect that audiotaping may have on other students' willingness to participate openly in classroom discussions. While encountering instructor resistance may produce immediate feelings that one's rights are being denied, students who are able to isolate the issue as a "process" dilemma are more likely to negotiate acceptable means of accessing information shared during a class session.

Table 15.1 Negotiating equity accommodation: a template for transition training

People & Perceptions The "*Who?*"	• Who are the conversation partners/stakeholders and what roles/positions do they represent? • What are each stakeholder's goals, responsibilities, and concerns and how might these be shaping the current dialogue? • How can perceptions be identified and reframed to facilitate dialogue from a shared perspective (both intra- and interpersonally)?
Principles & Power The "*Why?*"	• What are the underlying principles that are currently being employed to guide decision-making? • How might these principles need to be affirmed, challenged, or reframed in the current situation? • How are power and authority being displayed (e.g., individual, contextual, perspectival)? • How might each person's position and rights be acknowledged and affirmed within a framework of shared empowerment and collaboration?
Pathways & Processes The "*How?*"	• What are the typical or currently recommended pathways to achieve the desired outcome? • What alternate pathways might be suggested? • What are possible challenges or barriers to use of alternate pathways and how might these be addressed? • How can discussion of pathways and processes be respectful of the required outcome?
Product & Profit The "*What?*"	• How does each stakeholder conceive of or identify the final product? • Are there any discrepancies regarding what skills, results, outcomes, etc., must be demonstrated or incorporated to achieve the final product? • How might each of the stakeholders want to profit from the activity or interaction? • How might product and profit be reframed or negotiated to reflect an outcome that is acceptable and that achieves benefit for all stakeholders?

Product and profit: the "what?" component

Product and Profit have to do with the goal, outcome, or objective of an activity; what it should look like, what acceptable alternatives might be appropriate and who is intended to profit from the outcome. Among other things, educators are concerned with appropriately preparing students for vocation or employment, which includes meeting criteria for certification, or successfully passing examinations. Employers are invested in cost, benefit, and return on investment (Dong et al., 2012; Gold et al., 2012). However, effective organizations are also focused on their employees, and providing an environment where all can thrive. Similarly, postsecondary instructors are interested in student wellbeing, and their role in shaping an individual in process of becoming. Separating out these parallel goals might enable students and employees to negotiate accommodations that facilitate outcomes that are satisfactory to and benefit each.

According to Test et al. (2005), self-advocacy requires skill in communication, knowledge of self and others, the ability to understand and articulate one's rights, and the ability to manage interactions. The discourse template outlined next might be useful as an additional tool for use by counselors and coaches in transition training to build self-advocacy skills in persons with disability in preparation for postsecondary and workplace settings (see Table 15.1).

Research indicates that persons with disability do not wish special treatment or unwarranted privileges, or to be viewed as using disability as an excuse. Rather they want to be given opportunity; the same opportunity for achievement and success that is afforded to their non-disabled peers. This may best be accomplished through a change in mindset regarding what it means to request accommodation.

Equity accommodation: a shift in perspective

Equity accommodation is a term that suggests a shift from a deficit-based depiction of accommodation in which a person with disability must disclose need and describe how it interferes with their ability to achieve, to a strength-based outcome-oriented conceptualization of accommodation. Equity accommodation ensures that each individual has access to that which is accorded to others in terms of an environment conducive to working, affordances and tools appropriate and necessary to complete a task, opportunities to secure additional knowledge or skill, and an atmosphere of valuing and belonging. Equity accommodation, therefore, is based on principles of parity, justness, correspondence, beneficence, and respect. Discourse using equity accommodation moves disclosure from "let me tell you what I can't do because of . . ." to "let me tell you what I can do with access to . . .".

Clearly, the introduction of a term such as equity accommodation will not preclude concern with what is reasonable, cost effective, or even possible within a particular situation. What it might do, however, is initiate a shift in thinking from viewing accommodation request as evidence of "dis"-ability to viewing access to accommodation as supporting or promoting ability.

Bickenbach (2009) suggested that disability discourse is shaped by "attitudinal, structural, political, social and cultural" constructs embedded in the systems in which persons with disability live, study, and work (p. 1121). Thus, movement toward equity accommodation might precipitate a systems level shift in conceptualizations of ability and disability, power and disempowerment, and ways in which certain identities are privileged in society.

Negotiating disability, identity, and disclosure in postsecondary or workplace settings is a complex and ongoing dilemma for persons with disability due to concern that disclosure will result in being ascribed a label fraught with stigma, casting doubts upon competence, aptitude, and worth, both as a student and as a future employee. Self-determination, an important set of skills for transition to adulthood, involves proficiency in self-advocacy. But self-determination is best enabled when situated within a systems framework in which equity is a guiding principle. When equity shapes decision-making regarding accommodation, persons with disability can shift from a cautionary, even fearful, stance toward disclosure to the more forward-thinking, opportunity-oriented query: "What might be possible if I tell you who I am?"

Note

Portions of this chapter were presented at the World Educational Research Association Focal Meeting, Edinburgh, Scotland, 2014, and at the American Educational Research Association Meeting, Philadelphia, PA, 2014. In addition, the negotiation template has been presented in graduate courses in education and leadership studies.

References

Baglieri, S., Bejoian, L. M., Broderick, A. A., Conner, D. J., & Valle, J. (2011). [Re]claiming "Inclusive Education" Toward cohesion in educational reform: Disability studies unravels the myth of the normal child. *Teachers College Record, 113*(10), 2122–2154.

Beckett, C., & Wrighton, E. (2000). "What matters to me is not what you're talking about" Maintaining the social model of disability in "public and private" negotiations. *Disability and Society, 15*(7), 991–999.

Bickenbach, J. E. (2009). Disability, culture and the UN convention. *Disability and Rehabilitation, 31*(14), 1111–1124.

Brislin, D. C. (2008). Reaching for independence: Counseling implications for youth with spina- bifida. *Journal of Counseling and Development, 86*(1), 34–38.

Brock, B. L. (2007). The workplace experiences of educators with disabilities: Insights for school leaders. *Educational Considerations, 34*(2), 9–14.

Carter, E. W., Lane, K. L., Cooney, M., Weir, K., Moss, C. K., & Machalicek, W. (2013). Self determination among transition-age youth with autism or intellectual disability: Parent perspectives. *Research & Practice for Persons with Severe Disabilities, 38*(3), 129–138.

Carter, E.W., Lane, K. L., Pierson, M. R., & Stang, K. K. (2008). Promoting self-determination for transition-age youth: Views of high school general and special educators. *Exceptional Children, 75*(1), 55–70.

Chaudoir, S. R., & Fisher, J. D. (2010). The disclosure processes model: Understanding disclosure decision making and postdisclosure outcomes among people living with a concealable stigmatized identity. *Psychological Bulletin, 136*(2), 236–256.

Cloke, K., & Goldsmith, J. (2011). *Resolving conflicts at work: Ten strategies for everyone on the job.* San Francisco, CA: Jossey-Bass.

Cohen, M., & Avanzino, S. (2010). We are people first: Framing organizational assimilation experiences of the physically disabled using c-cultural theory. *Communication Studies, 61*(3), 272–303.

Crooks, V. A., Chouinard, V., & Wilton, R. D. (2008). Understanding, embracing, rejecting: Women's negotiations of disability constructions and categorizations after becoming chronically ill. *Social Science and Medicine, 67*, 1837–1846.

Dalgin, R. S., & Gilbride, D. (2003). Perspectives of people with psychiatric disabilities on employment disclosure. *Psychiatric Rehabilitation Journal, 26*(3), 306–310.

Davidson, J., & Henderson, V. (2010). "Coming out" on the spectrum: Autism, identity and disclosure. *Social and Cultural Geography, 11*(2), 155–170.

Davidson, J. A., McElwee, G., & Hannan, G. (2004). Trust and power as determinants of conflict resolution strategy and outcome satisfaction. *Peace and Conflict: Journal of Peace Psychology, 10*(3), 275–292.

de Vet, E., Waitt, G., & Gorman-Murray, A. (2012). "How dare you say that about my friend": Negotiating disability and identity within Australian high schools. *Australian Geographer, 43*(4), 377–391.

Dong, S., Oire, S. N., McDonald-Wilson, K. L., & Fabian, E. S. (2012). A comparison of perceptions of factors in the job accommodation process among employees with disabilities, employers, and service providers. *Rehabilitation Counseling Bulletin, 56*(3), 182–189.

Evans, W. (2013). "I am not a dyslexic person I'm a person with dyslexia": Identity constructions of dyslexia among students in nurse education. *Journal of Advanced Nursing, 70*(2), 360–372.

Gil, L. A. (2007). Bridging the transition gap from high school to college. *Teaching Exceptional Children, 40*(2), 12–15.

Gold, P. B., Oire, S N., Fabian, E. S., & Wewiorski, N. J. (2012). Negotiating reasonable workplace accommodations: Perspectives of employers, employees with disabilities, and rehabilitation service providers. *Journal of Vocational Rehabilitation, 37*, 25–37.

Hibbs, T., & Pothier, D. (2006). Postsecondary education and disabled students: Mining a level playing field or playing in a minefield? In D. Pothier & R. Devlin (Eds.), *Critical disability theory: Essays in philosophy, politics, policy and law.* Vancouver, BC: University of British Columbia Press.

Huws, J. C., & Jones, R. S. P. (2008). Diagnosis, disclosure, and having autism: An interpretative phenomenological analysis of the perceptions of young people with autism. *Journal of Intellectual & Developmental Disability, 33*(2), 99–107.

Jones, M. (2006). Teaching self-determination: Empowered teachers, empowered students. *Teaching Exceptional Children, 39*(1), 12–17.

Kelepouris, C. (2014). Transitioning students with disabilities into higher education. *Brigham Young University Education and Law Journal, 2014*(1), 27–39.

Lash, B. N. (2013). Research from the heart: Chancing labels and exposing a private identity. *Health Communication, 28*, 422–424.

Madaus, J. W. (2008). Employment self-disclosure rates and rationales of university graduates with learning disabilities. *Journal of Learning Disabilities, 41*(4), 291–299.

Magnus, E., & Tøssebro, J. (2014). Negotiating individual accommodation in higher education. *Scandinavian Journal of Disability Research, 16*(4), 316–332.

Matthews, N. (2009). Teaching the "invisible" disabled students in the classroom: Disclosure, inclusion and the social model of disability. *Teaching in Higher Education, 14*(3), 229–239.

Newman, L. A., & Madaus, J. W. (2015). Reported accommodations and supports provided to secondary and postsecondary students with disabilities: National perspective. *Career Development and Transition for Exceptional Individuals, 38*(3), 173–181.

Palmer, S. B. (2010). Self-determination: A lifespan perspective. *Focus on Exceptional Children, 42*(6), 1–16.

Riddell, S., & Weedon, E. (2014). Disabled students in higher education: Discourses of disability and the negotiation of identity. *International Journal of Educational Research, 63*, 38–46.

Roberts, K. D. (2010). Topic areas to consider when planning transition from high school to postsecondary education for students with autism spectrum disorder. *Focus on Autism and Other Developmental Disabilities, 25*(3), 158–162.

Rocco, T. S. (2001). Helping adult educators understand disability disclosure. *Adult Learning, 12*(2), 10–12.

Roessler, R. T., Neath, J., McMahon, B. T., & Rumrill, P. D. (2007). The relationship of selected supply-and-demand-side factors to forms of perceived discrimination among adults with multiple sclerosis. *Rehabilitation Counseling Bulletin, 50*(4), 203–215.

Scorgie, K., Kildal, L., & Wilgosh, L. (2010). Post-secondary students with disability: Issues related to empowerment and self-determination. *Developmental Disabilities Bulletin, 38*(1/2), 133–145.

Shaw, L. R., Chan, F., & McMahon, B. T. (2012). Intersectionality and disability harassment: The interactive effects of disability, race, age, and gender. *Rehabilitation Counseling Bulletin, 55*(2), 82–91.

Stetsenko, A., & Arievitch, I. M. (2004). The self in cultural-historical activity theory: Reclaiming the unity of social and individual dimensions of human development. *Theory & Psychology, 14*(4), 475–503.

Stone, D., Patton, B., & Heen, S. (2010). *Difficult conversations: How to discuss what matters most.* New York, NY: Penguin.

Test, D. W., Fowler, C. H., Wood, W. M., Brewer, D. M., & Eddy, S. (2005). A conceptual framework of self-advocacy for students with disabilities. *Remedial and Special Education, 26*(1), 43–54.

Trainor, A. A. (2010). Adolescents with disabilities transitioning to adulthood: Implications for a diverse and multicultural population. *The Prevention Researcher, 17*(2), 12–16.

Valle, J. W., Solis, S., Volpitta, D., & Connor, D. J. (2004). The disability closet: Teachers with learning disabilities evaluate the risks and benefits of "coming out." *Equity and Excellence in Education, 37*, 4–17.

Wehmeyer, M. L. (2004). Beyond self-determination: Causal agency theory. *Journal of Developmental & Physical Disabilities, 16*(4), 337–359.

Wilgosh, L., Sobsey, D., Cey, R., & Scorgie, K. (2008). Life management of postsecondary students with disabilities. *Developmental Disabilities Bulletin, 36*(1/2), 199–224.

Worley, D. W., & Cornett-DeVito, M. M. (2007). College students with learning disabilities (SWLD) and their responses to teacher power. *Communication Studies, 58*(1), 17–33.

Chapter 16

Promoting courage in children

The role of coaching

Maria Cristina Ginevra and Sara Santilli

In the last decade, thanks to the contribution of positive psychology, a paradigm shift has emerged and studies have been carried out according to a "positive view" of development in childhood. This perspective contrasts with more traditional approaches that have focused on children's deficits or pathology, such as antisocial conducts or affective disorders. It introduces a more affirmative and strength-building approach and promotes a series of strengths acting as buffers against mental illness, such as courage, future-mindedness, optimism, interpersonal skills, hope, perseverance, and flourishing (Catalano, Berglund, Ryan, Lonczak, & Hawkin, 2004; Roberts, Brown, Johnson, & Reinke, 2002). These skills and resources should be promoted and developed as soon as possible in children, to prepare adults to cope with a complex reality, as current society is, characterized by globalization, uncertainty about the future, and insecurity (Nota, Ginevra, & Santilli, 2015).

Among these personal resources, courage is one of the most widely valued attributes in recorded human history (e.g., Dahlsgaard, Peterson, & Seligman, 2005) and has been found to be linked to several positive developmental outcomes (Leontopoulou & Triliva, 2012; Muris, 2009).

This chapter aims at examining the construct of courage in childhood, emphasizing the role that it may have in children's development, especially in relation to the threats and challenges of the current social context. After an analysis of the definitions and typologies of courage, an international review on this topic on childhood will be presented. Moreover, assessment instruments and specific suggestions for practitioners interested to promote courageous actions in children will be provided.

Definitions and classifications of courage

Even if courage has been portrayed as a trait or a stable disposition, recent approaches have conceptualized it as a behaviour (Luthans, Youssef-Morgan, & Avolio, 2015), highlighting its common features: intentionality, risk, motivation to achieve a noble goal, and fear (Ginevra & Capozza, 2015; Pury & Hensel, 2010).

Numerous definitions can be found in literature about courage (Rate, Clarke, Lindsay, & Sternberg, 2007): Rachman (1990), for example, defined courage as the willingness and ability to deal "a fearful situation despite the presence of subjective fear and psychophysiological disturbances" (p. 12). Another complex and multidimensional definition of courage was provided by Woodard (2004), who conceptualized courage "as the ability to act for a meaningful (noble, good, or practical) cause, despite experiencing the fear associated with perceived threat exceeding the available resources" (p. 174).

Notwithstanding an operational definition of courage has not been found in literature, its multidimensionality is well documented (Pury et al., 2014). Specifically, Putman (1997) theorized three types of courage: physical, moral, and psychological. He defined physical courage as the act to handle a physical risk, moral courage as integrity in the face of risk, and psychological courage as acting despite risks associated with psychological wellbeing. Furthermore, Pury, Kowalski, and Spearman (2007) distinguished between general courage that regards behaviors considered courageous for anyone (i.e., the individual acts in a courageous way compared to how others would act in the same situation) and personal courage that involves courageous actions given by the individual's contextual difficulties. Precisely, authors indicated that high levels of confidence and low levels of fear featured a general courage behavior, instead of a personal courage behavior that includes elements of fear and individual limitations.

Courage as a protective factor against children's contemporary fears

As previously specified, some authors include the feeling of fear for the existence of courage (e.g., Rachman, 1990; Woodward & Pury, 2007), but others propose that it is a shared, but not needed, characteristic (e.g., Becker & Eagly, 2004; Pury et al., 2007). In any case, fear seems to be the subjective answer to the personal threat or risk included in nearly all definitions of courage.

The fear is considered to be an integral and adaptive emotion, with a strong survival value for development. Therefore, it should not be regarded as a pathological or dysfunctional response and should be differentiated from clinical fears or phobias (Gullone, 2000).

During the development, fears tend to have a moderate intensity and be relatively short-lived. A review by Gullone (2000) showed a developmental pattern of normal fear, from fears of stimuli in one's own immediate environment to fears related to social relations, and political or economic issues. Beginning from first infancy until the age of 4–5 years, it has been shown an increase in fear of strange persons, being abandoned by parents, darkness, ghosts, and animals. The years of primary school (6–11 years) coincide with the emergence of fears related to natural phenomena, such as thunder and earthquakes, and to social rejections, such as failure and criticism. Last, fears of late childhood into adolescence are more global and abstract, such as nuclear war, violence, and terrorism

(Burnham, 2009; Gullone, 2000). In this regard, a study by Gullone (2009) on contemporary fears of children and adolescents age 7–18 years, found that the most common fears were related to terrorist attacks, having to fight in a war, and experiencing tornadoes/hurricanes. According to Burnham (2009), these fears could emerge because of (a) war, (b) exposure to violent episodes in TV shows, (c) natural disasters, (d) diseases that happen in the social context, and (e) societal changes and outside influences, such as exposure to real violence or cyberbullying.

Even in the Italian context, Telefono Azzurro and Eurispes (2008), suggest that as early as children age 7–10 years face social and political fears: fear of being kidnapped (22.6%), to being approached by strangers (16.3%), terrorist attacks (16.2%), violence (13.5%), or being bullied (12.6%).

If some of the described fears seem typical of development and related with survival phases, as the phobia of strangers, others, like the fears associated with the social context, they are the result of a learning process and are strongly influenced by the messages that children receive from the media, school, and family context (Burnham, 2009; Querzè & Pini, 2011). In relation to the fears experienced during childhood, courage is conceptualized as a protective mechanism, because courageous children tend to expose themselves to challenging events, use coping strategies to overcome the feared stimulus or situation, and this reduces the perception of fearfulness associated with the stimulus or situation (Muris, Mayer, & Schubert, 2010; Pury & Hensel, 2010). In relation to the relevant role of courage for the personal fears, this construct in children is detailed next.

Courage in children: an international review

Although the construct of courage has been conceptualized since 400 B.C. by philosophers like Aristotle, Socrates, and Plato, it has not been extensively studied by psychological literature (Dahlsgaard et al., 2005). Muris and colleagues (Muris, 2009; Muris et al., 2010) are beginning to examine the relationship between courage and anxiety disorders.

Muris et al. (2010) showed that children age 9–12 years appeared to comprehend the concept of courage and had performed one or more courageous actions, especially "performing physically risky action," "preventing injury of another person," and "dealing with a feared animal." Moreover, they found that courage in children was positively associated with extraversion, openness/intellect, and negatively with generalized anxiety, separation anxiety, social and school phobia.

In an additional study, Muris (2009) further investigated the construct of courage in children, finding that children conceptualize it as making an action despite having fears – e.g., "You do something scary." He observed that children's personal courage was negatively associated with their general levels of anxiety symptoms, especially in situations involving separation from caregivers and social encounters with other people.

In the Italian context, Ferrari, Ginevra, Santilli, and Di Maggio (2016) explored the construct of courage in a sample of 263 (139 boys and 124 girls) elementary school students, with a mean age of 9.5 years (SD = 0.51; range 8–11 years). Specifically, using Nota and Soresi's (2015) interview (see next section), they found that the vast majority of children (i.e., 82 %) reported to have performed a courageous action at some point during their life. Exploratory cluster analysis with Iramuteq (Ratinaud & Marchand, 2012) was run to analyze the children's courage situations. The classification obtained according to these criteria was composed of four classes that contain a total of 212 texts equivalent to 81.54% of the total. The four classes identified corresponding to four lexical worlds (Reinert, 1997) selected from the different topics covered in the children's courage stories. The first cluster included 25% of the total text and the words characteristics of this cluster were all related to psychological risks (such as "dark," "sleep," "light," "night"). Examples of courageous situations described by the children regarded "During holidays, I had to sing in front of almost a whole holiday village! I did not want to sing because I am ashamed to sing in public, but when I was alone on the stage blinded by the spotlights and the music started, I started singing anyway." (Participant n. 3), or "My two-year-old cousin was afraid to go into a dark room. I was afraid too, but I went with her to quiet her" (Participant n. 12). The second cluster included 25% of the total answers and characteristic words were related to physical risks (such as "sea," "rock," "plunge"); examples were the following: "There was a rock in the sea where I would like to dive but I did not dare, however, then I grabbed it and I dove" (Participant n. 155); "I was scared, but I leaped from a rock of 7.40 feet" (Participant n. 206). The third cluster included 19% of the total texts and its characteristic words were all related to moral risks (such as "peer," "helping," "school," "defending"). Examples of moral courage were the following: "Once my classmate was beating my friend, I went between them and I said: stop beating" (Participant n. 146); "I protected a girl from some children who were teasing her. I told to them to shut up and stop" (Participant n. 10). The fourth cluster included 31% of the total texts and the words characteristic of this cluster were related to a mix of psychological and physical risks (such as "child," "beat," "help"). In all the sentences that combined this last cluster, the predominant action (psychological or physical) was not evident, or both were presented. Following is reported an example given by participant number 186: "I caught a ball that was on the other side of the road where there were dogs barking which scared me," or by participant number 11: "I helped my sister even though I'm afraid of the dark. For scouts at summer camp I was close to those who feared."

Overall, these results are in line with Putman's (1997) conceptualization of different types of courage and with Muris's (2009) findings. It seems that Italian children described more frequently actions in coping with physical and psychological risks, then psychological and physical specific risks, and last moral risks. Additionally, the authors verified differences in terms of type of courageous actions described compared to the rate of fear experienced and how courageous was that action, finding that children rated higher fear levels for and evaluated more courageous actions in coping with moral and psychological risks.

In another study, Ginevra (2016), involving 421 elementary school students, examined the relationship among courage, life satisfaction, resilience, hope, and student covitality – conceptualized as the synergistic experience of wellbeing that results from the interaction of zest, gratitude, zest, optimism, and persistence. Specifically, courage, assessed with the Italian adaptation of the "Courage Measure for Children" (see next section; Muris, 2009; Nota & Soresi, 2015), positively correlated with life satisfaction, assessed with "Satisfaction with Life Scale" (Diener, Emmons, Larsen, & Griffin, 1985), resilience and hope, assessed with the instrument "Pro.Spera" (Nota & Soresi, 2015). In addition, it was positively linked to student covitality, assessed with the questionnaire "Positive experience at school scale" (Furlong, You, Renshaw, O'Malley, & Rebelez, 2013), suggesting that courageous children more likely experience global positive school situations.

Overall, on the one hand, the few studies conducted on courage in childhood highlight that children experience courageous behaviors, especially in coping with physical and psychological risks, and that courage is related to more adaptive personal development; on the other side, these studies justify and stimulate further research on this topic, especially through crosscultural studies, to examine the role of courage on other health and career outcomes.

Instruments to assess courage in children

Considering the importance that courage may have in development and psychosocial wellbeing, practitioners should pay particular attention to analyze and strengthen it. We will describe some qualitative and quantitative measures that may be used in coaching activities to examine children's ability to face their fears and implement courage actions also with the aim to plan specific intervention activities.

One of the most used questionnaires in the literature is the Courage Measure for Children (Muris, 2009), which assesses the propensity to act courageously in children age 8–11 years. It is an instrument composed of 12 items on a 4-point Likert scale (1 = *not at all true*; 4 = *completely true*). Examples of items are: "I try to face my fears," "I act so brave," "I do things even if they seem dangerous." The analyses conducted by Nota and Soresi (2015) for the adaptation of the instrument to the Italian context suggested a monofactorial structure explaining 36.33% of total variance with an internal consistency index of .81.

Muris (2009) developed a series of vignettes illustrating fearful scenarios which require a child to give courageous performances. Examples of vignettes are as follows:

> Imagine you're alone at home one evening. Your parents went to the movies and they told you that they will get back home in a few hours. It's dark outside and there is a lot of wind, so you go to close all the windows and drapes. Do you feel a bit scared to be at home alone? Suddenly the doorbell rings. . . . Do you open the door to see who it is?

> Just imagine having a rabbit. At one point late one evening it starts to rain and thunder very hard. You regret that your rabbit is outside and you would like to bring him inside. Just when you decide to go outside, you see a flash in the sky and hear very loud thunder. Sounds scary. Would you go in the garden in that storm to get the rabbit?

Children are asked to respond using a 4-point Likert scale (1 = *not at all true;* 4 = *completely true*).

The author proposed also a semi-structured interview in which, after providing Rachman's (1990) definition of courage, children are asked to tell the most courageous action they have ever done and to evaluate it in terms of how much courage was required on a 9-point Likert scale (1 = *no courage at all* to 9 = *very much courage*) and how much fear they experienced on a 9-point Likert scale (1 = *not at all afraid* to 9 = *very afraid*).

Based on this qualitative procedure, Nota and Soresi (2015) recently developed the interview "The courage of children," in which the child is stimulated to write a courageous situation he/she was involved in. The instrument aims specifically to consider the indications that the stories collected provide about settings, characters, and actions to bring out the specific contexts in which the factual stories belong. The stories described by participants can be analyzed considering the following three broad categories developed by Koerner (2014): settings, where the story is narrated (in a school, in a classroom, in a house, etc.); characters (family, schoolmates, friends, etc.); characters' actions (facing difficulties, conflict and violence, encouraging changes, working, helping, etc.). Then the children are invited to retrospectively rate on two separate Likert scales how much fear they had felt at that time (1 = *no fear at all*, 9 = *a lot of fear*) and how courageous they think other individuals would rate their act (1 = *not at all courageous*, 9 = *very courageous*). This interview can be introduced in school activities aimed to increase positive relationships in classrooms based on collaboration, solidarity, and inclusion. The different productions and the analysis of narratives can also be discussed in groups and a "secretary" may be nominated to write down the different elements included in the definitions and statements.

The analysis of strengths allows one to elaborate a personalized report for each child, in which the variables considered and the scores obtained in these dimensions are described. When the children are handed the reports, they are encouraged to reflect on their resources and identify their strengths. Small-group or individual educational activities can be designed and specific intervention activities can be developed that can be used for further discussion.

Actions to increase courage: the role of coaching

After dealing with assessment, we think it is appropriate to address the issue of intervention and focus attention on the role of coaching as one of the most efficacious interventions to support the development of courage in childhood. Killion and Harrison (2006) conceptualize coaches as professionals who, rather than working directly with children, assist teachers and parents in increasing successful implementation of evidence-based practices with them. Specifically, by building a collaborative relationship, a coach operates by making the most of teachers' and parents' competences and guides them in setting learning and development goals and in planning strategies to pursue them (Dillard, 2015).

In describing the actions taken by coaches to help teachers and parents, Friedman, Woods, and Salisbury (2012) make reference to: (a) *Conversation and sharing information*: this is a bidirectional conversational strategy during a session with the aim to establish and maintain a relationship between caregiver and coach, which allows the sharing of information, comments, questions and answers on the program; (b) *Observation*, at the very beginning of the coaching activity, of what usually goes on in school and family daily contexts; (c) *Use of teaching strategies* to support parents and teachers in strategy implementation and in maintaining child participation in the coaching activity; (d) *Problem solving/reflection*: the coach and the caregiver co-describe the child or the routines to come up with new ideas and alternatives on how to improve or generalize a strategy.

Regarding courage, Goud (2005) maintains that a coach can train teachers and parents to help the children (a) enhance self-efficacy of handling the risk; (b) emphasize the purpose of courageous behavior; and (c) reduce their perception of risk.

(a) Enhancing self-efficacy in handling risk

Self-confidence is a primary strength in countering fears and risks. In order to instill self-efficacy, exposure to persons who demonstrate courageous behaviors is particularly relevant. Although direct models are the most powerful, vicarious modeling (e.g., reading stories, watching videos and cartoons, hearing about courageous behaviors) can also be effective. Coaches can help parents and teachers present stories of courageous peers who have succeeded in facing their fears and, through these stories, discuss with children the issue of fear (Villella, 2013). Specifically, stories about Putman's (1997) classification of courage should be presented, especially about coping with physical and psychological risks, as these are most frequently described by children (Ferrari et al., 2016). Children should be helped to identify strategies and resources used by the characters to overcome their fears and train them to apply them to school and family situations. Additionally, stories of general and personal courage should be designed (Pury et al., 2007). This latter, in particular, should be chosen in relation to a child's personal limitation and subjective fears experienced.

In addition to stories, video modeling can be used as an efficacious procedure to stimulate courageous behaviors; children could watch clips in which a character demonstrates the targeted behavior despite his or her perceived risks. Popular cartoons or movies for children should be chosen, with short clips rather than whole episodes being selected, to focus children's attention on the targeted behaviors (Macpherson, Charlop, & Miltenberger, 2014).

It is possible to enhance self-confidence also by setting up situations that envisage successful experiences for children and helping them recognize the successes achieved. Additionally, self-confidence can be increased also by verbal persuasion: learning to handle their own fears needs encouragement in persevering or increasing perseverance. Encouragement, as a form of social support, can give an individual motivation to apply psychological, physical, or moral courage (Pury et al., 2014). Parents and teachers can be trained to encourage children to face the risks that come their way, and to provide constructive feedback about their performance. Self-encouragement could also be promoted, as this strategy has been seen to be effective before performing a courageous act (Pury et al., 2014).

(b) Emphasizing the purpose of courageous behavior

Rather than being helped to improve their ability to meet their goals in the face of fear-eliciting risks, children should be supported in the school and family contexts to assess how worthwhile or noble these goals are. A courageous behavior involves a "good" purpose for oneself or others, distinguishing itself from other constructs and behaviors, such as bravery, intrepidity, and thrill-seeking (Pury et al., 2014; Rate & Sternberg, 2007). Therefore, coaches should help parents and teachers to train children to examine the merit of goals by using the principles of utility, or the idea that something is good when it positively affects other individuals, and autonomy, or the idea that choice for individuals is a dominant good, albeit respecting other people.

(c) Reducing the perception of risk

An appropriate evaluation of courage includes risks related to the courageous act (Pury et al., 2014). Promoting self-efficacy and strengthening a sense of purpose are powerful resources for counteracting fears. However, children should be encouraged to talk about their fears, distinguish reasonable fears, associated with an objective risk for the person's safety, from irrational ones, which do not involve any actual threat. They should be supported to identify and review any catastrophic thought – i.e., an excessive and unreasonable fear of succumbing to a threat or a perceived danger (Zampone, 2015).

In this connection, teachers and parents, guided by the coach, could illustrate a series of unpleasant situations that the children may come across in their family or school life and ask them to reflect on possible ways to deal with them. They could then train them to recognize possible irrational thoughts and question them based on evidence against them by giving alternative explanations to the events, and guiding the children to evaluate the likelihood of each connection between actual events and to envisage less catastrophic scenarios. When direct handling of some fears could lead to great social of physical risks for the child – e.g., contrasting acts of bullying against a schoolmate – it is important to stimulate indirect handling of the situation. In other words, to make children understand that courageous actions include also reporting unpleasant situations to significant others rather than handling these situations themselves.

Conclusions

Based on positive psychology, in this chapter we addressed the construct of courage as a crucial resource for children's psychosocial wellbeing. We examined the relationship between courage and fear in children, paying particular attention to the threats of the current context and the role of courage in overcoming them. Then, we described qualitative and quantitative instruments that can be used by practitioners to assess courage in childhood, and proposed suggestions and strategies found in the literature to promote courage.

What presented so far highlights the importance of early interventions to the advantage of courage in order that direct experiences of fear in the family or school context or indirect experiences through crime news in the media may not negatively influence the tendency to act to the benefit of oneself or others (Zampone, 2015). Such experiences of fear may trigger in children feelings of disinvestment in the future, of discomfort, of bewilderment as well as hostile behaviors and prejudice toward those that find themselves in a vulnerable condition (Nota, Ginevra, & Santilli, 2015). In our current context, characterized at the social, political, and economic levels by complex interdependent relationships impossible to manage based on simple causal processes, professionals must aim to improve the ability to act in a courageous way. This would result in increased perception of being able to cope not only with the fears of the "present" but also with the stressors associated with uncertainty about the future (Leppma, Szente, & Brosch, 2015).

References

Becker, S. W., & Eagly, A. H. (2004). The heroism of women and men. *American Psychologist, 59*, 163–178.

Burnham, J. J. (2009). Contemporary fears of children and adolescents: Coping and resiliency in the 21st century. *Journal of Counseling & Development, 87*, 28–35.

Catalano, R. F., Berglund, M. L., Ryan, J. A. M., Lonczak, H. S., & Hawkins, J. D. (2004). Positive youth development in the United States: Research findings on evaluations of positive youth development programs. *The ANNALS of the American Academy of Political and Social Science, 591*, 98–124.

Dahlsgaard, K., Peterson, C., & Seligman, M. (2005). Shared virtue: The convergence of valued human strengths across culture and history. *Review of General Psychology, 9*, 203–213.

Diener, E., Emmons, R. A., Larsen, R. J., & Griffin, S. (1985). The satisfaction with life scale. *Journal of Personality Assessment, 49*, 71–75.

Dillard, J. D. (2015). *The self-reported impact of instructional coaching on middle school teachers' practices in an urban Georgia school district* (Doctoral Dissertation). Georgia State University. Retrieved from http://scholarworks.gsu.edu/cgi/viewcontent.cgi?article=1141&context=eps_diss

Ferrari, L., Ginevra, M. C., Santilli, S., & Di Maggio, I. (2016, July). *The courage in a group of Italian children*. Poster session presented at 31st International Congress of Psychology, Yokohama, Japan.

Friedman, M., Woods, J., & Salisbury, C. (2012). Caregiver coaching strategies for early intervention providers: Moving toward operational definitions. *Infants & Young Children, 25*(1), 62–82.

Furlong, M. J., You, S., Renshaw, T. L., O'Malley, M. D., & Rebelez, J. (2013). Preliminary development of the positive experiences at school scale for elementary school children. *Child Indicators Research, 6*, 753–775.

Ginevra, M. C. (2016, October). *Coraggio in età evolutiva* [Courage in children]. Paper presented at the Italian Conference of Italian Associational of Vocational Guidance, University of Padova, Italy.

Ginevra, M. C., & Capozza, D. (2015). Il coraggio: dalle definizioni ad alcune considerazioni per le attività di counselling [Courage: From definition to some suggestions for counselling activities]. In L. Nota & S. Soresi (Eds.), *Il counselling del futuro* (pp. 111–122). Padova, Italy: Cleup.

Goud, N. H. (2005). Courage: Its nature and development. *Journal of Humanistic Counseling, Education & Development, 44*, 102–116.

Gullone, E. (2000). The development of normal fear: A century of research. *Clinical Psychology Review, 20*, 429–451.

Killion, J., & Harrison, C. (2006). *Taking the lead: New roles for teachers and school-based coaches*. Oxford, OH: National Staff Development Council.

Koerner, M. M. (2014). Courage as identity work: Accounts of workplace courage. *Academy of Management Journal, 57*(1), 63–93.

Leontopoulou, S., & Triliva, S. (2012). Explorations of subjective wellbeing and character strengths among a Greek university student sample. *International Journal of Wellbeing, 2*, 251–270.

Leppma, M., Szente, J., & Brosch, M. J. (2015). Advancements in addressing children's fears: A review and recommendations. *The Professional Counselor, 5*, 261–272.

Luthans, F., Youssef-Morgan, C. M., & Avolio, B. J. (2015). *Psychological capital and beyond*. New York, NY, US: Oxford University Press.

Macpherson, K., Charlop, M. H., & Miltenberger, C. A. (2014). Using portable video modeling technology to increase the compliment behaviors of children with autism during athletic group play. *The Journal of Autism and Developmental Disorders, 45*(12), 3836–3845.

Muris, P. (2009). Fear and courage in children: Two sides of the same coin? *Journal of Child and Family Studies, 18*, 486–490.

Muris, P., Mayer, B., & Schubert, T. (2010). "You might belong in gryffinder": Children's courage and its relationships to anxiety symptoms, big five personality traits, and sex roles. *Child Psychiatry & Human Development, 41*, 204–213.

Nota, L., Ginevra, M. C., & Santilli, S. (2015). Life design and prevention. In L. Nota & J. Rossier (Eds.), *Handbook of life design* (pp. 183–199). Göttingen: Hogrefe.

Nota, L., & Soresi, S. (2015, October). *Procedure di valutazione della speranza, dell'ottimismo e del coraggio nei bambini* [Assessment instruments of hope, optimism, and courage for children]. Paper presented at the Italian Conference of Italian Associational of Vocational Guidance, University of Padova, Italy.

Pury, C., & Hensel, A. D. (2010). Are courageous actions successful actions? The Journal of Positive Psychology: Dedicated to Furthering Research and Promoting Good Practice, 5, 62–72.

Pury, C., Kowalski, R., & Spearman, J. (2007). Distinctions between general and personal courage. *Journal of Positive Psychology, 2*, 99–114.

Pury, C. S., Starkey, C. B., Breeden, C. R., Kelley, C. L., Murphy, H. J., & Lowndes, A.T. (2014). Courage interventions: Future directions and cautions. In A. C. Parks, S. M. Schueller, A. C. Parks, & S. O. Schueller (Eds.), *The Wiley Blackwell handbook of positive psychological interventions* (pp. 168–178). Hoboken NJ: Wiley-Blackwell.

Putman, D. (1997). Psychological courage. *Philosophy, Psychiatry and Psychology, 4*, 1–11.

Querzè, A., & Pini, L. A. (2011). *Voci dalla paura: Riflessioni e analisi di un'emozione complessa.* Milano, Italia: Franco Angeli.

Rachman, S. J. (1990). *Fear and courage* (2nd ed.). New York: W.H. Freeman and Co.

Rate, C. R., Clarke, J. A., Lindsay, D. R., & Sternberg, R. J. (2007). Implicit theories of courage. *Journal of Positive Psychology, 2*(2), 80–98.

Rate, C. R., Sternberg, R. J. (2007). When good people do nothing: A failure of courage. In J. Langan-Fox, C. L. Cooper, & R. J. Klimoski (Eds.), *Research companion to the dysfunctional workplace: Management challenges and symptoms: New horizons in management* (pp. 3–21). Northampton, MA: Edward Elgar Publishing.

Ratinaud, P., & Marchand, P. (2012). Recherche improbable d'une homogène diversité: le débat sur l'identité nationale [Improbable research for a homogeneous diversity: The debate on national identity]. *Langages, 3*, 93–107.

Reinert, M. (1997). Les "Mondes lexicaux" des six numéros de la revue Le Surréalisme au Service dela Révolution [The "Lexical Worlds" of the six issues of the journal Surrealism in the Service of the Revolution]. *Cahiers du centre de recherche sur le surréalisme* (Mélusine), *XVI*, 270–302.

Roberts, M. C., Brown, K. J., Johnson, R. J., & Reinke, J. (2002). Positive psychology for children. Development, prevention and promotion. In C. R. Snyder & S. J. Lopez (Eds.), *Handbook of positive psychology* (pp. 663–675). Oxford: Oxford University Press.

Telefono azzurro ed Eurispes. (2008). *9° Rapporto nazionale sulla condizione dell'infanzia e dell'adolescenza* [9th national report on childhood and adolescence]. Retrieved from www.azzurro.it/sites/default/files/Materiali/InfoConsigli/Ricerche%20e%20indagini/sintesirapportoinfanziaadolescenza9.pdf

Villella, R. (2013). *Corso di coraggio per bambini paurosi* [Course on courage for fearful children]. Roma, Italy: San Paolo S.r.l.

Woodard, C. R. (2004). Hardiness and the concept of courage. *Consulting Psychology Journal: Practice and Research, 56*, 173–185.

Woodward, C., & Pury, C. (2007). The construct of courage: Categorization and measurement. *Consulting Psychology Journal: Practice and Research, 59*, 135–147.

Zampone, F. (2015). *Allena il tuo coraggio. Esercizi per essere felici* [Train your courage. Exercises to be happy]. Firenze, Italy: Giunti.

Conclusion

Ideas for the future of counseling and coaching

The aim of this volume was to invite all those interested in counseling and coaching to look at them also in light of the need for change and innovation, which are increasingly considered as indicators of ecological validity and social relevance in research works and interventions.

Many reflections on the nature of counseling and coaching and the possible areas of intervention proposed in this volume move in this direction, thanks to the attention paid to both individuals and groups, institutions, agencies, and organizations, privileging the pursuit of preventive goals whenever possible. Besides including actions typical of the so-called help relationships, of support to reflexivity, of the search for new personal meanings, and boosting people's resources and strengths, counseling and coaching will have to massively consider the life contexts of individuals. It is paramount to learn to better exploit and use research suggestions and also counseling techniques and strategies different from traditional ones. We are thinking, for example, of online supports and mobile technology (smartphones and tablets), which can facilitate assessment, maintenance of obtained results, and control over the risk of relapse. They could also allow a wider range of interventions and possible supports, cost effectiveness, easier involvement of individuals and contexts, identifying those that for whatever reason can find it difficult to access the services or may dislike face-to-face relationships (Mohr, Burns, Schueller, Clarke, & Klinkman, 2013). An example has been given by Robinson and Serfaty (2008) who reported the positive results observed in a group of female university students diagnosed with bulimia nervosa who had benefited from an interaction solely based on electronic mail. This can be seen as an "extreme" intervention, but, albeit upholding the value and the importance of interpersonal contact and relationship, we feel we can underscore the merit of these means to facilitate, for example, handing out homework, which is often resorted to in counseling and coaching practices, sharing materials (e.g., written and audio files), sending encouragement to stay on course in pursuing "resolutions", and the activation of actions that can make more likely the achievement of planned and set goals. Other advantages that may come from the intentional use of specific software or applications ("apps") could involve distance monitoring actions, audio- and video-recording of events, gathering statements and observations, using suggestions, passing on requests for help and supports, etc. We also wish to recall that in an increasingly more sophisticated way, texting via SMS (Short Message Service) or via WhatsApp allows the sharing of images, videos, and voice recordings that can be used to send brief prompts to clients on coping strategies to be used, forward motivational or encouraging texts, supply contacts in case of special need or in emergencies, remind clients of actions to carry out or of appointments, etc.

All of these tools and their applications open interesting perspectives that we should consider with increasing attention both in research and in practice. Obviously, it means that these issues will have to be addressed intentionally and in depth also during training, as special care must be taken in using a language that avoids misunderstandings, in handling feelings and emotions, in guaranteeing people's privacy, in making sure the person can access the internet and is familiar with the technologies to be used to avoid creating further barriers for the client.

Another thought underlying the collection of contributions included in this volume is the conviction that to avoid superficial generalizations, counseling and coaching actions must be "context-centered" and be directed, at any one time and in a privileged way, at least at one of the most important reference areas: (a) health and wellbeing, (b) learning and education, (c) vocational guidance and work, (d) prevention and participation in community life. We believe this to be important because in these different areas difficulties, urgencies, and types of intervention and support to be administered may differ significantly. Likewise, we think it is important to reiterate, also in these conclusive considerations, that it does not make much sense to think of a counselor or of a coach as a professional able to handle any typology of individuals or difficult events, and neither to make a complete and exhaustive list of professional competences to be used and certified for all possible events. What could possibly be an across-the-board condition for those that engage in counseling and coaching actions is the acceptance of a precise deontological code requiring interventions that aim to increase and mobilize people's resources and strengths, reinforce their abilities to cope with challenges and difficulties, while at the same time showing interest in and empathy toward the meanings and values that, based on their own culture, individuals attribute to their own contexts and resources (Gelso & Woodhouse, 2003).

That was also underscored by Polo and Soresi (2015) in reporting part of the interview used at the *Larios Laboratory*, University of Padova, to specify the actions a client is willing to undertake to achieve the desired change. In the interview, the client is invited to confidently consider the successful strategies he or she has resorted to in the past: "*Several researchers believe that the times we are going through require people not to give in, to handle difficulties with confidence and decision so that things can change and improve. Surely, you have already experienced difficult situations in your life which you were able to deal with, and you have certainly accomplished demanding tasks.*

(a) Can you briefly say what happened and what it was about?
(b) On those occasions, which of your abilities and personal resources did you turn to? Who (what) helped you most?
(c) What helps and supports (if any) would you have liked to receive?

> There have surely been things that you were successful at, that you are proud of because of the way you managed to do them. . . . Could you describe one of them to me? . . . Don't think of any superhero things, just something that you yourself were surprised at having done. Could you describe one to me?
>
> Very well . . . Do you remember what you had to do so that it would happen?" (p. 21)

With this volume we also wanted to focus attention on the current situation, on the "depression" warning issued by the World Health Organization (2011), and the vigorous request for "modern" low-cost services able to cater the help and support needed due to the intertwining of diverse aspects and factors, not merely psychological and individual ones. So that counseling and coaching can respond adequately and efficaciously to the new uncertainties and the new risks that the future, sometimes in threatening tones, seems to aim at large groups of the population, they must be able to renew themselves and be willing to have their innovations undergo stringent operations of evaluation. And innovation can only be ground in experimenting and spreading multidisciplinary and interdisciplinary approaches and projects. In this connection, the literature includes a wealth of in-depth arguments on how to differentiate between *pluridisciplinarity* (copresence and juxtaposition of a number of disciplines on research, education and training, or intervention), *interdisciplinarity* (interaction of several disciplines in studying, intervening in an area, or pursuing a goal) and *transdisciplinarity* (which, by means of collaborations among disciplines, attempts to identify a clearly common theme able to originate a completely new and novel epistemological philosophy). However, in our conclusive reflections, we will consider all these nuances in terms of *multidisciplinarity*. This is certainly a difficult challenge to handle, but what seems fairly certain today is that it is not advantageous to "erect barriers" between different knowledges, diverse disciplines and professionals by continuing to strongly defend one's own specificities and "excellences" in a shortsighted and self-referential way, and sometimes from markedly corporatist perspectives.

As scholars interested in counseling and coaching, we should perhaps start to talk less about "professional identity" and begin to think in terms of multiple identities, also to be able to present heterogeneous reflections and proposals to communities, labor organizations, the world of health, of training and of inclusion. As we have repeatedly stated, the professional needed in the future will have to be better able to use technology; privilege short, efficacious, low-cost preventive interventions; address small and large groups; respect all forms of diversity; and be able to interact with all those figures (teachers, parents, entrepreneurs, voluntary associations, social workers, etc.) who have significant responsibilities in the contexts, including stakeholders and policymakers, to start an alliance.

In all that, and in view of a future that we hope will be better than the present, counseling and coaching should decide "which side to be on", surely by continuing to aspire to increase people's self-determination and empowerment, but, however, not forgetting the responsibilities and values typical of sharing, of solidarity, and of social commitment. In the exchanges that we have with those asking for our intervention and support, we think it is urgent and timely to include markedly "environmentalist" reflections, propositions, and goals. These should contribute to allow an eco-social reading of individual themes, with pluralistic and inclusive visions capable to contrast the logic markedly oriented toward profits and competition that over the last decades has multiplied personal discomforts and created dangerous inequality levels and particularly vulnerable eco-systems (Jackson, 2017).

By constantly bearing in mind the *me* and the *you*, the person and the context, the counseling and coaching of the future could then dialogue and associate with scientific sectors and professionals who are similarly oriented toward sharing and respecting each and every person and their contexts. Fortunately, this idea of sharing is starting to materialize (Righetti, Nota, & Soresi, 2016) and more attention is being paid to those that encourage attentive consideration of the beneficial effects, especially among the most vulnerable individuals, of an economy really and truly ethical and civil (Zamagni, 2016) and of a fair and sustainable concept of development (Di Rienzo, 2011). The ability of strongly taking on greater responsibility as concerns wellbeing, inclusion, conservation of the environment and of the public goods (air and water, first of all), and protection of biodiversity, at the same time also involving the policymakers, will give counseling and coaching the ecological and social recognitions that we think they deserve (Bennholdt-Thomsen, 2012).

It follows that a higher sense of responsibility in daily life, in actions carried out at home, at work, and in the community, can lead to attentively considering also reciprocal support and "free" giving, in accordance with the so-called gift economy that many could be interested in (Vaughan, 2015). If, on the one hand, though a gift waste can certainly be decreased, on the other hand, information, knowledge, and respect can be shared and networks attentive to altruism and to alternative forms of social recognition can be created. That has certainly a lot to do with a vision of counseling and coaching truly interested in community wellbeing and in prevention.

As the editors of this volume, we would like to give our grateful thanks to all the colleagues that have contributed to its drafting and accepted the challenge we had issued: the criticalities of the present in light of a future that could be "desirable" in their fields of study and application. The future, including also that of counseling and coaching, is indeed difficult to predict and will likely surprise most of us, but all the same we must be ready to consider it with attention, worry, and hope. If it is true that the past does predict the present to some extent and that the latter anticipates future developments, we can also assume that our representations of the future, of what we desire, can significantly influence the present by stimulating new analyses and triggering innovations to be experimented and evaluated. Thus, both researchers and professionals engaged in counseling and coaching could become, and this is what we wish, "change agents", not simply satisfied with describing discomforts and dealing with a few, maybe "private", difficult situations, but also having the courage, if necessary, to clearly point to the causes of problems and introduce original and innovative modalities to address them. It will mean new commitments and new responsibilities, since among the people that today could benefit from the help and support that we have focused on in this volume, many seem little projected toward the future, often concentrated almost exclusively on the present and on pursuing short-term gratifications instead of reflectively distinguishing between the essential and the superfluous, between the transitory and the permanent.

People's wellbeing, their right to self-determination and high-quality inclusion must be adequately defended . . . and when signs of deterioration and the presence of marked discomforts are glimpsed, they should be reported first of all by the operators engaged in the help professions. Counselors, coaches, educators, voluntary and social workers, but not only them of course, should show that they are ready to become the defenders of the quality of life of individuals and the livability of their contexts. In other words, we think that those that intend to help people cope successfully with their daily difficulties and become more resilient should have the role of "sentinels" in defense of individuals' rights and wellbeing. These sentinels should act to alert contexts (e.g., health, education and training, labor and social participation) and urge them along so that they can take care of unfavorable events and of the threatening approach of "enemies" and negative circumstances (in medicine there are "sentinel cells" and "sentinel events") which might undermine individuals' right to wellbeing, to self-determination, to inclusion, especially of those who are more vulnerable and more greatly at risk of marginalization. *Wellbeing sentinel* and *inclusion sentinel* seem to us particularly appropriate titles for this extra task that we would like all counseling and coaching professionals to take up. From an etymological perspective, the term sentinel (*sentinelle* in French, *sentinella* in Italian, *sentinela* in Spanish) comes from *sentina* (bilge) the lowest "living" part of a boat, the part in constant contact with seawater in its natural context, where infiltrations and seepages tend to collect, which, if not properly monitored, could even cause its sinking and so its end. On ancient Roman ships, a man (the sentinel) was assigned to the constant control of the bilge and his job was to warn everybody in case of threatening seepages.

We would really like every community and all our educational, formative, and social contexts (schools, corporations, places of aggregation) to include watchful "wellbeing and inclusion sentinels" and we would like the first to accept this important scientific and social task to be those professionally dealing with counseling and coaching, who would thus have the chance to keep a close watch on the levels of wellbeing and inclusion of the contexts in which they live and work, and who would then be the first to warn of threats to rights and values.

References

Bennholdt-Thomsen, V. (2012). La politica della prospettiva di sussistenza [The perspective of the policy subsistence]. *Dep, Deportate, esuli, profughe, 20*, 53–64.

Di Rienzo, M. (2011). *Voci dalla rete: Come le donne stanno cambiando il mondo* [Voices from the network. How women are changing the world]. Udine, IT: Multiverso – Forum Edizioni.

Gelso, C. J., & Woodhouse, S. (2003). Toward a positive psychotherapy: Focus on human strength. In B. W. Walsh (Ed.), *Counseling psychology and optimal human functioning* (pp. 171–197). Mahwah, NJ: Lawrence Erlbaum Associates.

Jackson, T. (2017). Prosperity without growth: Foundations for the economy of tomorrow. London: Routledge.

Mohr, D. C., Burns, M. N., Schueller, S. M., Clarke, G., & Klinkman, M. (2013). Behavioral intervention technologies: Evidence review and recommendations for future research in mental health. *General Hospital Psychiatry, 35*(4), 332–338.

Polo, A., & Soresi, S. (2015). Il counselling in un'epoca di crisi economica e disagi: Il contributo della psicologia positiva [Counseling in times of economic hardship and crisis era: The contribution of positive psychology]. In L. Nota & S. Soresi (Eds.), *Il Counselling del futuro* (pp. 13–28). Padova, IT: Cleup.

Righetti, A., Nota, L., & Soresi, S. (2016). Un sistema di welfare per tutti . . . nonostante la crisi economica [A welfare system for all . . . despite the economic crisis]. In S. Soresi (Ed.), *Psicologia delle disabilità e dell'inclusione* (pp. 375–384). Bologna, IT: Mulino.

Robinson, P., & Serfaty, M. (2008). Getting better byte by byte: A pilot randomised controlled trial of email therapy for bulimia nervosa and binge eating disorder. *European Eating Disorders Review, 16*(2), 84–93.

Vaughan, G. (2015). The gift in the heart of language: The maternal source of meaning. London, UK: Mimesis International.

World Health Organization. (2011). *Impact of economic crises on mental health*. Copenaghen: WHO Regional Office for Europe.

Zamagni, S. (2016). Il bene comune come berillo intellettuale in economia [The common good as beryl intellectual in economics]. *Archives of Philosophy, 84*(1), 161–176.

Index

Note: Page numbers in *italics* denote references to Figures and Tables.

For Product Safety Concerns and Information please contact our EU representative GPSR@taylorandfrancis.com Taylor & Francis Verlag GmbH, Kaufingerstraße 24, 80331 München, Germany